RETURN TO WINTER

RETURN TO WINTER

RUSSIA, CHINA, AND THE NEW COLD WAR AGAINST AMERICA

Douglas E. Schoen and Melik Kaylan

ENCOUNTER BOOKS *e* NEW YORK • LONDON

First American edition published in 2014 by Encounter Books,
an activity of Encounter for Culture and Education, Inc.,
a nonprofit, tax exempt corporation.
Encounter Books website address: www.encounterbooks.com

Manufactured in the United States and printed on
acid-free paper. The paper used in this publication meets
the minimum requirements of ANSI/NISO Z39.48–1992
(R 1997) (*Permanence of Paper*).

First paperback edition published in 2015.
Paperback edition ISBN: 978-1-59403-843-3

THE LIBRARY OF CONGRESS HAS CATALOGUED
THE HARDCOVER EDITION AS FOLLOWS:
Schoen, Douglas E., 1953– , author.
Return to winter: Russia, China, and the new cold war against America /
by Douglas E. Schoen and Melik Kaylan.
pages cm
Originally published in hardback in 2014 as: The Russia-China axis : the new cold war
and America's crisis of leadership.
Includes bibliographical references and index.
ISBN 978-1-59403-756-6 (hardback)—ISBN 978-1-59403-757-3 (ebook)
1. United States—Foreign relations—21st century. 2. United States—Foreign relations
administration—21st century. 3. National security—United States.
4. Russia (Federation)—Foreign relations—China. 5. China—Foreign relations—Russia
(Federation) 6. World politics—2005–2015. I. Kaylan, Melik, 1962– , author. II. Title.

JZ1480.S358 2014
327.47051—dc23
2014002441

Contents

Authors' Note

We wrote most of this book before the recent, unfolding events in Ukraine, as well as before further developments confirming the existence of a Russian-Chinese alliance. These events and others, in our view, only confirm the validity and relevance of our arguments, but we offer this foreword as a more current take on the state of affairs as we go to press (2014).

Foreword

"Now Russia-China cooperation is advancing to a new stage of comprehensive partnership and strategic interaction. It would not be wrong to say that it has reached the highest level in all its centuries-long history."

—VLADIMIR PUTIN[1]

"[Russia's and China's] enhanced partnership marks the first emergence of a global coalition against American hegemony since the fall of the Berlin Wall."

—CHARLES KRAUTHAMMER[2]

"The Sino-Soviet rift that brought the two countries to the brink of nuclear war in the '60s has been healed rather dramatically."

—STROBE TALBOTT[3]

"The echoes of the non-aggression pacts of the 1930s get louder in this age of American retreat."

—*WALL STREET JOURNAL*[4]

"If not letting America have its own way is Mr. Obama's objective, he is an unparalleled foreign-policy success."

—JOHN BOLTON[5]

"This will be the biggest construction project in the world for the next four years, without exaggeration," Vladimir Putin said in Shanghai in May 2014, as he raised a glass to drink a toast with Chinese president Xi Jinping.[6]

The two leaders were celebrating the signing of a 30-year, $400 billion natural-gas deal between their countries—the biggest in the history of the natural-gas industry. Under the terms of the deal, Russia would supply the Chinese with natural gas for the first time—38 billion cubic meters of gas per year, through pipelines and other massive infrastructure investments. The Chinese would gain a major new source of energy, and a cleaner-burning fuel, in a country facing major pollution problems. Russia would acquire a massive new customer base for its gas, at a time when Europe seeks to diversify from Russian sources. The deal, Putin said, was "an epochal event" in the relationship between the two nations. For his part, President Xi, always the less voluble of the two leaders, spoke of expanding commerce with Russia. "We are determined that trade between our countries will reach $100 billion by 2015," he said. Moscow hopes to double that figure by 2020.

The agreement had been in the works for a decade, but some commentators saw it solely in the context of a current crisis: the Western reaction against Russia after its illegal annexation of Crimea in Ukraine, and the threat that war might break out between Russia and Ukraine. "The crisis in relations with the West over Ukraine has made ties to Asia, and particularly relations with its economic engine, China, a key strategic priority," the *New York Times* asserted, discussing Putin's interest in China.[7]

That sounded perfectly logical. It was also perfectly wrong.

The truth is, Putin's trip to Shanghai was only the latest evidence of an unfolding alliance between Russia and China that most observers are only now starting to acknowledge. The gas deal was so momentous that it would have been impossible to ignore; but the signs of Russian and Chinese collaboration are everywhere, and they have been mounting for more than a decade.

"Russia-China cooperation is advancing to a new stage of comprehensive partnership and strategic interaction," Putin said on the eve of his visit to Shanghai. "It would not be wrong to say that it has reached the highest level in all its centuries-long history."[8] He was preparing to sign "a record package of documents" and agreements between the two countries, covering trade, investment, energy, infrastructure development, Asia-Pacific cooperation, and cultural exchange.[9] "We are aiming at the creation of special areas of advanced economic development with an investment-friendly environment," Putin said.[10] Indeed, Putin has turned to China for financing, trying to roll back limits on Chinese investment in the Russian economy in the hope of luring cash into industries from housing to infrastructure to natural resources. Russia seeks China's help to build a bridge to the Crimean peninsula.

This expanding trade is part of a larger story: Russia and China, once Communist adversaries during the Cold War, now increasingly act in concert. Beijing tacitly supported Russian moves in Crimea by abstaining from a vote in the United Nations, even though Moscow's actions violated a stated core principle of Beijing's foreign policy: non-interference. The two countries also lined up on the same side at the UN regarding the Syrian civil war.

Militarily, the two nations are cooperating and collaborating like never before. In May 2014, the Russian and Chinese navies held large-scale joint drills in the East China Sea—sending a message, most experts felt, to Japan, which has found itself in increasing tension with Beijing. "Moscow and Beijing have found advantages in working together to diminish U.S. influence and create greater room for them to pursue international economic and strategic interests," Brian Spegele and Wayne Ma noted in the *Wall Street Journal*. "Mr. Putin is widely depicted in Chinese official media as a powerful leader unafraid to take on the West."[11]

That's not how the Chinese view American leaders, to put it mildly.

In spring 2014, Defense Secretary Chuck Hagel, on an official visit to Beijing that included a tour of China's first aircraft carrier, stood at a press conference with his counterpart, Chinese Defense Minister Chang Wanquan. With the media looking on, Wanquan made sure the Pentagon chief understood that the Chinese military had no fear of American power. "With the latest developments in China," Wanquan told Hagel, "it can never be contained."[12]

In different ways, Russia and China also effectively tolerate, and even facilitate, the interests and goals of rogue nations—Iran, North Korea, Syria, and others. They use their political influence to assist these nations' efforts to procure nuclear power or weaponry, to avoid international punishment for egregious human-rights abuses, and to prop up anti-Western dictators and even terrorist groups. Despite lingering differences and suspicions, Russia and China have become both newly aggressive in their own spheres and newly cooperative as partners and allies. They have forged a powerful new alliance that marks, as Charles Krauthammer rightly suggests, "the first emergence of a global coalition against American hegemony since the fall of the Berlin Wall."[13]

Put simply, this coalition has the potential to permanently and fundamentally alter international relations. It was envisioned as, and it has functioned as, a counterweight to liberal democracy generally and the United States specifically. "The unipolar model of the world order has failed," Putin says, referring to what he sees as American hegemony. "Today this is obvious to everyone."[14] The Russia-China alliance—we call it a new Axis—already possesses extraordinary power, as is clear not just with new economic and trade agreements and military cooperation but also in the areas of nuclear proliferation and cyber warfare. Individually and together, Russia and China seek to undermine the social, economic, and political framework of democratic societies and our alliances in a way that has yet to be fully understood.

Their efforts to do so are emboldened immeasurably by a United States that is losing the confidence and trust of its allies and partners around the world. From Europe to the Middle East to the Far East, American policy is muddled, irresolute, and even feckless—as was powerfully symbolized in June 2014 when the Obama administration stood by as the Islamic State of Iraq and Syria (ISIS), the al-Qaeda offshoot, quickly overran cities in Iraq. Our allies doubt American commitment and resolve, question or outright oppose our policies, and are increasingly looking elsewhere—or within—for sustenance and support. Even nations historically aligned with us are making tentative outreach elsewhere. The United States has no clear strategy other than retrenchment and the minimization of genuine threats. We seem unwilling to acknowledge what our adversaries our doing. Unless we fundamentally change the foreign-policy approach we have followed under President Obama, we will continue to lose ground—as will the cause of democracy and freedom around the world.

These, then, are the subjects of the book you are about to read: the Russia-China alliance, the dangers that it poses, and the desperate need for a cogent and committed American response. Without unduly flattering ourselves, let us be frank: We tried to sell the idea of this book for years before we found a taker. We'd rather have been wrong than right. Now that more Americans are paying attention, there might yet be a chance to reverse the tide.

ON THE MARCH: RUSSIA, CHINA, AND THE ROGUES

On May 9, 2014, Russian President Vladimir Putin coasted into the Crimean port of Sevastopol on a naval launch, gliding past Russian warships arrayed to greet him. It was Victory Day, the Russian holiday commemorating the Soviet Union's triumph over Nazi Germany. Over the years, Putin has made the occasion a great celebration of Russian nationalism. He had spent the morning in Moscow attending a military parade in Red Square, an old Soviet practice he resurrected in 2008. His visit to Crimea came two months after he led Russia's illegal annexation of the Ukrainian territory—a move condemned not only by Ukraine's government but also by much of the world. In his remarks at Sevastopol, Putin roused his audience with patriotic themes.

"I think 2014 will also be an important year in the annals of Sevastopol and our whole country, as the year when people living here firmly decided to be together with Russia, and thus confirmed their faith in the historic truth and the memory of our forefathers," he said, in remarks broadcast nationally.[15] Putin called Victory Day "the holiday when the invincible power of patriotism triumphs, when all of us particularly feel what it means to be faithful to the Motherland and how important it is to defend its interests."[16] After the speech, Russian jets flew over the crowd, through what mere months before had been Ukrainian airspace.[17]

While Putin was in Crimea, Deputy Prime Minister Dmitri Rogozin celebrated Victory Day in Moldova's breakaway pro-Russian region of Transnistria, declaring Russia the "guarantor of security" for what he provocatively called "the republic of Transnistria," echoing the language Russia has used to justify intervention in Ukraine.[18] On May 11, in a referendum widely denounced by the West, 90 percent of voters in the eastern Ukraine provinces of Donetsk and Luhansk voted for secession from Ukraine.[19] Pro-Russian activists were soon saying that they wanted to become part of Russia; annexation might be only a matter of time.

Regardless of what ultimately happens in Ukraine, the Russian seizure of Crimea has fundamentally changed the international power balance. Despite the sanctions that have been put in place, Russian aggression and assertiveness have yet to be deterred, and the United States and its European allies have no clear consensus on how to proceed. For the first time, the essential principles of the NATO alliance have been called into question—with implications for Eastern and Central Europe, and indeed for the world.

While the world anxiously watched the Ukraine situation, an 80-ship Chinese fleet sailed into waters claimed by Vietnam to install a billion-dollar oil rig in the energy-rich South China Sea. When Vietnam's coast guard arrived, the Chinese flotilla responded with force, ramming at least one Vietnamese ship and firing water cannons at others.[20] Then, later in May, a Chinese vessel rammed and sank a Vietnamese fishing boat in the disputed waters.[21] China claims 90 percent of the South China Sea as its own, rejecting the United Nations Convention on the Law of the Sea and staking claims to dozens of islands and reefs that Beijing claims are historically Chinese.[22]

New examples of Chinese assertiveness in regional waters occur regularly. As this book went to press, Chinese jet fighters armed with missiles "buzzed" two Japanese reconnaissance planes in the two countries' overlapping air-defense zones over the East China Sea. The Chinese fighters got within 100 feet of the Japanese planes, in what the Japanese defense minister described as a dangerous act that would increase tensions between the two nations.[23] Those tensions have been rising for years. In late 2013, China unilaterally imposed an "air-defense identification zone" in the East China Sea in airspace that overlaps with Japanese and South Korean airspace, and it threatened any aircraft that penetrated the zone.[24] The incident with the Japanese planes could mark a new and more dangerous stage in the standoff.

China has been acting more provocatively toward its Asian neighbors for years. Beijing recently began a construction project in the disputed Spratly Islands, despite a long-standing agreement with the Philippines and other nations in the region not to build on these disputed landmasses. The Philippines filed a formal protest, and the action worsened relations with Vietnam, already angered by the oil-rig incident. It wasn't clear what the Chinese were building in the Spratlys—only that Beijing insisted that its right to do so was purely a matter of "Chinese sovereignty."[25] In March 2014, China blockaded Philippine marines stationed on Second Thomas Shoal, an uninhabited atoll China claims for itself.[26]

While some foreign-policy observers may believe that Beijing is acting recklessly, it's more likely that these provocations are all part of a broader strategy to undermine U.S. authority in the region by picking small, winnable fights. "China is seeking to prove to its neighbors that containment cannot work and that the U.S. cannot be relied upon to defend them," wrote David Pilling in the *Financial Times*. "If it can do so, they and Washington will have to acknowledge that the status quo is untenable. It is a dangerous strategy. It is also a clever one."[27]

"China is deliberately doing these things to demonstrate the unsustainability of the American position of having a good relationship with China and maintaining its alliances in Asia, which constitute the leadership of the United States in Asia," says Professor Hugh White, a former senior Australian defense official.[28]

Russia and China are also formidable combatants in one of the 21st century's primary battlegrounds: cyber warfare. The Justice Department's May 2014 indictment of five Chinese officers of the People's Liberation Army (PLA) for cyber espionage only confirms what has been poorly understood up until now, but which we assert vigorously in Chapter 3: that a state-sponsored cyber war against the United States is being directed at the highest levels of the Chinese government. Russia, too, is a key cyber player: Hackers almost certainly affiliated with Moscow have been behind some of the most destructive private-sector cyber attacks of recent years.

Americans had only to note the two countries in which Edward Snowden stopped when he was on the run from the United States after he leaked American intelligence secrets: first China, then Russia, where he was eventually granted asylum. Those who dismiss the strong likelihood that Snowden was an agent of either the Russians or the Chinese are deluding themselves.

As Russia and China flex their muscle, rogue nations have often looked to one or both of them for support—tacit or explicit. Syrian dictator Bashar al-Assad stands in a stronger position than he has for years, thanks in no small part to Vladimir Putin's staunch support. President Obama threatened Assad with missile strikes in August 2013 after the dictator used chemical weapons against rebel groups and civilians, but at the last moment Obama completely reversed himself, making the term "red line" into an international synonym for spinelessness.

Likewise, the Islamic theocracy that runs Iran is closing in on achieving its goal of becoming a nuclear power. This time, it hasn't been American irresolution that is to blame, but American commitment—a commitment to a fatally flawed nuclear accord that will all but assure the Iranians of getting what they want. Finally, a new Defense Intelligence Agency report shows that North Korea has nuclear weapons capable of delivery by ballistic missiles. The murderous regime, propped up by China, threatens the peace and stability not only of Asia, but the world.

All these challenges are serious, complex, and multifaceted, and it would be foolhardy to assume that even under the finest leadership, the United States could solve them all with the best conceivable outcomes in each case. At the same time, however, there is no question that these problems have been exacerbated and made much more dangerous and destabilizing by failed American leadership—or, more accurately, by an abdication of American leadership.

AMERICA IN RETREAT

It's not often that congressional leaders emerge from a White House meeting with the president of the United States and call their visit "bizarre," but that's how Senator Bob Corker of Tennessee described his sit-down with Obama-administration national-security officials in May 2014. Listening to them talk about Syria, Afghanistan, and the Nigerian Islamist terror group Boko Haram, Corker was amazed by how far off course American foreign policy had drifted. "I realized last night that the administration has no policy in Syria, has no strategy in Syria," Corker said.[29]

It isn't just Syria, either. The Obama administration has no clear counterterror policy in the wake of Snowden's damaging leaks of national-security information in 2013. It has no clear coordination with American allies and no coherent approach to upgrading and modernizing our defenses. It has no articulated doctrine on when, where, and how to use force in the world, and how to offer credible deterrents to antidemocratic regimes and groups.

Consider that Obama ran for reelection in 2012 in substantial part on his foreign-policy record, touting especially his decision to order the operation that killed Osama bin Laden. Al-Qaeda, the president said often, was "on the run," and the War on Terror was winding down. "This war, like all wars, must end," he said in a speech at the National Defense University in 2013. Only recently has he begun to acknowledge the obvious: that the terrorism threat is not declining but growing around the world, not only in Afghanistan and Iraq but also throughout the Middle East and Africa. Writing in the *New York Times*, Mark Landler rightly underscored the contradiction of a president whose view of the world has "darkened," even as he has "settled on a minimalist foreign policy."[30]

Indeed, just days after he had pledged in his 2014 commencement address at West Point to tackle terrorism anew, Obama announced the release of five senior Taliban commanders in exchange for American POW Bowe Bergdahl.[31] Serious questions surround Bergdahl's capture in 2009 and whether his actions constituted desertion. But even if Bergdahl had been an unambiguous hero, the president's decision to free dangerous, high-ranking Taliban fighters would be profoundly troubling. Simply put, it is too high a price to pay, and it will almost surely come back to haunt American forces in the region, as well as our policymakers. Once again, Obama shows that he can talk a good game on American national security, but his execution leaves something to be desired.

"It's a case for interventionism but not overreach," says Obama's deputy national-security adviser, Ben Rhodes, in an attempt to clarify the muddle that characterizes the administration's approach.

Nice try. The truth is, even when the administration's words and stated principles sound clear, its policies are inconsistent and frequently incoherent. President Obama's America is a passive, confused, and ineffective superpower. Some years ago, one administration insider tried to describe Obama's approach as "leading from behind." But America isn't leading at all.

America is in retreat internationally, just as the need for U.S. leadership is greater than at any time since the end of the Cold War. It bears repeating: The world's superpower has no foreign-policy vision or strategy—unless one believes that Obama's doctrine of "Don't do stupid stuff" is visionary or that his resolute selling of his policies as anti-Bush and anti-war is a workable framework for dealing with a dangerous world.[32] Even when we do determine to pursue something, we lack will and follow-through. Our abdications know no borders: We're being kicked off the International Space Station by the Russians, and the administration has even urged us to surrender control of the Internet to a shadowy global consortium. The U.S. presence in the world has become so passive that the thuggish, brutal leader of Nigeria's Boko Haram, flaunting the group's monstrous abduction in April 2014 of hundreds of schoolgirls, released a video in which he dared Americans to retaliate. Any American force, even a small team of Marines, would make quick work of these Islamist fanatics. But like Vladimir Putin—and like Xi Jinping and Bashar al-Assad and Hassan Rouhani and Kim Jong Un—Abubakar Shekau knows that the Americans aren't coming for him.

In short, President Obama has manifestly failed to provide effective foreign-policy leadership—and this failure is due in large part to the president's own inclinations to de-emphasize American primacy and then expect the world to follow his vision for it.

"Obama's surprisability about history, which is why he is always (as almost everyone now recognizes) 'playing catch-up,' is owed to certain sanguine and unknowledgeable expectations that he brought with him to the presidency," Leon Wieseltier wrote in the *New Republic*.[33] Indeed, Obama seemed to crave a world in which American power is no longer essential, but the world doesn't share that wish. "There are many places in the world where we are despised not for taking action but for not taking action," Wieseltier observed. "Our allies do not trust us. Our enemies do not fear us. What if American preeminence is good for the world and good for America? Let's talk about that."[34]

General Wanquan's warning to Chuck Hagel about American inability to "contain" China was unfortunately correct—especially because, even as the international situation becomes less stable, America is slashing its defense budget. The Army is projected to shrink to its smallest size since before World War II. As the Brookings Institute's Robert Kagan argued at a recent Council on Foreign Relations meeting, our budgetary challenges don't require such extreme cuts.[35] "For diplomacy to succeed, it must be supported by a strong and credible defense," former Secretary of Defense and CIA Director Leon Panetta wrote in the *Wall Street Journal*. "Now is not the time to weaken our military, but that is exactly what's happening."[36] Indeed, we will always need enough troops to fight wars; it's absurd to argue otherwise and fall back on Predator drones and our expertise in cyber warfare.

This military retrenchment is all the more baffling in light of what Russia and China are doing militarily (explored at length in Chapter 4). Russian defense spending is set to rise 44 percent over the next three years,[37] and its naval budget, barely 10 percent of America's just a few years ago, is now approaching 50 percent of the American outlay.[38] In June 2014, four Russian strategic bombers conducted practice runs near Alaska; two of the bombers triggered U.S. air-defense-system warnings after they came within 50 miles of the California coast. A retired American Air Force general, Thomas McInerney, who served as Alaska commander for the North American Aerospace Defense Command, said that he couldn't remember a time when Russian strategic bombers had come that close to the American coast, and he blamed the episode on America's "unilateral disarmament, inviting adventurism by the Russians."[39]

China, meanwhile, will spend more on defense by the end of 2015 than Britain, France, and Germany combined,[40] and Beijing is set to overtake the U.S. in its number of naval "major combatant vessels" by 2020.[41] Hawkish officers in the People's Liberation Army (PLA) call for "short, sharp wars" to assert Chinese interests.[42] The hawks seem to be winning the policy debate: Whereas in the past, China's policies in the South China Sea have been erratic, leaving neighbors guessing as to when the next provocation would come, more recently, as we've seen, China has pursued an unyielding approach to its territorial claims, provoking high-profile clashes with Vietnam, the Philippines, and others. Beijing appears determined to pursue a strategy of hardline aggression in the Asia Pacific.[43]

The Chinese buildup comes in the context of Beijing's efforts to redefine the alliance system in Asia—loosening the grip of the U.S. on its Asian neighbors and asserting its primacy over the region. Xi Jinping made this explicit in May 2014 in a speech in Shanghai, in which he outlined a "new regional security cooperation architecture" that excluded the U.S. Admiral Sun Jianguo, the PLA general staff's deputy chief, was more blunt: According to the *New York Times*, he described the American alliance system in the region as "an antiquated relic of the Cold War."[44] And at the Shangri La security dialogue in Singapore, Major General Zhu Chengdu openly criticized American hegemony in the Pacific, warning ominously: "If you take China as an enemy, China will absolutely become the enemy of the U.S."[45] The simple conclusion is inescapable: Asia is for Asians—and Russians. American defense cutbacks aren't confined to conventional armed forces. We are also rolling back our nuclear armaments under the leadership of a president who has made no secret of his goal of someday reaching nuclear zero. That's a goal not shared, needless to say, by adversaries of America and the West.

Obama's high-minded yet strangely aloof and out-of-touch approach is evident in his reaction to Vladimir Putin, as it is in his foreign policy generally. Obama regards Putin's behavior with a combination of condescension and naiveté: "Mr. Putin's decisions aren't just bad for Ukraine," he says. "Over the long term, they're going to be bad for Russia."[46] He fails to consider that from Putin's perspective, aggression in Ukraine makes good strategic sense. In seizing Crimea, Putin has "acquired not just the Crimean landmass but also a maritime zone more than three times its size with the rights to underwater resources potentially worth trillions of dollars," William J. Broad detailed in the *New York Times*.[47] Obama also conveniently overlooks Russian success in turning more nations in Eurasia against the open, democratic Western model. According to a new report from Freedom House: "Ten years ago, one in five people in Eurasia lived under Consolidated Authoritarian rule, as defined in the report. Today, it's nearly four in five, and the trend is accelerating."[48]

Set against those real-world gains, why would Putin lose any sleep over Obama's haughty disapproval? Indeed, as Putin himself said of Obama recently: "Who is he to judge, seriously?"[49]

Obama's detachment has long distressed champions of American power, who often reside right of center on the political spectrum. The president's supporters dismiss those critiques, but it's not so easy to shrug off the criticism coming from two former Obama defense secretaries: Panetta (who also served as CIA chief) and Robert Gates.

"When the president of the United States draws a red line, the credibility of this country is dependent on him backing up his word," Panetta said last year, after Obama had backed down from confronting Syria at the 11th hour.[50] In his memoir, published early in 2014, Gates harshly criticized the commander in chief, particularly for what he saw as Obama's failed leadership and commitment to the war in Afghanistan. Obama, "doesn't believe in his own strategy, and doesn't consider the war to be his," Gates wrote. "For him, it's all about getting out."[51]

As Obama's international failures become more manifest and more consequential, it isn't just the Right or the neocons who are speaking out. Critics on the Left are worried, too. "What's frustrating to me sometimes about Obama is that the world seems to disappoint him," said *New Yorker* editor David Remnick—an Obama biographer and admirer—on the MSNBC program *Morning Joe*.[52] "Under Obama, the United States has suffered some real reputational damage," David Ignatius wrote at the *Washington Post*. "I say that as someone who sympathizes with many of Obama's foreign-policy goals. This damage, unfortunately, has largely been self-inflicted by an administration that focuses too much on short-term messaging."[53] And *Foreign Policy* editor David Rothkopf wrote in September 2013: "Even the most charitable of interpretations by the president's most loyal supporters (and I voted for him twice, so I count myself in that group) would have to rank the past couple of months as among the worst of his administration in terms of national-security policy mismanagement."[54]

It's no wonder that the United States has been outflanked at every turn by strong leaders such as Putin and Xi. They believe in what they're doing, and they have clear strategies and specific initiatives in the military, political, economic, and international realms that they purse with vigor and principle. At the present time, nothing like this can be said for the United States. Our paralysis and weakness have broad-ranging effects—clearing a path for our adversaries to advance their interests, while leaving our allies puzzled, angry, and vulnerable.

EMBOLDENED ADVERSARIES, WEAKENED ALLIES

When red lines are crossed in Syria, when Libya deteriorates, when Crimea is taken effortlessly in the face of clear U.S. treaty obligations, our allies around the world lose confidence and faith in our policies, in our commitments, and in us. The evidence is everywhere.

We are losing what allies we had in the Middle East. Consider: Saudi Arabia, one of America's key partners in the region, was elected to a seat on the UN Security Council in 2013—and declined to accept it. The Saudis cited the inability of the UN to put a stop to Iran's nuclear program and blamed the UN for allowing Syria "to kill its own people with chemical weapons . . . without confronting it or imposing any deterrent sanctions."[55] When our own allies have no faith in international security mechanisms such as the UNSC, it signals a crisis of confidence in the international system, the system so long backed by the confidence and authority of the United States.

We have no relationship to speak of with Egypt, for generations a staunch American ally. That country is in undeniably worse shape than before the revolution that ousted Hosni Mubarak. New Egyptian president Abdel Fattah el-Sisi is no friend of the United States; in fact, he has a strong and deepening relationship with Putin. Egypt is planning to buy Russia's cutting-edge MiG-35 fighter jet, and the two countries have agreed to hold joint military exercises. Russia is engaging in "arms-supply diplomacy" across the Middle East in an effort to take advantage of the power vacuum left by America's pull-back from the region.[56]

Another formerly close American ally, Turkey, has been blaming Washington for months for its domestic unrest. Under the increasingly autocratic leadership of Recep Erdogan, Turkey is moving away from the United States. Erdogan even filed an extradition request for Fethullah Gulen, a political rival living in Pennsylvania. Erdogan knows that America will deny this request, but the rebuff will set the stage for Erdogan to take advantage of rising anti-Americanism as he goes into upcoming presidential elections.[57] Like other Middle Eastern leaders, Erdogan has calculated that siding with America may no longer be a winning strategy.

In Afghanistan, where America spent an unfathomable sum in blood and treasure to defeat the Taliban, the current government is eager to distance itself from America's faltering global leadership. This past March, Hamid Karzai, who owes his presidency to America's efforts to promote democracy in that country, endorsed Russia's illegal annexation of Crimea.[58] Brazenly, Karzai chose to announce his position at a meeting with an American congressional delegation.[59]

Even Iraq, the country that America sought to remake, at enormous human, financial, and political cost to ourselves, is moving away from the U.S.—and toward a closer strategic alliance with Iran. The two countries concluded a sale of arms worth roughly $200 million in February 2014, the latest sign of a deepening relationship between the two majority-Shiite countries. Iraq might even be permitting Iranian shipments of weapons to Syria, directly undermining American efforts to support moderate anti-Assad rebels.[60] (Of course, all bets are off if ISIS, made up of Sunni rebels and al-Qaeda fighters, continues its gains and winds up toppling the Maliki government. That will present different problems, perhaps even worse ones, for the U.S.)

Indeed, the carnage in Syria continues unabated, and the international community is powerless to put a stop to it. The United States, devoted to staying out, is not exerting meaningful leadership to sway an outcome. The Syrian conflict has become a proxy for Iranian power, as Tehran has recruited and paid impoverished Shiite Afghanis to fight for Assad.[61] The Syrians have violated the chemical-weapons accord numerous times, including by using chlorine against rebels and civilians. French Foreign Minister Laurent Fabius said publicly that the United States, Britain, and France were wrong to call off airstrikes against Assad in August 2013. Fabius says that he has evidence that Syria has used chemical weapons 14 times since September 2013. Damascus has missed the deadlines for disgorging the chemical weapons it still possesses, and it may be hiding other stockpiles.[62]

We have offered no credible threat that would curtail the development of nuclear weapons in North Korea and Iran. China continues to defend and support the murderous regime in Pyongyang, whose sickening crimes against its own citizens were detailed in a chilling United Nations report in February 2014.[63] North Korea continues to expand its nuclear arsenal and threatens to provoke a nuclear arms race in East Asia.[64]

Our highly touted nuclear accord with Iran now appears all but certain to fail, as the terms of the deal leave Iran far too much leeway for uranium enrichment and will allow the Iranians to keep inspectors from visiting sites such as Parchin, where it is believed they are researching detonators that would convert nuclear fuel into nuclear bombs.[65] The West's deal-making has been not just incompetent, but destructive: In the process of making these craven attempts to put a good face on the Iranian situation, we have managed to alienate Israel, Saudi Arabia, Egypt, and Turkey. Abandoned hope for any Israeli–Palestinian peace deal is another price paid for our misadventures.

We're not doing much better reassuring our Asian allies, all of whom have felt the brunt, one way or another, of Chinese assertiveness. Obama's April 2014 Asian tour was meant to placate Japan and the Philippines, but he was subdued in his assurances, lest he offend Beijing. "President Obama obviously wants to avoid any appearances that this is part of a new Cold War with China," said Mark Thompson, director of the Southeast Asia Research Centre at City University of Hong Kong. "But this is a tricky balancing act because this is increasingly how the U.S.'s traditional allies that he is visiting are viewing things."[66] Thus the Philippines welcomed an agreement that would allow base access to American warships, planes, and troops for the first time since 1992, when the U.S. gave up its bases on the archipelago. But even this is hardly a warm embrace: We're using Philippine bases, not reopening our own. The message seems to be, "We do need you, but only on our terms." The Americans were quick to say that the decision had nothing to do with China, but most observers saw through that disclaimer.

Perhaps the most anxious Asian ally is Japan, which has found itself increasingly in Chinese crosshairs—and worried about whether Washington will really be there if trouble breaks out. In a press conference with Obama, Prime Minister Abe was less than enthusiastic about the alliance. Abe said: "We want to make this a peaceful region which values laws, and in doing this, strengthening of our bilateral alliance is extremely important. On this point, I fully trust President Obama."[67] But Abe has rapidly built up Japan's military, seeking to "make Japan a more equal partner with the U.S. in policing Asia"—hardly a sign of confidence in America's ability to keep the peace.[68] He is also building a web of security and defense relationships with other Asian states, independent of U.S.-led initiatives, because he lacks faith in America's willingness to use its alliances against China.

Most worryingly of all, Abe is reaching out not only to countries such as the Philippines and Vietnam but also to Russia. Looking at the China-Russia gas deal as a model, members of Abe's party are pushing for a $6 billion pipeline that would supply Japan with Russian gas. The new pipeline would make Japan dependent on Russia for nearly a fifth of its annual supply.[69] Putin will probably travel to Russia in the fall of 2014, and Abe hopes that the two countries can sign a peace deal that would normalize relations for the first time since World War II.[70] If the deal comes off, it would mark a potentially tectonic shift in the Pacific power balance.

Finally, in Europe, uneasiness about American commitments is rampant. Obama's humiliation on Syria has left European leaders wondering if he has a bottom line on anything, and our key allies increasingly doubt the strength and future of the NATO alliance—as their reaction to the crisis in Ukraine shows. The British refuse to go along with sanctions against Putin, looking to "protect the City of London's hold on dirty Russian money."[71] The German business establishment is more interested in protecting billions in trade and energy business with Moscow than in saving Ukraine. And perhaps most notoriously, the French are dismissing American concerns about their plans to go forward with sale of *Mistral*-class warships to Russia. For France, the decision makes good economic sense for its struggling shipbuilding industry, but the costs to the world could be enormous: The Mistrals will give Moscow capabilities it has never possessed before. If it had had Mistrals in 2008, Russian naval chief Vladimir Vysotsky said, Moscow would have won its war against Georgia in "40 minutes."[72] And France isn't just selling Russia the warships; it's also training hundreds of Russian naval personnel to operate them. Put simply, a NATO ally is actively assisting Russia to beef up its military capabilities, even as NATO countries in Eastern Europe prepare for more Russian aggression.[73] U.S. objections have done nothing to dissuade the French; one imagines that, in an earlier time, American disapproval might have meant something.

So withered has the American reputation become in Europe that the continent's far-right parties, which won big in parliamentary elections in May 2014, celebrate Putin as their political inspiration. Aymeric Chauprade, for example, of France's National Front, calls Russia "the hope of the world against new totalitarianism."[74] The National Front's Marine Le Pen said of Putin: "He's aware we are defending common values." When asked what values specifically, Le Pen replied: "The Christian heritage of European civilization."[75] Nigel Farage, the leader of Britain's far-right party, UKIP, says that he admires Putin most among world leaders. Greece's Golden Dawn party, Austria's Freedom Party, and Hungary's Jobbik also strongly prefer Putin to an America they frequently denounce. One might dismiss this fact if these parties had remained marginal, as they were only a few years ago. Now, their appeal and influence are growing.

INDISPENSABLE NATION, DISPOSABLE LEADERSHIP

On May 28, 2014, President Obama delivered the commencement speech at the United States Military Academy at West Point, attempting—yet again—to lay out a clear and decisive foreign-policy vision and answer the mounting chorus of critics. And, superficially at least, he succeeded. He declared that "America must always lead," spoke of his devotion to American exceptionalism, called America the "indispensable nation"—a phrase first coined by Madeleine Albright—and pledged support for our allies and for the cause of democracy. But notwithstanding the rhetoric, the speech offered no clear mandate for action, no clear framework for a strong and committed American presence in the world. Peel away the rhetoric, and the message was retrenchment and abandonment of responsibility.

When even the *New York Times* judges that the speech "did not match the hype, was largely uninspiring, lacked strategic sweep, and is unlikely to quiet his detractors, on the right or the left,"[76] it's a safe bet that the speech failed. The *Financial Times* joined the chorus of critics: "There was precious little to convince U.S. allies that Mr Obama is ready to step up his diplomatic agenda a gear or two." Indeed, Obama's omissions were glaring, with "barely a mention of how he would deal with China's maritime boldness, nor of Russia's neo-imperialist boundary-setting," the paper added. "He did not mention the foundering trade negotiations in the Pacific and across the Atlantic."[77] And so on.

The speech failed because, at heart, it was defeatist; and in this, it reflected clearly on its author. Despite his occasional clarion calls to American greatness, Obama's dominant tone was one of paring back the traditional post–World War II mission of the United States in the world. Where we have been, for 70 years, the world's lead actor in protecting democratic governments, adjudicating disputes, and putting teeth into UN resolutions, Obama would have us walk back from this into a much narrower definition of American capabilities, interests, and options. He offers nothing that will dissuade our allies from their growing conviction that they cannot count on a paralyzed United States. John Bolton put it well when he wrote that Obama "has somehow managed to combine the worst features of isolationism and multilateralism."[78] Indeed, a president so committed to multilateralism that he won't act alone—even with compelling reasons to do so—is a president willing to hamstring American power, in a world in which other actors (such as Russia and China) feel no such compulsion to ask for permission. No wonder that, barely a week after the president's speech, Iran's supreme leader, Ayatollah Khamenei, gave a speech of his own in Tehran—under a banner reading "America cannot do a damn thing"—in which he proclaimed that Obama has "renounced the idea of any military actions" against Iran.[79]

Traditionally, when a great issue has come to the fore demanding American action, American presidents have spoken to the world in clear and unequivocal language—saying, in effect, "We will handle this." Obama, by contrast, says, "We will look into this and get back to you"—and then he does neither. For years, he has fostered the growing sense that America wishes to disentangle itself from leadership in the world. He seems unwilling or unable to recognize that when America steps away from leadership, the world becomes more dangerous.

We remain convinced that strengthening, renewing, and promoting democratic institutions worldwide is a fundamental mission of the United States. This means championing U.S. and Western values whenever and wherever we can—through means such as the Voice of America—and providing far more robust assistance to democratic groups around the world while imposing tough penalties and sanctions on antidemocratic forces. Despite recent setbacks, the democratic ideal remains strong around the world, and the United States makes a profound mistake when it fails to promote democratic institutions globally to its utmost capacity. This diffidence is not only wrongheaded; it also carries ominous implications for our influence and authority around the world. It may be that democratic institutions are being tested in ways we never expected them to be. But it is the institutions and the politicians that are failing, not the democratic ideal or democratic values. If anything, those values become more essential in the face of autocracy, authoritarianism, and repression—as made clear by the courage and resolve of freedom-seeking people in Istanbul, Kiev, and Moscow, and around the Middle East. Exasperated with the Obama administration's failures, some are tempted to look to 2016 for a change in the American approach. And yet, a crisis-ridden world will not cooperate with our desire to sit out until better leadership arrives. Two more years in the current climate is too long to wait. Somehow, the United States must regain a clear sense of foreign-policy mission. In our view, this mission means reassuming American preeminence—in our defense capabilities, in our stewardship of Western alliances, and in our articulation of democratic values. The longer we delay in righting our course, the more difficult the task will be.

These truths are gaining acceptance across the American political spectrum. In May 2014, former Defense Secretary Robert Gates gave a commencement address at Georgetown. Gates said that the United States remains the country that the world looks to for advancement of the cause of freedom, liberty, and democracy. Yet, at a time of growing threats around the globe, we have degraded our defense capabilities severely. As Gates reminded his listeners, "soft" power means little without hard power to back it up. *The Economist*, always a fair and nuanced critic of the president, has made a similar point: "Credibility is about reassurance as well as the use of force. Credibility is also easily lost and hard to rebuild." Arguing that Obama has been an "inattentive friend" to American allies, the magazine also invoked his Syrian retreat to underline that he had "broken the cardinal rule of superpower deterrence: You must keep your word."[80]

Obama has often defended his approach by pointing to the growing isolationist sentiments of the American electorate. Polls do show such leanings, as they have for years, but the case for engagement remains compelling—and needs only a president who can make the public argument for it. Indeed, in an NBC/Wall Street Journal poll in which respondents voiced isolationist sentiments, 55 percent nonetheless agreed that it was important for the U.S. to project an "image of strength."[81] In our view, this suggests that isolationist sentiment is only skin-deep. We believe that, recent discouragements aside, most Americans still identify with assertion over accommodation—and with standing up for our principles, our values, and our broader interests.

This should not be confused with advocacy of endless war or of an overly intrusive United States. Rather, what we must do is offer credible deterrence again. As this book went to press, the Justice Department announced the indictment of five officers of the Chinese People's Liberation Army for violations of cyber security. The charges are almost certainly symbolic—Beijing isn't going to extradite these gentlemen to Washington for a trial—and more important, they are incomplete. We made no mention of going after government officials or Chinese businesses that enable and facilitate these hackers. However, at least the charges suggest accountability, recognition, and acknowledgment; all are essential if America is to grasp what it faces and begin fighting back.

In this book, we have outlined a bold and multifaceted set of initiatives the U.S. should implement if we are to begin restoring our place in the world as the bulwark of freedom, liberty, and democracy. Yet no matter how many good ideas are offered, strong leadership remains essential. The Obama administration has been hesitant, halting, and hamstrung.

This simply must change. Unless the United States rebuilds a robust defense, clearly asserts its interests and values, assures its allies, and offers unapologetic leadership, we will fail. And our failure will carry with it a huge price: the collapse of the post–World War II international architecture. To avoid such a scenario, the United States—still the world's only "indispensable nation"—must reassume its rightful role as the world's only superpower.

Superpowers, as Robert Kagan wrote recently, "Don't get to retire."[82]

Time is short, but it is not too late—yet.

Preface to the Paperback Edition

Authors' note: We are writing this updated preface to the new edition of The Russia-China Axis, *now titled "Return to Winter: Russia, China, and the New Cold War Against America," in early summer 2015—at a time when events around the world only strengthen our convictions about the arguments we make in this book. What follows is a brief overview of what has occurred since the book's first edition appeared last year.*

One year ago, when we published *The Russia-China Axis*, we felt strongly that we had written a book compelling in its analysis, accurate in its appraisal, and prescient in its warning that the United States was at mounting risk from a new, anti-Western alliance between Moscow and Beijing. We believed that the new Russia-China partnership, across every international front, spelled enormous risk for the United States and the Western democracies, and we tried to sound the alarm that the West, especially America, has shown no strategy and no will to take it on. In our view, the United States and its allies are at greater risk than at any time since the end of the Cold War.

A year later, at the risk of sounding immodest, we can only say: We were right.

Across every front, Russia and China continue on the march. The Russians changed the borders of Europe for the first time since World War II, with their illegal annexation of Crimea, and they are poised to destabilize and possibly even annex substantial additional parts of Eastern Ukraine. The Baltic states of Estonia, Latvia, and Lithuania, as well as large parts of the Arctic, appear to be next on Putin's hit list. Moscow is increasing its defense budget exponentially and upgrading its nuclear arsenal, and sending the message regularly to Washington and the European capitals that it is ready to confront us. Even as the Obama administration has tried to celebrate its ill-considered nuclear agreement with Iran, for example, Russian president Vladimir Putin has sold Tehran a missile-defense system that will fortify the Iranians against retaliatory attacks should they violate the agreement's terms—an inevitability, to those who see the regime's intentions clearly. Even more alarming has been Russia's escalating military involvement in Syria, where it has deployed troops and heavy weapons to provide support for Bashar al-Assad's regime.

Meanwhile, the Chinese are pursuing outright expansionism in the East China Sea and the South China Sea, where they are flouting international law and making brazen claims that, if conceded, would put one of the world's primary shipping lanes almost entirely under Chinese direction. Beijing is also engaging in a massive military buildup—especially of its naval forces—and is aggressively upgrading its nuclear posture. And Beijing continues to tolerate a nuclear North Korea, arguably putting the world at risk.

Russia and China are adept practitioners of the dark arts of cyber warfare. Both countries have been implicated in recent years in major attacks against American targets. And both Beijing and Moscow have moved boldly—and with distressing effectiveness—to make common cause, politically and economically, with American adversaries around the world, from the Middle East to Latin America.

More quietly yet equally if not more troubling, Russia and China have pursued systematic economic expansionism internationally—including in the West, and including in America's backyard. Chinese and Russian state-owned firms, their subsidiaries, and shell companies operating under different names have headquarters or offices in hundreds of locations around the world, constituting what a consultant to Western defense organizations calls "the fifth theater"—economic and financial. Meanwhile, at the state level, China and Russia are busy forging economic deals around the world, whether in Africa, where the Chinese have become the continent's largest trading partner and are leading massive infrastructure investment, or in Latin America (Monroe Doctrine be damned), where the Chinese have become the continent's top export market and leading creditor. And the Russians have busily pursued economic and trade deals, including significant sales of military hardware to U.S. adversaries.

The Russians and Chinese are tightening their economic relationship with each other, too. In 2014, they signed a $400 billion natural-gas pipeline deal that Putin called "an epochal event" in relations between the two countries. This year, the state-owned China Railway Group announced that it would partner with Russia in constructing a high-speed rail connection between Moscow and Kazan, one of Russia's largest cities.

No wonder Putin exulted that Russian-Chinese relations have reached a level "unprecedented in history."[1]

What unites all of these efforts is a common goal: to thwart the United States and the Western alliance at every turn, providing a counterweight in the form of a more autocratic, anti-Western system of political arrangements and individual rights. We wrote *The Russia-China Axis* to offer readers a glimpse at how this all worked and to raise the alarm about how ill-prepared the United States seems to be to confront it. Since the first edition appeared last year, the assertiveness and sometimes outright provocation of the two partners has continued—individually, or in tandem with each other or with rogue actors—and the consequences for the United States and its allies grow graver by the day.

Yet the challenge that Russia and China present still seems largely unrecognized by our political leaders, to say nothing of the public at large. We must confront it if America is going to maintain its pre-eminent position in the world. That task is made incalculably more difficult by a dynamic that we have observed, and lamented, for years: Chinese and Russian aggression, assertiveness, and strategic clarity, on the one hand; and American retrenchment, lack of commitment, and strategic ineptitude, on the other. We see it across the board—whether in our wholly inadequate and uncommitted effort to fight ISIS, our refusal to engage in tough diplomacy with Iran on the nuclear deal, or in our passive and ineffective global diplomacy, with our own allies and also as regards the shrewd and determined moves that Putin and Xi Jinping are making around the world.

The bottom line is this: Russia and China know what they want, are determined and organized in how they are pursuing it, and are meeting, by and large, with substantial success in their goals. None of this can be said about the American response, let alone about any proactive American vision for leadership in the 21st century. Until this changes, it's hard to feel optimistic. Our adversaries would be formidable on their own; working together, they cast a long shadow over the American future.

A DEEPENING, STRENGTHENING ALLIANCE

On May 17, 2015, originating from Novorissiysk on the Black Sea, the Russian and Chinese navies began weeklong joint naval exercises: Sea Cooperation 2015, as the Russian Defense Ministry billed it. Ten ships from the two countries participated, anchored by the *Moskva*, Russia's Crimea-based guided-missile cruiser, which served as headquarters for the drills. The goal of the exercises was to "strengthen mutual understanding between the navies . . . regarding boosting stability, countering new challenges and threats at sea," said Russian deputy navy commander Aleksandr Fedotenkov. "The joint drills are not aimed against third parties and are not connected with the political situation in that region," the Russian Defense Ministry said.

Despite those disclaimers, no observer, watching the navy ships pass in tandem, could miss the message: that the Russia-China alliance, once viewed as unthinkable, continues to deepen, with profound consequences for the world. The exercises take place as Russia continues to stare down the United States and its Western allies about Moscow's annexation of Crimea in 2014 and its continued destabilization of Ukraine, and as China is confronting the United States and its Asian allies in the Pacific, where Beijing's aggressive moves against neighboring countries seem to be challenges to regional security. What better time than now, then, and what better place than the Mediterranean—on NATO's southern perimeter—for Russian president Vladimir Putin and Chinese president Xi Jinping to advertise the strength of their growing partnership?

Sea Cooperation 2015 took place a week after Russia's annual Victory Day ceremonies commemorating its triumph in World War II over Germany. This year marked the 70th anniversary of that historic moment, so the celebrations were grander than usual. Russian soldiers marched in period garb, and 2,000 surviving Red Army veterans of what Russians call the Great Patriotic War were bused in to Moscow for the ceremonies. But because of Putin's aggression in Ukraine and violation of international law in annexing Crimea, no head of state from the Western democracies agreed to attend.

That was okay with Putin, though—because he had Xi sitting by his side.

The Chinese president was the most high-profile world leader in Moscow, where he joined Putin on the reviewing stand and watched not only Russian troops but a Chinese honor guard, too—which marched past the two leaders singing "Katyusha," a Russian war ballad. Along with the troops and pageantry, Putin wheeled out an impressive new tank, the Armata, considered by some to be the Russian army's new "secret weapon," and a new ICBM launcher. In his Victory Day speech, Putin made sure to get a dig in at the West and at the United States in particular.

"In past decades, we have seen attempts to create a unipolar world," Putin said, referring to what he sees as American attempts to control the affairs of other countries.

If the joint naval exercise wasn't the largest of its kind, and the Victory Day parade mostly pageantry and symbolism, the two events nonetheless underscore the Russian-Chinese partnership, which is far more substantive, in all major categories—military cooperation, economic and trade agreements, cyber-security issues, dealings with rogue nations, and mutual support in international venues such as the United Nations. This cooperation would be concerning enough on its own to American interests and those of our allies, but independently, Russia and China are also engaged in what amount to stare-downs with the United States in critical spots in the world.

FLASHPOINTS

Russia's aggression in Ukraine could be poised to reach a crucial stage. Troubling signs suggest that we could soon see a major Russian incursion. The Ukrainian government in Kiev has already lost more than two dozen towns to the Russian-backed separatists since early 2015. Ukraine president Petro Poroshenko has warned that 50,000 Russian troops remain massed on the Ukraine border—despite Moscow's repeated attempts to deny aggressive intent—while some 40,000 separatists or Russian loyalists are operating inside the country. Those numbers taken together represent an increase of 50 percent from the same time in 2014.

The separatist militants have repeatedly violated the Minsk II cease-fire agreement, provoking armed confrontations and shooting at Ukrainian positions.[2] The Kiev-based government in Ukraine now claims that Russia violates the cease-fire 50 to 80 times a day. Moscow's proxies in Ukraine have shelled Avdiyivka in eastern Ukraine, a town still held by the Kiev government, and also fired on Ukrainian forces near the port of Mariupol. Moscow's allies have brought in heavy weaponry, including tanks—again in direct violation of Minsk. Russian special forces have infiltrated Ukraine, and the Russians have maintained surface-to-air missile systems in areas prohibited by the agreement.[3] And a report from a Virginia-based cyber-security firm indicates that Russia has been waging a cyber war against Ukraine all along.[4]

In the words of a senior Western diplomat: "The familiar pattern is recurring. Russia makes high-level assurances that it wants peace, and meanwhile stokes the violence on the ground with fighters and arms."[5]

All the signs point to a Russian escalation. The proof will come in Moscow's deeds, not its denials. But it's worth remembering that Russian actions in Ukraine have already crossed a Rubicon before now—several Rubicons. The annexation of Crimea itself was thought unthinkable—until Putin went in and did it. Then, in summer 2014, while Moscow was supplying the separatist rebels in Donetsk and Luhansk with tanks, rocket launchers, and advanced air-defense systems, one of those air-defense systems shot down Malaysian Airlines Flight 17, killing 298 civilians.[6] Forensic evidence implicates Russian regular forces, as opposed to separatist rebels, for the incident, according to an independent report from a German research organization.[7] The episode aroused memories of Moscow's downing of Korean Air 007 in 1983, which took place during some of the frostiest days of the Cold War.

Recent years seem to have liberated Putin to be more frank and unapologetic about his aims. He has publicly acknowledged that he ordered the annexation of Crimea weeks before that region's referendum on independence,[8] and he admitted that he was willing to put Russian nuclear forces on alert during the Crimea crisis.[9] Putin might also feel emboldened because his back-against-the-wall stance against the West has bolstered his political popularity at home, where his approval ratings remain very high. Western sanctions on Russia for its behavior in Ukraine show little sign of working, even after multiple rounds, the most recent following the downing of Flight 17.

Respected, sober political analysts, such as Graham Allison and Dimitri K. Simes, writing in the *National Interest*, warn that a U.S. response to Russian aggression in Ukraine could potentially lead to war. (Conflicting accounts even suggest that Putin has threatened to use nukes if the United States intervenes in any substantial way.) A Russian–American war seems inconceivable to many, but Allison and Simes caution that "when judging something to be 'inconceivable,' we should always remind ourselves that this is a statement not about what is possible in the world, but about what we can imagine." How many of us imagined that one day Putin would dare to send two Russian nuclear bombers into American airspace over Alaska? That's what he did in May 2015.

Allison and Simes, longtime observers of Russia, say that they are "more concerned about the drift of events than at any point since the end of the Cold War."[10] In a sign of what may come next, the Prosecutor General's Office of Russia has begun a so-called investigation into "the legality of the independence" of Estonia, Latvia, and Lithuania—the Baltic States that were the first to break from the Soviet Union.[11]

Meanwhile, Putin's budding ally in Beijing is also moving aggressively, if more quietly, to expand Chinese influence and put pressure on American allies in Asia. The most visible, consequential, and troubling area of Chinese activity is in the South China Sea, where a newly assertive Beijing is staking claims to disputed island archipelagoes while building—and fortifying—artificial islands. In effect, China is laying claim to sovereignty over the South China Sea, a direct threat to the law of the seas, as well as to the United States and its Asian allies—whether Japan, the Philippines, Malaysia, South Korea, or Vietnam, the latter not technically an American ally but a country with a long history of difficulty with China. These countries dispute China's claims and assert counterclaims of their own, but none have the strength and force to pursue their aims as does Beijing. Only America can thwart Chinese designs.

One key flashpoint is the Spratly Islands, home to rich fisheries as well as oil and gas deposits. The territory is disputed: China, Vietnam, Malaysia, and the Philippines all make claim to it, and they occupy pieces of the island.[12] In April 2015, satellite images revealed that China is "building a concrete runway" on the Spratlys that would "be capable of handling military aircraft," including fighter jets and surveillance aircraft.[13] This was only the latest evidence of Chinese militarization there: Satellite photos in February showed that China had actually constructed an 800,000-square-foot island on top of Hughes Reef in the Spratlys. China has stationed helipads and anti-aircraft towers on both islands.[14] It's all part of its broader strategy to build serviceable land areas in the archipelago to serve Chinese military and territorial pursuits.

What's at stake here has global ramifications, not only for international security but also for the global economy. If Beijing got its way, its new claims of territory in the South China Sea would convert about 80 percent of the South China Sea and its islands from international waters to Chinese possessions.[15] The South China Sea is home to some of the world's busiest shipping lanes, through which passes a substantial portion of the world's commerce. If China converted these waters to its jurisdiction, America and its Asian allies would be forced to heed Chinese dictates.

Tempers have been flaring—between Beijing and its Asian neighbors, especially in the Philippines, and also between Beijing and Washington. In May 2015, the Obama administration sent a surveillance plane over Fiery Cross Reef, a portion of the Spratlys where one of the Chinese airstrips is being constructed. The surveillance prompted a tense face-off with Chinese naval forces, which ordered the American plane to leave the airspace, and Beijing filed a formal diplomatic complaint.

The words heated up when China released a policy paper detailing its new military strategy, which made clear that its future plans centered around a vast expansion of its naval forces. The document accused China's neighbors of provocations in the South China Sea, and it also warned America, though not by name. "Some external countries are . . . busy meddling in South China Sea affairs," it said. "It is thus a long-standing task for China to safeguard its maritime rights and interests."[16]

Around the same time, a provocative editorial in *Global Times*, a Chinese tabloid, hinted at a showdown with the United States. The editorial argued that conflict between the two great powers was inevitable if the United States didn't stop interfering in China's affairs in the South Pacific. "We do not want a military conflict with the United States, but if it were to come, we have to accept it," the editorial said.[17]

Up to now, Beijing's aggression has been enabled by a muddled and diffident American response. Though President Obama touted his "Asian pivot" as a key plank in his foreign policy, he has put no muscle behind it. Obama's speeches stress the importance of Asia, but he has sent no substantial increase of naval forces into the region to bolster our beleaguered allies there, all straining to hold their own against Chinese pressure. Navy data show that the U.S. will deploy an average of only 58 ships to the Western Pacific, and that the number will increase barely 10 percent by 2020.[18]

Obama's inattention has been interpreted as weakness, and it worries American allies, including Japan and the Philippines—who, perhaps in part because of it, have taken some provocative actions of their own, making the standoff with China more volatile and increasing the risks of escalation or a dangerous incident.

As we go to press, there are some hopeful signs that the United States is awakening to the Chinese challenge. Obama seems to have decided to confront the Chinese more directly—at least by way of demonstrating that Washington has no intention of ceding the South China Sea to Beijing. In May, the Pentagon began exploring options for enforcing freedom of the seas in the South Pacific; these include patrolling American ships within 12 nautical miles of those islands and sending American warplanes over the artificial islands that China is building. The goal would be to send a more concrete warning to Beijing than we have delivered before. But even these steps pose risks. What does the U.S. do if the warning isn't heeded? Already, China has announced that its determination to say the course in the Spratlys is as "firm as a rock."[19] If the U.S. doesn't follow through, it will once again leave its allies feeling vulnerable, and we will have lost face again in an international dispute, as Obama did in 2013, when he backed down from his heralded "red line" warning in Syria.

Clearly, the Obama administration recognizes that its passive approach in the South China Sea has failed and that something must change. It seems likely, though, that American aims are relatively modest: to dial down Chinese aggression. The airstrip and many of China's man-made islands are near completion; the Chinese won't abandon them. The U.S. and its allies are probably going to have to live with that, but through concerted effort, they should work to get Beijing to relinquish its wildly ambitious talk of colonizing the South China Sea and converting international sea lanes into Chinese territorial waters. In short, American options here are limited, which is why we need leadership and strategic vision more than ever. Dangerous as it could prove to be, the situation in the South China Sea holds more potential for constructive resolution than the crisis in Ukraine: American and Chinese interests are more intertwined than America's and Russia's, and in Xi, Washington faces a leader as formidable as Putin but less driven by motives of honor and revenge. American statesmanship has an opening here. All we need is statesmen.

ENABLING AND FACILITATING ROGUE REGIMES

On a separate front, Russia and China's facilitation of leading rogue actors has sown discord and instability around the world.

In April 2015, the Obama administration announced a preliminary agreement with the Islamic Republic of Iran to limit Iran's nuclear program, allowing Iran to keep its nuclear facilities open under strict limits. But those limits would be in place for only the first decade of the accord, and even under these, the only assurance that the Americans could provide was that Tehran could not "race for a nuclear weapon in less than a year." In short, the agreement all but guaranteed that Iran would soon have a nuclear capability. The agreement was reached through the administration's willful disregard of stubborn facts about the Tehran regime's behavior and intentions.

Nuclear experts warn that the deal will be impossible to verify, given Iran's history of noncompliance with similar agreements.[20] Ray Takeyh, an Iran expert at the Council on Foreign Relations, notes that Iran will enjoy "a sizeable enrichment capacity, and none of its facilities will be shuttered as was once contemplated." And Takeyh points out that the 10-year "sunset clause" is the real key to understanding the agreement. After 10 years, he says, "all essential restriction on Iran's enrichment infrastructure" will expire, thereby allowing Iran to develop highly advanced nuclear capabilities.[21] "What is often missed," he adds, "is that Iran's ingenious strategy is to advance its program incrementally and not provocatively."

Skeptics of the deal could hardly be encouraged by the increase in provocative behavior from Iran since the deal was announced. In April, Iranian Revolutionary Guard ships fired warning shots and then intercepted and seized a Marshall Islands vessel in the Persian Gulf, only days after Iranian patrol ships surrounded an American vessel.[22] The United States directed a destroyer toward the area, along with patrol aircraft.[23] And the Obama administration's reassurances to Israel about its continued security were belied when Ayatollah Khamenei, discussing the Iran deal shortly after its completion during a speech in Tehran, warned: "I'd say [to Israel] that they will not see [the end] of these 25 years."[24]

Iran's aggression in the Gulf mirrors that of China's activities in the South China Sea. In fact, China has enabled much of Iran's naval activities, in addition to providing other military assistance: "Over the years, China has supplied Iran with anti-ship cruise missiles, surface-to-air missiles, combat aircraft, fast-attack patrol vessels, and technology to produce ballistic missiles and chemical weapons," writes Tzvi Kahn, a Senior Policy Analyst for the Foreign Policy Initiative.[25] Iran's naval commander visited China to discuss broader military cooperation shortly before the incidents in the Gulf.[26]

Preparing for both Iranian and Chinese naval threats is straining the U.S. Navy's current force structure.[27]

At the same time, Russia, long a partner of Tehran's, has just announced the sale of an $800 million, S-300 missile-defense system to Iran. Coming just as Iran began formalizing the nuclear deal with the United States, the missile-defense sale is illustrative. It suggests that Iran is emboldened by the arrangements it has made with Washington, while also preparing itself, defensively, for any consequences of breaching the agreement—especially since the Americans insist that the "military option" remains "on the table" should Iran violate the terms. Putin just made it easier for Iran to do so.

"That deal represents a lot of money to Russia and a system Iran wants," said Russian expert Tom Nichols, a professor at the Naval War College. "From their perspective, why bother waiting? What price would be paid if they do it? This is what happens when other countries in the world feel they can act as if the United States doesn't exist." The missile-defense deal, he continued, was "yet another moment where Russia and Iran underscore the reality that they can do whatever they like, unconstrained by a disengaged United States."[28]

The S-300 sale reflects a deepening alliance between Moscow and Tehran that has developed over certain shared goals, all of which revolve, in some form or another, around checking American influence in the Middle East and around the world. Thus, Moscow has worked assiduously to help Tehran get closer to where it can reach its "breakout" nuclear capacity—after which point, a whole new reality will take shape. That explains why Tehran has dragged out the talks so long; time is its ally, and the Russians are helping them build more nuclear facilities. In 2014, Moscow announced agreement to help Iran build two more nuclear reactors in Bushehr. Moscow and Tehran have also found common cause in Syria, where they support the Assad regime, and they have played an indispensable role in its survival. Both countries are working together to blunt international sanctions against them—Iran because of its nuclear program, Russia for its annexation of Crimea and violation of Ukrainian sovereignty. The two countries have reached an agreement for Russia to market $20 billion of Iranian crude oil on the world market, weakening the U.S. effort to shut down Tehran's oil revenues.

According to Amir Taheri, the Russians have a phrase, *fortochka Obama*: the "Obama window of opportunity." It refers to the sense among many internationally that there will never be a better time than now to make advances and claims, while the United States is saddled with such dilatory leadership. As Taheri summarizes: "By the time the 'fortochka Obama' is closed, Moscow and Tehran hope to have consolidated a firewall spanning a vast territory from the Baltics to the Persian Gulf, shielding them against what Putin and Iranian 'Supreme Guide' Ali Khamenei designate as 'American schemes.'"[29]

The "fortochka Obama" has been left wide open in Syria, where 2,000 Russian troops have been deployed[30] along with tanks and dozens of aircraft[31] to prop up Assad's government and supplement his military. Russia has also begun to lay the groundwork for even wider involvement, building an additional weapons depot and military facility north of the city of Latakia, Assad's stronghold.[32] Putin claims he is backing Assad only to defeat ISIS, because the West has done little to stem the rise of the would-be caliphate. But the facts tell a different story: Putin is playing both sides of the Syria crisis, while America sits on the sidelines. The FSB, Russia's security service and replacement for the KGB, has established a "green corridor" to allow would-be Russian jihadists, especially from Chechnya, to reach Syria and join up with ISIS.[33] While Putin backs Assad overtly and ISIS covertly, America has spent $500 million to train a grand total of "four or five" rebels, according to Senate testimony from General Lloyd Austin.[34] In Syria, Putin saw the window of opportunity and climbed through.

Russia must sense that same window of opportunity when it comes to North Korea, with whom it has recently entered into a highly touted "year of friendship," in 2015, during which the two countries will explore deepening their economic and political ties. What some have called a "pariah alliance" would unite two of the most destabilizing actors on the world scene. We have yet to see how substantial the ties become, but, at minimum, a closer embrace with Moscow will help

Pyongyang defy American attempts to isolate and punish the Kim regime.[35]

The Russian outreach may be doubly important to North Korea these days, since China, Pyongyang's principal sponsor in the world—often its only sponsor—has shown increasing impatience with Kim's refusal to make economic reforms and especially with his continued pursuit of nuclear weapons. Most recently, North Korea test-launched a submarine-based ballistic missile, showing capabilities greater than what most observers had projected and leading analysts to believe that the regime could have a submarine fleet equipped with such missiles within five years.

But what has long caused the most worry around the world is the regime's nuclear-weapons production capabilities. In a remarkable meeting with U.S. nuclear specialists in April, Chinese nuclear experts warned that Pyongyang's ability to produce nuclear weapons has advanced well beyond American estimates. The Chinese now believe that the North may have as many as 20 warheads and the capacity to double that count within the next year, via its stocks of weapons-grade uranium.[36] Already, the United States is concerned about the North's ability to mount a nuclear warhead on an Intercontinental Ballistic Missile that, while untested, would have a range of over 5,000 miles—far enough to reach the West Coast of the United States. The U.S. believes that the North has exported nuclear technology to Syria as well as missile components to Iran and Yemen. What's striking about the recent developments is that the Chinese themselves seem worried; up until recently, they had generally dismissed North Korea's capabilities. But according to Siegfried Hecker, a Stanford University nuclear scientist who attended the meeting with the Chinese experts, "They believe on the basis of what they've put together now that the North Koreans have enough enriched uranium capacity to be able to make eight to 10 bombs' worth of highly enriched uranium per year."[37]

To be sure, we should be skeptical of Chinese concerns. Beijing has long maintained a complicated, good cop–bad cop relationship with its troublesome Communist ally. For example, despite its recent criticisms of the North Korean nuclear program, Beijing—through a secretive, Hong Kong–based business—is providing Pyongyang with massive amounts of foreign exchange, which is critical for the ongoing viability and stability of Kim's secretive regime.[38] The Chinese have an interest in propping up that regime, if only to prevent the chaos—including a likely refugee flood—that would follow any governmental collapse. The Chinese would prefer a more stable government, but North Korea continues to serve Chinese interests as an economic vassal and as a counterweight to South Korea and a threat to the United States. North Korea's growing nuclear capabilities should motivate Washington to bolster security—including a robust missile defense. We should not count on getting any help from China.

CYBER WARFARE, MILITARY AND NUCLEAR BUILDUPS, ECONOMIC EXPANSION

The Russia-China axis, as we call it in this book, is not just worrisome because of individual military flashpoints, as in Eastern Europe or in the Pacific; and not only because of both countries' consistent and expanding facilitation of rogue actors. It is also a cause of great concern because, in multiple other arenas, both countries are aggressively fortifying themselves for growth and assertion around the world.

For years, both countries have been eating America's lunch in the game of espionage and cyber warfare. We devote two chapters of this book to their efforts in these areas. As we went to press, the Obama administration revealed one of the largest breaches of federal-employee data in history, concerning at least 4 million current or former government workers. The breached data was held by the Office of Personnel Management, and the target appeared to be

Social Security Numbers. No allegations were made, but intelligence officials believe that the attack originated from China—though they're unsure whether it was state-sponsored.[39] The massive breach of OPM data comes on the heels of a report that last year, Russian hackers penetrated the White House's unclassified computer systems and swept up some of President Obama's email correspondence; the hackers also accessed the systems at the State Department[40] and the Pentagon.[41]

To get a sense of what the stakes are here, recall the controversy that erupted early in 2015 when congressional investigators discovered, shortly before Hillary Clinton announced her presidential candidacy, that she had used a private server to send emails when she served as secretary of state from 2009 to 2013. That arrangement was unusual enough, but what made it worse was that Clinton revealed that she had culled through the 60,000 or so emails she had received during this period and decided that only about half were public records; she deleted the remaining 30,000 or so. She made the decision unilaterally; an outcry ensued from those who maintain that Clinton herself should not be the sole arbiter of what correspondence belongs in the public record. That's the political aspect of the issue, and it will play out during the presidential campaign.

But what about the chance that those emails—deleted and undeleted—could have been accessed by hackers from foreign countries or intelligence organizations? On Fox News, Megyn Kelly asked Lieutenant General Michael Flynn, former head of the Defense Intelligence Agency, about the likelihood that "the Chinese, the Russians hacked into that server and her email account."

"Very high," Flynn said. "Likely. . . . They're very good at it. China, Russia, Iran, potentially the North Koreans."[42]

Flynn isn't alone in that assessment. Despite Hillary's confident claims that her server suffered no security breaches, independent systems analysts, bloggers, and hackers probed the server and uncovered serious security lapses.

In short: It may well be that the Russians and Chinese are the only ones who have the 30,000 emails that Hillary deleted. That is a bone-chilling possibility in and of itself. Yet more broadly, as we show in this book, it is clear that in a host of other areas—commercial, military, governmental—the Chinese and Russians have compromised American security in ways that we never thought possible.

Compromising American security seems to be a particular pleasure of Putin's, as he showed when he let his planes buzz Alaska—part of a pattern of increasing aerial provocations over the last year, in which Russian strategic bombers have intruded into American airspace at twice the normal rate of recent years.[43] Some interpret the gestures as warnings from Putin to the United States to stay out of Ukraine; the incursions also reflect Putin's growing confidence in his military might, which he has been building up in recent years. Putin has embarked on a decade-long modernization of the Russian military called New Look, which has had remarkable success in updating and transitioning the country's armed forces to a model more in line with today's war-fighting demands: smaller, more tactical forces; updated, modern weaponry and equipment; and a move away from conscription to a contract-based, professionalized military. Putin has spared no expense in bringing these changes about: "We should carry out the same powerful, all-embracing leap forward in modernization of the defense industry as the one carried out in the 1930s," he told the Russian Security Council in 2012.[44] His military investments have been Russia's largest since the end of the Cold War, and they show every sign of bearing fruit.

Of possibly even greater concern is Russia's nuclear posture. Russia holds a 10–1 advantage over NATO countries in nonstrategic nukes, and Moscow has been busy violating the 1987 INF Treaty, most recently with a test launch of a ground-launched cruise missile (GLCM), a sophisticated weapon difficult to track. It is "absolutely a tool that will have to be dealt with," in the words of a NATO commander. "Militarily, a new mobile GLCM with a range between 500 and 5,000 kilometers, which is what the Russians reportedly tested, enables Russia to threaten U.S. allies in Europe, the Middle East, and East Asia," says Senator James Inhofe. "It also puts important targets in China, India, Pakistan, and other countries within range of Moscow's nuclear force."[45]

And yet, the Obama administration negotiated the New START nuclear treaty with Putin while Russia was violating the earlier INF agreement.

China is also ramping up its nuclear capabilities. In spring 2015, Beijing announced that it was enabling its long-range ballistic missiles to carry Multiple Independent Reentry Vehicle (MIRV) technology—nuclear-arms terminology for placing multiple warheads on a single missile. Beijing has possessed MIRV technology for years but not operationalized it until now, suggesting that its strategic calculus has changed. The upgrade might mean a doubling of the number of warheads that China could fire at an enemy. "China's little force is slowly getting a little bigger, and its limited capabilities are slowly getting a little better," said Hans M. Kristensen, director of the Nuclear Information Project at the Federation of American Scientists.[46]

It is important to recognize that China's assertiveness here, as in other areas, is not episodic or circumstantial, but systematic. Case in point: China's remarkably bold aggression in the South China Sea, which includes a willingness to thwart international law in constructing artificial islands and claiming sovereignty over international shipping lanes. Troubling as all that is, it's part of a broader vision, which the Communist Party in Beijing even translated and released to the world in spring 2015: a planning document that spelled out China's vision of building a "blue-water" navy—meaning one that can move offensively, not just defend national coastal waters.

Historically, the Chinese land forces were dominant. The country only recently built its first aircraft carrier. But the planning document makes clear that Beijing has prioritized the creation and maintenance of a world-class naval force: "The traditional mentality that land outweighs sea must be abandoned, and great importance has to be attached to managing the seas and oceans and protecting maritime rights and interests," the document said. "It is necessary for China to develop a modern maritime military force structure commensurate with its national security and development interests."[47]

The focus was confirmed by Xu Guangyu, a retired Chinese major general. "As China continues to rise," he said, "it has enormous interests around the globe that need protection, including investments, trade, energy, imports, and the surging presence of Chinese living abroad." And for Washington's benefit, Xu went on: "China will actively build up its military capability and deterrence, just to make sure no one dares fight with us. The United States cannot expect China to back off under pressure. It needs to know that the consequences would be unthinkable if it pushes China into a corner."[48]

China is boosting its military budget by 10 percent this year alone, to $144 billion, though some observers believe that that figure is not all-inclusive. Much of the new funding is going to the naval modernization. The United States, meanwhile, oversees a navy at its smallest since the end of the Cold War.

The priorities expressed in the 2015 planning document are, in turn, a reflection of an even broader vision, what Xi has called the China Dream: a goal to become the world's preeminent military power, surpassing the United States, by 2049, the 100th anniversary of the Chinese Communist revolution. "We must achieve the great revival of the Chinese nation," Xi said in 2013. "We must ensure there is unity between a prosperous country and a strong military."[49]

China is on the march in other areas, including massive economic and infrastructure investments in the Third World, especially Africa. Beijing forged the new Asian Infrastructure Investment Bank, persuading more than 50 nations, including many U.S. allies, to join a venture that would rival the U.S.-dominated World Bank. And closer to home for the United States, South America now has China as it leading export destination outside Latin America, surpassing the U.S.—a sobering but little-noted fact.[50] In 2012, meanwhile, Russia wrote off $20 billion in debt for several African countries, as part of its strategic push into the continent, which it sees as a lucrative export market and as a potential partner in raw-materials exports. Moscow is eager get into the race for investment in Africa, where it lost much ground after the end of the Cold War. This past spring, Russia offered to help Greece with its latest financial crisis—on the condition that the Greeks agree to route Russian oil into Europe. In economics as in everything else, Vladimir Putin plays to win.

Most troublingly, both Russia and China have taken aggressive steps to invest in and form political alliances in Latin America—traditionally America's backyard. Not all of this is new: Russia had meddled aggressively in Latin America during the Cold War, and Putin forged a powerful alliance with Venezuelan dictator Hugo Chávez and has stayed close to his successor, Nicolás Maduro. Russia and Venezuela announced joint military drills in the Southern Caribbean Sea for later this year, and rumors persist that Moscow plans to sell Caracas military aircraft.[51] In March 2015, Putin's foreign minister, Sergei Lavrov, visited Cuba, Colombia, Guatemala, and Nicaragua—countries that have famously fraught relations with the United States. Nicaragua wants to buy Russian-made fighter jets—to the concern of its neighbors,

Costa Rica and Honduras. One analyst said the move could spark "a small-scale arms race" in the region.[52] Russia and Argentina might soon close a deal under which Moscow would lease 12 Sukhoi Su-24 Fencer aircraft to Buenos Aires in return for beef and wheat. Rumors of that deal prompted the British Defence Ministry to launch a review of air defenses on the Falkland Islands.

Russia is clearly determined to make clear to the West that it remains a global power—and not a mere "regional power," as President Obama dismissively described it. Struggling under the Western sanctions and exclusion from the G8 after the Ukraine crisis, Russia is looking for new partners—and it tends to find them among nations already hostile to the United States. Moscow even appears ready to get involved in some long-running Latin American disputes, whether the U.S. blockade of Cuba or the Falklands–Malvinas Islands standoff between Argentina and the United Kingdom.[53]

China is already Latin America's biggest creditor. Earlier this year, Xi pledged massive new direct investment commitments for Latin America, and Chinese companies announced a slew of new deals in the region. At least for now, the Chinese push seems more economic than political, but like Moscow, Beijing is doing business with the regional players most at odds with Washington: Venezuela, Argentina, Ecuador, which all have a harder time getting loans from Western banking institutions, especially the American-dominated World Bank. China is setting itself up as an alternative funder for Latin America. The leading beneficiary has been Venezuela, which has supplied oil to Beijing in exchange for funding for economic and infrastructure-development projects.[54] Last year, Xi visited Venezuela and formally upgraded the two countries' relationship to a "comprehensive strategic partnership."

In the economic sphere, as in others, the United States has not kept pace with its determined adversaries, with one encouraging exception:

The Obama administration has boldly pushed for passage of the Trans Pacific Partnership (TPP), a trade deal involving the United States and mostly Asian nations as well as others, including Canada—but excluding China. "China wants to write the rules for the world's fastest-growing region," the president said. "Why would we let that happen? We should write those rules."[55] He has shown this kind of vision and purpose only rarely during his presidency, however.

THE CLOUD OF WAR AND THE URGENCY OF ACTION

It has become a commonplace in recent years to observe that the American public is "tuned out" when it comes to foreign policy and that during election time foreign-policy issues—with the exception of terrorism—tend not to engage voters. Certainly there is some truth to this, and in recent years the tendency has become exacerbated by a growing distaste, at least among a portion of the voting public, for international involvement on the part of the United States. President Obama's call to "do some nation building here at home" has resonated with Americans who rightly worry about our mounting list of domestic problems, from spiraling budget deficits and unfunded entitlement programs to failing public schools and crumbling infrastructure. It's a time-honored American tendency to want to turn away from the problems of the world.

But if there is a single prevailing point that we wish to stress in the book you are about to read, it is that the time when Americans could afford such isolationist impulses (if we ever could) has passed. A second common refrain of recent years—that we live in an interconnected world—cuts against the first. In this interconnected world, the United States remains indispensable, even if our conduct in recent years has suggested otherwise. It is our hope that, after reading *Return to*

Winter: Russia, China, and the New Cold War Against America, you will share our view that the United States must reassume world leadership in the face of mounting threats and challenges—both for its own good and for the peace and security of the world.

While America Slept

"That is why the strategic partnership between us is of great importance on both a bilateral and global scale. [Russia–China relations are] the best in their centuries-long history. They are characterized by a high degree of mutual trust, respect for each other's interests, support in vital issues. They are a true partnership."

—VLADIMIR PUTIN[1]

It was a dramatic, even spellbinding, scene. A Russian honor guard stood at attention and martial music played as the jetliner taxied into Moscow's Vnukovo Airport. As millions of Russians watched live on television or at their computers, seemingly every cameraman and print reporter in the country jostled for position—something like when the Beatles arrived at Idlewild Airport. And then, finally, the sighting: Xi Jinping, China's new president, touched Russian soil for the first time.

The hype didn't end at his arrival. Those millions of Russians continued to watch live as Xi went directly to the Grand Kremlin Palace, where, for the first time in memory, Russian cavalry units greeted a visiting dignitary. They watched as Russian president Vladimir Putin greeted Xi warmly. They watched as Xi's glamorous wife, a renowned singer and actress, carried herself with poise and elegance. The day played out on television almost like a royal wedding. And in many ways, it was. The pomp reflected reality: China and Russia have increasingly become devoted to each other.

Like smitten newlyweds, the two leaders even parroted each other's lines. "China will make developing relations with Russia a priority in its foreign-policy orientation," Xi said before arriving in Moscow.[2] Said Putin: "Russian-Chinese relations are a crucial factor of international politics. Our trade is growing, both countries are involved in large humanitarian projects, and all of that serves the interests of the Chinese and Russian people."[3]

"The fact that I will visit Russia, our friendly neighbor, shortly after assuming presidency is a testimony to the great importance China places on its relations with Russia," Xi told Chinese journalists before departing. "The two sides have had closer strategic coordination on the world stage."[4] Putin agreed: "The strategic partnership between us is of great importance on both a bilateral and global scale." The Russian-Chinese partnership, Putin added, was "characterized by a high degree of mutual trust, respect for each other's interests, support in vital issues." It was "a true partnership,"[5] and Russian-Chinese relations were "the best in their centuries-long history."[6] Xi spoke of the two nations as close friends who treat each other with "open souls."[7] He even expressed his love of Russian literature and culture.

What's happening here? Russia and China, suspicious neighbors for centuries and fellow Communist antagonists during the Cold War, have been drawing closer and closer together because of a confluence of geostrategic, political, and economic interests. The overwhelming evidence suggests that an unprecedented partnership has developed.

The world is seeing the formalization and strengthening of a historic new alliance—a Russia-China Axis that presents the leading national-security threat to the United States in this young century, against which we seem almost willfully unprepared. Few appreciate the full nature of the threat; far fewer are even aware of it. Some who are, such as journalist Joshua Kurlantzick, see the Russia-China cooperation as part of an adverse trend for democratic governance, which is losing ground around the world to autocracy.[8] But the significance of the Russia-China Axis is even broader.

Russia and China now cooperate and coordinate to an unprecedented degree—politically, militarily, economically—and their cooperation, almost without deviation, carries anti-American and anti-Western ramifications. Russia, China, and a constellation of satellite states seek to undermine American power, dislodge America from its leading position in the world, and establish a new, anti-Western global power structure. And both Russia in Eastern and Central Europe and China throughout Asia are becoming increasingly aggressive and assertive, even hegemonic, in the absence of a systematic U.S. response—notwithstanding the Obama administration's "strategic pivot to Asia." For now, the most obvious example of American impotence is the Russian repossession of Crimea in March 2014 and the seemingly inexorable preparation for further territorial claims in Ukraine. Here as elsewhere, Russia, with the quiet but clear backing of China, has called America's—and the West's—bluff, with little consequence.

In short, there is a new Cold War in progress, with our old adversaries back in the game, more powerful than they have been for decades, and with America more confused and tentative than it has been since the Carter years.

Those in the Russia-China Axis now operate against American and Western interests in nearly every conceivable area. Their efforts include the following:

- Overseeing massive military buildups of conventional and nuclear forces, on which they often collaborate and supply each other, as well as of missile defense—on which they have signed an agreement of partnership
- Conducting aggressive and often underhanded trade and economic policies—in everything from major gas and oil deals to

collaboration with newly developed nations on creating alternative international financial institutions

- Taking aggressive action to consolidate and expand territorial claims in their spheres of influence, often in violation of UN norms: Russia in Central Asia and its "near abroad"; China, with its belligerence toward various disputed islands in the East and South China Seas and also toward its Asian neighbors
- Facilitating rogue regimes, both economically and militarily, especially in regard to nuclear weaponry. China has kept the deranged North Korean regime afloat for years with economic aid and enabled Pyongyang's nuclear pursuits by its refusal to enforce UN sanctions. Russia has bankrolled Iran's nuclear program and also acted as Syrian dictator Bashar al-Assad's strongest ally, showering his regime with weapons systems, bases, and funding—even as Putin has played a key role in spearheading the diplomatic agreement calling for Assad to turn over his chemical weapons.
- Using energy resources and other raw materials as weapons in trade wars
- Acting as the two leading perpetrators of cyber warfare worldwide—activity almost entirely directed against U.S. or Western targets
- Waging a war of intelligence theft and espionage against the West—an effort that has gone on for years but was epitomized in 2013, when China temporarily sheltered, and then Russia accepted for asylum, American NSA contractor and intelligence leaker Edward Snowden
- Facilitating, albeit indirectly, terrorist groups such as Hamas and Hezbollah
- Standing together at the UN, as when the Russians vetoed—and the Chinese abstained from voting on—a Security Council resolution declaring the Crimea referendum invalid[9]

Indeed, Russia and China exacerbate virtually every threat or problem facing the United States today—from terrorism to the war in Afghanistan to instability in the Western hemisphere and the possibility of a nuclear-armed Iran.

We understand why, to some ears, this argument might sound extreme or unfounded. The recent warmth between the two regimes masks a long history of division and hostility, most recently during the Cold War, when the Sino–Soviet split divided the Communist world. The relations of the two countries reached a nadir in 1969, when tensions between them nearly led to all-out war. But since Mikhail Gorbachev's visit to China in May 1989, and especially since the fall of the Soviet Union a few years later, growing strategic affinity has prompted stronger bilateral ties. To be sure, the two nations remain rivals as well as partners in the Far East. The Russians, in particular, worry about Chinese expansionism and the penetration of Chinese refugees into their sphere of influence. The Chinese worry about Russian desires to merge the former Soviet republics into some kind of alternative European Union, thus threatening Chinese economic opportunities in Central Asia.[10] It's certainly possible that their shared interests could erode under the pressure of competition and divergent goals.

We understand, too, that Russia and China have compelling economic and political reasons for maintaining strong ties with the United States: All three nations share key mutual interests, such as steadying global financial markets and combating Islamic terrorism. Russia and China have even voted America's way recently in the UN—on North Korean nuclear proliferation, for example. But these factors only obscure a much longer track record of oppositional and even aggressive action that shows every sign of becoming a formalized, dangerous alliance. Russia and China have mastered the art of a kind of geopolitical two-step: doing the bare minimum necessary to create the impression of cooperation (voting for sanctions on North Korea, for instance) while doing nothing substantive to truly cooperate (not lifting a finger to enforce those same sanctions). Often, the two partners adopt intermittently conciliatory positions to provide themselves with deniability on major international crises—not just in North Korea, but also in Iran and Syria. Indeed, Assad's use of chemical weapons against his own people in August 2013 was a case in point. American blundering and lack of resolve left an opening for Russia to play conciliator-in-chief by proposing a diplomatic solution to the crisis, although President Obama and Secretary of State John Kerry had initially pushed for a military strike. But when Kerry inadvertently stated that Assad could avoid the attack by turning over his chemical weapons to inspectors, the Russians saw their chance and stepped in, announcing their support for that plan and offering their assistance in brokering it. (Unsurprisingly, China supported Putin's plan.) The agreement did hold off the American attack—but also almost certainly bought Assad time to hide and move his chemical-weapons supplies before inspectors could come in. Indeed, Assad missed his first deadline—December 31, 2013—to turn over the first tranche of Syria's chemical weapons, forcing Norwegian and Danish ships sent to collect the weapons to turn back.[11] The UN blamed security concerns and bureaucracy for the delay, and, in typical fashion, the State Department sought to play down the issue. "As long as we see forward progress that's what's most important here, and we have," Marie Harf, the State Department's deputy spokesperson, said.[12] But how the process will unfold remains to be seen, and Assad continues to consolidate his power as the June 2014 presidential elections approach.

The Syria crisis showed the Axis powers (especially Russia) in a new light: They protected a mutual ally and in the process presented themselves as peacemakers trying to walk the Americans back from yet another military intervention in the Middle East. And, in fact, two years into the crisis, Putin's staunch backing of Assad has now accomplished a nearly complete reversal of fortune for the regime: Whereas the expectation two years ago was that Assad would go—it was just a matter of time—he's now an essential partner in the process, whatever happens.

No wonder that *Forbes*, in its 2013 annual survey of the world's most powerful people, selected Putin as Number One, elevating him above President Obama. "Who's more powerful: The omnipotent head of a corroding but still feisty power or the handcuffed head of the most dominant country in the world?" the magazine asked. "This year's snapshot of power puts the Russian president on top. Putin has solidified his control over Russia ('dictator' is no longer an outlandish word to ponder) and the global stage. Anyone watching the chess match over Syria has a clear idea of the shift in the power towards Putin."[13]

Nevertheless, in Washington, there seems to be little urgency and even less understanding about the burgeoning Russian-Chinese alliance. Our leaders appear unwilling or unable to grasp the magnitude of the situation and the inadequacy of their approach. American policy has been weak, bordering on negligent—the approach of a nation that seems to be conceding power and the ability to shape events.

As this book went to press, the United States stood passively by as Russia, following its annexation of Crimea, continued to interfere overtly and covertly in Ukraine, sponsoring pro-Russian militias in the country's east and south. Faced with Ukraine's pleas for military assistance, President Obama responded with a meager offer to provide military rations—and even those were slow in coming.[14] Unable to generate consensus among its NATO allies and unwilling to act decisively on its own, America seems to have all but conceded Ukraine to the Russian political orbit. *Washington Post* columnist Anne Applebaum quoted an exasperated Canadian diplomat who said, "It's like watching a hockey game with only one team on the ice."[15]

Even before these events unfolded, President Obama was sending similar signals—not only as regards Ukraine but also in connection with the mounting challenges the United States faces on many fronts. In his State of the Union speech in January 2014, for instance, Obama made clear that the U.S. was practically withdrawing from the field. He put no emphasis on confronting our enemies and made no explicit mention about the need to compete with China and Russia. The administration's much-heralded "pivot to Asia" got just one sentence, and the president's comments about the Middle East were perfunctory—save for his reference to Iran, where Obama made it clear that he would do everything in his power to support an agreement that contains such egregious loopholes that the Iranians can continue to enrich uranium at low grades, keep tens of thousands of centrifuges, and restart their full-blown enrichment program on less than a day's notice. The difficulty of enforcing even the best deals with such adversaries was illustrated a day after Obama's speech, when reports surfaced that the Russians have tested a medium-range cruise missile, in violation of the landmark 1987 arms-control treaty.[16] The 1987 treaty was thought to be sound; by contrast, few but the most devoted Obama defenders see the Iranian agreement as anything but reckless, a virtual giveaway to an outlaw regime that will endanger the United States and its allies.

Unfortunately, our allies have become accustomed to such disappointments. Indeed, rather than strengthening relations with American allies, the Obama administration, through its clumsy handling of the NSA wiretapping scandal, has found itself having to apologize to governments from Brazil to France to Germany for unauthorized monitoring of leaders' and citizens' phone calls. Indeed, reports have suggested that the NSA has monitored as many as 35 nations. The United States continues to prove far more adept at taping our allies and alienating our strategic partners than at developing and articulating a coherent policy in concert with them. "Fuck the EU," Victoria Nuland, assistant secretary of state for European affairs, was caught on tape saying, expressing her contempt for European efforts to quell the crisis in Ukraine.[17] German chancellor Angela Merkel, already alienated by American wiretapping, called the comments "completely unacceptable."[18] Meanwhile, a German newspaper editor opined that Vladimir Putin "should certainly be laughing himself stupid" over the latest fracas.[19]

As the Western alliance frays and the U.S. becomes less powerful, Russia and China become more aggressive in the advocacy of their interests. They grow stronger while we do nothing to stand in their way and arguably become weaker. The stakes are enormous. If we don't build awareness of what Russia and China are up to, greatly improve our understanding of their actions and motives, and take steps to defend ourselves and protect our interests, we will see our economic and political well-being threatened. And we'll watch as the international order tilts toward authoritarianism and away from democratic ideals and freedoms.

That would be a tragedy for America and for the world.

CHAPTER 1

The New Terrain

"In my opinion, the competition between China and the U.S. in the 21st century should be a race, that is, a contest to see whose development results are better, whose comprehensive national power can rise faster, and to finally decide who can become the champion country to lead world progress."

—GENERAL LIU YAZHOU, CHINA[1]

"What preserved peace, even in Cold War conditions, was a balance of forces."

—VLADIMIR PUTIN[2]

"After my election, I have more flexibility."

—PRESIDENT BARACK OBAMA[3]

Xi Jinping's visit to Moscow in March 2013 was dramatic, but the event was a long time coming. It was foreshadowed, in fact, more than a decade earlier, in 2001—the historic year that saw the 9/11 attacks on New York and Washington and the launch of America's War on Terror. Those attacks fundamentally transformed American foreign policy and American relations with both countries and the rest of the world. But while America geared up to fight a shadowy, multinational enemy, Russia and China were playing a much older, more traditional game: the time-honored practice of two strong nations identifying common interests and formalizing an alliance.

In June 2001, in Shanghai, the two countries created a kind of alternative NATO: the Shanghai Cooperation Organization (SCO). Evolving out of a predecessor organization, the Shanghai Five, and originally something of a vague concord between Russia and China, the SCO has developed more recently into a comprehensive effort to strengthen economic, military, and cultural ties and to provide mutual security. Vladimir Putin has called the SCO "a reborn version of the Warsaw Pact."[4] Unlike the old Warsaw Pact, however, which excluded China, the SCO is a joint Russian-Chinese alliance that includes the four "stan" countries that have tilted against democracy: Uzbekistan, Kazakhstan, Tajikistan, and Kyrgyzstan. Putin has made clear in recent years that he now sees the SCO as an explicit response to Western attempts to expand NATO—an effort that he views as a betrayal after his cooperation with the West, especially after 9/11.

Working together in the SCO, Russia and China have forged strong relationships with enemies of the U.S., such as Iran (which has observer status), and with those that have contentious relationships with the U.S., such as Pakistan (which has applied for full membership). The SCO has also allowed observer status to India, Afghanistan, and Mongolia; Turkey became a "dialogue partner" in 2013.[5] For Iran, in particular, SCO membership would guarantee stability in its relationships with Russia and China and further its interests in Central Asia.[6] Because of the SCO, the United States has a difficult time building consensus on nuclear nonproliferation, drug trafficking, trade rules, and a host of other issues.

That difficulty would probably grow if the SCO's membership became much larger—a likely possibility. Its member states already cover an area of more than 30 million square kilometers, with a combined population of 1.46 billion. If India were to join, the organization would contain the two most populous countries. "The leaders of the states sitting at this negotiation table are representatives of half of humanity," said the host of the SCO's 2005 SCO summit. That was a bit of an overstatement at the time, but the words may soon reflect reality.

Only a month after the SCO's founding, Russia and China signed the Treaty of Good-Neighborliness and Friendly Cooperation, the most significant agreement between the two powers since the historic 1950 compact signed by Stalin and Mao. The 2001 pact was a 20-year strategic treaty in which both parties formalized their shared positions on sovereignty issues and their opposition to "uni-polarity," code for American influence abroad. The treaty made sense to both powers for many reasons. First and foremost, it increased their leverage internationally in relation to United States power, which was at a historic high. Both countries saw American unilateralism as a threat to their interests and traditional spheres of influence.

The treaty also served individual needs on both sides. The Russians' greatest need was for capital investment, and the Chinese had capital to burn. The Russians, meanwhile, had massive energy reserves and a willing and needy buyer in the Chinese. The Chinese were also eager to buy Russian military technology. All in all, for the Russian economy, the treaty was vital. For the Chinese, modernizing their armed forces and securing stable energy supplies were two of the most pressing national issues. The treaty helped fulfill both needs.

Few observers at the time, however, understood the significance of the alliance between the two longtime foes. "If China and Russia decide to get into bed with each other," Ralph A. Cossa had written in the *New York Times* a few years earlier, "the appropriate response is to wish both of them pleasant dreams, since each will surely feel compelled to sleep with one eye open."[7] Such skepticism about a Chinese-Russian partnership made sense at the time. After all, with so much adversarial history between them, how close could the two nations get?

Yet, with the benefit of hindsight, it now seems clear that the seeds were planted during those years for the culminating moment of 2013, when Xi visited Moscow to so much political pomp and ceremony. By the time they met in Moscow, Xi and Putin were seeking more than just expressions of friendship. They were pursuing a substantive agenda of cooperation and partnership, signing at least 35 agreements covering a range of issues—economics, travel and tourism, agriculture, banking, science and technology, military technology, and geopolitical cooperation. These agreements represent only the latest illustration of a Russian-Chinese collaboration that has been deepening for years— most of it in opposition to U.S. interests. Let's take a look at the key areas.

FACILITATING ROGUE REGIMES AND FORGING A "LEAGUE OF AUTOCRACIES"

Vladimir Putin was riding high in February 2014, as Russia hosted the Winter Olympics in Sochi. It was the first time Russia had ever hosted a Winter Games, and Putin was determined to revel in every minute of it. And so he hosted a lavish reception in the Atrium ballroom of the Rus Sanatorium, a structure that dates to the Stalin era. Yet, as the *Wall Street Journal* put it drily, "Mr. Putin's guest list ha[d] some big gaps." While most prominent Western leaders stayed away, Putin entertained President Xi along with then-President Viktor Yanukovych of Ukraine, President Aleksander Lukashenko of Belarus—and North Korea's second-highest-ranking official, even though Pyongyang was sending no delegation of athletes to Sochi.[8] If, as the old saying has it, we know someone by his friends, Putin's Olympic reception provided a fresh reminder.

"It takes time for societies and policymakers to understand that a major shift in global affairs is afoot. But what we see clearly, in recent months, is the emergence of a new constellation of powers," wrote William C. Martel in *The Diplomat*. The new grouping includes China, Russia, Iran, North Korea, Syria, and Venezuela. On the surface, these nations are surely distinct; in some cases, indeed, they have conflicting interests. But for the most part, they are united in that their economic and geostrategic goals are inimical to U.S. interests. "There are two common fears that animate the policies of these authoritarian governments," Martel noted. "One is their apparent fear of democracy, freedom, and liberty, which each of these societies work aggressively to curtail. Second, these authoritarian regimes fear the power and influence of the United States and the West."[9] Thus, they are eager to work together when possible, or at minimum stay out of one another's way. As Russian Foreign Minister Dmitri Lavrov said of China: "We appreciate Beijing's measured and impartial stance on the Ukrainian crisis, as well as China's manifest understanding of all its manifold aspects, including the historic ones."[10]

Russia and China are both directly and indirectly supporting and facilitating the efforts of U.S. adversaries around the world—especially the Iranian and North Korean nuclear programs. Russia provides technical assistance and nuclear know-how to Tehran and has sold advanced weapons to defend Iran's nuclear sites from air strikes. Russia is Iran's biggest provider of foreign weapons, supplying $3.442 billion in total arms sales since 1991.[11] The Russians have also assisted Iran in constructing its Bushehr I nuclear reactor, which critics say is abetting Iran's pursuit of a nuclear bomb. The Russians have used their position on the UN Security Council to argue against a military strike on Iran or the imposition of harsh sanctions.[12] That stance seemed to soften in 2012, when both Russia and China voted in favor of UN sanctions against Iran. On the surface, it looked as if they had finally come around to seeing things the West's way. In reality, the action was almost certainly motivated by a common desire on the part of Russia and China to keep Iran from ever aligning with the United States. Permanent enmity between the U.S. and Iran, in their thinking, is the best way to keep the Americans out of Central Asia.

Under the terms of an "interim" six-month agreement reached in Geneva in November 2013, Iran pledged to freeze and even curb some nuclear activities in exchange for an easing of economic sanctions. The Obama administration trumpeted the accords as a major step forward, and they are—for Iran. As John Bolton, a former UN ambassador, wrote, the deal accomplished three major Iranian goals: First, it "bought time to continue all aspects of its nuclear-weapons program the agreement does not cover." These include centrifuge manufacture, weaponization research, and the ballistic-missile program—hardly trivial areas. Second, Iran "gained legitimacy" by being welcomed back into the international community. And third, Tehran has escaped, perhaps forever, the crippling impact of U.S. economic sanctions; the more time passes, the more difficult it will be to reimpose them.[13] The lessening of U.S. sanctions will wind up boosting the Iranian economy by at least $7 billion, and perhaps much more. In short, the agreement is woefully, dangerously inadequate. It fails to rein in the Iranians' ability to enrich uranium; nor does it force them to get rid of their centrifuges or even to slow their heavy-water reactor. For all practical purposes, the Iranian program carries on.

Time will tell whether opponents of the agreement in Washington can mend the damage done. A bipartisan majority in Congress wants tighter sanctions against Iran now, but President Obama opposes them. Polls show that the American public has deep reservations about the deal and overwhelmingly mistrusts the Iranian government as partners in any agreement.[14] If something positive is to be salvaged from these dealings, the U.S. will have to rediscover its negotiating power. Certainly it cannot count on the Russians to halt their support of Iran's nuclear program, despite Moscow's role in the negotiations as a member of the P5+1.[15]

China does business with Iran as well and singlehandedly props up a North Korean regime that seems to be ever more volatile and dangerous. The Chinese have refused to discourage Pyongyang from building up its stockpile of nuclear warheads or from developing even more sophisticated and deadly nuclear weapons that could hit Alaska or the U.S. West Coast.

While China positions itself as a supporter of sanctions against North Korea, it does nothing to help enforce them. At heart, China doesn't want the North Korean problem resolved. An intimidating, unpredictable North Korea keeps South Korea in check and the Americans off balance in the Far East, while terrifying such staunch American allies as Japan and the Philippines. This is all to the good, from the Chinese perspective. More recently, it is true, the North Koreans got too provocative even for China's tastes, and the Chinese have been working behind the scenes to rein them in. But they do this to protect their strategic interests, not out of solidarity with the West.

China's facilitation is also essential to perhaps the most disturbing alliance of all: the long-running Iran–North Korea "axis of proliferation," as Claudia Rosett calls it in *Forbes*. In this weapons trade, North Korea for the most part is the seller and Iran the buyer, though the two rogue nations also work together on developing missile technology.[16]

All of these efforts are part of a broader Russian-Chinese goal: to build a counter-Western alliance of antidemocratic nations, what might be called a League of Autocracies—quite the opposite of the "League of Democracies" John McCain has called for.[17] These autocratic nations include not only North Korea and Iran but also Syria, Venezuela, Sudan, and Myanmar (Burma), among others. Both Russia and China sell arms to state sponsors of terrorism and have strengthened the hand of such terrorist groups as Hamas, Hezbollah, and even al-Qaeda affiliates in hopes of weakening the United States and thwarting its strategic goals.

In one of the deadliest places in the world—Syria—the Russians and the Chinese are, again, strongly aligned with each other and against the U.S. and Western powers. The Russians have a base in Syria and came under fire from the international community in 2013 for supplying weapons to the Bashar al-Assad government as it continued to suppress a rebellion, although Russia's representatives defended their actions by claiming the U.S. was supporting the rebels. It's becoming increasingly clear that the Russians will do just about anything to discredit the American view. To this end, in an op-ed in the *New York Times* after Assad used chemical weapons against his own people, Putin pleaded for "caution" from the U.S. as he argued for delaying a military strike. He wrote: "From the outset, Russia has advocated peaceful dialogue enabling Syrians to develop a compromise plan for their own future. We are not protecting the Syrian government, but international law."[18] He went on to argue that it is dangerous for Americans to see themselves as exceptional.

Putin's presentation of Russia as an honest broker was starkly at odds with the facts. Indeed, during the March 2013 chemical-weapons attack in Aleppo, when the Americans called for a UN investigation into the claims of both the government and the rebels, the Russians supported only the claims of the Assad government.[19] Further, the Russian envoy to the UN openly mocked U.S. concerns by reminding the Americans of their erroneous claims about chemical weapons in Iraq a decade earlier.

Both Russia and China have vetoed proposed UN Security Council resolutions that sought to put pressure on Assad (and more recently, they helped block a Security Council resolution affirming the sovereignty and national borders of Ukraine). Russia has supplied $928 million in weapons to Syria since 1991.[20] China, for its part has repeatedly said that it opposes forceful foreign intervention in Syria and has called for a political solution.[21] Both Axis nations have generally been wary of what they perceive as American attempts at regime change.

Meanwhile, the Obama administration, still in "reset" mode, shows little sign that it understands the challenge the Axis poses or has any intention of addressing it. The U.S. is withdrawing from the Middle East and retreating from commitments it made to allies there and in Western and Eastern Europe. Our disengagement from the world couldn't come at a worse time.

CYBER WARFARE

In the area of cyber warfare, America has done somewhat better. Here, at least, American officials show some recognition of the enormity of the challenge facing us. In fall 2012, former Defense Secretary Leon Panetta warned that the U.S. could someday face a "cyber Pearl Harbor." Panetta also said, "It's no secret that Russia and China have advanced cyber capabilities." That was an understatement.

In fact, Russia and China are the world's leading practitioners of cyber warfare. They work overtime to sabotage and subvert military, economic, and infrastructure assets of nations they view as adversaries—and to loot their systems of military intelligence, diplomatic information, and corporate trade secrets. The Russians have brought down the technology infrastructure of Georgia and Estonia; Chinese hackers affiliated with the Army of the People's Republic have infamously been identified as the culprits in massive attacks on U.S. banking, security, infrastructure, and even military systems.

In his January 2012 unclassified Worldwide Threat Assessment before the Senate Select Committee on Intelligence, Director of National Intelligence James Clapper named Russia and China as the state actors most active in stealing secrets from the United States and attacking us through cyberspace.[22] If Panetta's dreaded cyber Pearl Harbor materializes, one or both of the Axis nations will almost certainly be behind it.

In a political sense, a cyber Pearl Harbor has already happened. The leaking of national-security secrets in June 2013 by Edward Snowden, and the refuge he was given, first by the Chinese and then by the Russians, ought to remind skeptics of the potential costs and dangers we face in this area. Though both nations were careful to profess that they didn't support Snowden's actions, their protection of him should make clear, too, that Moscow and Beijing would take any chance available to undermine American power and international influence. And they don't need to rely solely on their own efforts to do this.

In late September 2013, the U.S. announced that Iran had successfully hacked into unclassified Navy computers running email services and internal intranets. It showed a new sophistication from Iranian hackers, suggesting they now have the capability to break into U.S. military systems. They had previously focused their attacks on U.S. banks and other private networks, and the U.S. didn't consider Iran a major cyber player. How did the Iranians ramp up their capabilities so quickly?

"They're getting help from the Russians," said cyber-security specialist and former State Department official James Lewis in a *Wall Street Journal* story that cited "current and former officials" who believe that the Iranians have developed "a growing partnership with Russian cybercriminals."[23]

MILITARY AND NUCLEAR BUILDUPS

"What preserved peace, even in Cold War conditions," Vladimir Putin has said, "was a balance of forces."[24]

On the fundamental measure of national security—military readiness—the Axis nations are building up while the U.S. is slashing its defense budget through the imposed sequestration and other automatic cuts. While the U.S. pursues wholesale reductions, the Axis pursues wholesale augmentations; while we allow our equipment, materials, and technologies to degrade, they pursue constant upgrades. Perhaps most worryingly, while the American president advocates so-called nuclear zero—a world without nuclear weapons—the Russians and Chinese bolster their atomic arsenals.

While all signs point to a strengthening Russian-Chinese relationship and more formalized cooperation and coordination, the United States is pulling back from its commitments and leaving allies from Japan in the Far East to Poland in Eastern Europe worried and vulnerable. As we have seen in Ukraine, the Russians have already taken advantage of this vulnerability. In the Far East, it may only be a matter of time before the Chinese attempt to do the same. While the Russians and Chinese make demands, the United States makes concessions. And while the Russians and Chinese pursue what they dubiously call "a new, more just world order," the United States backs away from world leadership, hiding behind the illusion of "leading from behind." It all adds up to a calamitous American message: The U.S. simply has no coherent national defense strategy.

Obama's broader disarmament agenda, both in offensive and defensive capabilities, is at odds with treaty commitments he made to our allies. His anti-nuclear ambitions are music to the ears of the Axis, but they leave the U.S. increasingly vulnerable. As former Senator John Kyl puts it: "The U.S. is now stuck with numbers and technology capable of dealing only with low-level threats."[25]

On the other side, things couldn't be more different. Putin gave Xi an honor he has allowed no other foreign leader: a visit to Russia's strategic-defense command headquarters and "war room." He even let Chinese media film the visit, as Xi observed giant computer screens of military intelligence.[26]

One key aspect of the Sino-Russian strategic partnership, military exchange, involves Russian arms sales to China and high-technology sharing. China's weapons purchases from Russia over the past 20 years account for $29 billion of its $34 billion in arms imports.[27] For the

Russians, this ongoing exchange has two major objectives: bolstering the former Soviet defense-industrial complex following the USSR's collapse, and arming a country that shares the goal of weakening U.S. control in the region.

The Chinese, meanwhile, have grown their military power exponentially over the last two decades, projecting force across Asia to the borders of India, with new naval ports imposed on client countries. Some Western estimates put Chinese military spending second only to the Americans', at $200 billion annually,[28] having grown from $20 billion 10 years ago.[29] The Chinese have even begun threatening stalwart Western allies in the Pacific and East Asia—warning Australia, for example, that it would be "caught in the crossfire" if the nation went ahead with plans to offer a base for U.S. Marines.[30] The Chinese have bullied the Philippines over the Spratly Islands, and they are engaged in a tense provocation with Japan over the disputed Senkaku Islands (called the Diaoyu Islands by China)—an ongoing battle which has made starkly clear America's declining power in the region. By the late 2020s—a little more than a decade from now—Chinese ships should outnumber American ships in the Pacific.[31]

In July 2013, an armada of Chinese and Russian warships sailed through the Sea of Japan in joint naval exercises that included live firing. Beijing called it the largest joint exercise the Chinese military had ever undertaken with another country. The Chinese fleet commander said the goal was to strengthen "strategic trust" with Russia—and that seems to be how it was received. "This shows unprecedented good relations between China and Russia," said Professor Wang Ning, a Russian Studies specialist at the Shanghai International Studies University. "It shows that the two countries will support each other on the global stage."[32]

All of this plays neatly into what has come to be called the China Dream: a goal shared by both top military leaders and Communist Party officials to surpass the U.S. as the world's preeminent military superpower by 2049, the 100th anniversary of the Chinese Communist revolution. Xi calls it simply "the dream of a strong nation," but the dream is inseparable from military prowess.

"To achieve the great revival of the Chinese nation, we must ensure there is unison between a prosperous country and strong military," Xi has said.[33] He has spared no resource to focus the military on "combat readiness" and "fighting and winning wars." No one need spell out whom the war would be fought against. There is only one candidate: the United States, China's only Pacific and East Asian rival.

"In my opinion," writes General Liu Yazhou, "the competition between China and the U.S. in the 21st century should be a race, that is, a contest to see whose development results are better, whose comprehensive national power can rise faster, and to finally decide who can become the champion country to lead world progress."[34]

Meanwhile, Russia is using its petro-wealth to rebuild its conventional military while also modernizing—and greatly expanding—its nuclear arsenal. Already, Russia's nuclear weapons outnumber America's. The 2008 Georgian war made clear, or should have made clear, that the Russians intend to reclaim the entirety of their old Soviet sphere of influence. The West's failure to lift a hand to help a democratic ally in that struggle emboldened Russian confidence.

"TELL VLADIMIR": THE U.S. ABDICATION ON MISSILE DEFENSE

On the surface, it was a customary scene: a pool of journalists waiting for the start of a news conference with President Obama and Russia's then-president, Dmitri Medvedev, in March 2012. But sitting close together beforehand, the two leaders shared an impromptu exchange inadvertently caught by a "hot" microphone.

"It's important for him to give me space," Obama told Medvedev, referring to Vladimir Putin, who had just won election to succeed

Medvedev as Russia's next president. "This is my last election. After my election I have more flexibility."

"I understand. I will transmit this information to Vladimir," Medvedev said.

Then, as the two men sat back in their chairs, barely audible over the videotape, Obama could be heard saying, sotto voce: "Tell Vladimir."

Obama and Medvedev were trying to iron out a long-running dispute between the two countries on American plans to deploy a missile-defense system in Eastern Europe—a system that the U.S. conceived mainly as protection against Iranian nuclear ambitions. The United States insisted that the missile-defense shield was intended to counter Iranian nuclear ambitions; Russia claimed that the real target of American missile-defense plans was Moscow. What mostly spooked the Russians about the American plan was the missile shield's final phase, then in development, which would allow the U.S. to use interceptors to shoot down long-range ICBMs, a core part of Russia's nuclear arsenal. Those U.S. plans angered Putin, who saw them as an encroachment on his sphere of influence and a betrayal of his cooperation with the West after 9/11—much as he had seen a betrayal in the American plans to expand NATO. He made clear that he would resist the American missile-defense effort at any cost.

"When we talk about the missile-defense system, our American partners keep telling us, 'This is not directed against you,'" Putin said. "But what happens if Mr. Romney, who believes us to be America's No. 1 foe, is elected as president of the United States? In that case, the missile-defense system will definitely be directed against Russia as it is technologically configured exactly for this purpose."[35] General Nikolai Makarov, who was then Russia's chief of the general staff, said of the missile-defense standoff: "A decision to use destructive force preemptively will be taken if the situation worsens."[36]

Happily for the Russians, the situation didn't worsen: In March 2013, just before the Xi-Putin summit meeting, President Obama blindsided them, and American allies, with a unilateral retreat on missile defense. The U.S. announced that it would deploy 14 new missile interceptors on the West Coast or in Alaska, in response to the increasingly bellicose words and deeds of North Korea—but that the U.S. would pay for this redeployment by canceling the last phase of the planned missile shield in Poland and Romania. That last phase, which involved interceptors, had concerned Putin most. Thus the United States, in the absence of any concessions from Russia, had scuttled the most vital aspects of its missile-defense plan for Eastern Europe. (Some GOP senators are urging the administration to reconsider the policy and restart the Bush-era plan for the missile shield, especially in light of the Kremlin's aggression against Ukraine.[37])

The announcement illustrated how strategically off-balance the U.S. remains under President Obama. The missile-defense shield had been geared to protect the region against prospective Iranian nukes, which Iran pursues with Russian assistance. There is no sign that the Iranian danger has lessened; on the contrary, it has grown. Thus, the shield is more needed than ever, but with North Korea acting up, the U.S. merely pulled resources from one dangerous area and shifted them to another. This is not leadership; this is lurching from crisis to crisis.

It's hard to overstate the magnitude of Obama's capitulation—one, it's important to note, that came as a surprise to the Russians, who had no inkling that the U.S. was about to back down. The move telegraphed, yet again, that America lacks a clear strategy and sense of what it is trying to accomplish in the world. Meanwhile, Russia and China show every sign of having clear plans.

Xi and Putin have moved closer together on missile defense, as they have in so many other areas; their expression of unity on the issue may have been the single most important document they signed at their March 2013 summit. The two leaders pledged to work together while voicing common concerns about the deployment of missile-defense systems around the world. They were talking about the U.S., although they didn't say so.

On the surface, the Russian-Chinese statement of concern about missile defense could have sounded like a note of weakness, a futile complaint against American power. It may have been, too, but for Obama's big announcement a week earlier, making clear just how "flexible" he intended to be. This American and Western "flexibility"— really, an abdication of responsibility—will only make America's eventual task harder, should we ever wake from our neo-isolationist slumber.

ECONOMIC COOPERATION

Among the agreements signed during Xi's March 2013 visit was a deal to proceed with the Power of Siberia natural-gas pipeline, which would provide energy-hungry China with Russian natural gas beginning in 2017. As part of the agreement, the Chinese gave up to $30 billion in loans to Rosneft, Russia's state-owned oil company, in exchange for a massive boost to their supplies of Russian oil. Both sides benefit: Russia obtains the capital needed to finish an acquisition of the British-Russian oil firm TNK-BP, while China secures the fuel source to power its workhouse economy.

More broadly, both Russia and China play leading roles in the efforts of the BRIC nations (Brazil, Russia, India, and China) to create an independent international financial structure—efforts that include starting a development bank and pooling their foreign reserves to protect against currency crises.[38] Independently, China has expanded its economic reach across not just Asia, where it projects its economic might through investment and trade, but also deep into Africa and Latin America. Russia uses its growing oil and energy industry to increase its state power and international political leverage, especially in Central Asia and Europe. Russia's economic ties with nations operating against U.S. interests—especially Syria, but also Venezuela, Iran, and North Korea—are broadening.

NATIONAL SOVEREIGNTY AND "NON-INTERFERENCE"

The Moscow meeting also included several expressions of agreement on a less specific, but hugely significant principle: what both nations speak of as non-interference in the internal affairs of other nations. Xi urged China and Russia to "resolutely support each other in efforts to protect national sovereignty, security, and development interests." At the Moscow State Institute of International Relations, he said, "We must respect the right of each country in the world to independently choose its path of development and oppose interference in the internal affairs of other countries."[39] Those were friendly words to the ears of Vladimir Putin, who has long opposed what he considers internal interference—code language for U.S. involvement in Central Asia and the Middle East. (He shows no such compunction, of course, when it comes to his own interventions.) Now, the Chinese find the concept of national sovereignty amenable as well, given their concerns about American support for Japan in the South China Sea and other strategic concerns in the Far East. It was all part of a broader expression of "strategic partnership" that included support for each other's territorial claims and goals. In a press conference with Xi, Putin even referred to Japan and Germany as "the defeated powers" from World War II.[40]

A WAKE-UP CALL

In spring 2013, the world braced for a potentially catastrophic war on the Korean Peninsula. North Korea's mysterious young leader, Kim Jong Un, was systematically cutting ties with the South, making threatening statements, and preparing a new missile launch. While periodic provocations from North Korea have become almost commonplace over the last two decades, the crisis unfolding in March and April 2013 seemed more severe, and it highlighted how destructive the leadership gap in Washington is becoming for our national security. While the Obama administration seemed to take the Pyongyang crisis seriously, it appears to lack an understanding of the bigger picture—the role China plays here and elsewhere, and the broader challenge all these crises present to U.S. interests.

There are exceptions to the general lack of understanding. "Chinese behavior has been very disappointing," said Senator John McCain. "Whether it be on cyber security, whether it be on confrontation on the South China Sea, or whether it be their failure to rein in what could be a catastrophic situation." Warning that accidental war could break out on the Korean peninsula, McCain blamed China as an enabler of the North Korean regime and its nuclear program. "China does hold the key to this problem," McCain said. "China could cut off their economy if they want to."[41] (From time to time, China does put the hammer down on its troublesome ally, as in May 2013, when Beijing announced that its biggest foreign-exchange bank, the Bank of China, would stop doing business with North Korea's Foreign Trade Bank, which the U.S. has accused of facilitating transactions linked to weapons of mass destruction.[42])

McCain's frank talk is refreshing, but the Arizona senator is one of the few engaging in it. Far too few lawmakers on either side of the aisle are willing to put themselves on the line about the fundamental foreign-policy challenges facing the United States, though we desperately need American political leadership here—it makes a difference. During the height of the Chinese currency manipulation, for instance, Senator Sherrod Brown's persistent criticism had a real impact; China has much modulated its practices in this regard. Likewise, former Secretary of State Hillary Clinton's defense of U.S. firms overseas—where, as she put it, they felt that the "deck was stacked against them"—has helped open markets for American companies.[43]

Leadership means not only speaking up, but also taking real action—and yes, taking action involves risk. But it also holds the promise of finding solutions. We don't have the luxury of talking around these problems. America's oft described "intervention fatigue" should not, and cannot, result in responsibility fatigue: the responsibility for our safety and prosperity and our obligation to the free world, which looks to us for leadership.

Millions look to us as custodians of their defense against aggression and intimidation. They also look to America to uphold the principles we share: democracy, human rights, transparent government, and the rule of law. In short, if we believe in protecting our principles and privileges as American citizens, we must start thinking and acting to address these challenges. If we also wish to maintain our role as champion of such principles around the world, we must conduct ourselves accordingly. That is what we had to do during the Cold War. In this new era, we must make ourselves literate in our new, uncomfortable burdens.

Americans must begin by acknowledging the realities. It took us too long to grasp the threat from militant Islam. When we finally did, we ignored the far more powerful adversaries waiting in the wings who were marshaling their strength and pretending to offer support while studying our weaknesses and exploiting our exhaustion. Russia and China emerged immeasurably stronger from America's War on Terror. America, on the other hand, emerged deep in debt and uncertain of its calling.

America's misadventures in Iraq and Afghanistan have created the impression of American weakness. Our Axis rivals drew predictable conclusions. They saw that the interventions resulted in years-long chaos and in vast, untenable expenditures. They witnessed the spectacle of the lone superpower bogged down by insurgents. And they recognized a chance to reassert themselves. In his book about the rise of China, *The Contest for Supremacy*, Princeton professor Aaron L. Friedberg describes the opportunity China saw in American duress: "In the words of a People's Liberation Army–sponsored journal . . . 'Simply put, the United States has begun to enter a period of relative decline.' While the United States wallowed, other potential power centers would continue to grow and 'of course, China first of all.'"[44] The official Chinese Communist Party newspaper even gloated in a 2009 article: "U.S. strength is declining at a speed so fantastic that it is far beyond anticipation."[45]

Why do we find ourselves so unprepared at this moment in history?

There is plenty of blame to go around in the post-Soviet history of American foreign policy. Both Republicans and Democrats in Washington have helped forge our current predicament. The West missed many chances to disarm the Russian Bear in the post–Cold War era and to force Russian concessions on other issues. The potential for chaos, as first the Soviet Empire collapsed and then Russia itself began to fray, was perhaps too daunting. Bill Clinton seldom criticized Moscow throughout the 1990s, at the time of Russia's greatest post-Soviet weakness, to avoid exacerbating instability. George W. Bush was taken in by Putin's charisma, infamously proclaiming that he had looked the Russian leader in the eyes and gotten "a sense of his soul."[46] Bush allowed himself to be lulled into a false security that Putin shared his democratic goals. But at least Bush understood that Putin *had* strategic objectives, even if he misjudged what they were. President Obama doesn't seem to appreciate that Russian activities are part of broader geopolitical goals. He dismisses Putin's tough-guy "shtick" and says that he acts like the "bored kid in the back of the classroom."[47] This is a terribly foolish, cynical way to talk and think.

Likewise, we abstained from any confrontation with China after the Tiananmen Square massacres. U.S. companies had too much invested in China's stability. We told ourselves for years that economic prosperity in China would, sooner or later, lead to greater democratization.

A decade later, after 9/11, as we focused all our attention and national will on Islamist terrorists, Moscow rebuilt its challenge—aided by President George W. Bush's overstretch into Iraq and Afghanistan and by our vital need to view Putin as an ally. Meanwhile, political negligence and economic dependence left us mostly passive in the face of mounting Chinese power. Finally, as President Obama struggles to nurse the U.S. economy back to health, he has shown almost no inclination to confront Russia or China. For two decades, it has been a sorry litany of missed chances, poor choices, and hubristic acts of weakness. As a result, we face a challenge more formidable than any since the height of Soviet Communism—certainly one that is more formidable, over the long term, than that presented by al-Qaeda. There is no scenario in which militant Islam can dominate the globe.

The Axis partners are capable of just that and have deployed their resources precisely to that end—even as they recognize the complexity of the world they live in and the limitations on their own efforts. Both Russia and China, of course, maintain relationships with the United States that are often cooperative in certain areas. Moscow and Washington have made substantial progress in trade and investment relations, which will be aided further by Russia's joining the World Trade Organization. China and the United States are also economic partners; the Chinese have also taken part in joint military exercises with the United States to increase familiarity and lessen chances of conflict or misunderstanding in common international waters. Unlike the non-state actors of the Islamic world, Moscow and Beijing are in the business of survival. Martyrdom does not interest them. They don't go about provoking manifestly stronger adversaries—and they recognize, for the time being, the United States' clear, if dwindling, military edge. But they will exploit weakness whenever it serves their interests—politically, economically, militarily, and also by proxy, where their willingness to make mischief often has the bloodiest consequences.

Indeed, in some ways, it is the Axis's behavior in the most dangerous, unstable regions of the world today—North Korea, Syria, Iran, and Latin America—that demonstrates the most about Russia and China's intentions and long-range strategies. Let's examine the Russian and Chinese facilitation of rogue regimes, which shows how their actions further a well-conceived strategy while American vacillation and inconsistency show our lack of anything like a big-picture plan.

CHAPTER 2

Rogue Regimes:
How the Axis Uses Proxies to Win

"I've been known to be an optimist, but here are the Russians sending [the Syrians] up-to-date missiles, continued flights of arms going into Syria. Putin keeps our secretary of state waiting for three hours. . . . It doesn't lend itself to optimism, all it does is delay us considering doing what we really need to do. The reality is that Putin will only abandon Assad when he thinks that Assad is losing. Right now, at worst it's a stalemate. In the view of some, he is succeeding."

—JOHN McCAIN[1]

"China should be named and shamed for its role in enabling North Korea to remain and grow as a threat. North Korea is one of the most sanctioned countries on the planet, but Beijing (with only brief exceptions) has effectively watered down and otherwise dulled the impact of international sanctions on North Korean 'stability.'"

—STEPHEN YATES[2]

"Moscow has formed partnerships with China, Iran, and Venezuela to prevent the U.S. from consolidating a regional order under its auspices. Like the USSR, its predecessor and inspiration, today's Russia pursues key allies in the Middle East and Latin America, such as Syria, Iran, and Venezuela, with whom it can jointly frustrate American and Western efforts to consolidate a peaceful regional order."

—ARIEL COHEN AND STEPHEN BLANK, THE HERITAGE FOUNDATION[3]

"For more than a decade, Pyongyang and Tehran have run what is essentially a joint missile-development program."

—GORDON G. CHANG[4]

The setting was elegant: the dining room of New Century, the richest equestrian club in Moscow. The fare was extravagant: smoked trout, duck liver, venison soup, rhubarb sorbet, veal cheeks, and pear soup with caramel. The audience was distinguished: a gathering of members of the Valdai Club, a group of international academics and journalists that had flown in for the annual dinner with Vladimir Putin, Russia's once and future president. It was December 2011, and Putin was poised to retake the reins of power, once the formalities of the March 2012 elections were completed.[5]

Putin conducted a wide-ranging discussion with his audience, covering everything from the Russian government's loss of public trust to his own indispensable leadership. He lambasted the United States' plan to build a missile-defense system that, in his view, posed a deliberate threat to Russia's national security. "You ask me whether we are going to change," he said, directly addressing the Americans at the event. "The ball is in your court. Will you change?" Then Putin said something that could not help but make headlines around the world.

The only reason the United States had any interest at all in relations with Moscow, he said, was that Russia was the only country that could "destroy America in half an hour or less."[6] It would be difficult to find a statement more revealing about Putin's true position regarding the United States.

By this, we do not mean to suggest that Putin has any intention of launching a nuclear attack on America. We refer to his general disposition toward the United States: We are not only an adversary; we are an enemy. Moreover, as Putin well knows, one can pursue the destruction of one's enemy without initiating an Armageddon. And perhaps the most effective means of doing so is to facilitate and support the tactics, policies, and general well-being of rogue nations hostile to the United States. As the record of the last few decades shows, Russia and its Axis partner China have become expert at doing just this.

For many years now, Russia and China have directly facilitated the interests of North Korea, Iran, and other rogue nations such as Syria and even, in America's backyard, Venezuela. Notwithstanding moves like that of the Russians to write the UN resolution on Syria's chemical weapons or that of the Chinese to rein in North Korea on nuclear testing, both nations believe it is in their long-term good to undermine American interests and power.

They do this under the cover of a doctrine they call "non-interference": States should be able to do what they wish, whenever they wish, inside their own boundaries. The two nations that benefit most from this seemingly high-minded doctrine are Iran and North Korea, both of which enjoy extensive economic, political, and military ties with the Axis nations—Russia in particular with Iran, and China in particular with North Korea. As this chapter will show, the Axis nations have played an ongoing role in strengthening and facilitating the interests of these regimes.

Making matters even worse, Russia and China, by supporting these rouge states, have also facilitated terrorism. It is beyond dispute that Hezbollah has gotten weapons from Iran—in many cases, almost certainly Russian-made weapons. North Korea almost certainly sent to Syria the technology that built the nuclear plant that Israel destroyed in 2007. The non-interference doctrine has made it much easier for traffic in arms and military technology to flourish between these regimes. As if Russian backing of Iran and Chinese support for North Korea weren't bad enough, there is also compelling evidence that Iran and North Korea, in concert with their sponsors and independently, have begun working together on developing nuclear-weapons technology.

In short, whether around the world or closer to home, Russia and China have done the bidding of forces inimical to U.S. interests, democratic values, and international stability. This chapter will explore how each key rogue regime has thrived with Axis backing and will examine the motivations that drive Russian and Chinese support of them.

NORTH KOREA

China wanted a "new type of great power relationship" with the United States, said Chinese president Xi Jinping in June 2013, as he prepared to meet President Obama for the "shirtsleeves summit" in Los Angeles. Xi wanted to make clear, he said, that China, as the world's rising power, could work constructively and profitably with the U.S., the world's established power. In part, his message was cautionary: He wanted the Americans to take China seriously and to understand that the relationship between the two nations had to be forged on mutual respect—not the mutual fear that, he said, had often led to wars between established and rising states.

As a sign of his good faith, he pointed to the "big gift" he had recently given Washington: his public pressuring of the North Korean regime to enter nuclear talks, very much against Pyongyang's wishes.[7] Xi's intervention with the North Koreans was indeed welcome, as far as it went. But even the wording Xi used—a "big gift"—gives away that from his perspective, reining in North Korea is an American interest, not a Chinese one. More crucially, Xi's apparent change of heart about Pyongyang and his assurances to Washington are part of a long historical pattern in which both China and Russia say one thing to America's face and then turn right around and resume their support of rogue regimes.

It is well known that only one country can exert any serious influence on the behavior of the North Korean regime: China. The alliance between the two nations dates back to the early days of the Cold War, when Mao famously described the relationship as being as "close as lips and teeth."[8] Since then, it's gone through its share of bumpy patches, but China has never fully abandoned Pyongyang—and it has a decades-long track record of supplying the North Koreans with weaponry, economic aid, and diplomatic cover. If every rogue nation had that kind of support from its sponsor, the world would be more unstable than it is currently. At best, China acts as a braking influence on Pyongyang, and even then, only when the North Koreans' behavior becomes so volatile that it threatens China's broader interests. For the most part, this happens when the Kim regime acts recklessly on the nuclear issue, as it did repeatedly in 2013.

In February 2013, the Hermit Kingdom launched its third nuclear test, this time of a "miniaturized and lighter nuclear device with greater explosive force than previously." In April, the regime ratcheted up its threats against the United States and its "puppet," South Korea, with a series of moves. It warned foreigners to evacuate South Korea so they wouldn't be caught in a "thermonuclear war." The country's KCNA news agency predicted that once war broke out, it would be "an all-out war, a merciless, sacred, retaliatory war to be waged by North Korea."[9] That warning followed on the heels of the North's decision to suspend the activity of its 53,000 workers at the Kaesong industrial park that it runs with South Korea, the last vestige of cooperation between the two countries. Kim also threatened to scrap the 1953 armistice ending the Korean War and to abandon the joint declaration on denuclearization of the Korean Peninsula.

Then in April and May, Kim's regime launched a series of short-range missiles into the East Sea (just off the Korean Peninsula's east coast) and at least one missile into the Sea of Japan.[10] The regime even released a hysterical, but disturbing, fictional video depicting missile strikes on the White House and the Capitol in Washington. From its graphics to its music and almost parodic voice-over, the video was absurd; it might even have been funny, in a *Team America* sort of way.

As another manifestation of the regime's madness, though, it left few observers laughing.

Kim's behavior got so out of hand that in March, China and the U.S. co-authored UN sanctions against Pyongyang covering banking, travel, and trade.[11] Xi's foreign minister, Yang, stood alongside Secretary of State John Kerry in April 2013 and said, "China is firmly committed to upholding peace and stability and advancing the denuclearization process on the Korean peninsula."[12] In May, Xi told the North Koreans to return to diplomatic talks about their nukes.[13] As Xi put it bluntly: "No one should be allowed to throw a region and even the whole world in chaos for selfish gain."[14] His tough words made clear how exasperated the Chinese had become with North Korea—what some call China's "Pyongyang fatigue."

The U.S. was encouraged. But a closer look at China's North Korean track record makes clear that the Chinese never truly move against North Korea. Xi's gestures notwithstanding, they continue to support the regime in all the ways that really matter. Without the Chinese, Pyongyang couldn't even keep its lights on. Beijing supplies nearly all the fuel for the outlaw regime and 83 percent of its imports: grain, heavy machinery, consumer goods, you name it. The Chinese also supply the luxury goods, including pleasure boats and glamorous vehicles for the North Korean elite. Despite its leading role in authorizing the 2013 UN sanctions, China has kept this trade going—much of it in violation of those same sanctions. In light of all this, it's hard to see China's decision to cut off the North Korean bank accused of weapons dealing, mentioned in Chapter 1, as much more than a throwaway gesture.[15]

The North Koreans, if anything, are "doubling down," as the *Wall Street Journal* put it in April 2013, on their Chinese dependence, suggesting that they have confidence in the steadfastness of their Beijing sponsor. Almost all of the nation's recent economic development, such as it is, is owing to Chinese support, including deals signed by Chinese mining firms eager to get in on North Korea's largely untapped mineral wealth, which some recent reports estimate may be worth as much as $6 trillion. Other Chinese investments have included transportation, power generation, and infrastructure. Roughly two-thirds of North Korea's joint ventures with foreign partners are Chinese.[16]

"North Korea's lifeline to the outside world," says the *Daily Telegraph*'s Malcolm Moore, is the port city of Dandong, on the Chinese border.[17] About 70 percent of the $6 billion in annual trade between the two countries flows through Dandong. The black-market economy, meanwhile, may be even larger than the official trade. Even after the 2013 sanctions, trade continued unimpeded in Dandong, despite China's shuttering of the Kwangson Bank, which had channeled billions in foreign currency to Pyongyang.

Only the Chinese can enforce what the UN has put in place. But, as Moore writes, North Korea's elites continue to get whatever they need in Dandong: "Their shopping list includes luxury food and fine wine, Apple iMacs for Kim Jong Un, 30, as well as Chinese-built missile launchers and components for their nuclear arsenal."[18] Trucks leave the city every day transporting grain, fertilizer, and consumer goods to North Korea.

The 2013 UN sanctions also stipulated weapons seizures. But as one Western diplomat put it, "that will remain a largely ineffective measure until the Chinese implement it."[19] Don't bet on that happening. North Korea still makes money off its lone export—weapons. The regime sells Soviet-era technology on the black market, especially to some bankrupt African nations. Although this trade is often intercepted during inspections of North Korean ships, some of it gets through, and it almost certainly couldn't do so without Chinese acquiescence.[20]

In September 2013, Beijing released a 236-page list of equipment and chemical substances banned for export to North Korea—"fearing," as the *New York Times* noted, "that the North would use the items to speed development of an intercontinental ballistic missile with a nuclear bomb on top."[21] This seemed an encouraging sign of Beijing's willingness to clamp down on Kim's regime and his nuclear ambitions, especially as Western officials have long known that sanctions cannot work without Chinese enforcement. But the list also revealed just how extensive Beijing's knowledge is of the North Korean nuclear program. And it's one thing to make a list, another to enforce it. Finally, these embryonic gestures of cooperation, if cooperation it is, must be balanced against a much longer and ongoing track record of adversarial behavior. (Just two months later, the *New York Times* reported on a U.S. study detecting new construction at a North Korean missile-launch site—including satellite imagery suggesting that North Korea may have begun producing fuel rods for its recently restarted five-megawatt reactor.[22])

"Washington is looking to China to rein in the North Koreans. Unfortunately, Beijing has been busy giving the Kim regime the means to rock the world," China scholar and security expert Gordon Chang writes. Case in point: the KN-08, an intermediate-range ballistic missile.[23] The KN-08 presents a special threat to the U.S. While it lacks the range of some other missiles in Pyongyang's arsenal, it does not require the weeks of transport, assembly, and preparation of those longer-range missiles. Rather, it is mounted on mobile vehicles more difficult to destroy before they fire their missiles.

"And guess what?" Chang asks. "It is China that recently transferred to North Korea those mobile launchers, a clear violation of UN Security Council sanctions."[24] When Defense Secretary Chuck Hagel announced in March 2013 that the Obama administration would deploy 14 additional interceptor missiles in Alaska, he cited the KN-08. In effect, as Chang and others have pointed out, in selling this system, the Chinese have given the North Koreans the means to target American cities. China's transfer of the KN-O8 to North

Korea makes clear that Beijing really has no serious intentions of restraining Kim.[25] Those who see the Chinese as a willing partner with the U.S. in the effort to rein in the outlaw Pyongyang regime must contend with this consistent pattern of behavior. The U.S. should not be surprised. Beijing did not move against Pyongyang in 2010, either, when the regime sunk a South Korean frigate, the *Cheonan*, killing 46, and when it shelled Yeonpyeong, a South Korean island. The Chinese response in both cases was to stand by North Korea, its longtime ally. And in February 2014, China blasted a UN report on North Korea's systematic human-rights violations, indicating that it would use its Security Council veto to prevent any legal action against North Korea or its leaders.[26]

Clearly, China wants the North Korean regime to survive more or less intact. Why? China's support for North Korea is purely strategic and self-interested. Keeping the Korean Peninsula divided, and remaining an ally of North Korea, helps China maintain its authority in the region. Keeping Pyongyang in business not only staves off the possibility of facing a democracy on the border (or worst of all, a unified, pro-Western Korea), it also avoids regime collapse, which would lead to a host of problems China wishes to avoid: a refugee crisis at its doorstep, for one; the possibility that nuclear material would fall into the hands of the black market or terrorists, for another.[27]

Would China prefer to deal with a more stable actor in Pyongyang? Certainly. But China benefits even from today's unwieldy North Korean regime, which keeps its neighbors off balance while presenting a constant challenge to U.S. influence in Asia. From China's perspective, these benefits offset a multitude of sins. China's history makes clear that it does not share Western goals with regard to North Korea.

Unfortunately, policymakers in Washington *still* seem unable to recognize this. As U.S. State Department spokesman (now assistant secretary of state for Europe and Eurasia) Victoria Nuland put it in

2012: "[Kim] Jong Un can plot a way forward that ends the isolation, that brings relief in a different way of life and progress to his people, or he can further isolate them. . . . He can spend his time and his money shooting off missiles, or he can feed his people, but he can't have both."[28]

But Nuland is precisely wrong: Chinese support makes it possible for Kim Jong Un to "have both": to threaten the world while also getting what he needs to stay in power. Kim's regime "is like a honeybee," Michael Totten writes. "It can sting only once, then it dies. But it's like a honeybee the size of a grizzly bear."[29] That it can do so owes entirely to Chinese facilitation, influence, and support—all of which continue, despite cosmetic gestures and words.

The other half of the Axis does its fair share to support North Korea as well. Russia is pursuing a wide-ranging plan to boost its economic presence in Asia, which includes a proposal to build a gas pipeline through North Korea, providing the isolated country with $500 million in transit fees each year. In September 2012, Russia agreed to write off nearly all of North Korea's $11 billion in debt, accrued during Soviet times when the Kremlin worked overtime to bolster ties with its neighbor. Years in the making, the deal will forgive 90 percent of the debt and reinvest $1 billion as part of a debt-for-aid plan to develop energy, health care, and educational projects in North Korea. Free of debt, North Korea will also be able to engage in more commerce with Russia.

Russia's status as the world's other nuclear superpower, and North Korea's unquenchable interest in nukes, makes Moscow's relationship with Pyongyang a crucial issue to U.S. security. Some, like the Brookings Institution's Steven Pifer and Michael O'Hanlon, see U.S. pursuit of nonproliferation agreements with Russia as essential to ensuring that these weapons don't wind up in North Korean hands. "Pursuing one more U.S.-Russia bilateral treaty," they write, "can further reduce long-range or strategic nuclear systems to perhaps 1,000 deployed warheads on each side."[30] Perhaps, but Russia has a poor record of compliance with such agreements. The U.S. must understand that Moscow is no more interested in reining in Pyongyang than China is.

IRAN

"I would rather have a nuclear Iran than a pro-American Iran," scholar Georgy Mirsky once heard a Russian diplomat say.[31] If there is a single phrase that sums up the Axis attitude toward Tehran—especially the Russian attitude—this is it.

Those words describe more eloquently than any diplomatic communiqué or policy brief how Russia sees its interests when it comes to Iran's ongoing nuclear-weapons showdown with the United States. Along with its partner China, Russia has steadily argued against a military strike on Iran's nuclear infrastructure while thwarting the effectiveness of UN sanctions against Iran's nuclear program, sanctions that Moscow itself has voted for.[32] Sergei Ryabkov, the Russian deputy foreign minister, even published a 2012 study in a Russian security journal titled "Further Sanctions Against Iran Are Pointless."

That's a handy self-fulfilling prophecy: Sanctions against Iran have proved as pointless as Russia and China can make them. Neither power supports sanctions that would genuinely force the Iranian regime to reconsider its nuclear policies; they block sanctions that would impose embargoes on energy or arms. Instead, Russia and China put their stamp of approval only on narrowly tailored penalties that would supposedly prevent Iran from weaponizing its nuclear energy.[33] Yet even this goal has not been achieved.

"Today is a historic day and will be remembered in history," said Ali Akbar Salehi, head of Iran's Atomic Energy Organization in August 2010, as he marked the start-up of the Bushehr nuclear power plant, a core component of Iran's "peaceful nuclear program." As Salehi spoke, trucks rumbled into the site, carrying tons of uranium to be loaded into the reactor, signaling the beginning of its operational capacity. Over the next two weeks, the trucks loaded 80 tons of uranium fuel into the reactor core.[34] The 1,000-watt reactor began providing electricity to Iran in 2011.

The Bushehr reactor, situated on the Persian Gulf coast, wouldn't exist today without Russia. Its construction, development, and operation are the product of nearly two decades' worth of Iranian cooperation with the Russian business and scientific establishments. And Russia is considering whether to help the Iranians build a second reactor there.

Meanwhile, clandestine Russian involvement has been essential to Iran's development of a heavy-water reactor in Arak, which at full capacity will be capable of producing weapons-grade plutonium. Russian support for the Iranian program is so extensive that some Iranian facilities are simply adapted from Russian designs. This is the case for the Arak reactor, based on a design by NIKIET, the same firm that designed the Soviet Union's first reactors. The Arak reactor, and the enlarged version of it planned at Darkhovin, will be capable of producing weapons-grade plutonium.[35]

Iran has refused to cooperate with UN inspectors' requests for information about the Arak reactor's design and other specifications while insisting that it has no intention of weaponizing these capabilities.[36] The United States is asked to take such claims on faith—despite Iran's long history, especially under President Mahmoud Ahmadinejad, of making threats to annihilate Israel and otherwise confront the Western democracies.

The Russian-Iranian alliance is rich in irony, given a long history of antagonism between the two nations that lasted until the end of the Cold War. After the Cold War, however, the old adversaries came to realize that they had more goals—and more fears—in common than not. Today, three core concerns hold the alliance together:

- A mutual wish to reduce American influence in Central Asia, where both countries would like to increase their clout—a goal that seems more attainable with the U.S. strategic retreat under President Obama
- A mutual interest in opposing radical Sunni movements, such as al-Qaeda and the Taliban. Though these organizations are best known for their opposition to the West, their historical and religious roots make them anti-Shia (Iran is a predominantly Shiite nation) and anti-Russian as well.
- A mutual desire to oppose and defeat secessionist movements—in Iran, from the Kurds, and in Russia, from the Chechens—and to clamp down on internal dissent against their own regimes[37]

Understanding these shared interests is crucial if the United States is to grasp fully why the Russians act as they do. From the U.S. perspective, Iran is simply a rogue regime: It is working to develop nuclear weapons, despite UN sanctions; it is the world's leading nation-state sponsor of terror, especially of Hezbollah in Lebanon; it is the staunch ally of the Assad regime in Syria; and it oppresses and even kills its own people when they attempt political expression. To be sure, President Rouhani has made substantial headway in dispelling this image of Iran. In pitching a new, moderate Iran, Rouhani told the United Nations General Assembly in September 2013, "No nation should possess nuclear weapons, since there are no right hands for these wrong weapons."[38] He made a sharp contrast with his predecessor, Mahmoud Ahmadinejad, who came to New York last year to criticize Israel, deny the Holocaust, and suggest that the 9/11 attacks were the handiwork of Americans. That said, Rouhani called on Israel to give up its nuclear weapons and sign the Nonproliferation Treaty while insisting on Iran's right to a civilian nuclear program.

The Obama administration has tried repeatedly to get Moscow's help in increasing pressure on Iran. And although the Russians cooperated at the negotiating table in connection with the November 2013 Iranian nuclear accords, the agreement, as we noted in Chapter 1, is fatally flawed and will do nothing to halt or even hamper Iran's nuclear program. Benjamin Netanyahu justifiably called the agreement "the deal of the century" for Iran.[39] Somehow American negotiators saw fit to allow Tehran to continue enriching uranium and proceed with major components of its nuclear program—centrifuges, weaponization, and ballistic missiles—all while Iran continues to deny access to its military sites, particularly the Parchin base, where weapons work is believed to have taken place.[40] Yet the United States is moving ahead with its $7 billion in sanctions relief.

But the Russians see things differently. For them, Iran is a bulwark against American meddling and influence. Tehran's intransigence and its challenge to U.S. regional prerogatives force the Americans into enormous expenditures of capital, resources, and diplomatic energies. As Russian scholar Alexei Arbatov notes, Moscow views Iran as a growing "regional superpower" that can balance the power of Turkey and American military and political encroachment in the Black Sea/Caspian region and the Middle East.[41] Vladimir Putin also places Iran at the center of American plans to intervene in the Middle East. He believes, according to former Kremlin adviser Sergei Markov, that the U.S. is actually trying to destabilize the region, and he is convinced that the best policy is to bolster Iran and assure its leadership that it will not meet Libya's fate.[42]

The Russian-Iranian relationship has many components. Economically, the two countries have a trade relationship worth about $4 billion annually, much of it military trade. Russia is Iran's biggest source of foreign weapons, supplying $3.4 billion in arms sales since 1991. The trade has helped Iran modernize its defenses while serving as a shot in the arm for Russia's military-industrial sector, helping it survive many lean years.[43]

Putin and the former Iranian president, Mahmoud Ahmadinejad, not only collaborated to protect the Assad regime in Syria, they also worked "to dominate Iraq—Russia, by signing oil and arms contracts; Iran, by bribing politicians and tribal chiefs and maintaining sleeper cells in the Shiite-majority provinces," argues Amir Taheri. He points out that Iran hosted a Russian naval task force that was making a "goodwill" call on the Strait of Hormuz, through which passes a quarter of the world's oil. If Russia and Iran together gain the upper hand in Lebanon, Syria, and Iraq, they could secure "a contiguous presence from the Mediterranean to the Persian Gulf." All of this would also put more pressure on NATO ally Turkey and weaken the West in the region.[44]

But the nuclear alliance is most worrisome. The Russian-Iranian nuclear relationship began in the 1990s, when a troubled Russia began transferring nuclear technology and expertise to Iran. Russian scientists were soon traveling to Iran as part of an extensive, clandestine network, offering the Iranians assistance with missile and nuclear-weapons programs. A mid-2000s CIA report issued this finding: "Despite some examples of restraint, Russian businesses continue to be major suppliers of WMD equipment, materials, and technology to Iran. . . . Specifically, Russia continues to provide Iran with nuclear technology that could be applied to Iran's weapons program." The head of Israeli intelligence accused the head of the Russian Atomic Energy Ministry of using Iran as a source of employment for Russian nuclear scientists and also as a source of foreign reserves, desperately lacking in Russia at the time.

At the urging of the U.S., Russia scaled back some of its work with Iran in the late 1990s, cancelling a number of technology-related contracts. And as more information came to light about Iranian intentions to acquire a nuclear bomb, Russia became more hesitant—at least in public—about its support. Iranian nuclear engineers continue to train in Russia, but under tighter protocols.[45]

Still, it's important not to miss the forest for the trees here. By the time Russia began scaling back its support of Iran, it had already transferred significant quantities of information to Tehran. The ongoing work at Bushehr proceeds under the older contracts, and the Iranians have accumulated enough expertise to carry it on for years. Moscow trained hundreds of nuclear scientists to operate the plant, despite the urging of the U.S. and other Western nations to abandon the project. Hundreds of Iranians have been trained in Russia.[46] The Russian nuclear-energy firm Rosatom operates the Bushehr plant today, supplies all fuel from Russian sources, and recovers all spent fuel, which is processed and disposed of in Russia.[47] The Russians have no intention of walking away from Bushehr. If anything, they will expand their presence: Rosatom suggested in May 2012 that it would consider Iran's request to help construct a second reactor there. In April 2014, Iran announced that it has signed a protocol with Russia to start construction of the second reactor.[48]

Just as China's scolding of North Korea by no means suggests a fundamental shift of policy, Russia's role in brokering the Iranian nuclear accords should not be read as a serious rupture in the Russia-Iran nuclear alliance, which has endured many bumps in the road. Perhaps the low point came in 2010, when, under President Dmitri Medvedev, the Russians voted for another round of UN sanctions against Iran. But as noted earlier, those sanctions were weak and watered-down at Russian insistence.[49] And even this agreement came only with enticements from the U.S., including the lifting of bans on Russian arms exports and an agreement not to block sales of Russian arms to Iran.

The 2010 sanctions, along with the Russians' agreement not to sell Iran the SS-20 missile-defense system, represented the high-water mark for the U.S.-Russian "reset." Since then, and especially since Vladimir Putin retook presidential power in 2011, the Russians have resumed their strong support for Iranian nuclear and military procurement while making only occasional complaints. In January 2011, the Russians did voice disapproval over reports that the Iranians were enriching uranium at Qum. The foreign ministry said that Iran was "continuing to ignore the international community's demands on dispelling concerns about its nuclear activities."[50]

But these toothless public statements cost the Russians nothing, and they generally do nothing to interfere with Iranian nuclear pursuits. The Russians can gesture toward international cooperation on Iran, as they have recently, but as we've noted above, the accords do not necessarily mean that Iran's nuclear program will be diminished—let alone destroyed—by the new rules and regulations. It follows that Russia's real attitude is well summarized by Yevgeny Satanovsky, president of the Moscow-based Middle East Institute. The Russians are frustrated, he says, because their cooperation with various Western initiatives in the past produced nothing positive, from Moscow's perspective. "The West has no credibility here anymore," he writes. "The view is that Russia must chart its own course based on its own interests; if we don't look out for ourselves, who will?"[51] Indeed, after the Russians repossessed Crimea in early 2014, and the Americans levied sanctions in response and then expanded their scope, Moscow made clear that it *would* look out for itself. Deputy Foreign Minister Sergei Ryabkov warned that if the West didn't back off, the Russians would link their cooperation on Iran negotiations with the Ukraine situation. "If they force us into that," Ryabkov said of Western officials, "we will take retaliatory measures."[52]

*****

"China will not hesitate to protect Iran, even with a third World War," said Chinese Major General Zhang Zhaozhong in 2011.[53] The general's stunning statement came during the same month that China provided Iran with the most advanced intercontinental ballistic missiles the nation had ever obtained, along with the technical expertise needed to operate them.[54] Where most American observers tend to think of Russia as more closely aligned with Tehran, they can no longer overlook the substantial and growing Chinese-Iranian alliance—particularly on military and economic matters.

According to Gordon Chang, Chinese companies have violated international treaties and UN rules by selling equipment and materials to Iranian companies. Indeed, Beijing regularly exploits its dual role as Iranian benefactor and permanent member of the UN Security Council. Since 1991, China has sold more than $2.2 billion of arms to Iran.[55] China's exports to Iran include fighter jets, main battle tanks, and naval vessels, as well as roadside bombs, landmines, air-defense systems, and armored personnel carriers.[56]

The most disturbing interchange involves nuclear materials. China remains Iran's top source of nuclear and missile technology.[57] Chang traces the trade back to 1974, when China began helping Pakistan develop an atomic weapon as a hedge against Indian nuclear ambitions. Chang believes that Pakistani nuclear scientist A.Q. Khan sold China's nuclear technology to rogue states—including Iran and North Korea—almost certainly with Beijing's knowledge. Indeed, a North Korean engineering team took up residence at Khan's lab and stayed for years, with the approval and assistance of senior Pakistani military and political leadership. And an Iranian team of scientists, returning from a visit to Beijing, paid a visit to Khan's lab in 1995, which strongly suggests Chinese involvement in facilitating personal contacts between Pakistan and its customers. Moreover, Chinese companies played a leading role in Pakistan's development of the P2 centrifuge, the core mechanism of enrichment technology in Iran and North Korea.

In 2012, Ahmadinejad, then the president of Iran, attended the SCO summit, where Iran has observer status, to emphasize economic and strategic ties and to appeal for political support as Iran dealt with pressure from the U.S. and the West over its nuclear ambitions.[58] Ahmadinejad found a receptive audience. Much like Russia, China sees an anti-U.S., potentially nuclear-armed Iran as strategically useful in balancing American regional ambitions in the Middle East.[59] As with Russia, China's role in the P5+1 negotiations over the Iranian nuclear deal amounts to less than meets the eye.

China's support for Tehran goes well beyond the nuclear issue. China's main rationale for supporting Tehran, even more than political self-interest, is economic self-interest. For China, energy security is paramount, and energy has become the foundation of Chinese-Iranian relations. In 2011, China was the largest importer of Iranian crude oil, taking in 543,000 barrels per day.[60] The oil connection is particularly vital: The Iranians have enough oil to remain a key China supplier for years to come. Meanwhile, due to its limited oil-refining capacity, Iran is also heavily dependent on China for refined oil and gasoline imports. China has proved loyal, making up sanction-induced shortfalls in Iranian gasoline imports. For instance, in the summer of 2010, when the U.S. and EU sanctions lashed Iranian gasoline imports, China upped its gasoline sales to Iran, providing the regime with half of its gasoline imports for July—approximately 45,000 barrels per day.[61]

In recent years, China has become Iran's largest trading partner.[62] Between 2001 and 2010, Chinese exports to Iran grew almost sixteen-fold, to $12.2 billion, while Iranian exports to China in 2010 totaled $16.5 billion.[63] China has also ramped up its economic investments in Iran. About 70 Chinese companies now operate in the country. As of 2010, China was financing $1 billion worth of city-improvement projects in Tehran, including the expansion of its subway and highway system.[64]

The Chinese economic powerhouse has proved vital to Iran's survival as the West's crippling sanctions—which include expelling Iran from the global banking network—have pushed the regime to what some see as an impending breaking point. Iranian oil sales, which account for 80 percent of the government's revenue, have been cut in half by the sanctions. Since the sanctions permit Iran to use its oil-sales revenue to buy products only from those nations to which it sells, a flood of cheap Chinese products has inundated the country.[65] Without those cheap products, Iranian consumers would doubtless be struggling even more. At the same time, the situation plays right into China's hands, increasing Beijing's political influence and economic power within Iran.

"THE AXIS OF PROLIFERATION": THE IRAN–NORTH KOREA–PAKISTAN PIPELINE

"It's very possible that the North Koreans are testing for two countries," a senior American official told the *New York Times* early in 2013—the other country being Iran. He spoke after an Israeli publication ran an article, "Why Iran Already Has the Bomb," which argued that North Korea and Iran were working together to develop nuclear weapons. By this line of thinking, North Korea's successful nuclear test meant that, for all intents and purposes, Iran had acquired a nuclear weapon as well.

Sound far-fetched? Not to close observers of the situation.

Iranians have been present at every North Korean nuclear and missile test.[66] Iranian engineers attended the North's April 2012 launch of the Unha-3 long-range missile. That launch failed, but the Iranians helped analyze the failure and address the problems.[67] "For more than a decade, Pyongyang and Tehran have run what is essentially a joint missile-development program," says Gordon Chang. And North Korea "almost certainly provides missile flight-test data to Iran."[68]

Are the Iranians using North Korea as a conduit for their own nuclear ambitions? Hard evidence so far is lacking, but the connections and circumstances all point to the fact that North Korea is selling the Iranians nuclear technology in a mutually beneficial relationship that gives the Iranians the know-how they need while providing Pyongyang with economic and political assistance. Despite some advancement on this front, at least vis-à-vis Iran, an Iran–North Korea nuclear-proliferation nexus would negate American efforts to restrict Iran's weapons-development programs, because North Korea already has a nuclear weapon and could transfer it at will.[69]

The likely Iran–North Korea collaboration underscores an important point: The United States is up against a series of Axis relationships, not just that involving Russia and China or those involving their rogue-state clients. The rogues *themselves* work together, both in concert with and independent of their sponsors.

In 2011, Al Jazeera reported on a leaked UN report indicating that "North Korea and Iran have been exchanging ballistic-missile technology in violation of UN sanctions." The report suggested that the two countries transferred prohibited technologies "on regular scheduled flights of Air Koryo and Iran Air." Even more explosively, it indicated, through several diplomats who insisted on anonymity, that a third country had served as an outlet for the transfers—China.[70]

The growing Iran–North Korea partnership masks the fact that, on the surface at least, the two nations appear about as different from each other as can be imagined. North Korea is an impoverished, secular dictatorship in Asia, while Iran is a Middle East theocracy with a growing middle class. The basis of their relationship is not history or culture, but rather a common enemy and a willingness to work with each other in spite of international isolation. Iran provides North Korea with foreign currency, which, due to oil sales, it has in reasonable abundance, while North Korea sends Iran missiles and other weapons technologies unobtainable elsewhere.[71]

It is this nexus that Claudia Rosett refers to as the "axis of proliferation." As Rosett points out, the two nations make nearly perfect partners:

> Iran, with its visions of empire, has oil money. Cash-hungry North Korea has nuclear technology, an outlaw willingness to conduct tests, and long experience in wielding its nuclear ventures to extort concessions from the U.S. and its allies. Both countries are adept at spinning webs of front companies to dodge sanctions. Both are enriching uranium. The stage is set for North Korea, having shopped ever more sophisticated missiles to Iran, to perfect and deliver the warheads to go with them.[72]

In September 2012, a North Korean delegation traveled to Tehran to attend the Non-Aligned Movement (NAM) summit. During the summit or shortly afterward, North Korea and Iran signed a Scientific Cooperation Agreement, described by North Korea's state-run Korean Central News Agency as covering "cooperation in science, technology, and education." The agreement strongly resembled the one North Korea signed with Syria in 2002, which led directly to the Syrians' development of a nuclear reactor to produce plutonium for nuclear weapons. That reactor, based on the North Korean one in Yongbyon, was nearly finished by 2007, when Israel destroyed it with an air strike.[73]

At the NAM summit, North Korea was represented by the same official—head of North Korea's parliament, Kim Yong Nam—who headed the North Korean delegation to Syria in 2002. Parties to the agreement signed between the two countries included not only Iran's former president, Ahmadinejad, but also the head of Iran's Atomic Energy Organization, Fereydoun Abbasi-Davani—blacklisted by the UN in 2007 for his involvement in "nuclear or ballistic missile activities."[74] As the agreement was signed, Iran's supreme leader, Ali Khamenei, told Kim Yong Nam: "The Islamic Republic of Iran and North Korea have common enemies since the arrogant powers can't bear independent governments."[75] No one needed to be reminded of who the arrogant powers were.

Troubling as all of this is, it gets worse: Strong evidence points to both countries' participation in what Rosett calls "the evolving global webs of illicit proliferation activities." Both countries were involved, for example, in the nuclear-proliferation network run by Pakistani nuclear scientist A.Q. Khan. These proliferation webs depend heavily on Chinese influence, and Beijing has facilitated these procurement efforts in multiple ways, whether as direct provider or middleman.

There is also compelling, if not yet confirmable, evidence that Iran and North Korea have shared expertise on tunnel construction for military purposes. In 1974, South Korean forces discovered a highly sophisticated system of massive tunnels located under the Demilitarized Zone (DMZ) between North and South Korea. Equipped with railroads, electricity, and vehicle transports, it was 35,000 meters long.[76] A generation later, in the wake of the Israeli–Hezbollah war of 2006, Israeli forces discovered large networks of tunnels close to the Israeli border that were extraordinarily similar to those constructed under the Korean DMZ. As part of its schemes to bring in foreign capital, North Korea in the past has been known to lend out its tunneling expertise for a price.

Ronen Bergman, a senior officer in the Iranian Revolutionary Guard who defected, said, "Thanks to the presence of hundreds of Iranian engineers and technicians, and experts from North Korea who were brought in by Iranian diplomats . . . Hezbollah succeeded in building a 25-kilometer subterranean strip in South Lebanon." Indeed, Beirut officials believe it likely that Iranian sources passed the tunnel-construction blueprints on to Hezbollah, having obtained them first from North Korea.[77]

Barring an almost impossible coincidence, the tunnels in Lebanon were based on North Korean plans—meaning that either the North Koreans built the tunnels or Iran passed the plans on to Hezbollah. Either way, the tunnels episode makes clear how Iran and North Korea, already dangerous enough themselves, can serve as enablers of technology proliferation for still more dangerous, unpredictable third parties. In this case, the technology involved only tunnels. Next time, it might involve nukes.

SYRIA

"We have never changed our position on Syria and we never will"—thus Alexander Lukashevich, the Russian Foreign Ministry spokesman, summarized Moscow's outlook in December 2012, just as the international community seemed to be moving toward a consensus that Assad's days as Syria's president were numbered. Like the Russian diplomat who said he'd rather have a nuclear Iran than a pro-American Iran, the statement reveals Russia's true priorities and loyalties. They may talk encouragingly and make a few half-helpful gestures, but in the end, they will stay on the side of their ally and client.

Recent developments—including Russia's move to author the UN resolution on Syria's chemical weapons—don't change the reality of Lukashevich's words. The resulting UN resolution contained no threat of force if Syria failed to comply with the disarmament terms. And while Assad will have to surrender his chemical weapons, Putin also took steps to keep the Syrian regime well armed otherwise. A major Reuters report in January 2014 reported that Russia had "stepped up supplies of military gear to Syria, including armored vehicles, drones and guided bombs, boosting President Bashar al-Assad just as rebel infighting has weakened the insurgency against him." The supply of arms from Moscow came shortly before peace talks were scheduled to begin in Switzerland.[78]

Such behavior has been par for the course for Putin. He continues to insist, for instance, that the chemical-weapons attack in August 2013 may not have been the work of Assad. He said: "We talk all the time about the responsibility of the Assad regime if it turns out that they did it, but nobody is asking about the responsibility of the rebels if they did it. We have all the reasons to believe it was a clever provocation."[79]

Neither the U.S. nor the UK and France have expressed the slightest doubt that Assad perpetrated the attack. Russia's ties to Syria make it difficult to take Moscow's skepticism seriously. Putin has brilliantly used the crisis to paint himself as international peacekeeper. He also tapped into American war exhaustion. "At the time we tried to talk to the UK prime minister about our doubts on Iraq, but they didn't listen, and look at the result," he said. "Every day dozens of people die. Do you understand? Every day. What's the result?"[80]

Russia is a longtime supplier of weapons to Syria, and throughout the civil war, Moscow sold Assad enough arms, both offensive and defensive, to help the dictator stay in power. The Russians' arming of Assad not only took place at the same time they were publically calling for peace talks, but it also flew in the face of their own statements warning the West not to arm the rebels. "In our point of view, it [arming the Syrian opposition] is a violation of international law," Russian Foreign Minister Sergei Lavrov said in March 2013.[81] By Russian thinking, international law has nothing to say about arming the Syrian regime. The significance of Russian weapons in Syria has implications far beyond Syria's borders; because the Russian shipments may also be shared with Assad's terrorist ally, Hezbollah, they also have the potential to cause widespread havoc in the region. "If Hezbollah and Iran are supporting Syria and propping the [Assad] regime up, then why shouldn't it transfer those weapons to Hezbollah?" asked senior Israeli defense official Amos Gilad. "You don't even have to be an intelligence expert, it makes sense that they will. If Hezbollah can put its hands on them, it will."[82]

Russian (and Chinese) support for Assad is perhaps the most blatant example of the double game that Moscow and Beijing have played for years. In public, they call for peace conventions and author UN resolutions; behind the scenes, they back the Syrian regime to the hilt. Russia and China have stood with Syria for years, undermining the efforts of international institutions to mediate the conflict and bring an end to the bloodshed.

The Syrian saga has moved quickly since the chemical-weapons attack of August 2013, but all along, Russia and China have remained unswerving in their efforts to protect an important ally. By July of 2012, the two nations had blocked three UN resolutions since the uprising against Assad began. Among these were a British-sponsored initiative that would have placed sanctions on the Syrian government for failing to go through with a peace plan, including a cease-fire and demands that the Syrian government stop using heavy weapons against the opposition. The British plan also suggested the basis for a political transition. The Russians blocked a Security Council fact-finding trip to Jordan, Turkey, and Lebanon to deal with the refugee crisis. Moscow said the trip was beyond the Security Council's mandate.

"I don't believe Syria would use chemical weapons," Lavrov said in February 2013. "It would be a political suicide for the government if it does."[83] Six months later, Assad proved Lavrov wrong.

The Russians did all they could in the immediate aftermath of the attack to help Syria. They made only the most grudging concessions: They issued a public statement urging the Assad government to cooperate with UN investigators, while in the same breath they alleged that the Syrian opposition, not Assad, was behind the attack. "It is now up to the opposition, which should guarantee safe access for the mission to the alleged place of the incident," said the statement from the Russian Foreign Ministry.[84] Lukashevich also fingered the opposition for the attack, saying, "This criminal act had an openly provocative character." As evidence, he pointed to a YouTube video about the chemical attacks, time-stamped hours before they began in Syria. "So the talk here is about a previously planned action," he concluded.[85]

Lukashevich overlooked something embarrassingly obvious: YouTube, run out of California, time-stamps all its videos, regardless of the time zone where they originate, by U.S. West Coast time, which is 10 hours behind Damascus.[86]

Even after the YouTube confusion had been explained, Foreign Minister Lavrov hammered away at the same theme. "There is information that videos were posted on the Internet hours before the purported attack, and other reasons to doubt the rebel narrative," he said days later. "Those involved with the incident wanted to sabotage the upcoming Geneva peace talks. Maybe that was the motivation of those who created this story. The opposition obviously does not want to negotiate peacefully."[87]

Lavrov was right about one thing: After the chemical attack, any hope for a Geneva peace conference was gone. But even Russian advocacy for the peace conference had amounted to less than met the eye. One reason they felt comfortable organizing the conference was that they knew it would fail, in no small part because they had insisted on Iran's participation. "One must not exclude a country like Iran from this process because of geopolitical preferences," Lavrov said. "It is a very important external player."[88] All the while, Russia maintained its assistance to Assad.

Lavrov's advocacy for the peace conference came almost simultaneously with news that the Russian navy was bulking up its military and naval presence in the Mediterranean and the Black Sea, sending more than a dozen warships to patrol waters near Tartus, home to Russia's only naval base in the Mediterranean. Analysts called the buildup one of Russia's "largest sustained naval deployments since the Cold War."[89] Observers in the U.S. and Europe saw the Russian deployment as less about defending Syria and Assad per se—though it would certainly help do that—and more about warning the West, and Israel, not to make another Libya out of the Syrian conflict.

The naval show of force wasn't only about ships. At the same time, the Russians announced that they would proceed with sales of advanced anti-ship cruise missiles, known as Yakhonts, to the Syrians. Russia had provided an earlier version of the missiles years before, but the new models are equipped with state-of-the-art radar systems. The updated Yakhonts would allow Assad's military to "deter foreign forces looking to supply the opposition from the sea, or from undertaking a more active role if a no-fly zone or shipping embargo were to be declared at some point," said Nick Brown of *Jane's International Defense Review*. "It's a real ship killer."[90]

If that weren't bad enough, it became clear in May 2013 that the Russians would almost certainly go ahead with the delivery to Syria of the highly advanced S-300 surface-to-air defense system. Thanks to Russian construction, technology, and know-how, Syrian air defenses were already highly advanced, but the new system could shoot down guided missiles and present a formidable, perhaps prohibitive, obstacle to warplanes trying to enter Syrian airspace. The U.S. persuaded Moscow to back off selling the S-300 to Iran—for which the Iranians eventually sued Moscow—but the Americans could not convince Russia to do the same regarding Syria.[91]

The issue of Syrian air defense bears on another threat: the likelihood that the Assad regime is transferring Russian arms, including the Yakhont missiles, to Hezbollah in Lebanon—a transfer that Israel, for one, regards as a fact. In late April 2013, Russian Foreign Minister Mikhail Bogdanov met in Beirut with Hezbollah's secretary general, Hassan Nasrallah. Sources close to the meeting said that it concerned "the role of Russia in protecting the forces that are close to it" as well as the "matching ideological, economic, geostrategic, and security-related interests of Moscow and local forces" in the region.[92]

For Israel, the meeting was dispositive. The Israelis reportedly conducted airstrikes inside Syria in early 2013 targeting suspected weapons shipments to the terrorist group.[93] But it was later revealed that the Israelis had never entered Syrian airspace; they had instead used a tactical maneuver called "lofting" to launch bombs across the border to the target about 10 miles inside Syria.[94] If the Israelis were unwilling to challenge the regime's existing air defenses, imagine the difficulties of doing so when Damascus is able to deploy the S-300 system. Israeli incursions into Syrian airspace may become prohibitive—and the Assad regime's ability to move weaponry to its Hezbollah allies will be strengthened. Thus, supposedly "defensive" Russian systems enable Assad and his terrorist allies to go on the offensive.

American policymakers need to understand how the Russians see the situation in Syria. To the U.S., Assad is a bloody dictator who has to go. But the Russians have much at stake in keeping Assad in power. Moscow stands to lose up to $5 billion in arms sales if or when the regime falls. Russian companies have major investments in Syrian infrastructure and tourism. Taken together, Russia has close to $25 billion worth of interests in Syria. Syria is not only home to the Russian naval base in Tartus; the two countries have also agreed to return the former Soviet naval base in Latakiye to Russian control.[95] Currently, more than 600 Russian technicians are working to update these Soviet-era bases.

Russia also sees compelling geostrategic reasons to support Assad. These include fear of "the spread of Islamic radicalism and the erosion of its superpower status in a world where Western nations are increasingly undertaking unilateral military interventions," as Russian defense analyst Ruslan Pukhov explained it in 2012.[96] There is no question that Russia and China remain bitter that Western forces ignored their opposition to intervention in Libya and the ousting of Colonel Qaddafi. Desperate to stay in power, Qaddafi offered China and Russia a stake in the Libyan oil industry in exchange for support in 2011. For years before Qaddafi's fall, Moscow had close military and commercial relations with Libya[97]—and since Qaddafi's demise, Russia has lost $4.5 billion in contracts.[98] Both Russian and Chinese representatives told the *Financial Times* that they would have vetoed UN Security Council Resolution 1973—the one establishing a no-fly zone over Libya—if they had known how broadly it would be interpreted. Then-President Dmitri Medvedev publicly stated that the West "simply deceived Russia" with its Libyan intervention.[99] "Russia's current Syria policy," wrote Pukhov, "basically boils down to supporting the Assad government and preventing a foreign intervention aimed at overthrowing it, as happened in Libya."[100] Forcing Assad to turn over his chemical weapons through the UN resolution does nothing to change the fundamental calculus.

Some, like Georgy Mirsky, say that Russia's anti-Western animus is like a reflex, a resurgence of the old Soviet mentality.[101] It's not all anti-Westernism, though. The Russians are pragmatic skeptics, contemptuous of American democratic aspirations. What they see in Assad is a secular (if brutal) dictator fighting off forces of radical Islam that, if they prevail, could destabilize the entire region. Its long experience with Islamists in Chechnya and elsewhere has motivated Moscow to protect Assad from that outcome. "In Moscow," Pukhov wrote, "secular authoritarian governments are seen as the sole realistic alternative to Islamic dominance."[102]

Finally, the Russians know that if Assad falls, then Iran, their most important ally in the region, will be weakened—as will Russian influence. Moscow has already seen the ouster, over the last decade, of its allies Saddam Hussein and Qaddafi. It cannot afford to stand by and watch another Western intervention weaken its regional interests.

Beijing's support for Assad, meanwhile, seems comparatively mysterious to outside observers. China enjoys a healthy $2.2 billion annual trade relationship with Syria—no match for what it does in trade with the other Gulf Arab states (roughly $90 billion annually). China's Iran commitments dwarf its Syrian investments. But China opposes a repeat of the Libyan model as strongly as the Russians do, and Beijing vetoed the UN resolutions alongside Russia in order to stand in solidarity against the West generally and the U.S. more specifically. Beijing also worries about the repercussions of regime change in Syria, as an op-ed in the Chinese *People's Daily* newspaper, an organ of the Chinese Communist Party, made clear:

> Though China has a less direct stake in Syria than Russia, the collapse of Syria will result in the West further controlling the Middle East, and Iran taking direct strategic pressure from the West. If war broke out in Iran, China would have to rely more on Russia for energy, bringing in new uncertainty to the Sino–Russian strategic partnership.[103]

Like Russia, then, China backs Assad for self-interested reasons that have little to do with actual support for the Syrian president. But while Russia has major economic and strategic interests to protect in Syria, China's stake is less vital. Rather, Beijing is standing in solidarity with Moscow in their mutual opposition to interventionism, while also supporting Russia's notion of regional "stability." Beijing knows what it's getting in Assad, and it is content with his remaining in power. Finally, in blocking U.S. and Western efforts to intervene, the Chinese help support a regime that, at little cost to themselves, causes their American rivals nothing but trouble.

VENEZUELA

"I like kitties and puppies and little animals," Vladimir Putin said matter-of-factly in 2012. It's true: The Russian strongman has a soft spot for animals, as a trove of Web photo galleries makes clear. And so it stands to reason that he wouldn't give puppies as gifts to someone unless he felt strongly about them—and Putin felt very strongly about Hugo Chávez, the longtime Venezuelan dictator. In the last year of their long partnership, Putin gave the Latin American strongman a three-month-old Russian black terrier puppy, along with a private message. When Chávez died in March 2013, Putin's condolence telegram was striking for its heartfelt praise: "He was an uncommon and strong man who looked into the future and always set the highest target for himself."

Although it's too early to predict the shape of post-Chávez Venezuela, the early signs are for continuity—and that means a strong Venezuelan relationship not only with Russia but also with China. Both countries have sent signals that they wish to work closely with Chávez's successor, Nicolás Maduro. The feeling seems to be mutual.

"We are not going to change one iota of the fundamental themes of President Chávez's policies," Venezuela's energy minister, Rafael Ramirez, told a local TV station not long after Chávez's death. "We have a very important strategic relationship with China, which we're going to continue deepening and cultivating. It's the same with our cooperation with Russia.... Chávez's policies are more alive than ever, and we will push ahead with them."[104]

During his tenure, Chávez made Venezuela an archenemy of the U.S., and he possessed the means and the motivation to harm the United States like few others could. He built strategic alliances not only with Russia and China, but also with Cuba, Iran, and Syria. While much of the international community was busy condemning Bashar al-Assad for massacring his own people, Chávez sent large shipments of oil to the Syrian leader, in defiance of international sanctions. Venezuela became deeply involved in drug trafficking and money laundering while providing staunch support for Hamas and Hezbollah. Chávez severed ties with Israel in 2009 to protest its offensive against Hamas, and in 2010, he hosted an extraordinary secret summit in Caracas for senior members of Hamas and Hezbollah, along with Palestinian Islamic Jihad.[105] "Hezbollah's presence in Latin America is growing significantly with the support of the Chávez regime in Venezuela," Roger F. Noriega, assistant secretary of state for Western Hemisphere Affairs under President George W. Bush, told the Committee on Homeland Security.

Chávez called Iranian leader Mahmoud Ahmadinejad his "brother," partnered with him in a joint Iranian-Venezuelan bank, and declared that he would consider any attack on Iran an attack on Venezuela. And indeed, should the U.S. take military action against Iran, the quickest route of retaliation would be through Venezuela—close enough to the U.S. that intercontinental missiles wouldn't be needed. Ahmadinejad placed agents from the Iranian intelligence apparatus in Venezuela to advise the army as well as the intelligence service. For years, Venezuela operated a weekly flight from Teheran to Caracas, bringing untold numbers of Iranians into the country.

Chávez's Venezuela had few stronger allies than Putin and Russia. The two countries forged a joint Russian-Venezuelan bank venture in 2009 to pursue bilateral projects, especially involving energy; Pdvsa, Venezuela's state-owned oil company, partnered with Russia's Gazprom. The bank was headquartered in Moscow with an office in Caracas. On military matters, cooperation was close. Before Chávez died, Russia granted Venezuela a $4.4 billion loan to purchase Russian weaponry and "defend its sovereignty," in Chávez's words. Venezuela pursued a separate $6 billion loan for infrastructure. Russia also sold Chávez battle tanks and missile systems.

Russia's investment in the Venezuelan oil industry grew steadily during Chávez's tenure. In May 2013, two months after Chávez died, Venezuela and Russia formed a joint venture to produce 120,000 barrels of oil a day by 2016 in two fields of the Orinoco Belt of heavy oil, regarded as the one of the world's largest hydrocarbon reserves. That agreement came with another Russian loan, this one for $1.5 billion, to finance the development of the field. Some critics are skeptical that the relationship can survive post-Chávez, but Russia has much to lose in Venezuela by allowing the alliance to languish and everything to gain by remaining committed. The projects that Moscow signed with Chávez are worth at least $30 billion. Venezuela has reason to stay close to Moscow, too: It is Russia's largest importer of arms, and Moscow promises to maintain its arms deals with Caracas.[106]

"As for our future relations with Venezuela," Putin said, "they will depend primarily on the Venezuelan people, the future president, and the country's leadership."[107] Time will tell, but don't bet on this relationship breaking up.

Meanwhile, China has pledged to continue its "strategic alliance" with Venezuela, post-Chávez, which includes increased oil exports to China and massive Chinese investment in Venezuelan oil-producing infrastructure. Without question, oil is the key driver of this relationship, though it is not the only one.

As late as 2005, Venezuela was sending only a few thousand barrels of oil per day to China. But China's thirst for oil and Chávez's hunger for loans drew the two nations closer. After getting a $36 billion loan from Beijing, Chávez stepped up shipments drastically. Venezuela now provides 500,000 barrels a day to China, a total projected to reach 1 million barrels per day by 2015. In addition, China National Petroleum is a key player, along with the Russians, in developing the Orinoco oil field. After a series of deals with the Chinese that would help him expand Venezuela's oil production, Chávez said, "Never before has

Venezuela had such a fruitful and positive relationship with a great power like China." [108]

At the same time, China has also stepped into the breach left by the U.S. ban of arms sales to Venezuela. Beijing has sold Caracas new military transport planes as well as Chinese-built trainer jets and ground radar. The two countries have hundreds of other bilateral agreements not involving military technology specifically, but a wide range of infrastructure projects. These include mining deals, satellite construction, irrigation systems, agricultural-processing plants, housing complexes, and railway infrastructure.

The questions for the Chinese post-Chávez are the same the Russians are asking: Can the relationship survive the leader's death? Early indications show a strong commitment by both countries to keeping the alliance going. In May 2013, the Chinese vice president, Li Yuancho, visited Caracas to meet with Maduro and discuss a host of ongoing and future projects, including ventures involving telecom and other technologies. "This visit has been very fruitful," Maduro said. "We will never forget the loving support that China gave to our Comandante [Chávez]. We will be loyal to the work that has been done." [109] Like the Russians, the Chinese have strong incentives to keep a good thing going.

CONCLUSION

While much of what we've discussed in this chapter has a gloomy cast, we'd like to close on a somewhat more hopeful note. The U.S. should recognize that when it takes concrete action—even if insufficient and not sustained—it has produced results. Not dramatic results, necessarily, but results: American pressure convinced the Chinese to rein in the North Koreans in the spring of 2013, at least to some degree, defusing what had been an increasingly tense situation. Dogged American diplomatic efforts persuaded the Russians to agree to a Geneva conference to mediate the Syrian conflict. More recently came the UN resolution requiring Assad to turn over his chemical-weapons supply. As we've made clear above, we're skeptical that these efforts represent genuine changes in Russia's and China's postures toward these rogue regimes, but in all cases, they were better than nothing. Broader and more sustained action should prove even more effective. (Of course, U.S. engagement doesn't always lead to positive outcomes, as indicated by the nuclear accord reached with Iran in November 2013. As we noted previously, by all indications, this accord is likely to prove hugely beneficial to Tehran but disastrous for the United States, Israel, and the Western democracies. We share the views of other observers who see the deal as part of a long-term strategy on Tehran's part to "concede to interim demands in order to secure principles that will favorably define a final, comprehensive agreement."[110])

Still, America's moderate recent successes should remind us of a timeless lesson: Applying pressure is the *only* way to achieve positive results. Russia and China are not to be persuaded by American "resets" or other conciliatory postures, but they will listen, because they must, when they understand that we are committed to actively defending our positions. There is no substitute for what Hillary Clinton called "coercive diplomacy," or what might be called muscular multilateralism: American efforts, sometimes in concert with others, to defend our interest and principles around the world. There is no substitute, in the end, for American engagement. "Leading from behind" just doesn't cut it.

Up to now, unfortunately, our leaders in Washington have not yet fully absorbed this lesson; they show intermittent signs of reengaging, but then they pull back again. Russia and China never pull back. They have always got the pedal down, full throttle, and we lose precious time and squander options with our dithering.

Russia and China are, to put it bluntly, playing a double game: They work with the United States and the international community on broad efforts and thus preserve their political deniability and their economic and political relationships with the United States; at the same time, they thwart the will of the international community by backing the world's most dangerous regimes. Neither Iran nor North Korea could long survive without Axis support. Russia, Iran, and Syria are close partners economically and militarily, and their alliance only grows closer as the United States backs off from confrontation and engagement. American passivity not only emboldens our adversaries; it also leaves our partners unsettled and prompts them to look elsewhere for support or blame us for their troubles. President Putin has made himself an ally of General al-Sisi, Egypt's top military officer, who will run for president in May 2014. Putin encouraged him to do so. It would be a "very responsible decision," he said, "to undertake such a mission for the fate of the Egyptian people." He made his support explicit: "On my own part, and on behalf of the Russian people, I wish you success." Putin made these comments during al-Sisi's February 2014 visit to Moscow, which was accompanied by news of impending arms deal with Russia worth $2 billion, bankrolled by Saudi Arabia and the United Arab Emirates.[111] Meanwhile, feeling betrayed by American dithering on Syria, Turkey blamed Washington for its domestic unrest.

At every juncture, we seem to be losing, and it is not clear what we're actually negotiating—let alone what our goals are. We will discuss specific steps that the United States can and should take in our concluding chapter. But more important, even, than our particular policies is the mindset behind them. Until Washington's foreign-policy apparatus once again embraces America's central role in the world, the United States and its allies will operate at a disadvantage.

Of course, the Russian and Chinese effort on behalf of rogue regimes is far from the only avenue in which they threaten American security. Both countries are actively pursuing an entire range of policies designed, if not wholly, then at least in substantial part, to negate or transcend U.S. influence. Unfortunately, Washington has been no better at recognizing these other threats—the most immediate and troubling of which is cyber warfare.

CHAPTER 3

Cyber Security:
The New Battlefield

"I call it the Wild West, because you can be anywhere and do anything and be effective. . . . All you need is an Internet connection."

—GENERAL WILLIAM SHELTON, COMMANDER OF AIR FORCE SPACE COMMAND[1]

"Cyber-networks are the new frontier of counterintelligence. If you can steal information or disrupt an organization by attacking its networks remotely, why go to the trouble of running a spy?"

—JOEL BRENNER[2]

"The problem is 1,000 times worse than what we see."

—ALAN PALLER, RESEARCH DIRECTOR, SANS INSTITUTE[3]

"We have a national problem and it is significant. The next big issue will be a cyber 9/11. I've been sounding the alarm, and I've been doing this now for 20 years. We are going to have a cyber event that is catastrophic."

—RETIRED VICE ADMIRAL MIKE MCCONNELL[4]

"It's fair to say we're already living in an age of state-led cyber war, even if most of us aren't aware of it."

—ERIC SCHMIDT, GOOGLE CEO[5]

The press called it "the shirtsleeves summit": President Obama and Chinese president Xi Jinping meeting for bilateral talks in the unlikely setting of Sunnylands, an estate in Rancho Mirage, California, built by the billionaire Walter Annenberg. The beautifully landscaped grounds, at the intersection of Bob Hope and Frank Sinatra Drives, might encourage a more informal dialogue, Americans hoped, and build trust between the two leaders. And it seemed to be working: At one point, Obama and Xi talked privately for almost an hour as they sat in the shade on a bench made of California redwood—a personal gift from the president to his Chinese guest.

"The president had very good discussions in an informal atmosphere—uniquely informal atmosphere—with President Xi," said Tom Donilon, Obama's national-security adviser. "If you go back through studying each of the encounters between an American president and the leadership of China since President Nixon's historic meeting in February of 1972 in China, I think the uniqueness and the importance of a number of aspects of this encounter really come to the fore," he said.[6]

And the summit did produce some results: most substantively, an agreement to cooperate closely in pressuring North Korea to give up its nuclear program.

But on another issue—one with perhaps more "uniqueness and importance" than any other discussed—there was no progress between the two leaders. In fact, there was barely an acknowledgement, on the Chinese side, that the issue existed. This was the matter of cyber warfare and cyber hacking, which Obama had promised the American people he would make a top priority at the talks. The subject had become a flashpoint in U.S.–China relations: The previous fall, outgoing Defense Secretary Leon Panetta had warned of a possible "cyber Pearl Harbor" caused by computer hackers who were trying to bring down critical infrastructure systems.

Moreover, as Obama and Xi sat together in Sunnylands, the Edward Snowden affair was breaking in the media. The day before

Obama and Xi arrived at the estate, *The Guardian*, a British newspaper, broke the story that the National Security Agency had obtained
access to voluminous data from the systems of private Internet-based
companies, including Google, Facebook, Apple, and others. It was all
part of an undisclosed government program called PRISM, under
which the NSA could collect data including search history, emails,
file transfers, and Web chats.[7] New angles kept appearing: The British
equivalent of PRISM was Tempora, under which the British Government Communications Headquarters conducted massive electronic
surveillance and freely shared their findings with the NSA. As an
uproar began, the source of these bombshell findings unveiled himself:
American Edward Snowden, a former CIA employee and, at the time,
an "infrastructure analyst" for NSA contractor Booz-Allen Hamilton.
Snowden made the disclosures from Hong Kong, where he had gone
under the guise of receiving epilepsy treatment; once there, he spilled
the goods on the classified U.S. government programs to *Guardian*
journalist Glenn Greenwald.

That's right—the most notorious national-security leaker in recent
American history fled to China for shelter and protection. And, after
the Hong Kong government rejected American pleas to extradite
him, Snowden flew off to Moscow. There, he sheltered for weeks in
the transit area of Moscow's Sheremetyevo Airport—while Russian
president Vladimir Putin, like the Chinese, refused to extradite him
to the United States.

We'll explore the Snowden case in more detail in our "Intelligence
Wars" chapter, but its explosion into the news just as Obama was
attempting to press China on cyber hacking and thievery could not
have been more symbolic. The Snowden leaks exposing vital national-
security programs, and the American failure to get him back for prosecution, represented a huge win for Russia and China—all the more
so when Snowden, in effect, told the Chinese that we were spying on

them, confirming their accusations against the U.S. The Snowden fiasco also mirrored the general ineffectiveness of U.S. efforts to confront its adversaries on the cyber issue.

Sitting with Xi at Sunnylands, Obama detailed a number of massive cyber attacks against American targets and made clear that the U.S. had no doubt they came from China. He warned Xi that Chinese cyber attacks would directly threaten the American–Chinese relationship, especially economically. But the president found Xi as immovable as Mao. Xi would protest only that China suffers cyber intrusions, too; he gave no quarter, made no admissions, and pledged no cooperation. Donilon, for his part, claimed that Obama had raised the issue with some force—Donilon made no mention of Xi's response, which was unpromising. It was more of a one-way phone conversation than a negotiation.[8]

While Xi seemed tight-lipped about the subject, his actual message couldn't have been clearer, and it was based in the most traditional kind of power politics: I'm going to keep doing what I'm doing because it benefits me, and because the price to you of trying to stop it is too high. In other words, China's cyber war against the U.S. would continue.

Obama's attempt to confront Xi came on the heels of stunning news reports earlier in 2013 that made clear the extent and sophistication of Chinese-based cyber attacks on every major aspect of American life—financial institutions, private-sector businesses, military systems, government servers, political groups, and infrastructure and power grids. These attacks have been going for years, but only recently has definitive evidence linked them to China. It is now undeniable that China is the leading global practitioner of cyber warfare.

However, the Chinese are not alone. Their Axis partner, Russia, also excels at cyber sabotage and aggressive technological attacks, though the Russians' expertise takes different forms. Proof of Russia's involvement in attacks on the American mainland has so far been lacking, but independent Russian hacker groups—if they really are independent of Moscow—have launched audacious, damaging attacks on U.S. and Western financial targets. The hacking of American retailer Target in December 2013, the largest of its kind in U.S. history—involving 40 million stolen credit card numbers—originated from Russian computers.[9]

Like Xi, however, Putin dismisses questions about cyber attacks, scoffing at the mention of "hackers" as if they were beneath his notice. And he maintains his denials that Russia was behind the sabotage that disabled Estonia in 2007 and Georgia in 2008, bringing havoc to these countries at a time when they challenged Moscow. The Chinese have attempted nothing on this scale to date.

Finally, there is Iran, which, remarkably, has launched what is believed to be the most destructive attack yet on a private-sector target: the "Shamoon" virus, which brought down 30,000 computers of the Saudi oil giant Aramco in 2012.

Cyber security may well be the ultimate battleground in our conflict with the Axis forces—cyber assault is the most immediate threat the U.S. faces, as well as the one we understand the least. Moreover, it is an area in which our key adversaries excel, in different ways. On this playing field, the power imbalances between America and the Axis are meaningless: In cyber war, the strength of your military and the size of your GDP and navy are irrelevant. What matters is whether you and your intelligence assets have the technological chops and the political daring to launch sophisticated attacks on the world's only superpower. Russia, China, and Iran have already shown that they have all the capabilities and a good share of the political daring. They are defiant and unrepentant when challenged.

To be sure, from an offensive perspective, the United States has displayed its mettle. The U.S. possesses the most sophisticated cyber-war capabilities in the world, as it demonstrated in 2009, when the

Stuxnet virus disabled the Iranian nuclear facility at Natanz. Washington denied responsibility, but most experts are confident that Stuxnet was an American operation. So are the Iranians, who launched the Shamoon virus at least partly in retaliation.

The issue for the U.S., then, is not whether it can launch effective attacks, but whether it can defend itself against them. For all the worries that Americans and their political leaders have about protecting the country against military or terrorist attacks, an invisible and virtual enemy could inflict far more extensive damage on the nation. The ball here, as elsewhere, is in America's court: The intentions and behavior of its two primary adversaries could not be more consistent, confrontational, or transparent. It is past time that Washington got serious about the looming cyber catastrophe.

THE VULNERABILITY

Richard Clarke must be accustomed, by now, to giving dire warnings—and to being ignored until it is either too late or precariously close to being so. The man who spent the years before 9/11 warning, mostly in vain, about the threat posed by al-Qaeda eventually turned his attentions to cyberspace. In 2010, his book *Cyber War*, written with Robert Knake, described potential attacks of unimaginable scope, complexity, and destructiveness and laid out how the U.S. remains undefended. And, as he had in the years before 9/11, he sketched a graphic scenario:

> Several thousand Americans have already died, multiples of that number are injured and trying to get to hospitals. . . . In the days ahead, cities will run out of food because of the train-system failures and the jumbling of data at trucking and distribution centers. Power will not come back up because nuclear plants have gone into secure

lockdown and many conventional plants have had their generators permanently damaged. High-tension transmission lines on several key routes have caught fire and melted. Unable to get cash from ATMs or bank branches, some Americans will begin to loot stores. Police and emergency services will be overwhelmed.[10]

Such an attack, if it came, would render America more helpless than it had ever been in wartime, and would make the toll of 9/11 seem like child's play. Could it really happen? Clarke insisted it could: "A sophisticated cyber war attack by one of several nation-states could do that today, in *fifteen minutes*, without a single terrorist or soldier ever appearing in this country."[11]

It took a while for official Washington to embrace his alarm. In 2010, when Clarke's book came out, President Obama's then–cyber chief, Howard Schmidt, scoffed: "There is no cyber war," he said. "I think that is a terrible metaphor and I think that is a terrible concept. As for getting into the power grid, I can't see that that's realistic."[12] But as the evidence piled up and our lack of preparedness became more evident, that complacency began to lift.

Leon Panetta has spent decades in public life. His style is reserved and matter-of-fact. A political jack-of-all-trades, he has served in Congress and in the White House as chief of staff; he has also been CIA director and defense secretary. So when he stepped to the podium in October 2012 at the Intrepid Sea, Air, and Space Museum in Manhattan to address a business audience, few expected that he would deliver the most resounding warning of his political career—one that Americans desperately needed to hear.

"A cyber attack perpetrated by nation-states or violent extremist groups could be as destructive as the terrorist attack of 9/11," Panetta said. "Such a destructive cyber terrorist attack could paralyze the nation." As an example, he pointed to Iran's Shamoon attack on Saudi

Aramco, which employed a "wiping" mechanism and a so-called kill switch to eradicate system memory in 30,000 computers, rendering them useless. The virus replaced essential system files with the image of a burning American flag. The business executives in attendance didn't need prodding to imagine the impact of such an attack on their companies. But Panetta warned of darker scenarios.[13]

Broad-based infrastructure attacks, he warned, "would cause physical destruction and loss of life, paralyze and shock the nation, and create a profound new sense of vulnerability." He described how sophisticated computer hackers—especially from Russia, China, and Iran—could bring down portions of the nation's infrastructure. "An aggressor nation or extremist group could gain control of critical switches and derail passenger trains, or trains loaded with lethal chemicals." Panetta said. "They could contaminate the water supply in major cities, or shut down the power grid across large parts of the country."[14]

Panetta's words reflected a growing awareness among American officials. Earlier in 2012, in an unclassified Worldwide Threat Assessment before the Senate Select Committee on Intelligence, Director of National Intelligence James Clapper listed cyber threats as just behind terrorism and nuclear proliferation in the list of strategic threats to U.S. security and economic interests. He named Russia and China as the state actors most active in stealing secrets from the United States through cyberspace.[15]

"We are going to have a cyber event that is catastrophic," warned retired Vice Admiral Mike McConnell in early 2013, describing an attack that would cripple U.S. banks and financial institutions.[16] And Tom Donilon called out China directly for cyber theft on "an unprecedented scale," ending the Obama administration's long-running public reluctance to identify perpetrators.[17]

It was about time: The attacks have been going on for years.

Item: In March 2012, the Department of Homeland Security warned that a major cyber attack against U.S. gas companies was under way and had in fact been going on for four months. The department called it a "gas pipeline sector cyber intrusion campaign" and warned that it was directed against multiple companies.[18]

Item: In January 2013, servers at the Energy Department's Washington headquarters were attacked, though department officials said that that no classified information was compromised.[19] The attackers stole personal employee information of the kind that could be used for criminal purposes, though investigators suspected that the attackers had broader goals, including gaining access to classified information.[20] Americans should be profoundly alarmed that departments of the federal government are being hacked.

Hackers' most disturbing potential targets are the military and the industrial sectors and national infrastructure that make normal life possible. If adversaries can interrupt industrial functioning, they could make their moves and create chaos before the U.S. could respond. Imagine, for example, hackers bringing down the FAA's flight computers or sabotaging the U.S. power grid. An attack on water infrastructure could render whole regions uninhabitable, while sabotaging power lines could take out telecommunications, emergency services, and utilities. The American economy and infrastructure are so embedded in technology—more and more of it stored in the so-called cloud—that such actions would be destructive and deadly. That's why Panetta's doomsday scenarios focused on infrastructure disruptions. And China has already conducted the necessary network mapping and computer reconnaissance of government and private networks to "cripple infrastructure and military command and control," say military sources.[21]

U.S. vulnerability also extends to its $14 trillion economy, and especially the nation's banking system, through which $13 trillion moves daily—backed not by gold or physical money but by the system of banking reconciliation.[22] A targeted, one-day attack on American credit card companies could cost $35 billion, while a full-fledged, sustained cyber assault could cost the United States some $700 billion.[23] (The 2013 Target hack, meanwhile, has already cost financial institutions more than $200 million, and that is not a final tally.[24]) Mike McConnell, the retired vice admiral quoted above and in the epigraph to this chapter, says that he is "personally acquainted" with people who have the capability of hacking into the banking system and compromising data. Some nation-states have this capability but not the intent, he says, while terrorist groups have the intent, but not the capability—yet.

"How long," he asks, "before those two come together?"

The danger extends throughout the private sector, beyond the obvious financial-industry targets. Law-enforcement officials weren't sure who launched the attacks against retailers (Neiman Marcus was another victim) in the 2013 holiday season, but they believe that they originated in Eastern Europe, "which is where most big cybercrime cases have been hatched over the past decade."[25] Stolen secrets or corporate intellectual capital impose huge costs on the most prominent firms—including Apple, Facebook, Twitter, and Microsoft, all of which reported that their employee computers or systems were hacked in 2012 or 2013. The U.S. has uncovered evidence of cyber attacks against 140 other American companies. Most of these attacks, as we'll detail later, have been linked to the Chinese military.

Surveying 56 companies and governmental organizations in a 2012 study, the Ponemon Institute, a Michigan cyber-security think tank, found that the average annualized cost of cybercrime to each was $8.9 million and that companies suffered 102 successful attacks per week. These attacks range from hacking into e-commerce platforms to stealing company financial records or customer data to "spear phishing," in which hackers target specific employees in order to obtain sensitive company information.[26] A report from 14 U.S. intelligence agencies described a sophisticated espionage campaign by Chinese spy agencies against major industries in the U.S.: biotechnology, telecommunications, nanotechnology, and clean energy. One U.S. metallurgical company lost technology to China's hackers that had cost $1 billion and 20 years to develop.[27] The Office of the National Counterintelligence Executive estimates that "losses of sensitive economic information and technologies to foreign entities" already represent between 0.1 percent and 0.5 percent of GDP.[28]

Clearly, then, the problem is real and serious, and most worryingly, we do not seem ready to combat it. What we do know, however, is the identity of the world's leading perpetrator: China.

CHINA'S MULTIFACETED CYBER WAR

"We can physically locate anyone who spreads a rumor on the Internet," bragged a salesman at a Beijing trade show, pushing his company's Web-monitoring services, which included highly advanced capabilities for tracking online postings and identifying who made them. Another official at the same trade show boasted that his company could hack into anyone's computer, "download the contents of the hard drive, record the keystrokes, and monitor cellphone communications, too."[29]

In America, such boasts would constitute a scandal; in China, they are a staple of public conversation at business conferences and in general media, part of a broader culture that accepts and endorses hacking. Chinese universities sponsor hacking competitions with businesses; talent scouts from the army attend, looking for fresh recruits. Chinese companies openly hire hackers to spy on their competitors and steal trade secrets. This is what the United States is up against when it comes to China's cyber-war practices: an adversary that is not only skilled at the tactic, but that also supports its use in government, spycraft, commerce, and crime.

China's status as the No. 1 cyber threat to the U.S. was confirmed in the 2013 National Intelligence Estimate, which warned that the U.S. faced an ongoing challenge from a massive, coordinated campaign of cyber espionage. Although the NIE identified three other countries—France, Israel, and Russia—as practitioners of economic hacking, the report concluded that these countries' efforts paled beside those of China. Few critics dispute this assessment. China is clearly at the cyber-war forefront, both in terms of the sophistication of its capabilities and the breadth of its targets.

Those targets can be grouped into three fundamental areas of American life: defense, business, and communications.

Hacking the Pentagon

Bob Gates has seen it all as a defense secretary and CIA chief, but Obama's Pentagon boss probably never thought he'd see the day that a visit to China would coincide with Beijing's first test flight of a stealth fighter—the Chengdu J-20. That's what happened when Gates went to Beijing in January 2011 to meet with former President Hu Jintao.[30] The visit was intended to help mend contentious U.S.–Chinese relations, but any attempt at diplomacy was immediately overshadowed by news of the test flight, stories and photos of which papered the normally highly censored Chinese media. Thus it could be reasonably construed that the Chinese (or at least the military) wanted Gates to know all about it. Amazingly, Hu seemed unaware of the test flight, or at least he affected to be. More disturbingly, the J-20 bore a striking resemblance to American designs.

Imagine if, during the Cold War, the Pentagon announced that the Soviet Union had stolen secrets to dozens of military programs, weapons systems, and battle plans. In an era of fallout shelters and nuclear-readiness drills, that news would probably have caused a national panic. Thankfully, nothing on that scale occurred.

But now it has.

Chinese hackers have gained access to design information for more than two dozen U.S. weapons systems, from missile-defense systems for Europe and Asia to combat aircraft and ships. These include many of the Pentagon's flagship weapons and technology programs: the Patriot missile system, the Navy's Aegis ballistic-missile-defense system, the F/A-18 fighter jet, the V-22 Osprey, Black Hawk helicopters, and the F-35 Joint Strike Fighter. It's not clear how much information on each the Chinese obtained. But American officials believe that the Chinese have at least two ways of exploiting what they obtained: first, to knock out communications and corrupt data in the event of a conflict; and second, to modernize their own weapons systems, a clear goal of the Chinese leadership, as shown by Beijing's massive increases in military spending.[31]

Most disturbingly, in a series of infiltrations that apparently went on for years, the Chinese stole enormous quantities of data concerning Lockheed Martin's F-35 Lightening II—the costliest, most complex jet fighter ever produced.[32] They may have already put the information to good use, as the world discovered in January 2011 when China tested the Chengdu J-20. To be sure, the J-20 is not yet at operational capacity—it cannot participate in real-world missions—but it emerged well ahead of schedule, and its appearance kicked up a storm of questions.[33] Secretary Gates had believed that the Chinese would not develop such a fighter until 2020; Chinese analysts put the date around 2017 or 2018. So the J-20 test flight surprised everyone.[34]

So much so, in fact, that China was accused of copying the designs for the plane. Military officials in China have dismissed these claims as a "smear campaign." A test pilot, Xu Yongling, boasted that the "J-20 is a masterpiece of China's technological innovation."[35] Innovative it may well be, but is the innovation native to China? Some analysts called the J-20 a "kludge," or a machine assembled from mismatched parts.[36] Others suggested that the Chinese borrowed the design from the Russians, while still others wondered whether they might have copied it from an American stealth fighter downed in Serbia during the 1999 U.S. military operations there.

The most troubling possibility—although one that is not proven—is that a series of cyber attacks on the Pentagon gave the Chinese the necessary know-how to construct the plane. These cyber attacks targeted the Pentagon's $300 billion Joint Strike Fighter program, a multinational project headed by the United States, between 2007 and 2009. The JSF program researched and designed the F-35 Lightening II. Although it has proved difficult to trace the origins of the attacks with certainty, former U.S. officials believe that the cyber attacks originated in China.[37]

The hackers were able to capture several terabytes of information about the electronic systems and design of the F-35, though precisely what they stole is not known. The most important computer-weapons systems were not touched; they are stored on hard drives not accessible from the publicly accessible Internet.[38] Only relatively unimportant parts of the F-35's coding were ever on the Internet, the Pentagon insists. "They'll have very little information other than how you maintain the aircraft," Jim McAleese, a former consultant for Lockheed Martin, said. "They'd know, for example, at what number of hours do the engines get checked, or the procedures for maintaining the stealth coding . . . they wouldn't have information about key parts."[39]

Is McAleese's relative calm about the situation well founded, or does he seriously misjudge what occurred? It's hard to know. Even if he's right, the program's multinational nature offered attackers multiple avenues for penetration: Turkey, for instance, suffered heavy data losses.

Moreover, some parts of the enormous project were contracted out to private companies. These, too, were targeted.[40]

In sum, we don't have a definitive reading on what hackers stole from the Defense Department in their attacks from 2007 to 2009; nor do we know what effect these attacks had on the development of the Chinese J-20. But consider that in March 2012, BAE systems, Britain's largest defense contractor, acknowledged that Chinese cyber attacks had successfully penetrated its network and that data on the F-35 project had been stolen.[41] And remember that, even by the estimates of Chinese analysts, the J-20, even in its not-quite-ready form, appeared years in advance of anyone's expectations.

"American U.A.V. technology is very sophisticated," Xu Guangyu, a retired military general and director of the China Arms Control and Disarmament Association, said in late 2013. "We can only envy their technology. Right now, we're learning from them."[42] His statement came as Comment Crew, a Chinese hacking group that has been linked to the People's Liberation Army, spearheaded a hacking operation dedicated to stealing our drone technology. The Chinese government is striving to put China at the forefront of drone manufacturing—something they seemingly can't accomplish without lifting our drone designs. More like "stealing from" the United States than "learning from" us.

The Chinese military has not released statistics on the size of their drone fleet, but analysts say they have thousands, making their drone force second only to the United States' 7,000.[43] And China's domestic-security apparatus—with a budget of $124 billion this year—has become keenly interested in drones, suggesting that they could become an integral part of China's surveillance system. All of this spells bad news not only for the U.S. but also for China's neighboring nations. Indeed, in early September 2013, China's navy sent a surveillance drone into the disputed Diaoyu Islands (called the Senkaku Islands by Japan), the first time China had ever deployed a drone into the

East China Sea. But it surely won't stop there. The Chinese will use drones to secure maritime sovereignty but, according to a report from the security think tank Project 2049, Chinese strategists have also discussed using drones in attack situations in the event of war with the U.S. breaking out in the Pacific.[44] The Chinese will take what they want. And they want our drone technology.

Finally, hackers are also targeting defense partners and suppliers. Lockheed Martin has identified China as the main suspect in what the company called a "sophisticated" attack on its systems. In December 2006, a major cyber attack forced the Naval War College in Rhode Island—where much military strategy against China is developed—to take all its computer systems offline. One professor at the school told his students that the Chinese had brought down the system.[45] Some hackers target defense firms, seeking to gain information on weapons systems; others target tech firms to steal valuable source code that powers software applications—the firms' bread and butter.[46]

In addition to the damage these attacks do to U.S. firms, the perpetrators use everything they obtain for their own purposes—that is, not only to weaken the United States but also to strengthen themselves. In an earlier time, aggressor nations helped themselves to the raw materials and energy stores of vulnerable nations. Today, our adversaries are helping themselves to our innovation.

The Mandiant Report and China's War on the U.S. Media

One calls himself UglyGorilla. He once kept a blog about his job as a People's Liberation Army hacker, in which he "lamented his low pay, long hours, and instant ramen meals."[47] Another goes by the moniker DOTA and appears to be a Harry Potter fan, frequently setting account-security questions such as "Who is your favorite teacher?" and "Who is your best childhood friend?" to the values "Harry" and

"Potter" and creating accounts such as poter.spo1@gmail.com. They sound like high school geeks, but they are at the forefront of a cyber-hacking effort of unprecedented scale and effectiveness.

Even doubters began to understand the reach and determination of the Chinese cyber-warfare effort with the stunning news in January 2013 that the *New York Times* had been extensively hacked over several months the year before. Chinese hackers infiltrated the paper's computer systems, stealing passwords for reporters and other employees by installing malware (malicious software designed to disrupt computer operations or gain access to systems) that provided entry to computers on the *Times* network. The hackers eventually gained access to the personal computers of 53 *Times* employees.[48]

What were they after? As it turns out, the attacks coincided almost to the day with the paper's extensive investigative report on the family wealth of former Prime Minister Wen Jiabao, which totaled more than several billion dollars raised from a host of businesses, from real estate to rubber manufacture to Ping An, one of the world's largest financial-services firms.[49] The Chinese government warned the *Times* that there would be consequences for its investigation, and soon enough, the paper discovered what those consequences were. The hackers broke into the email accounts of the paper's Shanghai bureau chief, David Barboza, the lead reporter on the Wen story, as well as the account of Jim Yardley, the paper's South Asia bureau chief. The *Times* claimed that the hackers did not obtain any crucial information, however.

To track the invaders and understand what was happening, the *Times* hired a computer-security consulting firm, Mandiant, which has been doing big business of late. The firm now serves 30 percent of the Fortune 500 firms and saw an amazing 76 percent increase in revenue in 2012. That's no accident. Mandiant is sweeping up clients victimized by Beijing's nonstop assault on private- and public-sector computer servers.

The Mandiant investigators weren't sure how the hackers broke into the *Times* system to install the malware, but their best guess was that they used some variation of a "spear-phishing" attack. Spear-phishing involves sending emails to employees that contain malicious links or attached files, often in the guise of useful information. The most sophisticated phish attacks can appear to come from someone in the recipient's address book, even a close colleague. Once the recipient clicks on the link or attachment, the hackers can install the malware, which often takes the form of "remote access tools," or RATs, which can pilfer oceans of data, from passwords to document files, and send them back to the hackers' Web servers.[50]

Shockingly, the *Times* attack was only the tip of the iceberg. As Mandiant made clear in a more comprehensive report, Chinese hackers targeted and penetrated just about every institution of American life. The firm documented attacks on 141 targets in the U.S. and around the world that occurred over six years—and "those are only the ones we could easily identify," said Kevin Mandia, founder and chief executive of the firm.

The targets ranged from the U.S. military and government to defense-industry firms, energy and communications infrastructure, think tanks, law firms, embassies, media companies—not only the *Times* but also Bloomberg, the *Washington Post,* and others—and manufacturing concerns. What's more, Mandiant traced the origins of most of these attacks: They came from a Shanghai office tower belonging to Chinese military intelligence and were predominantly the work of a unit of the People's Liberation Army known as Unit 61398.

Mandiant's 60-page report tracked the behavior of the most sophisticated groups in this unit, known as Comment Crew and Shanghai Group. Intelligence officials believe that both groups, along with other sophisticated Chinese hackers, have state sponsorship and are run from inside the Chinese intelligence apparatus. The Mandiant report made the Chinese connection official, despite Beijing's denials. "It is unprofessional and groundless to accuse the Chinese military of launching cyber attacks without any conclusive evidence," the Chinese Defense Ministry said in a statement—but Mandiant has the digital goods on the attackers.[51]

Comment Crew even broke into the systems of Telvent (now Schneider Electric), an information-technology and industrial-control firm that designs software for the remote management of power grids for gas-pipeline and power companies. The software controls access to valves, switches, and security systems. Telvent has remote access to more than *60 percent of oil and gas pipelines in North America*—and it keeps detailed blueprints of most. Comment Crew stole the project files.

"This is terrifying because—forget about the country—if someone hired me and told me they wanted to have the offensive capability to take out as many critical systems as possible, I would be going after the vendors and do things like what happened to Telvent," said Dale Peterson, head of Digital Bond, a security firm that specializes in industrial-control computers. "It's the holy grail."[52]

The Mandiant report was a landmark moment in the ongoing cyber war with China. As a result, soon after the *Times* broke the hacking story, many hackers in Unit 61398 went silent and removed their spying tools from the servers of the organizations they had infiltrated. Some of the group's most prolific and colorful hackers—not just UglyGorilla and DOTA, but others with names such as SuperHard—disappeared. Within a few months, though, Unit 61398 was operating at 60 to 70 percent of its original capacity, re-inserting many spying tools with minor alterations to the code while working from different servers.

Clearly, neither the Mandiant report nor the U.S. government's approach of "naming and shaming" is sufficient to stop China's cyber attacks. Something else would be needed. As Dennis Blair, President Obama's former director of national intelligence, put it: "Jawboning alone won't work. Something has to change China's calculus."[53]

Skeptics might ask, if the Chinese military, through its cyber hackers, can gain access to such critical U.S. information and infrastructure systems, then why haven't they tried to take them down? And since they haven't, how much is there to worry about? Perhaps these are merely exercises. Others say the attacks are purely about obtaining information. In the media examples, for instance, the Chinese wanted to learn what U.S. reporters knew about the inner workings of their government. Besides, even if the Chinese launched a major cyber attack that brought down, say, the U.S. banking system, they would be hurting only themselves—as prime owners of American debt, they are deeply invested in the U.S. economy. Sabotaging it would make no sense.

All of that sounds reasonable but assumes that there aren't other uses to such attacks and such access—blackmail, for instance, on the far end of the spectrum, or just coercive pressure on the less dramatic end. The U.S. is engaged in a number of diplomatic and potential military disputes with China involving its conflicts with our allies over islands in the South and East China Seas. We have a half-century-old impasse over Taiwan. And then there is the lingering North Korean situation. What if China were to use what it learned through cyber attacks as leverage against us in these matters?

"Would an American president respond with full military force if he knew that the Chinese would retaliate by turning out all the lights on the Eastern Seaboard?" Fred Kaplan asks.[54] Scoffing at these scenarios is foolhardy.

Corporate Sabotage, Hacking, and Spying

In 2010, the U.S. Navy received shipment of 59,000 microchips from China for installation in a wide range of American defense systems. The chips turned out to be counterfeits. The Navy discarded them, but the episode made American officials wonder.

What if, in the future, they didn't catch the mistake—if it was in fact a mistake? What if, with increased sophistication, the Chinese could sneak purposefully defective chips into its shipments? "Instead of crappy Chinese fakes being put into Navy weapons systems," Adam Rawnsley wrote in *Wired*, "the chips could have been hacked, able to shut off a missile in the event of war or lie around just waiting to malfunction."[55]

Regardless of what really happened in 2010, the Chinese are expert at a whole range of tools involved in cyber sabotage. They excel, for instance, at "backdoor" hacking—stealing data through the use of compromised computer parts. A "back door" is an embedded piece of computer code that makes it possible to hack into whatever processes the code controls. Such codes are notoriously difficult to remove.[56] Backdoors can be added to code or installed in a computer's physical machinery. Hardware-encoded backdoors are more threatening than software-encoded ones, because they can't be removed or detected by anti-virus software or reformatting. They can override any part of the software in the computer. Extraordinarily difficult to detect, they're built with "open-source" tools, making it much harder to identify the perpetrator.[57]

It's a problem that isn't going away, because the U.S. is no longer the sole global manufacturer of computer chips and has begun buying foreign-sourced chips. China manufactures a great deal of the material used in the U.S. for computers and digital transmissions. China's opaque manufacturing sectors, with links to the military and to the Communist Party, control some of these processes and are suspected of inserting a range of mechanisms into materials in order to monitor, interrupt, or sabotage U.S. networks.

In May 2012, Cambridge University researchers declared that Chinese hardware manufacturers were inserting backdoors into computer chips used in Pentagon weapons as well as in nuclear power plants and public transportation. A researcher, Sergei Skorobogatov, found the backdoor in a computer chip from Microsemi, a Chinese hardware maker. The U.S. government uses the Microsemi chip for civilian and military applications, including software that operates Boeing 787s and surveillance drones.

Skorobogatov described how he had found the backdoor and its "key," both inserted by the manufacturer: "If you use this key, you can disable the chip or reprogram it at will, even if locked by the user with their own key," he said. "In other words, this backdoor access could be turned into an advanced Stuxnet weapon to attack potentially millions of systems. . . . The scale and range of possible attacks has huge implications for [U.S.] national security and public infrastructure."[58]

The incident was far from isolated. In October 2012, the U.S. House Permanent Select Committee on Intelligence recommended that U.S. companies avoid hardware made by Chinese telecom giants Huawei and ZTE, saying that its use constitutes a risk to national security. Huawei and ZTE manufacture network hardware for telecommunications systems. The House report criticized both firms for not being forthcoming about their relationship with the Chinese government or how they conducted their operations in the United States.[59]

Backdoors allowing remote access have been found on ZTE devices, and the FBI is investigating the firm for stealing American intellectual property and selling it to Iran.[60] But in the end, Huawei may be the more dangerous actor. The firm's founder, Ren Zhengfei, served in the People's Liberation Army engineering corps in the 1960s. Some American executives believe that Huawei has stolen designs from Cisco; the two companies settled a lawsuit in 2004. In the U.S., after all, telecom companies have assisted with espionage. It's perfectly reasonable to worry that in China, where boundary lines between corporations and government are much fuzzier, such firms might be engaging in the same practices.[61]

Huawei officials even showed off their ability to hack into American telecom systems at a technology and intelligence conference in Dubai. They claimed that they did this only to eliminate "malicious data" and protect their networks, but the demonstration raised questions about what other uses the company may find for these capabilities.[62]

In short, China has become notorious for intellectual-property theft. By one estimate, cyber attacks of Chinese origin tripled in the third quarter of 2012 over the previous three years. There seems to be a direct correlation between the increased attacks and China's ambition to develop leading high-tech industries and compete against American businesses with low-cost products.[63] It mirrors Chinese military hacking, similarly motivated by the desire to improve their technologies by stealing U.S. secrets. China is well positioned here, since, as Richard Clarke notes, "China is very familiar with [America's] routers. Most of them are made by the U.S. firm Cisco, but made in China."[64]

The Chinese often perpetrate these thefts by using malware. They bombard U.S. companies and government agencies with these devices in an attempt to obtain industrial, military, or private-sector trade secrets. The attacks don't have to be large-scale to be effective. "My greatest fear is that, rather than having a cyber–Pearl Harbor event, we will instead have this death of a thousand cuts," Clarke says. "Where we lose our competitiveness by having all of our research and development stolen by the Chinese."[65]

In 2009, as Coca-Cola executives were negotiating what would have been the largest foreign purchase of a Chinese company—a $2.4 billion acquisition of Huiyuan Juice Group—Comment Crew broke into Coke's servers looking for information on the company's negotiating plans, sending company files back to Shanghai weekly.[66] Chinese regulators ended up barring the deal on antitrust grounds; what role the extensive hacking played in this decision is unknown. A few years later, Comment Crew penetrated RSA Security's systems, forcing the security company—manufacturer of the well-known SecurID tokens—to replace the tokens for its clients and augment its security products with new layers of protection.[67]

"The disparity between American and Chinese firms and their tactics will put both the government and the companies of the United States at a distinct disadvantage," says Eric Schmidt, Google's CEO. "The United States will not take the same path of digital corporate espionage, as its laws are much stricter (and better enforced) and because illicit competition violates the American sense of fair play."[68] Schmidt also calls China the world's "most sophisticated and prolific hacker."

Schmidt knows this subject well; his company was famously hacked by China in 2010. Those attacks were part of a broader corporate-espionage attack that targeted at least 34 other companies—including Yahoo, Symantec, and Adobe in the technology sector, and, in the industrial and defense sectors, Northrop Grumman and Dow Chemical. The attacks seemed to be focused on sectors in which China was lagging competitively or on firms that supplied critical materials or know-how to the U.S. defense industry.[69]

The 2010 cyber attacks set off a series of events that led Google to temporarily end its agreement with the Chinese government to censor certain search results, and the company physically moved its servers out of the country.[70] China also attacked Google accounts as a proxy for getting U.S. government information in 2011, when it hacked into hundreds of Gmail accounts, including those of some senior U.S. government officials. Google confirmed that the attacks originated from China.[71]

The Chinese have also used cyber warfare to target human-rights activists. The 2010 Google attacks included breaches of Gmail accounts belonging to two activists.[72] The Chinese have gone after political critics, including, in the U.S., Frank Wolf, a Republican House member and vocal lawmaker on Chinese human-rights issues. Wolf reported in 2006 that his office computers had been compromised and that similar attacks had compromised the systems of several other representatives and the office of the House Foreign Affairs Committee.[73] Wolf suspected the Chinese.

RUSSIA: STATE ATTACKS AND CYBER CRIME

A small country that had only recently won independence from Russian domination, Estonia had reason to be proud and optimistic in 2007. Not only had it secured its long-sought autonomy, but it also had one of the most wired economies in the world, in proportion to its size. In fact, some had started calling the place E-stonia. But that was before citizens got together and decided to remove the Bronze Soldier.

The military monument, a Soviet-era relic that commemorated the battle against the Nazis, served as a symbol of pride for the Russians. Estonians, however, saw it mainly as a boast of bygone Soviet glory, and they wanted it gone. After some interethnic disagreements, the government took it away.

The next day, sleeping viruses infecting thousands of computers came alive and began to ping messages to Estonian websites—signaling "denial of service" attacks, shutting down servers for hours at a time. Meanwhile, in Russia, the government accused Estonians of dishonoring the memory of Soviets who had fought against the Nazis, and Russia called for a boycott of Estonian goods. Angry Muscovites staged rowdy street protests and even went after the Estonian ambassador. The attacks continued for weeks and so flooded Estonia's digital traffic system that the country's crucial servers—which ran banks, telephone systems, road-traffic networks, and the like—began to overload and freeze up. Russia also suspended rail service.[74] Estonia had effectively ground to a halt—the first country to fall victim to a virtual war—and the Estonians had to call in NATO experts for help.[75]

"If you have a missile attack against, let's say, an airport, it is an act of war," said Madis Mikko, a spokesman for the Estonian Defense Ministry. "If the same result is caused by computers, then how else do you describe that kind of attack?"[76] The digital traffic was traced back through various layers of proxy-infected computers to originating programs in Russia. The Russians denied wrongdoing and refused requests to pursue an investigation of what had happened.

A year later, Russia invaded Georgia under the pretext of protecting the separatist zone of South Ossetia from attack by Georgian troops. As Russian tanks rolled in, a massive cyber attack on Georgia's Internet communications also got under way. Hackers effectively took over Georgia's strategic entry-exit routes of digital communication to other countries and used them to control government websites so that the president's own Web page became a Russian "zombie." Georgia's banking sector—its ATM, credit card, and money-transfer systems—shut down, as did its cellphone networks. Georgians could not get emails out of the country and could not log on to any foreign news sites, such as CNN or the BBC, to get information on what was happening. American experts saw clear evidence of the work of a St. Petersburg–based criminal gang known as the Russian Business Network, or R.B.N. Some of the attacks on Georgian systems were launched from computers the R.B.N. was known to control.[77] R.B.N.'s coordination with the Russian government has never been determined.

Whatever the Georgian authorities tried, including blocking incoming data from Russian servers, their antagonists proved to be a step ahead. Servers and routers from other countries unwittingly aided the attack, having fallen prey to pre-planted viruses. So complete, coordinated, and adaptable was the campaign that it could only have been a thoroughly thought-out war plan. But again, Moscow officials denied state involvement.

Meanwhile, a full-scale kinetic war unfolded on two fronts across Georgia's borders, with Russian Sukhoi fighter-bombers buzzing the skies over the presidential residence in the capital, Tbilisi, while bombing targeted areas along the Abkhazian and South Ossetian breakaway zones and overrunning sizable slices of Georgian territory. Overcommitted in Iraq and Afghanistan, the U.S. could do little more than send Secretary of State Condoleezza Rice to Tbilisi as a gesture of solidarity.

Cyber war is only partly about getting intelligence. It can also be a weapon of war, pure and simple—as Russia showed. Through this theatrical display of cyber muscle in Estonia and Georgia, Moscow demonstrated that its war-making ability no longer remained mired in the post-Soviet doldrums. Moscow sent a message to the world that the Russians had full mastery of new-millennium, high-tech, next-generation capability. If just a fraction of their cyber prowess could overwhelm their "near abroad" neighbors, they were also sending a warning to the U.S. directly. The Russians understood the rules of this new virtual battlefield, in which computers from all around the world could be commandeered to attack any chosen country. They understood, and they wanted the U.S. to know that they could conduct such operations with impunity.

The Internet, after all, by design grew as an open-ended structure. Only those countries consciously intending to control the flow of information, such as China, have tried deliberately to structure their alternate versions of the Web so as to create built-in choke points and control mechanisms. The U.S. and the West as a whole have no such defensive forethought woven into the architecture of their Internet. Ironically, the least wired of countries, such as North Korea, thus derive a huge cyber-war advantage from the openness of the West.

Along with the message Russia was sending about its cyber capabilities, one might also detect a subtler cultural one: See, they seemed to be saying to the Americans, you wanted this big, wide-open technology that would mirror your big, wide-open society and culture, but in the end, it leaves you defenseless. Your ideals may appear noble in the abstract, but they cannot weather hard reality and they merely lure your friends to disaster. Moscow showed how it could use the West's "open" cyberspace system to subvert democracy and reassert autocratic control.

The skeptical reader might at this point protest that America's capacity to defend itself must be vastly superior to that of the small countries that Moscow bullied. The avenues of communication in and out of and across the continental United States via satellites, undersea cables, fiber-optic systems, and routers must add up to many multiples of the comparable digital avenues in Estonia or Georgia. How much of the complex networks that crisscross the U.S. can be targeted in one concerted attack? If nuclear first strikes cannot hope to take out enough of America's infrastructure to prevent a devastating counter-strike, how could the cyber equivalent do so?

Such a question doesn't come to grips with the real-world scale of Internet connectivity and the rapidity with which computers communicate. The meticulous planning over weeks, months, and years that it takes to put viruses into geographical swaths of computers—viruses that can go undetected for long periods—suggests that an operation of this kind *can* succeed on a massive scale. We dismiss Moscow's successes in 2007 and 2008 at our peril.

Yet attacks on small countries in the Russian "near abroad" are not the end of the story. Though definitive proof is lacking, compelling evidence links Moscow with powerful cyber-espionage rings that have sprung up in recent years to sabotage business communications, steal financial data, and gain access to government and diplomatic information. The Target attack during the 2013 holiday season is currently the most notorious example, but there have been others, affecting both the private sector and government.

Or consider the long-running operation known as Red October, one of the most formidable online espionage operations ever mounted. Red October stole government and diplomatic secrets, as well as science research, from many countries from 2007 to 2012. Targets were mainly countries in Eastern Europe, Central Asia, and former USSR republics—but also countries in Western Europe and North America, including the U.S.[78] The operation became known when researchers discovered malware implanted not only on PCs and servers but also on mobile devices.[79] The puzzling thing, however, was that the network was discovered by a Russian IT-security firm, Kaspersky Labs. Kaspersky found Russian-language words in the software code and concluded that the attackers themselves were Russian, though they used some Chinese-made software.

Kaspersky researchers played victim to the attacks, in order to understand the operation better. They learned a lot, primarily that all of the attacks were launched through spear-phishing emails. When a recipient clicked on them, the malware, which Kaspersky Lab dubbed Sputnik, would be attached onto his computer. The hackers had created more than 1,000 modules and tools that could be downloaded through the "Sputnik" system.[80]

The key question about Red October is: Who was behind it? That question remains unanswered, and to be fair to Moscow, it might be someone else. Analysts have suggested multiple possibilities, some arguing that the attacks came from somewhere in the EU; others believe that they are the work of a private cyber-criminal network. But other signs—especially Russian language in the code—point to Moscow as the culprit.

"To be able to function and get the information that they've supposedly got, you have to be able to operate in an environment immune from imminent prosecution," said Laura Galante of Mandiant. "For something that goes after this type of information, that's a five-year-long operation, it's really suspicious that a completely private group of entrepreneurial hackers would have the funding to do that and have the same kind of attention to go on that long."[81]

Also daunting is Project Blitzkrieg, an audacious cyber-bank heist. Project Blitzkrieg came to public attention in late 2012, when the Internet security firm McAfee Labs warned about massive malware installations lying dormant in the computer systems of 30 of America's biggest banks and financial-services firms—including Fidelity, Wachovia, Citibank, ETrade, PayPal, Charles Schwab, Wells Fargo, and Capital One. Project Blitzkrieg was uncovered when another security firm, RSA, was monitoring a Russian chat room run by a hacker known as vorVzakone ("thief in law"). He was trying to recruit hackers to break into online bank accounts as part of a broader criminal scheme. During the chat, vorVzakone posted screenshots of his malware along with descriptions of his plan to recruit "botmasters" to wield "botnets"—a collection of Internet-connected programs—to attack the banks and authenticate wire transfers of millions of dollars.

"The goal—together, en-masse and simultaneously process large amount of the given material before antifraud measures are increased," vorVzakone wrote during the chat. The elaborate chat-room setup was first seen as a Russian sting operation to catch the hackers, but it later became clear that Project Blitzkrieg was a real criminal operation.[82]

"The targets are U.S. banks, with the victims dispersed across various U.S. cities," the McAfee report said. "Thus this group will likely remain focused on U.S. banks and making fraudulent transactions."[83] The plan was ingenious in its conception. Botmasters would co-opt a banking process with which millions of Americans are familiar—authentication of account activity. The hackers would use "phone flooding" equipment to prevent banks from confirming the legitimacy of wire transfers with customers; the banks wouldn't be able to reach them because the phone lines would be blocked. The hackers would call the banks on their own, claiming to be the accountholders, and verify the transactions.[84]

The malware could also clone victims' computers, allowing the hackers to set up a "virtual machine" in Russia with all of the same user cookies, software configurations, and the like. To the U.S.-based bank, transactions coming from that computer would appear to be happening in the U.S. and authorized by its actual U.S.-based customer.[85]

McAfee's exposure of Project Blitzkrieg may have caused vorVzakone to call off his attack or to move further underground. "Too hot, too much media attention," he wrote in one of his final messages. If he's gone, it's likely only temporarily. And, as with Red October, the same nagging question goes unanswered: Whom does he work for?

It might also be noted in closing that in Russia, as in China, a high premium is placed on developing computer skills among the young—much more so than in the United States. We simply don't train the way they do, as the results of the International Collegiate Programming Contest, held in St. Petersburg in 2013, showed. Russian IT University earned a perfect score, and seven of the top 10 finishers were former Warsaw Pact universities. Schools in Taiwan, Japan, and China rounded out the top 10. Only three U.S. schools cracked the top 20.[86]

CONCLUSION: WHAT TO DO?

When it comes to cyber security, the myopia in U.S. policy comes down to three core points: First, so far, we are more focused on offensive operations than defensive; second, we have not come to terms with the structural disadvantage an open society faces in this struggle; and third, our inability, or unwillingness, to confront the Axis, China in particular, is bound up with the same deficiencies that afflict our overall posture—namely, a preference for wishful thinking over acknowledgement of reality.

"The attackers are ahead of the defenders in cyber space," Deputy Defense Secretary William Lynn warned in 2011. "The technology for intrusions is far ahead of the technology for defenses, and we need to catch up."[87] Mike McConnell agrees: "All the offensive cyber capability the U.S. can muster won't matter if no one is defending the nation from cyber attack."[88]

While the U.S. offensive capability is probably unmatched at present, the defensive dimension remains dangerously weak. Washington's current cyber-command structure is mostly set up to defend the Pentagon and perhaps some government agencies, but not the private-sector infrastructure that makes our economy go. The question of security in this area has grown up largely within the military; but neither the Pentagon nor Homeland Security is currently geared to defend civilian infrastructure.[89] Though Washington has created a Cyber Command, no overarching body is assigning responsibility and coordinating efforts to plug the gaps. Thus, ramping up our offensive capabilities even further is in many ways beside the point. Until the U.S. figures out the defensive end of this, we remain hugely, even shockingly, vulnerable.

Of course, it's much harder for an open society to seal itself up against the kinds of assaults now being directed against U.S. networks. And "U.S. agencies and private companies have a lot more information that's worth stealing," as *Forbes* put it.[90] For our adversaries, the target is both vulnerable and valuable. There is no question that the U.S. faces an uphill battle in the cyber war, especially considering that our adversaries don't operate under the same constraints we expect our government to observe.

Pervasive in its manifestation and devastating in its effects, cyber war is also cheap to launch—a huge differentiator from the doomsday nuclear attacks we worried about during the Cold War or, more recently, even modest terrorist plots, which require some kind of funding and operational coordination. Not so here.

"It costs about 4 cents per machine," said Bill Woodcock of Packet Clearing House, which tracks Internet traffic. "You could fund an entire cyber-warfare campaign for the cost of replacing a tank tread, so you would be foolish not to."[91] So they're cheap, devastating, and, as we've also seen, difficult to track and prove—what's not to like?

We are on different terrain here, where no rules exist to guide us. Richard Clarke and others compare it with the first decade after the atomic bomb, when American and then Soviet scientists built these weapons of enormous destructiveness, but before politicians or strategists devised ways of thinking about them rationally: how to control them, deter their use, or limit their damage if a war couldn't be avoided.[92] That's where we are today. And as with the Cold War, our task in devising rules is made ten times more difficult when the parties who need to help set such standards are our adversaries.

Finally, there is the issue of our overall posture toward the cyber threat. The Obama administration lacks a coherent, overarching vision of how to confront the cyber threat at its multiple levels—as we saw when Obama failed to counter Xi's rebuffs at the Sunnylands summit. Obama's unwavering commitment to "good faith" negotiation over coercive diplomacy sends a message of weakness. The White House's "tough" statements are thin gruel; even the *New York Times* sees through them. The Obama-defending paper of record pointed out that the president, after declaring that "we know foreign countries and companies swipe our corporate secrets," refused to identify which countries he meant. He even added: "Our enemies are also seeking the ability to sabotage our power grid, our financial institutions, and our air-traffic-control systems."[93]

What an extraordinary admission to make, without a long and elaborate outline of ongoing or planned measures against such an adversary. The *Times* article went on to discuss the difficulty of identifying China as an enemy when the country is our banker and when, indeed, innumerable U.S. companies do business with Beijing and would quickly resent such a combative stance. The irony is that many of those companies suffer constantly from the very cyber shenanigans that are at issue.

Here, then, we can reemphasize the overarching theme of this book: that we confront a relentless enemy; that we have, to date, dared not call him an enemy and confront him openly; and that we must soon overcome our reluctance to do so. This is as true in the area of cyber warfare as it is in any other—and perhaps more so.

CHAPTER 4

Military Supremacy: America's Fading Edge

"Beijing's military buildup—its defense spending has more than doubled since 2006, and its armed forces now include nearly 1.5 million service members, according to Chinese officials—is driven by a sense that it needs to prepare for a possible showdown in the Pacific with the world's remaining superpower."

—*TIME*, JUNE 2013[1]

"The Russian armed forces need to be of a new quality, and that quality has to manifest itself in everything: combat preparedness, military planning, and military science. We are faced with the considerable task of creating a new look for the armed forces."

—VLADIMIR PUTIN, OCTOBER 2003[2]

"The readiness of our Armed Forces is at a tipping point. We are on the brink of creating a hollow force due to an unprecedented convergence of budget considerations and legislation that could require the Department [of Defense] to retain more forces than requested while underfunding that force's readiness."

—LETTER FROM JOINT CHIEFS OF STAFF TO SENATOR CARL LEVIN, CHAIRMAN OF THE COMMITTEE ON ARMED FORCES, JANUARY 2013[3]

"Countries that are winning do not have to close their embassies in 19 countries. This is a statement of impotence and incompetence on a grand scale, an admission that the United States cannot even defend its own embassies."

—NEWT GINGRICH, AUGUST 2013[4]

Originating from Vladivostok, the home port of Russia's Pacific Fleet, the armada moved in "ceremonial formation" through the Sea of Japan in July 2013. It stopped periodically for live firing drills and exercises in air defense, antisubmarine warfare, and surface warfare. The Russian fleet included a Kilo-class submarine as well as the guided-missile cruiser *Varyag*, which the *New York Times* described as "the flagship of its Pacific Fleet."[5]

But the Russians weren't traveling alone.

The armada was a joint one, and the partner was China, in what Beijing described as the largest military exercises that it had ever undertaken with another country. The Chinese fleet sent seven warships to the exercise, including missile frigates equipped with antisubmarine capabilities and a guided-missile destroyer outfitted with Aegis-quality radars that can guide weapons to enemy targets. Ding Yiping, deputy commander of the Chinese navy, said that the joint naval drills had been a complete success.[6]

"This is our strongest lineup ever in a joint naval drill," said the Chinese fleet commander, Major General Yang Junfei.[7] For Yang, the main goal of the exercises was to build "strategic trust" between the Russian and Chinese navies.[8] "This shows unprecedented good relations between China and Russia," said Wang Ning, director of the Center for Russian studies at the Shanghai International Studies University. "It shows that the two countries will support each other on the global scale."[9]

In Cold War days, military cooperation between Moscow and Beijing would have caused panic in Washington. But while the Axis countries are moving aggressively, jointly and apart, to rebuild and modernize their military might, the United States is pulling back—politically, financially, strategically—from its leading position in the world. We are on a course of retreat that, combined with the determined efforts of our adversaries to catch up, could lead to calamity.

The Russian-Chinese armada took sail partly in response to two interconnected challenges: first, the Obama administration's so-called Asian pivot, in which the Americans would reallocate focus and resources, military and otherwise, from Afghanistan, Europe, and the Middle East to Asia and the Pacific area; second, the dispute between China and Japan over the Diaoyu (in China)—or Senkaku (in Japan)—Islands. Knowing that more American resources would soon be arriving in the Pacific, Beijing picked a strategic time to let Washington know that China would not be sailing alone. Given that the strength of the U.S.-Japan alliance is too imposing for either Axis country to challenge on its own, approaching Japan in tandem made sense. A Russian-language version of a Chinese news portal essentially conceded that one of the exercise's purposes was to put pressure on Japan and the U.S.[10] It already may have paid dividends, considering the Americans' lackluster support for Japan in the fall of 2013 over the contested islands. (Russia also has a Pacific-island dispute with Japan, over what Moscow calls the Kurils and Tokyo calls the Northern Territories.)

The joint exercises were only the latest reminder of Russian-Chinese cooperation in a host of areas. What makes their growing military cooperation especially alarming is not only the facts and figures substantiating it—which we'll get to below—but also that it comes as the United States is in the middle of a massive military retrenchment. Since the end of the Cold War, the United States has enjoyed military superiority over all other nations—and not just in relation to each nation considered on its own. As many have pointed out for years, the U.S. spends more on defense than the rest of the world combined. This remains the case, but the margins are waning, and the Axis nations are catching up. Vladimir Putin has undertaken a top-to-bottom reconstruction of the Russian armed forces, while the Chinese spend something like six times more on their military than they did just 10 years ago.

Moreover, China and Russia (now the world's second- and third-highest military spenders) have something else that the United States lacks: strategy and the will to put it into practice. Both nations have taken dramatic steps in the last decade to improve their ability to contest American control of the high seas, and not only in the Pacific.[11] The Chinese aim to be the preeminent power in their coastal region, while the Russians are looking to restore the naval capabilities of the Soviet Union.

Contrast this with what we see on the American side. It's true that the U.S., through its "Asian pivot," has conceded that it needs to contain China to some degree. Some agree with that outlook; others find it a misplaced Cold War analogy. Either way, it is bound to fail in the absence of a coherent American strategic objective, one not likely to be realized, in any case, given the recent deep cuts to Pentagon spending.

As China and Russia beef up, Congress is set to cut nearly $1 trillion from the defense budget over the next 10 years.[12] Defense Secretary Chuck Hagel has said that these cuts will put American national security at "much greater risk."[13] Brookings foreign policy commentator Robert Kagan commented at a recent Council on Foreign Relations meeting that there is no justification for the heavy cuts to the defense budget.[14] While the full brunt of those cuts is a ways off, the military is already taking it on the chin thanks to the cuts negotiated during the sequestration of January 2013. That's what prompted Hagel's warning and also his decision to launch an internal study on both the short-term and long-term effects of spending cuts. What he and others have found so far is alarming: impaired combat-troop readiness; inability to modernize equipment and weapons and technology systems; and the need, potentially, to slash as many as five of the Air Force's tactical aircraft squadrons. Former Defense Secretary Leon Panetta warns that the effects of sequestration alone will leave the United States with our smallest ground fighting force since 1940, the smallest naval fleet since 1915, and the "smallest tactical fighter force in the history of the Air Force."[15]

The U.S. government shutdown in the fall of 2013 didn't help matters. "A week won't make a significant difference," said one Army officer. "Two weeks and you might start to see readiness issues." The shutdown lasted 16 days, causing extensive cancellation of reserve training, the cutoff of some veterans' benefits, and uncertainty about the status of some categories of military pay, including incentive compensation for troops serving in Afghanistan.[16]

So, yes, the United States remains the world's preeminent military power, retains an extraordinary advantage in military spending and capability, and begins from a position of strength—but we are decimating budgets with no clear goal, let alone a clear understanding of what we face on the other side of the cuts. Meanwhile, the Russians and Chinese have clear plans and strategies, and their military budgets reflect this. Our rivals are back in the game in a big way. They make no bones that America is the primary enemy. We show no such clarity in our thinking about them.

CHINA'S MILITARY BUILDUP

"China's military spending has been rapidly spiraling upward, and the growing amounts are unnerving Beijing's Asian neighbors and policy planners in the Pentagon, who are openly wary about the country's long-term intentions," reported the *Washington Post* in October 2012. That was, if anything, an understatement. In just seven years, China has more than doubled its defense spending, as Beijing takes unmistakable steps toward regional, and even global, superpower status. It's an ongoing, aggressive campaign that leaves many uneasy, from the oceans and seas of the Far East to the power corridors of Washington.

The buildup is even more troubling for the fact that we don't have an accurate picture of how much Beijing is spending, because so much of it is not available in transparent public records. Some spending, as the *Post* noted—such as the spending of the People's Liberation Army on research and space exploration—seems to occur entirely off the books. Two facts are nonetheless clear: The Chinese spend more than they say they do, and they spend more than they ever have before.

By some projections, China is on course to surpass the United States in total military spending by 2035. Beijing's publicly disclosed military spending of $106 billion in 2012 already makes China the second-largest military in the world after the United States, which spends roughly $700 billion annually.[17] Most Western analysts estimate that the real Chinese total is much greater. The Pentagon gives estimates in the range of $120 billion to $180 billion.[18] Figure 1 (below) provides both the PRC's public figures and the (much higher) U.S. Department of Defense estimates.

Whatever the real figure, it's all the more impressive given that its military outlays put China only at 11th among spenders as a proportion of GDP—in other words, the spending has lots of room to grow, especially given the robust Chinese economy. And China has learned the lesson of unsustainable defense expenditures from the USSR and thus refrained from committing too much of its economic wealth to the military. Still, the trajectory of Chinese spending has mirrored its robust economic growth. As recently as 2002, China spent only about $20 billion annually on defense. But from 2000 to 2011, it has averaged an 11.8 percent annual increase in officially disclosed military spending, according to Department of Defense estimates.[19]

China's military spending has had one overarching goal: to modernize and transform the People's Liberation army and navy (and to a lesser extent, the PLA air force) through investment in high-technology equipment, hardware, and training. With a particular focus on the development of long-range, high-precision strike capabilities that the U.S. has employed in Iraq and Afghanistan, China is developing its command, control, communication, computers, intelligence, surveillance, and reconnaissance abilities, along with other systems necessary to extend the effective reach of the People's Liberation Army well beyond China's borders.

The sweeping modernization program also includes investments in anti-ship ballistic and long-range cruise missiles capable of attacking U.S. aircraft carriers; air and missile defense; unmanned aerial vehicles; electromagnetic pulse weapons; a J-10 and J-11 fighter-jet fleet; an experimental stealth J-20 plane; new maritime-surveillance and targeting systems;[20] and a growing space program, which includes China's own satellite navigation network.

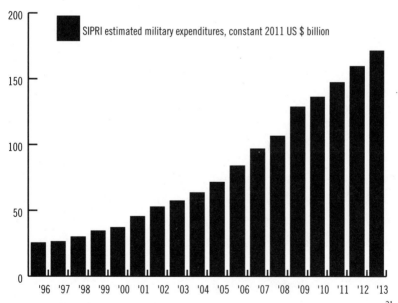

Figure 1: China's Annual Real GDP and Military Budget Growth, 1996 to 2009[21] (subsequent increases of 9.4% in 2010, 12.9% in 2011, and 11.1% in 2012[22])

The impact of these investments is already being felt in the Western Pacific, where the People's Liberation Army is engaged in a long-term program of naval, air, and missile modernization in order to allow it to undertake "anti-access/area denial" (or A2/AD) missions—any set of tactics or weapons that would deny an enemy from crossing or occupying an area of land, usually by destroying his military assets from a safe distance. What this means is that, in the event of an international incident in the Western Pacific—say, another Taiwan Straits crisis or a standoff over energy rights in the South or East China Seas—China would seek to deter the U.S. Navy from intervening or establishing control. We should note that China has not yet attained these capabilities. Truly effective A2/AD capability relies on systems such as highly accurate, long-range anti-ship ballistic missiles and significant aircraft-carrier forces, and China's investments in these systems may be several years from making them fully operational. But Beijing is clearly putting tremendous resources into their completion.

To this end, China conducted its first test of a new ultra-high-speed missile vehicle in January 2014. The hypersonic vehicle, which the Pentagon has dubbed WU-14, traveled at high speeds over China and represents a major step forward in Beijing's strategic military buildup. It could reach velocities 10 times the speed of sound when perfected. "We routinely monitor foreign defense activities and we are aware of this test," Marine Corps Lieutenant Colonel Jeffrey Pool said. According to Chinese military experts, the hypersonic-vehicle test is part of a broader effort to develop asymmetric capabilities that Beijing calls "assassin's mace" weapons—high-tech assets that would offset China's military disadvantages in a confrontation with the United States.[23]

The PLA Navy has also acquired a former Soviet aircraft carrier and is developing its own indigenous carrier.[24] China will thus become "the last permanent member of the UN Security Council to obtain a carrier capability,"[25] according to the Pentagon. The strategic significance of these carriers may be their ability to project air power well beyond China's traditional sphere of influence.

Finally, China has adopted a "shop till you drop policy toward submarines," as Robert Kaplan of the Center for a New American Security puts it.[26] (See Figure 2, below.) As of 2012, it had 34 modern attack submarines and 12 older models. The Office of Naval Intelligence estimates that "over the next 10 to 15 years . . . the force is expected to increase incrementally in size to approximately 75 submarines."[27]

No examination of Chinese military numbers is complete without a reminder of the broader context. Xi Jinping, who has warned often that China should be "prepared for war," has toured military installations extensively, taken hardline stands on China's territorial disputes, and wholeheartedly embraced the notion of the China Dream: "We must achieve the great revival of the Chinese nation, and we must ensure there is unity between a prosperous country and a strong military."[28] More recently, during Defense Secretary Chuck Hagel's April 2014 visit to Beijing, China's defense minister, General Chang Wanquan, told him: "We are prepared at any time to cope with all kinds of threats and challenges. The Chinese military can assemble as soon as summoned, fight any battle, and win." China, he warned Hagel, "can never be contained."[29]

The United States cannot afford to ignore the evidence—in dollars, words, and deeds—of China's newfound aggressiveness.

RUSSIA'S MILITARY BUILDUP

"I think that this shows we are firmly holding a position as one of the world leaders," said Mikhail Pogosyan, chief executive of Russia-based Sukhoi United Aircraft Corporation. He was speaking about the big splash that his company's designs made at the Paris air show in June 2013. A Russian jet hadn't been the draw of the crowd since Cold

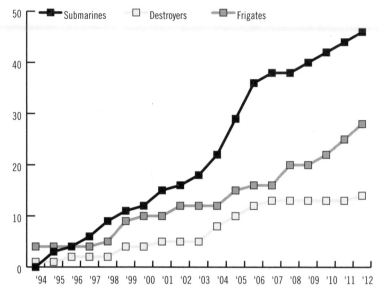

Figure 2: China: Cumulative Total Number of Submarines, Destroyers, and Frigates, 1994 to 2012[30]

War days, but the new Sukhoi Su-35 "carries new defense systems and missiles that—for the first time in years for a Russian aircraft—rival those made by Western suppliers," as the *Wall Street Journal* reported. The Sukhoi Su-35 "streaked across the sky here in flying displays . . . performing extreme maneuvers that few Western aircraft can achieve."[31]

"The battle for the air is heating up," said Alberto de Benedictis, CEO of British operations at Italian aerospace group Finmeccanica SpA.[32] And, indeed, it is.

The Su-35 isn't even Russia's most advanced jet. Moscow will soon roll out a fifth-generation model, the T-50, which it will co-produce with India. The T-50 aircraft has a longer range and greater maneuverability than the U.S. F-22; T-50s have already performed more than 200 test flights since January 2010.[33]

United Aircraft, like many other Russian aerospace firms, is capitalizing on the massive restructuring of the armed forces ordered by Vladimir Putin, a restructuring that has resulted in billions more in defense spending.[34] It's all part of a transformative new $755 billion commitment that Putin has made to restore the Russian military to something like its old Soviet glory. "The rearmament, after 20 years of stagnant defence budgets, is part of a new effort to transform the military into a professional force similar to America's or Britain's, breaking the model of a conscript army designed for mass battles with Napoleon or Hitler," wrote Charles Clover in the *Financial Times*.[35]

It was time to "make up for all those years during which the army and fleet were chronically underfinanced," Putin wrote in a February 2012 editorial published in a state-run Russian newspaper. "It's obvious we won't be able to develop our international position, our economy or democratic institutions if we cannot defend Russia. We must not tempt anyone with our weakness. . . . New regional and local wars are being sparked before our eyes. There are attempts to provoke such conflicts in the immediate vicinity of Russia's borders."[36] Putin's plan represented the largest Russian military investment since the days of the Cold War. Later in 2012, he drew an analogy to Stalinist times: "We should carry out the same powerful, all-embracing leap forward in modernization of the defense industry as the one carried out in the 1930s," he told the Russian Security Council.[37]

Russian military expenditures recently reached record highs for the post-Soviet era, having more than tripled over the last decade. Spending increased by 9.3 percent in 2011, reaching $71.8 billion, overtaking the military spending of both France and the United Kingdom and making Russia the world's third-largest military spender in the world in absolute terms, behind the U.S. and China.[38] It is also third in share of GDP among the world's largest military spenders. The total Russian

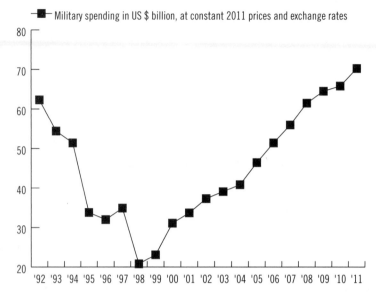

Figure 3: Russian Military Spending, in Constant 2010 Prices and Exchange Rates, 1992 to 2011 (Numbers for 2011 are adjusted for prices and exchange rates that year.[39])

military expenditure in 2011 is just above 10 percent of the U.S. total for the same year.

As Figure 3 above shows, Russia's military expenditures have risen steadily over the last decade, even during the 2008 global financial crisis, growing from a low of $20.5 billion in 1998. These figures are still well below the spending of the former Soviet Union[40]—but unlike the old Soviet Union, today's Russia has kept its spending increases proportionate with the country's economic growth. These spending hikes have roughly kept pace with the country's economic growth. Military spending has hovered around 4 percent of GDP since 1996—far below the Soviet-era figure, which was well above 20 percent in the early 1990s.[41] As a percentage of government spending, the figure has actually decreased, from nearly 20 percent in 2002 to 14 percent in 2009.[42]

The Russians have been able to spend so much less, proportionately, and get more, thanks to the improvement of the Russian economy since the end of the 1990s, which is largely due to huge new cash flows from rising oil and gas prices worldwide.[43]

What's happened over the last decade is something just short of miraculous, considering the moribund state of the Russian military after the collapse of the USSR. With the Communist Party's demise, Russian military investment cratered; procurement went almost to zero by the mid-1990s. In 1994, only 30 percent of Russian military equipment could be classified as "new," less than half the average figure for other developed countries. President Boris Yeltsin, lulled into complacency by warm relations with the West, took a lax attitude toward military preparedness and thus stood aside as the Russian military was gradually defunded.[44] The country had no coherent national-security policy, and the military was overrun by infighting between generals representing the conventional and nuclear forces. Moreover, those in command of conventional forces were busy fighting the last war; their planning, such as it was, focused on mass industrial warfare of the kind fought in WWII, with NATO countries as the presumptive adversary.[45] The Russians seemed to be living in a historical time warp.

By the time Putin took power on New Year's Eve, 1999, he was the proud heir of a seriously weakened military with aging equipment, abysmal research and development, and a top-heavy command structure filled with inexperienced senior officers and few junior officers.[46] The true costs and risks of this long deterioration became glaringly apparent to Russians in 2008, during the conflict in Georgia over the breakaway republics of South Ossetia and Abkhazia. Although Moscow prevailed, the performance of the Russian military was widely regarded as an embarrassment. The army's command-and-control structures failed to function, causing delays in deployment. Poor communications hampered Russian efforts as well, and aging Russian equipment and hardware fared poorly against the underdog Georgian army.[47]

The Georgian fiasco led to a 2008 announcement of comprehensive reform of conventional forces, which the government called the "New Look." The overarching principle was modernization: The Russians pledged to emphasize smaller (brigade-level) units, transition to "network-centric" warfare—that is, war-fighting based on information technology—and develop high-technology precision-strike capabilities, particularly through air power. Much of the New Look thinking was driven by the Russians' appraisal of US/NATO operations in the First Gulf War and in Iraq and Afghanistan in the 2000s.[48]

At the same time, New Look pushed for an across-the-board streamlining and downsizing of the Russian military to pare waste and inefficiency and improve effectiveness. The ground forces were targeted to go from 1,890 units to just 172—another departure from the old Soviet model of mass mobilization for a large-scale conventional war.[49] The air force would retain 180 of its previous 340 units, and the navy would reorganize to 120 units from 243.[50] The officer corps was to be slashed from 355,000 to 200,000 by 2012, with all of the cuts coming at ranks higher than lieutenant.[51]

An even broader goal was to move away from conscription toward the rapid professionalization of the army. Putin has promised that by 2017, two-thirds of Russia's army would be contract soldiers.[52] This element is crucial, because training for and maintaining unit readiness cannot be achieved when most soldiers are 12-month conscripts. The success of the U.S. armed forces has shown the efficiencies of an all-professional army.

Finally, in 2010, when he was still prime minister and had not yet reassumed the presidency, Putin announced a plan to modernize the Russian military's equipment. The goal is to do so by about 11 percent each year, eventually converting 70 percent of the inventory to modern weaponry by 2020. Thus the military-procurement program for 2011–2020 is heavily geared toward high-tech systems.[53] Recent Russian military purchases have also included unmanned aerial vehicles from Israeli Aerospace Industries, French navigation systems for Russian aircraft, and four new French-designed warships—the latter the first major weapons system sold by a NATO member to Russia, arousing controversy.[54]

Most analysis indicates that New Look has a long way to go toward achieving its goals, but the Ukraine crisis has shown that what Russia has achieved so far is substantial. Western analysts were struck by the high performance of Russian special forces in Crimea and Eastern Ukraine, as well as Russia's use of "21st-century tactics" and "hard and soft power"—including cyber warfare and sophisticated information campaigns. These are a far cry from the crude military tactics Moscow used in Chechnya in 2000.[55] Russia is clearly financially and politically committed to transforming its military into a 21st-century fighting force. Russia's determination and China's stand in stark contrast to the confusion of U.S. defense policy.

THE SUPERPOWER ADRIFT: AMERICA'S MILITARY PULLBACK

The attacks on the U.S. Consulate in Benghazi, Libya, in September 2012, which resulted in the death of ambassador Christopher Stevens and three other Americans, sparked one of the most intense political scandals of the Obama presidency. Why did the administration go public with the false story that an anti-Islamic video had caused the violence? How much warning did the administration have about the attack, and who was in or out of the loop? How could the consulate have been left so poorly defended, especially on the anniversary of the worst terrorist attack in American history?

The questions only multiplied when it became known that military personnel were available to assist in the rescue of U.S. Consulate staff, but they were essentially ordered to stand down. The devastating January 2014 Senate Intelligence Committee report, which concluded that the Benghazi attacks could have been prevented, confirmed this. As the press release accompanying the report said, "The committee found the attacks were preventable, based on extensive intelligence reporting on the terrorist activity in Libya—to include prior threats and attacks against Western targets—and given the known security shortfalls of the U.S. Mission."[56] In short, Americans were left to die.

Post-Benghazi, the U.S. military undertook studies of how to improve its rapid-response forces, including adding 10-men special-operations teams to each ship carrying a Marine Expeditionary Unit (MEU). These MEUs already number 2,200 Marines possessing expertise in skills ranging from special operations to reconnaissance. With or without the 10-men additions, the MEUs are lethal, professional, highly efficient fighting forces, the best in the world. They didn't save our people in Benghazi, not because they weren't good enough—but because they weren't available.

Mark Helprin explains:

> From World War II onward, the U.S. Sixth Fleet stabilized the Mediterranean region and protected American interests there with the standard deployment, continued through 2008, of a carrier battle group, three hunter killer submarines, and an amphibious ready group with its MEU or equivalent. But in the first year of the Obama

presidency, this was reduced to one almost entirely unarmed command ship. No MEU could respond to Benghazi because none was assigned to, or by chance in, the Mediterranean.[57]

Helprin calls the Benghazi catastrophe "a brightly illustrative miniature," and a "symbol of things to come." It's difficult to disagree when considering the scope of the U.S. defense retreat and defunding.

At the core of the issue is a planned trillion-dollar cut in defense spending over the next decade—a staggering sum with implications that cannot be overstated. Already some of this damage has been wrought even earlier than anticipated, because of Congress's failure in 2013 to pass a budget, which led to the sequester. On its own, the sequester imposed a 20 percent cut in military operating budgets. The impact is sinking in across the Pentagon and around Washington. In January 2013, the Joint Chiefs of Staff sent a letter to Senator Carl Levin, the chairman of the Committee on Armed Forces. In this letter, cited as an epigraph to this chapter, the chiefs warned: "The readiness of our Armed Forces is at a tipping point. We are on the brink of creating a hollow force due to an unprecedented convergence of budget considerations and legislation that could require the Department [of Defense] to retain more forces than requested while underfunding that force's readiness." The cuts would force all major branches "to ground aircraft, return ships to port, and stop driving combat vehicles in training."[58]

The combination of the long-range military cuts and the unanticipated hit from the sequester cuts led Defense Secretary Chuck Hagel to commission an internal study on the implications for the armed forces. The study, known as the Strategic Choices and Management Review, or SCMR (pronounced "skimmer" or "scammer"), laid out three main scenarios for how the Pentagon would deal with an upcoming decade of massive cutbacks. None are positive or desirable. Washington merely faces choices that range from bad to worse.

- The first scenario is the most optimistic: It assumes that seques-tration won't be necessary after Fiscal Year 2013, and that Con-gress will approve President Obama's long-term Pentagon budget, which would impose $150 billion in cuts, but mostly at the end of the decade.
- The second scenario is a halfway point between the best and worst cases, with an estimated $250 billion in cuts over the decade."
- The third scenario is the harshest: The long-term budget caps under sequestration will go into effect, wiping out another $500 billion from defense spending between 2013 and 2021—cuts that Pentagon leaders call "devastating" and "dangerous."

The optimistic scenario doesn't look likely as this book goes to press. Congress has shown little indication that it can come to an agreement that would end the sequestration cuts, despite the warnings of Hagel and other Pentagon officials that they are hurting military readiness.

"During a visit to Fort Bragg last week, I heard from infantrymen whose units were short on training rounds for their weapons," Hagel said in July 2013. "Each of the services have curtailed activities—flying hours have been reduced, ships are not sailing, and Army training has been halted. These kinds of gaps and shortages could lead to a force that is inadequately trained, ill-equipped, and unable to fulfill required missions."[59]

Indeed, Pentagon observers are warning that the Joint Chiefs' bleak post-sequester prediction about our "hollow force" has already come true. Only $37 billion of the $487 billion in cuts was imposed in 2013, but the effects have been devastating. A quick summary of the impact on the four main service branches:

- The Army would cut training and maintenance, and delay equipment readiness, for as many as 100,000 troops and would slash 40,000 flying hours for pilots. These cuts would create "a pool of unready units," in the words of General Ray Odierno, the Army chief of staff, and "there may not be enough time to avoid sending forces into harm's way unprepared."
- The deployment of the USS *Harry Truman* to the Persian Gulf, along with other Navy deployments, was delayed. Admiral Jonathan Greenert, the chief of naval operations, said: "We will not be able to respond in the way the nation has expected and depended on us."
- The Air Force grounded an incredible 33 squadrons, amounting to approximately 250 planes, and delayed maintenance and upgrade for the F-22, the F-15, and F-16 fighters. General Mark Welsh, the Air Force chief of staff, said: "We can't just all of a sudden accelerate training and catch up. It costs up to two-and-a-half times as much to retrain a squadron as it does to keep it trained."
- General James Amos, the commandant of the Marine Corps, said: "Bring in sequestration and we'll be down [from 23 planned infantry battalions] in the teens for battalions, and we will be very, very strained to be a one-MCO [major contingency operation] Marine Corps."

As Hagel outlined it, the choice comes down to quantity versus quality: The U.S. can have a much smaller force, but with the most up-to-date weapons, or we can have a massive force with older weaponry. We cannot, apparently, have both.

Having high-tech supremacy won't amount to much if we lack the troop force to mount and sustain critical large-scale operations. Having the manpower to project force around the world won't be sufficient to overcome the disadvantages of outdated equipment and technologies, which will place the lives of our people at risk. Needless to say, neither option is desirable. Neither has ever been necessary during America's entire time as a superpower, both before and after the Cold War. Only now do we face—through our own willful negligence—ultimatums that leave us so vulnerable. In short, with the ax it is taking to its military budget, the U.S. is entering uncharted territory.

"We would go from being unquestionably powerful everywhere to being less visible globally and presenting less of an overmatch to our adversaries," says the chairman of the Joint Chiefs, Martin Dempsey. "And that would translate into a different deterrent calculus and potentially, therefore, increase the likelihood of conflict."[60]

BEHIND THE BUILDUPS: AXIS STRATEGIES AND GOALS

Why should Beijing feel the need for such a military buildup? The only conceivable adversary on any serious scale is the United States. Yet the U.S. has certainly not impeded China's economic growth or in any way prevented China's vast populace from gaining employment, comfort, and affluence. On the contrary, precisely the reverse has been true: Without the investment of funds and know-how in the Chinese market over the last two decades by the U.S. and its allies, the China's economic miracle would never have happened. Beijing would not even be in a position to increase its armed might. So exactly what kind of threat is Beijing defending against?

The answer, alas, must be that Beijing's military buildup—despite propaganda to the contrary—is aimed at *offense*, at dominating its region by force. And considering the projection that in perhaps 20 years,

China's outlays will exceed the U.S. global military investment, one has to wonder whether China will stop at dominating *only* its region.

China's military expansion can be seen in terms of two broad goals—one historical, the other quite new. First, Beijing is determined to prevail in any cross-strait conflict with Taiwan. The Chinese still smart from U.S. Navy intervention in the Third Taiwan Crisis in 1996. Although many experts believe another such conflict is increasingly unlikely, the threat posed by Taiwan—and especially by American support of Taiwan—has been a powerful factor in Chinese strategic thinking since the Cold War. Thus Beijing's military-modernization effort has focused, at least in the short term, on developing military options in the event of an incident with Taiwan. The goal is to deter, or at least impede, U.S. naval and air forces.[61]

Second, beyond Taiwan, China also resents U.S. hegemony in the Asia-Pacific because it keeps China from assuming regional pre-eminence. Although it risks upsetting their largest export market, the United States, Beijing is pursuing a long-term military strategy: amassing enough deterrents, whether conventional or nuclear, to keep the U.S. from interfering in regional disputes.[62]

This second goal reflects China's global-superpower status, which has been taking shape for some time. A decade ago, then-President Hu Jintao announced a "new historic mission" for the People's Liberation Army, calling on the military not only to protect China's national interests but also to "adopt a larger role in promoting international peace and security."[63] That UN-style wording, though, is more of a cover for China's ambitions than a reflection of its desire to play global peacemaker.

Those broad regional and global interests also come to the fore in economic areas. Above all, the Communist Party stakes its claim to power on economic growth and on its track record of pulling hundreds of millions out of poverty since the late 1970s. The rise in living standards has led to heightened expectations. To satisfy the demands of its 1 billion-plus people, China must look abroad for resources and opportunities. A necessary precondition for that is a stable and secure regional and global environment.

Consider the Chinese stake in a number of crucial areas.

Shipping Interests: About 45 percent of all commercial goods, in terms of gross tonnage, cross the South China Sea. A large majority of this tonnage moves through the Strait of Malacca between Malaysia and Indonesia, a narrow strip of water that serves as the main shipping lane between the Indian and Pacific Oceans. Approximately 82 percent of China's imported crude oil flows through this strait. Thus China would be enormously vulnerable to any disruption in the area and has a vested interest in securing primacy over the shipping lanes surrounding the Strait of Malacca and the South China Sea.[64] Yet the U.S. Navy has traditionally played a critical role in securing global shipping lanes; it continues to dominate here. American leadership is making the Chinese increasingly uneasy.

Energy Interests: In 2010, China became the world's largest energy consumer, surpassing the U.S.[65] Most of its energy is imported from abroad. Thus energy security is a top priority. Given traditional American naval-lane preeminence, Beijing will have to act more assertively in defense of perceived security threats.

Indeed, China has already made sweeping territorial claims in the South China Sea that conflict with U.S. interests. Beijing's interest is understandable: The South China Sea contains, by one estimate, 900 trillion cubic feet of natural gas and 130 billion barrels of oil. Some liken it to a "second Persian Gulf,"[66] and Beijing may need it to be exactly that if the country is to continue fueling its economic expansion. Secure access would allow China to lessen dependence on the Strait of Malacca and on Middle Eastern oil, limiting the risk of supply disruptions. The Chinese are also embroiled in a dispute with the Philippines over the rights to the Scarborough Shoals, which sit atop oil and gas reserves.[67]

Territorial Disputes: Given the interests involved, it shouldn't be surprising that China and some other countries situated around the South China Sea have conflicting territorial claims to the resource-rich seabed and islands in the area. These islands are important mostly owing to the two interests cited above: shipping and resources. Emboldened by its growing naval capabilities, China has taken a more assertive stance in a number of these territorial disputes—not only its long-standing border dispute with India but also its maritime boundary disputes with Japan "over the East China Sea and throughout the South China Sea with Vietnam, Malaysia, the Philippines, Brunei, and Taiwan."[68]

Probably the most notable—and most volatile—current dispute involves the China–Japan standoff over the Senkaku Islands (or Diaoyu Islands, to the Chinese) in the East China Sea. Until its economy became a global pacesetter, Beijing made no noises about ownership of the islands. China's offshore power grabs center entirely around two things: claiming underwater oil and gas reserves, and protection of the sea-lanes that deliver China's energy supplies.

Relations between the two neighbors, never easy, have frayed even further in recent years. China's growing naval strength and newfound comfort at asserting its might internationally bode poorly for resolution. Touting their economic might, the Chinese believe that Japan must accept a "readjustment" in the power balance, including conceding ownership of the islands.

Nothing doing. Instead, on the 68th anniversary of the bombing of Hiroshima, the Japanese unveiled the *Izumo*, the largest warship the country has built since World War II. Because the Japanese Constitution forbids aircraft carriers and prohibits Japan's self-defense forces from taking offensive action, Tokyo called this ship a "helicopter carrier." The Chinese didn't buy it.

"It is an aircraft carrier, and Japan just called it 'a helicopter destroyer' to downplay its aggressive nature," said Zhang Junshe, of the People's Liberation Army Naval Military Studies Research Institute. He pointed out that the *Izumo* was much larger than many other countries' aircraft carriers and could be easily adapted for the support of F35-B fighters.[69]

China's Ministry of National Defense condemned the move, lambasting the "continuous military buildup" of its neighbor. "Japan should reflect on its history, adhere to self-defense and the promise of following the path of peaceful development," the bureau said in a statement, warning the international community to be "highly alert." In December 2013, Beijing struck back.

That's when the Chinese announced their decision to establish an "air defense identification zone" (ADIZ) over the East China Sea. It prompted Vice President Joe Biden to visit Tokyo to show support for Prime Minister Shinzo Abe and attempt to soothe our anxious ally. Beijing's unveiling of the ADIZ made clear that the Chinese were playing for keeps in the East China Sea. As Asia-Pacific expert Hugh White explains, Washington's Asian pivot was based on the "supposition that China wasn't serious about asserting their primacy—and Washington underestimated China's ambitions."[70] In the end, the Chinese military buildup can be viewed through the most traditional lens: Any growing power tends to seek expanded resources internationally, and that is what the Chinese are doing. With China's enormous population and economic growth, Beijing will only become more assertive on the world stage. Beijing is now pursuing what Robert Kaplan calls a "resource-acquisition" foreign policy, as opposed to a "missionary policy" (one based on ideas) such as that pursued by the United States and the former Soviet Union during the Cold War.[71]

"They will deal with any regime provided they can get natural resources," Kaplan says, "again for a totally legitimate purpose—to raise the standards of living for hundreds of millions of people into the global middle class."[72] Indeed, as Kaplan points out, China is following the trajectory of many great mercantile empires—first by securing land borders and then by building a capable navy, branching out, and securing natural resources necessary to feed a hungry economy. Mercantilism is an economic policy, as opposed to a military or for-eign-affairs doctrine. It emphasizes a positive balance of trade and accumulation of resources.

The military posture is a reflection of this reality, not the driver of it. Nonetheless, it cannot merely be accepted as a fait accompli. There is a realpolitik logic to what China is doing, but that doesn't mean that American policy should acquiesce, or that the U.S. should not take substantive measures in response.

*****

In its effort to create the New Look, the Russian Ministry of Defense is attempting, at least in part, to reignite the patriotic zeal Russians felt for the Soviet-era armed forces. Moscow promises not only a refur-bished military but also a new source of national pride. Its ambitious modernization program is a last-ditch attempt to break the cycle of weakness that has afflicted the Russian military since the collapse of the Soviet Union.

The clearest indication of where the priorities—and thus strate-gies—lie is, unsurprisingly, where the money is going. And what's most striking about the 10-year Russian military-modernization program is its de-emphasis on the Russian ground forces, once the heart and soul of the Red Army. In the Soviet era, the Red Army had been vital, because the USSR needed the ability to occupy its client states and credibly threaten a ground war in Europe. Now, Russian priorities are focused on protecting hydrocarbon export routes and bullying neighbors, tasks better accomplished through the sea or air. Thus, while the ground forces still must deal with internal terrorist and separatist threats, equipping and maintaining them does not require the large-scale investments of the past. In the new era, the focus is squarely on the navy and air force.

For the first time since the fall of the Soviet Union, the navy has received top billing in a Russian military budget. The 10-year budget provides for 30 new submarines (both nuclear and diesel), 32 frigates and corvettes, and 10 amphibious landing ships. These programs show a dramatic turn away from the anti–aircraft carrier, anti-NATO capabilities that were developed by the USSR and haltingly maintained until fairly recently. The Russian navy is also undertaking a massive reorganization that will shift ships and focus away from the Baltic and Northern Fleets to the Black Sea and Pacific Fleets.

The navy also purchased two *Mistral*-class amphibious assault ships from the French.[73] (For now, the $1.7 billion deal is going forward, though the French have made unconvincing threats about cancelling it if the Ukraine crisis is not resolved.[74]) These ships will most likely make their way to the Black Sea and Pacific Fleets, granting those flotillas amphibious capabilities that were not fully developed even under the Soviets. The Mistrals are capable of rapidly delivering hundreds of soldiers and dozens of vehicles to a target location via helicopter assault. After the 2008 Georgian war, and the failures of Russian equipment and technology that occurred, one can see why the Russians would value this new technology in their southern waters.

The naval procurements paint a picture of stark transition from a NATO-centric navy to an Asia-centric navy. Russia is beginning a new phase in its naval history, with the Pacific Ocean and Black Sea holding a place of privilege that they have not occupied since Imperial times.

Unlike most current Russian subs, which are part of the Northern Fleet and deployed—even today—as anti-NATO resources, the new *Borei*-class nuclear submarines will almost certainly be assigned to the Pacific Fleet upon completion. With the addition of the Boreis,

Russia's Pacific Fleet will become a powerhouse capable of rapidly delivering a truly frightening amount of nuclear firepower anywhere on the Pacific Rim. Naval power, especially seaborne nuclear power, is Russia's only remaining trump card in the Far East. The Kremlin wants to keep it that way.

There is a brewing conflict between Russia, Norway, Denmark, Canada, and the U.S. over rights to the Arctic seafloor, which is suspected to be rich in hydrocarbons.[75] A modern, rapidly deployable nuclear submarine force is essential if Russia wishes to defend its current Arctic holdings and pursue new claims. Additionally, Russia is hedging its bets that global warming will make the arctic coastline navigable, and it hopes to pursue trade opportunities along the mouths of the Yenisei and Ob Rivers.[76]

Russia's Arctic ambitions will only be strengthened by its active funding of GLONASS, its native Global Navigation Satellite System. It is currently the only operational alternative to American GPS. While it provides all the advantages for Russia that GPS does for the United States, GLONASS also has a strategic edge: GPS satellites orbit in such a way that high northern latitudes are susceptible to lack of coverage, presenting a critical vulnerability. GLONASS takes advantage of this, and its satellites orbit in such a way that they provide the most reliable and consistent coverage in the Arctic Circle.[77] With this edge in mapping, tracking, and exploration, Russian goals of Arctic dominance may be achievable.

While the Russian navy is turning its priorities away from the anti-NATO capabilities of the Cold War, the Russian air force still views its primary competitors as the NATO states. Russian leaders worry about the ability of Russia's aging air fleet to defend Russian airspace, and keeping Russian aerospace products commercially competitive with Western products remains a priority. The air forces are dead set on maintaining parity with NATO capabilities and equipment and to that end are fielding and developing world-class jets that can compete for foreign contracts.

Moscow is purchasing many MIG-35s and Su-35s, and, as noted earlier, both have outperformed NATO planes at international air shows and won lucrative contracts for their Russian manufacturers. In addition, if the PAK FA stealth fighter can stay on its development schedule, it will make Russia the second country to develop and field a native *fifth-generation* fighter design. The PAK FA is being developed by Sukhoi to be comparable to the American F-22 Raptor. Ultimately, Russia will maintain a cutting-edge air force because it is the only branch capable of global, meaningful power projection against every potential adversary, NATO included.

In sum, what the military reforms begun under Medvedev and continued under Putin indicate most clearly about Russian priorities is this: For the first time since the fall of the Soviet Union, Russia is ready, willing, and able to get serious about military modernization and buildup. The Russian 10-year plan is well funded to meet that challenge. It's up to Washington to make sure that the United States can say the same.

WHY AMERICAN MILITARY SUPERIORITY ISN'T ALL THAT IT SEEMS TO BE

The U.S. Pacific Command headquarters in Honolulu called it "Air Sea Battle 2028"—a huge war game that would "position U.S. air, naval, space, and special operations forces against a rising military competitor in the East Asian littoral with a range of disruptive capabilities, including multidimensional 'anti-access' networks, offensive and defensive space control capabilities, an extensive inventory of ballistic and cruise missiles, and a modernized attack submarine fleet," according to an Air Force memo. "The scenario will take place in a notional 2028."[78]

By the time it was over, U.S. planners had to be happy that 2028 was 20 years off, because the war game was an utter disaster. We lost to China at our own game, and the incident is widely regarded as part of the motivation for a shift in military strategy toward a concept known as Air Sea Battle (ASB). Losing the game also prompted the policy shift that became the Asian pivot itself.[79] Indeed, at the 2012 Shangri-La Security Dialogue, former Defense Secretary Leon Panetta said that the U.S. would commit 60 percent of its naval fleet to the Asia-Pacific by 2020.[80]

The 2008 war game slyly made mention only of a "rising military competitor" in the East Asian littoral, but that describes only one nation. Four years later, at the Marine Corps' 2012 war games, retired Marine Lieutenant General Wallace "Chip" Gregson made it explicit, saying of China: "They have the ability to stretch our defenses at the end of a long logistic line." He went on: "We've been accustomed to having secure lines of communication, since 1945." Now, in areas where we don't—such as Afghanistan, where Pakistan has closed off key supply routes—"that's messing us up," he said.[81]

Problem is, we haven't heeded the warnings of General Gregson. The programs the military originally devised in the wake of ASB 2028 have been cut or dramatically scaled back to the point that they do not come close to meeting our needs in the Pacific. The Obama administration's solution to this has been to deplete our forces in the Atlantic in order to keep our fleet in the Pacific strong.

American policymakers, and certainly American citizens, have usually taken solace in the United States' status as the world's only superpower, with a military that rates second to none in both expenditures and capabilities. In a literal, objective sense, this remains true. But, practically speaking, it means less than meets the eye. This is not only because our military superiority is now so greatly taxed, and probably facing severe retrenchment; it is also because the Axis nations have proven adept at devising tactics and weaponry explicitly calibrated to neutralize U.S. capabilities. Indeed, Vladimir Putin, in the 2012 article in which he called for the massive Russian military buildup, pledged also to deliver an "effective and asymmetrical response" to NATO's planned European missile-defense shield (issues we will cover in depth in the next chapter).[82]

Spending figures—in which the U.S. dwarfs the world—tell only so much. How we are able to use, or not able to use, our assets in the real world means much more. The Axis does not strive for or need anything like parity in military force or spending. They seek only effectiveness in neutralizing the American behemoth, and they are succeeding.

Consider the 2008 Georgian war. A rusting, severely underpowered branch of Russia's motorized armor proved sufficient to the task of invading and occupying a Western ally. Russian troops overran Georgia's ports and strategic highways. Warplanes bombed cities. The West did nothing about it. The U.S. refused to arm its Georgian ally with anti-aircraft and anti-tank missiles for fear of Russian retribution. So much for our overwhelming military superiority.

What manner of retribution would so intimidate the mighty U.S. military? The threat that Moscow could sell even more advanced weapons to Iran. The message would be: You defend Georgia against us, and we will defend Iran against you. The threat resonated hugely in the context of Iran's nuclear program, which the U.S. might, one day, need to bomb from the air. Israel had sold air-defense missiles to Georgia. The same Russian threat intimidated the Israelis, with the added threat that Russia could supply comparable weapons to Hezbollah. The Israelis, too, backed off.

So while the U.S. spends more on its military than the Axis powers combined, we could not or would not protect Georgia. Asymmetry, in the form of rogue-nation politics, deterred us from exercising our natural and measurable military advantages.

The future of that advantage, of course, is very much in question. Quite apart from the large funding reductions that it faces, the Pentagon must also come to terms with the Obama administration's Asia Pivot strategy. It remains to be seen what this will mean in terms of the holes left in the strategic theaters being de-emphasized, though so far, given European paralysis over Ukraine, the prospects are not encouraging. A lot rides as well on how much the West continues to depend on Middle Eastern oil. America's resources have limits—this much we have learned—and the Asia Pivot may mean that the U.S. will need to neglect other important areas.

Equally alarming, however, is the indication that with a fraction of U.S. spending, China has developed comparable military technology. Chinese citizens—unlike Americans—cannot vote and cannot push their government to reduce military spending or balance funding for civic and military projects so it's in synch with the public's preferences; we can therefore assume that Beijing can focus unhindered on its military ambitions. The U.S. cannot.

In the summer of 2012, at the height of the drone war against insurgents in Afghanistan, Americans woke to headlines saying that a reconnaissance drone had been captured by Iran—captured intact, so the Iranians claimed. A great deal of speculation ensued about whether Iran had indeed done so, and if it had, whether Tehran had leaked details of the drone's component parts to the Chinese. What we do know is that, within a few months, a mysterious drone appeared above Israel and was shot down by Israeli warplanes, and that, in Syria, the opposition reported that the besieged Assad government was using reconnaissance drones. We also know that in June 2012, the University of Texas at Austin demonstrated to the Defense Department how easily third parties could commandeer a drone.[83]

Consider, too, the state of the stealth technology on which the U.S. has spent tens of billions of dollars. Some 30 Stealth bombers costing up to $2 billion each are now operational. Yet during the Balkan war, the Serbians successfully shot down one such bomber, most likely with the help of Russian technology. According to local sources, Chinese operatives crisscrossed the region buying up pieces of the wreckage from farmers who had scavenged the matériel as souvenirs.

In January 2011, China conducted the first test of a stealth plane called the Chengdu J-20, hours before Robert Gates, then the U.S. secretary of defense, was due to meet with Hu Jintao, who was then China's premier (we discussed this incident as well in Chapter 3). Gates himself had projected that the Chinese would not develop such a warplane until 2020. Most experts see distinct similarities between the J-20 and several other non-Chinese designs, specifically Russia's Sukhoi-50 and America's two most advanced warplanes: the Stealth bomber and the F-35 Joint Strike Fighter (JSF), which is slated to cost the U.S. some $300 billion. And now here were the Chinese, potentially adapting something similar, for a fraction of the cost—and in collaboration with the Russians.

We'll probably never know the whole story behind the development and performance capability of China's stealth warplane, but there can be no doubt of its purpose. Most experts believe, based on the size of the J-20, that it is a bomber. You don't develop radar-evading systems for defensive uses. You don't rush to build a cutting-edge bomber to repulse invaders from your own shores. No one in China's periphery has asked for Chinese military hardware to help defend against outsiders. It's clear, then, that no one but China intends to use these non-defensive planes.

Of course, the way some might see it, this merely puts China's offensive capability on par with that of NATO and the United States. The analogy has no merit. NATO works in tandem with countries that fear Russian aggression; the U.S. collaborates with Asia-Pacific allies to defend against Chinese intimidation. Nobody is interested in invading Russia or China. The same cannot be said of Russian and Chinese ambitions with regard to their neighbors. Beijing pointedly tested a stealth bomber on the eve of a visit by the American defense secretary, leaving him free to conclude that such war-making capabilities are aimed at the U.S. and its allies. The same goes for announcements of new drone systems that can reach American bases in the Pacific.

The fundamental reality here is that the Axis has specifically devoted its resources to countering U.S. stealth technology and targeting systems.

The Russian weapons industry, in particular, has evolved an "asymmetrical" philosophy of countermeasures against U.S. strike capability. The approach is based on acceptance that Russian weaponry cannot match American might head-on but can effectively target vulnerable areas of U.S. defenses—air refueling, cockpit avionics, communications and weapons guidance, and, above all, expense. In short, Axis weaponry is calibrated to operate for the sole purpose of neutralizing the U.S. and its allies. The battlefield inequities have balanced out alarmingly.[84]

During the 2006 Israeli invasion of Hezbollah territory in Lebanon, for instance, the Israelis deployed some 350 to 400 Merkava tanks, thought to be invincible in such an encounter. Through the use of somewhat modern Russian weaponry, Hezbollah was able to damage 52 of them.[85] The crucial point to understand is the punishing cost differential. Whereas the Merkava tanks can cost more than $2 million each, the rockets that neutralized them cost less than $100,000. Even more alarmingly, Hezbollah knocked out an Israeli warship with missiles. The cost differential in that instance doesn't even need detailing. (In March 2014, the Israelis intercepted an Iranian ship carrying Syrian-made missiles bound for Gaza.[86])

Consider the conflict in Syria. A Turkish air-force fighter—an American-made F-4 Phantom—was shot down off the nearby Syrian coast in June 2012.[87] The Russians supply Syria heavily with both Russian personnel and anti-aircraft weaponry. Although it was only one instance, the incident lent some insight into what a "full theater" conflict might entail for the U.S. and it allies. At minimum, it would be prohibitively expensive. This kind of asymmetrical cost-benefit equation was enough to keep the U.S. from engaging the Assad regime actively or even imposing a no-fly zone.

In short, there is more than enough evidence of U.S. and Western inadequacy in the realm of technical superiority that we all take for granted. Perhaps *inadequacy* is not the right word; the problem, after all, is not with the weapons and technologies themselves, which rarely fail to perform as intended; it is in their vulnerability to asymmetric arms. Consequently, they do not give us the dispositive, conflict-ending advantage that we assume they will. Our complacency has little basis in objective reality.

Satellites in Space

In December 2013, China entered an exclusive club: It became just the third nation (after, naturally, the U.S. and Russia) to make a soft landing on the moon when the unmanned *Chang'e-3* probe landed after a 13-day journey. "The dream of the Chinese people across thousands of years of landing on the moon has finally been realized with *Chang'e*," said the state-run China News Service. "By successfully joining the international deep-exploration club, we finally have the right to share resources on the moon with developed countries."[88]

As Paul D. Spudis, a scientist at the Lunar and Planetary Institute in Houston, sees it, the mission of the *Chang'e-3* is to hone technology for future space exploration. "Although it will do some new science, its real value is to flight-qualify a new and potentially powerful lunar surface payload delivery system," Spudis told the *New York Times.*[89] China might be the only country in the world with an operating space station after 2020, when the International Space Station is set to be decommissioned. Beijing shows every sign of regarding space as just another arena in which to compete with, and perhaps surpass, the U.S.

That's one reason that the state-run *Global Times* in China sounded even more impassioned than usual in January 2013, defending the country's right to develop anti-satellite (ASAT) weapons in space. "It is necessary for China to have the ability to strike U.S. satellites," the paper's editorial read. "This deterrent can provide strategic protection to Chinese satellites and the whole country's national security." The Global Times saw ASAT capabilities as a way to even the odds against the U.S.: "In the foreseeable future, [the] gap between China and the U.S. cannot be eliminated by China's development of space weapons. The U.S. advantage is overwhelming. Before strategic uncertainties between China and the U.S. can disappear, China urgently needs to have an outer space trump card."[90]

And that is how Beijing has treated ASAT capability over the last decade. In 2006, China targeted high-powered lasers at American satellites passing over its territory. The purpose of the lasers was not entirely clear, but the Union of Concerned Scientists speculated that they could have been used to blind the satellites' delicate optical sensors or to track their motion. Satellites travel on predetermined pathways; tracking them could be the first step in targeting and incapacitating them with an ASAT.[91]

In January 2007, China used a ground-based missile to destroy a defunct weather satellite in orbit some 500 miles above the earth's surface. The exercise constituted the first test of its kind since the 1980s, when the United States and Russia developed the capability to shoot down orbiting satellites. The move seemed to suggest that

Beijing was entering a new phase of its efforts to counter American technological dominance—demonstrating to Washington that it could take down U.S. satellites.

"In my view, the Chinese are sending a strong signal here," said Jeffrey Kueter, president of the George C. Marshall Institute, a nonprofit defense think tank. "They're saying they can hold our space-based, war-fighting capability at risk, and are putting into doubt our ability to challenge them. They're a rising space competitor."[92]

Others agreed. "The Chinese are telling the Pentagon that they don't own space," said Michael Krepson of the Henry L. Stimson Center, another security think tank. "We can play this game, too, and we can play it dirtier than you. . . . [It] blows a hole through the Bush administration reasoning behind not talking to anybody about space arms control—that there is no space arms race. It looks like there is one at this point."[93]

That became more apparent in July 2013, when the rumors that the *Global Times* had discussed in January finally came true: The Chinese military launched three ASAT satellites into orbit, where they were observed "conducting unusual maneuvers in space, indicating the Chinese are preparing to conduct space warfare against satellites," as a U.S. official described it. One of the ASATs, equipped with what a space expert called "a robot-manipulator arm," was thought capable of attacking orbiting U.S. satellites—a capability that the official called "part of a Chinese 'Star Wars' program."[94] China's new capabilities in these areas—to the extent we understand what they are—have important consequences for the military and economic balance of power.

Satellites are America's eyes on the battlefield, "the soft underbelly of our national security," in the words of then-Representative Edward Markey.[95] They provide key communications support. An attack on 40 or 50 low-orbit satellites like the one China destroyed could blind the American military in a matter of hours.[96] China's ASAT capabilities specifically threaten America's photographic intelligence, electro-optical, and electronic-intelligence satellites that operate in low-earth orbit. In a hypothetical conflict between the U.S. and China, these systems would probably be targets for Chinese ASAT missiles. China could also equip its ASAT missiles with electromagnetic pulse or nuclear weaponry, creating an even more serious threat to these systems.[97] In short, ASATs are another in the growing arsenal of asymmetric weapons—and their development and use may have further-reaching consequences than any other.

CONCLUSION

In August 2013, as the violence in the Syrian civil war reached horrifying levels, the United States closed embassies and consulates in 19 countries in the Middle East and Africa after an abundance of terror threats that the government considered serious and credible. The countries involved produce one-third of the world's oil, yet the United States had basically announced that it could not defend its personnel in these nations. The widespread closures seemed to symbolize the decline of America's posture in the world—where we seem always to operate from a defensive crouch, confused, tentative, and unwilling to make hard choices to defend our interests in a dangerous world.

"Countries that are winning do not have to close their embassies in 19 countries," wrote Newt Gingrich, as we cited in the epigraph to this chapter. "This is a statement of impotence and incompetence on a grand scale, an admission that the United States cannot even defend its own embassies (and this is after decades of turning our embassies into fortresses isolated from local communities)."[98] Referring also to a series of prison breaks in Iraq, Afghanistan, Pakistan, and Libya, which set loose some 2,500 al-Qaeda-linked militants and other enemy fighters, Gingrich concluded: "So after 12 years of intense effort, two overt wars, dozens of minor skirmishes in Somalia, Libya, Mali, and other countries, widespread use of drones to kill people, and a massive investment in power projection and intelligence gathering, the fact is, our enemies are widespread, growing, and increasingly dangerous."[99]

Indeed, despite the extraordinary American military advantage, the U.S. is actually losing ground against the Axis in almost every area. In Washington, policy planners cut budgets with no plan for what they are trying to achieve; we lack not only an overarching strategy, but also a practical framework for what we decide upon. The Russians and Chinese, by contrast, while not immune to some policy confusion and disagreements of their own, are for the most part clear in their articulation of broad goals and consistent in the actions—economic, financial, strategic—needed to achieve them.

"History and the present tell us unambiguously that we require vast reserves of strength used judiciously, sparingly where possible, overwhelmingly when appropriate, precisely, quickly, and effectively," writes Mark Helprin. "Now we have vanishing and insufficient strength used injudiciously, promiscuously, slowly, and ineffectively."[100] Indeed: The shadows of what we face are rapidly materializing into real-world problems.

A skeptic might say: Even if the United States is pulling back on its military might, it still has its nuclear deterrent—not just an offensive nuclear arsenal but also the installations and technologies that protect the homeland against attack. How dangerous can things be? The answer: very dangerous, because (as our next chapter will show) we are systematically dismantling our offensive and defensive nuclear capacities as well.

CHAPTER 5

Nuclear Security:
They Build Up, We Build Down

"We closely watched last night's events. They were successful. We tested an intercontinental ballistic missile which I call 'a missile defense killer.' Neither modern nor future American missile defense means will be able to stop this missile from hitting its target directly."

—RUSSIAN DEPUTY PREMIER DMITRI ROGOZIN[1]

"Our policy, relentlessly pursued by the president, is to disarm. As China and Russia invigorate their defense industrial bases, we diminish ours. We are stripping our nuclear deterrent to and beyond the point where it will encourage proliferation among opportunistic states, endow China with parity, and make a first strike against us feasible."

—MARK HELPRIN[2]

"Historians will look back at the present moment with astonishment that Iran so skillfully outwitted the West. They will note the breathtaking naiveté of American and European officials who let a brutal theocracy undermine Western interests throughout the Middle East. At one of Iran's most vulnerable moments, America threw the mullahs a life-line; an ill-conceived nuclear deal . . . "

—DAVID KEYES[3]

"We build, they build. We stop, they build."

—REPRESENTATIVE MIKE ROGERS, QUOTING A FORMER
DEFENSE SECRETARY, ON TREATIES WITH RUSSIA[4]

Even by North Korea's standards, the threats sounded pretty dis-turbing. "Intercontinental ballistic missiles and various other missiles, which have already set their striking targets, are now armed with lighter, smaller, and diversified nuclear warheads and are placed on a standby status," said Army General Kang Pyo Yong at a mass rally in Pyongyang. "When we shell [the missiles], Washington, which is the stronghold of evils . . . will be engulfed in a sea of fire."[5] The inter-national community had grown accustomed to North Korean threats, but these seemed more serious. A few weeks earlier, the Pyongyang regime had threatened South Korea with "final destruction."[6]

Many were therefore not surprised when the news broke that the United States would deploy 14 new missile interceptors in Alaska in response to the bellicose words and deeds of North Korea. The additional interceptors would be installed by 2017 and, added to 30 already in place on the West Coast, would bring the U.S. total to 44.

"The reason that we are doing what we are doing," said Defense Secretary Chuck Hagel, "and the reason we are advancing our program here for homeland security is to not take any chances, is to stay ahead of the threat and to assure any contingency."[7]

What Hagel did not say was that the U.S. would effectively pay for the redeployment by cancelling the last phase of its planned missile shield in Poland and Romania.[8] That last phase, which had involved missile interceptors, had been the most vital. This decision, as noted in Chapter 1, was tantamount to unilateral American withdrawal from missile defense in Western Europe. For years, the Obama administra-tion had been saying that it was crucial to stop the Iranian pursuit of a nuclear bomb and to help defend our allies against it. Now, with no sign that the Iranian threat—aided and abetted by Russian support—had abated, we had pulled our resources out and moved them to the Pacific.

The U.S. retreat from missile defense is even more worrisome given our domestic failures in this area. In July 2013, at Vandenberg

Air Force Base in California, an advanced missile interceptor failed to hit its target over the Pacific Ocean—the eighth failed test of the U.S. missile-defense system in 16 tries. The U.S. hasn't held a successful test since 2008. It's hard not to see the flagging program as intricately linked with the Obama administration's blasé attitude toward missile defense—and its comfort level with starving the Pentagon, especially in the nuclear area.

Because the truth is, missile defense is only part of the nuclear equation. More broadly, the United States is retreating across the board when it comes to nuclear defenses and nuclear armaments, all while the Russians and Chinese expand their stockpiles—particularly of ballistic missiles—and modernize their capabilities. The fledgling nuclear programs in Iran and North Korea (with the North Koreans' considerably more advanced) will soon be capable of enriching uranium for dozens of warheads. Just one is enough to change the strategic calculus for their respective regions.

Against this determined armaments race, the United States has taken an equally determined stand to build down. President Obama's stated goal, over the long term, is to reach nuclear zero—a world without nuclear weapons. Ronald Reagan professed the same goal. But whereas Reagan believed the best way to get there was remaining strong and convincing our would-be adversaries it would be foolhardy to challenge us in the nuclear area (or any other), Obama seems to think that nations such as Russia and China will be persuaded to lay down their arms by seeing that we have laid down ours.

The Obama administration stunned many in 2010 by declaring that the United States would limit the instances in which it will use nuclear weapons—even in defense of the homeland—and that the Pentagon will *not* develop a new generation of nuclear weapons.[9] In 2013, three years after agreeing with the Russians to a limit of 1,550 deployed nuclear warheads, Obama declared his intention to cut the

U.S. nuclear arsenal by another one-third. It is this plan that retired Air Force Lieutenant General Thomas McInerney called *"the most dangerous thing I have ever seen an American president attempt to do."*[10]

Obama has delayed or outright terminated crucial defense programs. Besides the aforementioned European missile-defense shield, these cutbacks include scaling back programs such as the Airborne Laser program (which enables enemy-missile interceptions during the early launch phase) along with high-tech tools such as the Multiple Kill Vehicle and the Kinetic Energy Interceptor. The U.S. is delaying (or ignoring the need for) upgrades to nuclear ballistic-missile submarines and other crucial assets, and has not even made clear whether next-generation U.S. strategic bombers will be permitted to carry nuclear weapons.[11] Our nuclear capabilities remain more expansive than either Russia's or China's, but that advantage is eroding and won't last forever.

"As the stockpile shrinks in size," says Mike Rogers, chairman of the House Armed Services Subcommittee on Strategic Forces, "we have reached the point where further reductions take on immense importance to the nation's security."[12] Such is the extent of Washington's abandonment of our nuclear defenses—the arsenal that kept the peace during the Cold War and helped win it. Now, faced with equally determined if subtler adversaries, we seem to have forgotten the lessons of that struggle.

THE AMERICAN NUCLEAR RETREAT

In the 1964 film *Fail-Safe*, Henry Fonda plays an American president caught up in the ultimate Cold War nightmare scenario: He is informed that U.S. radar has picked up what looks to be an intrusion into American airspace by an unidentified flying object. The United States Strategic Air Command scrambles bombers toward pre-identified aerial points around the globe—they're called fail-safe points—to get into position and await a "go code" for launching attacks on Russian targets.

As the bombers near their destination, however, the flying object in U.S. airspace is identified: It's an off-course commercial airliner. U.S. Command tries to cancel the alert, but the message is bungled; instead of telling the bombers to desist, it sends the "go code." The bombers proceed to their targets, and U.S. Command cannot communicate with them, because Moscow has already jammed their signals. The U.S. bombers attack Moscow. Fonda as the American president is faced with an impossible choice: whether to brace for an all-out Russian counter-assault on multiple American cities—a nuclear holocaust—or order an American bomber to drop the same nuclear payload that hit Moscow on a U.S. city, in an effort to appease the Soviets and demonstrate good faith. Fonda opts for the second choice. The film ends with the bombs leveling New York.

Fail-Safe was a classic film of its time, tapping into the fears of millions in an age of Mutual Assured Destruction (MAD). If a remake were attempted today, Fonda's president might find himself in a different situation: that of being the superpower that lacks sufficient nuclear firepower to respond. If the United States keeps on its present course, destruction will remain part of the equation—but it will no longer be mutual.

At the height of the Cold War, the United States had a stockpile in the range of 32,000 weapons. Perhaps that was excessive; perhaps nothing like that number was needed. It's difficult to know. Today, however, we have gone so far in the other direction—toward disarmament, some of it unilateral—that we now have a different brand of excess. The United States, as this book goes to press, is on course to have a grand total of 1,550 deployed nuclear weapons on bombers, subs, and land-based missiles—the air, sea, and land components that make up the famous "triad" of our nuclear defenses. In fact, the administration is considering cutting one leg of the triad, perhaps the land-based component. Whether that happens remains to be seen.[13]

Experts regard the 1,550 nuke figure as much too small, considering all that our nuclear arsenal must enable us to do: Deter an attack on the homeland from Russia, China, and perhaps both; defend U.S. forces around the world; and protect more than 30 allies in Europe, the Far East, North America, and Australia. This is an awful lot to ask of a force facing such steep cuts. And it gets worse, because the Obama administration wants to cut further. The handwriting has been on the wall since the early days of Obama's presidency. As a candidate, Obama announced his interest in the nuclear-zero dream. As president, he began working toward it—at least as it pertained to the United States.

In April 2010, Obama unveiled a new chapter in his nuclear doctrine, setting limits on the situations in which the United States would consider using nuclear weapons. While American policy was once vague on this point, Obama made explicit promises not to use nuclear weapons and to stop developing new ones. He promised not to use nuclear weapons against non-nuclear states—even if they attacked the United States with chemical, biological, or Internet-based weapons.

"We are going to want to make sure that we can continue to move towards less emphasis on nuclear weapons," the president said, "to make sure that our conventional weapons capability is an effective deterrent in all but the most extreme circumstances."[14] This is an odd way for any head of state to prioritize his nation's defenses—by first announcing all of the weapons that he will *not* use. Obama's shift represented a sharp reversal of the policy that the Bush administration and most of Obama's predecessors had followed; they had always sought to maintain a strong nuclear posture. Even Obama's first secretary of defense, Bob Gates, opposed the new policy's ban on new weapons.[15]

Whether pursuing his disarmament goals unilaterally or as part of treaty arrangements with Moscow, President Obama has pressed the U.S. into aggressive disarmament. And even when he thinks he has Russian agreement, he doesn't seem to realize that (a) the deals he's made aren't good from the American perspective and (b) that the Russians aren't complying with them anyway. This is the situation that pertains with the latest major treaty signed between the two nations: New START.

The Fallacies of New START

"Even as this treaty allows Russia to strengthen their arsenal, President Obama remains hell-bent on weakening our own, while also suspending critical modernization of our strategic forces," wrote Representative Trent Franks, a member of the Armed Services Committee, in 2011. "By pandering to Russia repeatedly throughout his administration, this President has managed to weaken our defenses, to betray trusted allies like Poland and the Czech Republic, and to once again put American interests on the backburner."[16]

Franks was referring to the Russian-American New START treaty, signed the previous year, the successor treaty to previous Cold War pacts. Those who review seriously the treaty's terms would be hard-pressed to dismiss his conclusion: The treaty does nothing for American defenses while allowing the Russians to get away with proverbial murder. The terms of New START effectively allow Russia to continue to build up its arsenal even though the treaty's stated purpose is to reduce nuclear arms.

"Since New START has come into force," Franks writes, "Russia has been able to increase its nuclear armament yet still remain in compliance [with] treaty terms, which highlights precisely how ineffective the treaty truly is." New START is the capstone—so far—of President Obama's "good faith" negotiating strategy with the Russians.

The treaty formally commits the United States and Russia to reducing their stockpiles of delivery systems and strategic warheads to 1,550 each over the next seven years, and to resume on-site inspections.[17] The treaty language also includes a nonbinding statement regarding missile defense, in which the United States and Russia acknowledge different interpretations of what the treaty says: Washington maintains that New START does not limit missile-defense systems, while Moscow insists that it does.[18]

The treaty also includes reductions in delivery systems, such as launchers and bombers. The U.S. will make the larger cuts here, since its nuclear arsenal and delivery systems currently outpace Russia's.[19] In fact, the United States will have to eliminate 240 deployed strategic warheads compared with just 16 for Russia. And while the U.S. will have to reduce its strategic delivery vehicles, the New START caps are actually *above* Russia's current arsenal in this category—meaning that Moscow can *add* 184 such vehicles, while Washington has committed to reducing its stockpile.

It's vital to remember that the treaty passed ratification in the U.S. Senate only after President Obama promised to invest $85 billion over 10 years to update the aging U.S. nuclear arsenal and infrastructure, which by now is mostly outdated technology from the 1980s or even earlier. But congressional sequestration threatens any money for upgrades, and unless the fiscal picture changes, the American nuclear arsenal, without upgrades or replacements, will age and eventually become obsolete.

Another huge failing of New START is in the area of tactical nuclear weapons, a category in which Russia has as much as a 10-to-one numerical advantage.[20] Tactical nukes are weapons that can be used on the battlefield; they're highly destructive but of such a scale that they are practical for use in combat. New START does not address tactical weapons at all. In terms of the safety of Europe in particular, tactical nukes are more relevant than strategic missiles.

The Russians love tactical nukes: They have shown their willingness in the past to threaten their European neighbors by moving shorter-range tactical nuclear weapons to border regions.[21] It was shortsighted of the U.S to think that Russia would be genuinely committed to reducing tactical nuclear capabilities. They buttress Russia's military capabilities in such a way that the Russians can actually contend with, and even defeat, other major powers. Thus the Russians are quite pleased with New START, since the treaty leaves their tactical stockpile untouched.

For a time, New START improved Obama's relations with the Russians, but it placed the president in a weaker position from which to build America's arsenal, since Russian leaders believed the treaty to be more binding than their American counterparts did. Most important, they interpreted it as a legally binding limit on constructing missile-defense systems rather than as a directive to simply restrict the use of missiles themselves. "The first thing is that our American colleagues do not recognize the legal force of the treaty's preamble," said Konstantin Kosachev, chairman of the Russian parliament's international-affairs committee. "The preamble sets a link between strategic offensive arms and defensive arms."[22]

Since the signing of New START, Russia has sought to exploit loopholes in the treaty—something at which they have deep experience, as Washington knows. (In early 2014, for example, the Obama administration informed its NATO allies that the Russians have been testing ground-launched cruise missiles in violation of the landmark 1987 treaty banning such tests.[23]) Now the Russians seek to attach multiple warheads to individual missiles in a process called MIRVing (Multiple Independent Reentry Vehicles). It has the effect of making it more and more advantageous to strike first, thus increasing the danger of the Russian arsenal while keeping it within the bounds of the treaty.[24] If New START weren't bad enough, President Obama has proposed further reductions outside the treaty framework.

Beyond New START: Nuclear Zero?

In his 2013 Berlin speech, President Obama announced his intention to negotiate an additional one-third cut in nuclear stockpiles, which would allow the United States and Russia to lower the number of warheads to between 1,000 and 1,100 each, down from the New START limit of 1,550.[25] "I intend to seek negotiated cuts with Russia to move beyond Cold War nuclear postures," the president said. "At the same time, we'll work with our NATO allies to seek bold reductions in U.S. and Russian tactical weapons in Europe."[26] That's the category in which the Russians already hold a major edge.

While the cuts announced in Berlin are dramatic, they probably don't represent the bottom line in Obama's vision of a reduced American stockpile of nuclear weaponry. The administration has asked the Pentagon to draw up plans—at the very least, on an exploratory basis—to examine cutting America's nuclear arsenal by *another 80 percent*—bringing us down to, at the most aggressive estimate, somewhere between 300 and 400 total nuclear weapons. The last time the U.S. nuclear stockpile was that small was 1950, when the country was still in the early stages of ramping up its nuclear defenses.[27]

Shortly after the president's 2013 Berlin speech, Secretary of Defense Chuck Hagel announced that despite the reductions, the United States would continue investing in nuclear modernization and maintain its triad of bombers, intercontinental ballistic missile (ICBMs), and ballistic-missile submarines.[28] But funding for nuclear modernization is being cut by congressional sequestration—and the existing funding, says Representative Mike Rogers, chairman of the House Armed Services Strategic Forces Subcommittee, was already the "minimum required to accomplish this modernization." Rogers estimates that the administration is underfunding nuclear forces by between $1 billion and $1.6 billion annually. Programs taking a hit include the replacement of the *Ohio*-class ballistic-missile submarine, life-extension programs for W-78 and W-88 nuclear warheads, the long-range standoff cruise missile, and the submarine-launched Trident D-5—now two years behind schedule and not deployable until 2029 at the earliest. The cuts also canceled a plutonium lab in New Mexico, which Rogers sees as "one of the most urgently needed facilities."[29] Former Senator John Kyl picks up the trail of the damage from here:

> U.S. modernization programs—to extend the life of America's aging ballistic nuclear warheads and modernize its "triad" approach to defense against nuclear attack—are in trouble.
>
> Intercontinental ballistic missiles are the first leg of the triad. Although Russia is preparing to field a new generation of intercontinental ballistic missiles (one type of which can carry as many as 15 warheads), the Obama administration is still studying whether to develop its own modernized ICBMs.[30]

In effect, President Obama has announced his intention to work around the Senate's authority to ratify foreign treaties. Obama does not need to wait for another formal treaty to implement new reductions; he and Putin could make them more rapidly, through "parallel, reciprocal reductions of strategic warheads to well below 1,000 within the next five years."[31] With an aggressive second-term president eager to implement his agenda before time runs out, and who has never enjoyed positive relations with Congress, it's hard to know what unilateral moves Obama might yet make.

Why U.S. Nuclear Defenses Still Matter

To put it plainly, President Obama's proposed cuts would put the United States at enormous risk. Rogue nations such as North Korea and Iran seek to build larger nuclear arsenals, while allies such as Japan might move to build their own arsenals if they determine they can no longer depend on the U.S. nuclear umbrella. And Obama chooses to do all this in a dangerous world in which the trend is not to disarm, but to rearm.

"Our experience has been that nuclear arsenals—other than ours—are on the rise," says Jim Inhofe, the top Republican on the Senate Armed Services Committee. "A country whose conventional military strength has been weakened due to budget cuts ought not to consider further nuclear force reductions while turmoil in the world is growing." Senator Bob Corker, the ranking member of the Foreign Relations Committee, warned that "the president's announcement without first fulfilling commitments on modernization could amount to unilateral disarmament."[32]

It's dangerous in no small part because the Russians don't comply with the agreements they do sign. Representative Buck McKeon, head of the House Armed Services Committee, has raised the issue of the Russians' previous treaty violations in his criticism of President Obama's Berlin speech, saying that "the President's desire to negotiate a new round of arms control with the Russians, while Russia is cheating on a major existing nuclear arms control treaty, strains credulity."[33]

- Russia has been violating these agreements for years. Consider just its violations of the 1987 Intermediate-Range Nuclear Forces (INF) Treaty, which bans the two nations from "developing, testing, or possessing ballistic or cruise missiles with a range between 500 and 5,500 kilometers."

- Russian tests of the R-500 cruise missile, which may already be prepared for deployment, "falls within the INF's prohibited range," according to John Bolton.[34]
- Russia has rejected basic elements of the 20-year-old Cooperative Threat Reduction (CTR) Program, known as the Nunn-Lugar Program. Even though Russia received billions of dollars for eliminating Soviet-era missile, nuclear, biological, and chemical weapons, it now prohibits U.S. access to weapons sites while still seeking aid.
- Russia has violated the Conventional Forces in Europe Treaty, introducing "additional military forces into Georgia without host state consent and subsequent recognition of Abkhazia and South Ossetia as independent states."[35]

It's enough to remind one of what Ronald Reagan said famously 30 years ago: that the Russians "reserve unto themselves the right to commit any crime, to lie, to cheat." They're still doing it. Their pattern of noncompliance should not encourage Washington to believe that the Russians will implement its New START obligations.

And these cautions apply not only to Russia but also to the more volatile and dangerous proliferators, and potential proliferators, of nuclear weapons around the world—especially North Korea but also Iran and others. That is why, in February 2013, 20 foreign-policy experts and retired military officers wrote an open letter to President Obama urging him to reconsider his aggressive disarmament agenda:

> It is now clear that, as a practical matter under present and foreseeable circumstances, this [nuclear zero] agenda will only result in the unilateral disarmament of the U.S. nuclear deterrent. That will make the world more dangerous, not less.

According to published reports, you are considering further, draconian and perhaps unilateral cuts in the numbers of nuclear weapons in our arsenal. We respectfully recommend that this plan be abandoned in favor of the fulfillment of commitments you made at the time of the New START Treaty to: modernize all three legs of the Triad; ensure the safety and deterrent effectiveness of the weapons with which they are equipped; and restore the critical industrial base that supports these forces.

Doing otherwise will put our country, its allies and our peoples at ever-greater risk in a world that is, far from nuclear-free, awash with such weapons—with increasing numbers of them in the hands of freedom's enemies. It is unimaginable that that is your intention. It must not be the unintended result of your actions, either.[36]

Logic and history argue against all of President Obama's naive assumptions and his reckless insistence that the United States can maintain its current level of security without a large nuclear advantage. In fact, detailed scholarship indicates that states with an advantage in nuclear forces are more likely to win in nuclear crises against states with smaller arsenals.[37] President Obama's drastic reductions to the nuclear arsenal make it more likely that the United States will lose such confrontations in the future, should they arise. This is especially true when those states are so determined to arm up.

THE AXIS ARMS UP

Perhaps President Obama's eagerness to disarm would have some application in a world in which other powerful nations were equally or even more determined to reduce their arsenals. That is not the case, however, especially with the nations that view the United States as an adversary, as Russia and China often do, or as an outright enemy, as

Iran and North Korea do. All these countries, as well as Pakistan—our estranged "ally" in the War on Terror—are aggressively expanding and upgrading their nuclear stockpiles, delivery systems, and defenses. A review of their postures makes clear that Obama's anti-nuclear passions are a poor fit for this moment in history.

Russia

Dmitri Medvedev was ready to leave the political stage as Russia's president in May 2012. As part of his farewell, the president held a Kremlin ballroom ceremony to honor Russian citizens from all areas of endeavor. He awarded medals to a policeman, a theater director, the chairman of the Russian hockey federation, and dozens of other ordinary citizens. Then Medvedev approached the podium to speak, and he had a special message for the young. The next generation of Russians, he said, needed positive role models to inspire them toward "success in literature, art, education." Then he paused and added, "and nuclear weapons."[38]

That has to be one of the more creative segues any statesman has ever made, but Medvedev's linkage was not accidental; it was deeply revealing about Russia's attitude toward nukes. The way the Russians see it, an expansive nuclear arsenal is essential to their national goals. As Medvedev's speech shows, in contrast to China, Russia has never made any secret of the extent of its nuclear arsenal. In fact, the Russians take every opportunity to brag about it, and they have much to boast about it: The Russians maintain the world's largest nuclear arsenal, and unlike the Americans, they are determined to modernize and upgrade it.[39] Russia spends 40 percent of its total military budget—about $30 billion a year—on its nuclear program, most of it focused on developing less vulnerable nuclear-launch systems such as mobile ICBM launchers and new submarine-launched ballistic missiles (SLBMs).[40]

At the same time, Moscow has pressured the U.S. and its NATO allies in Europe not to install the updated missile-defense shield, as discussed when we looked at Obama's hot-mic promise of post-election "flexibility" vis-à-vis Russia. Moscow claims that the shield is an offensive weapon pointed against it, while NATO argues that it is for defensive purposes against third parties such as Iran. The U.S. has even invited the Russians to participate in the shield. The Kremlin rejected this offer and countered by explicitly threatening a preemptive strike against countries such as Poland that wish to deploy it. It was an echo of Soviet-era threats against Western Europe.

The Russians have been eagerly modernizing for years. In 2008, Medvedev announced that he wanted to build a "guaranteed nuclear deterrent system" and a "system of aerospace defense" by 2020, mostly in response to America's plans to move ballistic-missile defense systems into Eastern Europe. In order to "achieve dominance in airspace," Medvedev then said, "we plan to start serial production of warships, primarily nuclear-powered submarines carrying cruise missiles and multifunctional submarines."[41]

Four years later, an objective source (at least when it comes to Russia)—China's Xinhua News—reported that Russia's modernization was proceeding as planned, with Russia rearming to a level not achieved since the fall of the Soviet Union.[42] Those in Washington concerned with the American build-down have had plenty of signs to worry them from Russia's actions in recent years.

In March 2013, Russia launched an operational drill of its nuclear weapons. The drill tested the transport and deployment of strategic and tactical nuclear weapons near the European border, and came in the wake of increased test flights of Russian nuclear bombers over Guam and simulations of bomber runs over California and Alaska.[43]

In April 2013, the Russian government announced that work was under way on a new generation of rail-based ICBM missiles. Older

American-Soviet agreements prohibited rail-based launchers, but the New START treaty did not mention them. Additionally, Russia is working on a new generation of strategic bombers, to be completed by 2020.[44]

In May 2013, the Russian government announced that it would soon deploy the first of its newly designed Yars-M ICBM systems. The Yars-M is said to have a greater capacity to penetrate missile-defense systems such as those the Obama administration is setting up in Eastern Europe. The missile "is one of the military technological measures that the Russian military-political leadership has devised in response to the development of a global missile-defense system by the Americans," said Victor Yesin, a retired Russian strategic forces commander.[45]

Long before 2013, the Russians were using their marked advantage in tactical nuclear weapons to pressure and intimidate other nations. As we observed when looking at the New START Treaty, tactical nukes, where Russians have a huge numerical advantage, have come to play a vital role in Russian military thinking. While Russia and the United States have both heavily reduced their strategic stockpiles, tactical stockpiles have rarely been the focus of international treaties. As Russia's conventional forces continue to suffer from structural weaknesses, Russian strategists have come to see their tactical arsenal as a substitute for conventional strength in some cases.[46]

In 2009, Moscow launched an exercise along its borders from the Baltic States to Finland, with simulated use of such weapons accompanied by actual cyber attacks on the communications of nearby countries. In November 2011, Nikolai Makarov, the chief of the Russian general staff, stated that local conflicts could escalate to the use of tactical or strategic weapons: "The possibility of local conflicts practically along the whole periphery of our borders has increased sharply.... Under certain conditions I do not exclude the possibility that local and regional armed conflicts could turn into major wars, including the employment of nuclear weapons."[47]

Russia's stance on tactical nukes is shaped by its understanding of the geopolitical environment. Russia views these weapons as a key part of its defense not only against Europe or America, but also China or Japan. Unlike the United States, protected by wide oceans, Russia is surrounded by nuclear-armed states that it views as potential rivals. Unless Russia's view of its neighbors changes, it is unlikely that the government will abandon its tactical arms. And that goes double for the times when Russia is led by a determined nationalist such as Vladimir Putin, who promises to use military intervention (including preventive intervention) to protect Russian citizens "wherever they may be." One Russian expert refers to tactical nukes as weapons of "regional deterrence."[48]

The Russian posture shouldn't surprise the United States, especially given New START, which essentially reduced an American advantage in deployed strategic weapons to parity with Russia, while leaving untouched the Kremlin's advantage in tactical weapons. By reducing its nuclear advantage, the U.S. also allowed the Kremlin to rein in its own nuclear budget, which remains aggressive even though it no longer has to play catch-up as it did during the 1980s. The eased budgetary pressure allows Moscow to devote more money to modernizing its navy and air force, as detailed in the last chapter.

Finally, recent events demand that we view the Russian nuclear posture also in the context of the Budapest Memorandum on Security Assurances, signed by Russia, Ukraine, the United States, and Britain in 1994. In that agreement, Ukraine, then the world's third-largest nuclear power, agreed to give up *all* of its nuclear weapons—transferring them to Russia—in exchange for guarantees that the signatories would "respect the independence and sovereignty and the existing borders of Ukraine" and "refrain from the threat or use of force against the territorial integrity or political independence of Ukraine."[49] Twenty years later, Ukraine is a denuclearized nation threatened with absorption into Vladimir Putin's Russia—and the Budapest Memorandum has no binding power to compel the U.S. or Britain to do anything about it.

China

It took an act of God for the world to get any sense of how much China was building up its nuclear arsenal.

In 2008, a 7.9-magnitude earthquake rocked China's Sichuan Province, killing roughly 70,000 people and leaving more than 18,000 missing.[50] "It looked like toothpaste being squeezed out," said a local who described the collapse of buildings as if they were volcanic events. "No, it wasn't [magma]. It was these concrete pieces. The eruption lasted about three minutes."[51] In addition to the tragic loss of life, the event exposed to the world the extent of China's nuclear-weapons reserves.

Beijing sent nearly 150,000 soldiers, including radiation-containment specialists, to secure and conceal nuclear facilities scattered throughout Sichuan.[52] In the Chinese blogosphere and some Western outlets, rumors swirled that the quake had been caused by an accidental nuclear blast. That rumor could not be corroborated, but the event revealed the clearest picture yet of China's nuclear stockpile. Even with the new data, information about this stockpile remains scarce and shrouded in secrecy.

In 2006, we thought that China had 145 deployed warheads. That was probably a low estimate; conservative estimates put the figure around 350, which might also be too low. Experts such as the Russian general Viktor Yesin believe that the Chinese have closer to 1,800 warheads in their arsenal.[53] China could have up to 850 of these ready to be launched.[54] Whatever the real numbers are, the Sichuan quake made clear that the Chinese are running a far more sophisticated operation than most observers understood.

What we do know is that China is committed to growing its nuclear capabilities alongside expansion of traditional military forces. We know that China has taken steps to improve the ability of their nuclear installations to withstand an attack, beefing up their capacity to conduct a nuclear counterstrike.[55] These steps have included developing a watered-down version of the U.S. triad and increasing the use of mobile launchers. We know that China continues to develop new missile capabilities and upgrade older missiles, and continues to analyze and improve the structure of its nuclear-forces management.[56] This also includes building what some call an Underground Great Wall of China—stretching more than 5,000 kilometers through northern China—that houses nuclear weapons.[57]

China is also part of a pan-Asian arms race over short- and intermediate-range missiles, which has involved North Korea, India, Pakistan, and Iran. The U.S. and Russia are precluded from developing these missiles by the 1987 INF treaty.[58] We know that the Chinese will soon have five nuclear-powered submarines capable of launching a new class of nuclear-tipped missile, the JL-2, with an estimated range of more than 7,400 kilometers. The Pentagon calls this China's "first credible sea-based nuclear deterrent," which means that China now has two legs of its nuclear triad.[59]

We also know that China is well known internationally for announcing a "no first use" policy on nuclear weapons. By this, it means that it would use nukes only in response to a nuclear attack on China, and that China would not use or even threaten nuclear attack on any non-nuclear state. (President Obama emulated this stated approach in his Nuclear Posture Review.) That sounds encouraging, but as with everything that comes out of Beijing's official channels, one must be skeptical.

That became all too clear a few years back, when a senior Chinese general warned that if the U.S. attacked China with conventional weapons in a conflict over Taiwan, Beijing might retaliate with nuclear weapons. The general was then promoted.[60]

As it has with Russia, the Obama administration has treated the Chinese nuclear offensive with kid gloves. In exchange for Chinese help in containing Kim Jong Un's nuclear provocations in North Korea, Obama offered to rein in U.S. missile-defense activities. The offer included cancelling deployment of two destroyers, both outfitted with the Aegis missile-defense system, and also cancelling the delivery to Japan of another long-range missile-defense radar system. These offers were music to Chinese ears; Beijing had objected to both of these deployments. Of course, what the Obama administration sees as help with North Korea and steps toward improved relations with Beijing can only strengthen Beijing's hand in the region—and weaken the leverage, and the defenses, of our Pacific allies, especially Japan and Taiwan.[61]

Iran

The United Nations General Assembly has seen some remarkable displays over the course of its history, but the performance of Israeli Prime Minister Benjamin Netanyahu at the annual meeting in 2012 may have topped them all. Holding a crude, almost childish, diagram of a cartoon bomb, marked with horizontal lines much like a fundraising thermometer would be, Netanyahu explained that each line drawn across the bomb represented a stage in the Iranian nuclear program. The bottom line, about two-thirds from the bottom of the bomb, marked the point at which the bomb was 70 percent "full" of enriched uranium; the next line, 90 percent; and the final portion (topped off with a fuse) represented completion. Netanyahu said that the Iranians had reached the 70 percent stage—the cultivation of low-enriched uranium—and were well on their way to reaching the 90 percent stage, the cultivation of medium-enriched uranium.

Given their current pace of work, he said, the Iranians would probably complete this second stage by spring or summer 2013. Then all that would stand between them and their first bomb would be the final steps: the high-enriched uranium stage, which might take only a few months longer, he said. Iran would have the bomb at that point.

"Ladies and gentlemen, what I have told you now is not based on secret information," Netanyahu said. "It's not based on military intelligence. It's based on the public reports of the International Atomic Energy Agency. Anybody could read them."

Then, taking out a red marker, he asked: "If these are the facts—and they are—where should a red line be drawn?" His reply: "A red line should be drawn right here." With this, he drew the line across the neck of the bomb, at the border separating the end of the 90 percent stage from the beginning of the final stage, thus cutting off Iran's ability to complete its enrichment program.

"At this late hour," Netanyahu said, "there is only one way to peacefully prevent Iran from getting atomic bombs, and that's by placing a clear red line on Iran's nuclear-weapons program."[62]

Netanyahu's demonstration drew its share of mockery, but it accomplished its goal: Little else from the meeting made news. To those who found him belligerent and provocative, a criticism familiar to Netanyahu, he said: "Red lines don't lead to war; red lines prevent war. Iran uses diplomatic negotiations to buy time to advance its programme. The international community has tried sanctions, has passed some of the strongest sanctions. Oil exports have been curbed, and the Iranian economy has been hit hard. But we must face the truth that sanctions have not stopped Iran's nuclear drive."[63] Indeed, since 2000, the Iranians have sat down for nuclear talks six times; except for a temporary suspension of the enrichment program at one point, the talks have accomplished nothing. We're closer than ever to a nuclear-armed Iran.

The much-heralded U.S.–Iran "interim" nuclear deal, signed in November 2013, has done nothing to change this—on the contrary, it has all but guaranteed it. As we discussed in Chapters 1 and 2, the deal offers Iran at least $7 billion in sanctions relief for Iran in exchange for extremely modest concessions that nevertheless allow Iran to continue enriching uranium and proceed with major aspects of its nuclear program. Even with all these benefits, it took Iran just days to cross some of the "red lines" Obama claimed he had laid down—for instance, Iran's foreign minister, Mohammad Javad Zarif, announced that Iran will continue construction at its heavy-water research reactor at Arak.[64] And the Iranians couldn't resist tweaking the Americans publicly, taking issue with Washington's characterization of the deal.

"We did not agree to dismantle anything," Zarif defiantly told CNN, irked by what he saw as the Obama administration's misrepresentation of Iranian concessions.[65] Indeed, many in Congress already have buyer's remorse, as do U.S. allies Israel and Saudi Arabia—hardly common bedfellows. If reports in the British *Sunday Times* are accurate, the two countries were working together on a contingency plan to strike Iran's nuclear facilities, should the agreement fail to rein in its program.[66]

As this book goes to press, the Iranians appear to be approaching from "breakout capacity," or the ability to enrich sufficient uranium for a bomb and to do it quickly enough to avoid detection or preventive action.[67] A recent military-intelligence report concludes that Iran will have a missile capable of hitting the United States by 2015. "We should consider that Iran has a capability within the next few years of flight testing ICBM capable technologies," says General Charles H. Jacoby, commander of the Colorado-based U.S. Northern Command. "The Iranians are intent on developing an ICBM."[68]

There seems little short of military action that can stop the progress of the Iranian nuclear program at this point. The end of Mahmoud Ahmadinejad's regime offered short-term hope that some course correction might be possible, but those hopes have borne little fruit. Iran's president, Hassan Rouhani, sent early signals that he looked for a better relationship with the U.S., but his attitude toward Israel seems no different from his predecessor's. In dismissing Netanyahu's threat of a military strike in July 2013, Rouhani said: "Who are the Zionists to threaten us?" And he called Israel's threats "laughable."[69]

Even under a best-case political scenario—which we don't have—the Iranian program has progressed so far that only drastic steps can stop it. "In the end, Iran's nuclear program is advancing much more rapidly than any domestic political changes taking place inside Iran, and we will therefore be forced to decisively address the Iranian nuclear threat well before any new government comes to power," writes Matthew Kroenig, a former adviser on Iran policy in the Pentagon.[70]

We discussed in the "Rogue Regimes" chapter the intensive cooperation the Iranians have received from Russia on their nuclear program. Iranian scientists have also benefitted from the nexus of nuclear collaboration between Pakistan and North Korea, which effectively ran a joint program during the 1990s facilitated by Beijing. Iranian centrifuges are barely altered versions of Pakistani ones from the mid-1990s, and evidence indicates that Iran obtained these designs directly from Islamabad.[71] It's worth considering the role played here by our erstwhile ally in the War on Terror, Pakistan.

Pakistan

Pakistan—and by implication, China—is far and away the most dangerous and persistent proliferator of nuclear technology and arms in the world. Beijing seems intent on keeping Pakistan supplied with the latest in nuclear technology, and it is currently at work modernizing the country's arsenal, which is estimated to contain as many as 100 warheads. China is also helping Pakistan develop a new warhead for its missile arsenal and providing expertise in reprocessing spent nuclear fuel.[72]

Islamabad's Chinese partnership traces back to the 1970s, when Beijing—eager to buttress Pakistan against their mutual enemy, India—helped Pakistan develop an atomic weapon. Gordon Chang and others have argued that Pakistani nuclear scientist A.Q. Khan sold China's nuclear technology to rogue states—including Iran and North Korea—and that Beijing was almost certainly aware of this.[73]

In 1995, a group of North Korean engineers and Iranian scientists visited Khan's lab. They were returning from Beijing, which strongly suggests the Chinese were directly involved in facilitating personal contacts and technology transfers between Pakistan and its customers.[74] With help from Chinese companies, moreover, Pakistan developed the P2 centrifuge, the core mechanism of Iran and North Korea's enrichment technology. Within a year of this assistance—in the mid-1990s—Iran had obtained P2 designs and North Korea had actual P2 centrifuges.[75]

The cooperation has persisted: The Chinese and Pakistanis signed a secret agreement in February 2013 to build an additional nuclear reactor in Chashma, in Punjab Province, Pakistan's most populous. CNNC, the state-owned Chinese company also responsible for producing nuclear weapons, will build the reactor.[76] CNNC had previous links with Pakistan's nuclear program. Chinese firms have violated international law to supply Pakistan's program; two Chinese companies were fined in U.S. courts for exporting nuclear material used to construct a Pakistani nuclear plant in 2006 and 2007.[77]

It's unlikely that constructive signs will be coming from Islamabad anytime soon: The election of Nawaz Sharif as prime minister in 2013 was a highly discouraging development for the West. Sharif was prime minister during periods in the 1990s when Pakistan was actively cooperating with China and disseminating nuclear technology abroad.[78] Pakistani relations with the West have only worsened since he took office; Sharif seems determined to use the leverage that the nuclear program gives him.

And that leverage will be directed not only against India but also against the United States. Islamabad increasingly views the United States as a potential threat to its regional ambitions, and it is beefing up its capacities accordingly, especially by pursuing the nuclearization of its submarine fleet. Some reports suggest that the first Pakistani nuclear submarine will be operational within five to eight years.[79]

The instability of the regime in Pakistan—and the possibility of a terrorist organization getting hold of a nuclear device—remains the real stuff of Western nightmares.[80] So far, Sharif, like Pervez Musharraf before him, has been able to keep the nuclear arsenal secure, but Pakistan is so politically volatile that we can take nothing for granted. The country's political future is impossible to predict. Keeping their nukes contained, while blocking their international proliferation efforts as much as possible, might be the best the West can hope for in the short term.

North Korea

No other nation in the world has revealed the inadequacy of the Obama administration's policies more starkly than North Korea. Consider some recent developments:

- In February 2013, the North Koreans conducted their third nuclear test, exploding what Pyongyang called a "miniaturized and lighter nuclear device with greater explosive force than previously," though it was not as big as the Hiroshima bomb.[81] Previous tests took place in 2006 and 2009.

- North Korea has launched satellites into space, which suggests that with a few adjustments, they could develop an ICBM capable of hitting the United States in a relatively short period of time.[82]
- The North Koreans—courtesy of China—now possess KN-08 intermediate-range ballistic missiles, weapons that could be used to target American cities. As we explained in the "Rogue Regimes" chapter, the KN-08 has a shorter range than some other North Korean missiles, but it can be mounted on mobile vehicles and is thus not only more difficult to destroy but also much quicker to prepare for operation.[83]
- The North has the clearly demonstrated ability to enrich weapons-grade uranium and plutonium, and it has enough plutonium stockpiled for four to eight weapons.[84] A plutonium-based warhead could be rapidly fitted to one of their short-range missiles with little or no warning.[85]
- The Asan Institute, a Korean policy think tank, reported in September 2013 that North Korea had "advanced its indigenous atomic capabilities so much that it is not realistic to expect international sanctions and export controls to constrain its progress in developing a nuclear weapon."[86]

And yet in response to all of this, the Obama administration pledges "strategic patience," which ought to take its place on a short list of ridiculous policy names. This policy requires the North Korean leadership to show "positive, constructive behavior" in dismantling its nuclear program.[87] Unsurprisingly, North Korea has not complied. Worse, the United States' defense posture against Pyongyang's potential missile deployments has major holes. Apparently, officials inside the Pentagon believe that "North Korean missiles can already reach Alaska and Hawaii, and will soon be able to deliver nuclear warheads to Seattle and San Diego," wrote Larry Bell in July 2013.[88] That ought to prompt emergency measures. Instead, we seem to be muddling along, at best, to defend against this threat.

"The United States has missile-defense systems in place to protect us from limited ICBM attacks," said Defense Secretary Hagel in March 2013, as he announced the addition of the 14 missile interceptors in the Pacific. "But North Korea in particular has recently made advances in its capabilities and has engaged in a series of irresponsible and reckless provocations."[89]

No one would dispute Hagel's description of the North Korean regime's behavior. But what about those defense systems that would protect us from "*limited* ICBM attacks"? Why is the world's only superpower satisfied with partial defense? Herein hangs a tale of how the United States, the missile-defense pioneer, has abandoned this brave vision.

AMERICA'S ABDICATION OF MISSILE DEFENSE

What would Ronald Reagan have thought? The political father of Star Wars—what he called the Strategic Defense Initiative, a plan for national missile defense—would have been dismayed if he were watching at Vandenberg Air Force Base in California. There, in July 2013, a U.S. advanced missile interceptor failed to hit its target over the Pacific Ocean—the third straight failure of its kind. After 30 years of research and $250 billion of investment, the ground-based defense system has undergone 16 tests; only eight have been successful, the last one in 2008."[90]

The system's track record "has not improved over time," said Senator Richard Durbin of Illinois, wondering how the Pentagon can continue to assure the White House that the system will work when its tests are continual failures.[91] The system "is something the U.S. military, and the American people, cannot depend on," said Phillip E. Coyle, who once ran the Pentagon's weapons-testing program and is now with the Center for Arms Control.[92]

Perhaps it is unfair to note that the program's last successful test was in 2008, before President Obama took office. Whether or not that's a coincidence, the fact remains that the Obama administration has conducted a pullback on missile defense that matches its retreat on nuclear weaponry generally. And some Republicans, in particular, do blame the president for the flimsy state of America's current missile defenses. For them, the administration has simply taken its eye off the ball—as its decisions show.

Representative Mike Rogers, whom we've cited throughout this chapter, is explicit in blaming the administration's funding cutbacks for missile-defense failures. He points out that the 2013 test was the first since 2008—an eternity for any high-priority program. "Has anyone in this room ever kept a car in the garage for five years and then pulled it out one day and expected to go for a cross-country drive?" he asked. "Of course not. Unfortunately, that's what we've done with our only homeland defense system."[93]

Rogers notes that the administration has cut $6 billion from our missile-defense programs—a 16 percent cut from the Bush years—at a time when missile threats are growing. "This is not the time to stand still or regress as we have done in some respects lately: We continue to be challenged by increasing threats, budget scarcity, and the resulting test failures," Rogers said. "With regard to the nation's only national missile-defense program, it's been cut in half in almost ten years."[94] And yet that's nothing compared with the way the U.S. is leaving its allies high and dry on missile defense.

Deserting Europe

Long before Obama took office, the American plan to install a Ballistic Missile Defense (BMD) system in Eastern Europe had created severe tension with Russia. It was a major source of dispute between President

Bush and Vladimir Putin. The missile-defense system in Poland and the Czech Republic would, according to the Bush administration, protect against missiles launched by Iran. As we've noted, Moscow viewed it as a cover for Washington's intentions to strengthen its influence in the former Soviet satellites and alter the balance of nuclear power. The Russians made their displeasure clear.

"What can we do?" asked General Yuri Baluyevsky, then chief of the Russian military's general staff. "Go ahead and build that shield. You have to think, though, what will fall on your heads afterward. I do not foresee a nuclear conflict between Russia and the West. We do not have such plans. However, it is understandable that countries that are part of such a shield increase their risk."[95]

Over the years, unconfirmed reports have suggested that Russia periodically moves tactical nukes into its Kaliningrad Oblast (a small Russian exclave located between Lithuania and Poland); or Russia threatens to move these nukes whenever it wants to exert political pressure on its neighbors.[96] In 2007, General Vladimir Zaritsky, chief of artillery and rocketry for Russia's ground forces, suggested moving state-of-the-art Iskander missile platforms armed with nuclear weapons into Kaliningrad in response to the American missile shield. He said, "Any action meets a counter-action, and this is the case with elements of the U.S. missile defence in Poland and the Czech Republic."[97] In December 2013, Lithuania and Poland issued statements of concern that Russia had carried through on its rhetoric and stationed Iskanders in Kaliningrad—well within striking distance of much of NATO.[98] Putin denied the claims, saying, "We haven't made the decision yet" about the Iskanders.[99]

The Obama administration's first major betrayal of our European allies came in 2009, with the decision to scrap the Bush-era plan to install ground-based interceptor missiles in Poland—a technology that would have been able to deter ICBMs, SLBMs, and other offensive missiles. Instead, the U.S. would deploy a system of reconfigured SM-3 missiles, first on ships and later in Romania, to counter the Iranian missile threat.[100] SM-3s are part of the Aegis ship-based system, and they are only really effective against short- and medium-range missiles, not ICBMs. Obama claimed that the decision had nothing to do with Russia opposition; it was based, he said, on the notion that the reconfigured SM-3s could be procured more quickly than the bigger interceptors originally envisioned, and that they could shoot down missiles that already exist in the Iranian arsenal. The U.S. would upgrade the SM-3s in a four-phase plan that would, by 2020, be able to counter intercontinental ballistic missiles (ICBMs)—but the SM-3s would be operational against Iranian-type missiles much sooner than that.[101] Russia seemed guardedly pleased. President Medvedev said, "We appreciate the responsible approach of the U.S. president toward implementing our agreements."[102]

Thanks to WikiLeaks, we now know that the Obama administration did, in fact, renege on America's commitments to missile defense in Poland and the Czech Republic to appease Russia. The anti-secrecy organization obtained State Department cables from 2010 that show that Obama scrapped the plan "in hopes of securing Russia's support for sanctions against Iran." The release of the cables "confirmed Poland's worst suspicions and contradicted the administration's denials that the change in plans was prompted by concerns about Russia," writes Benjamin Weinthal, a correspondent for the *Jerusalem Post*.[103]

The administration justified its new missile-defense stance with a fresh intelligence assessment that Iran's development of long-range missiles was slowing down, meaning that the Bush plan's emphasis on interceptors for long-range missiles would not be essential. But Henry "Trey" Obering III, a retired Air Force lieutenant general and former head of the Pentagon's Missile Defense Agency, scoffed at that claim. Obering argued that Iran's satellite launch and solid-rocket tests in

2009—the same year Obama changed course—showed that Iran was making progress on long-range missiles. "I am very surprised by the new intelligence assessment," Obering said in 2009. "It is dramatically different from what we were told last spring. To me it flies in the face of what is observable." Obering believed that the administration's decision to cancel the ground-based interceptors was designed to boost a diplomatic offensive with Iran and the "reset" with Russia.[104] The reset, of course, has taken its place on the ash heap of history.

The change in policy caused a rift with U.S. allies. "After today," said Polish Foreign Minister Radek Sikorski when the announcement was made in 2009, "I think we all know that if we are to look to somebody, we have to look to ourselves."[105] After the WikiLeaks cables were published, Polish Prime Minister Donald Tusk commented: "I'm worried—if it really is true—that the U.S. made decisions about our security with mainly its relations with Russia in mind and not the objective security of NATO allies. If the first interpretations and leaks are confirmed, I can only have the satisfaction of being the first prime minister over the past 15 years who isn't so enchanted with our ally."[106]

A few years later, Poland announced that it would invest $400 million in its own missile-defense system, which, by 2023, will be integrated into the NATO missile shield. Once more, Russian officials threatened to deploy tactical weapons in Kaliningrad. Gener Koziej, the head of Poland's National Security Bureau, called the Russian threat "blackmailing which would have been impossible if Poland had powerful missile defense."[107]

We learned something else from the WikiLeaks cables: just how important American missile-defense plans are to the Russians, and how worried they are when we take any steps to further them (and Russian incursions into Ukraine demonstrate how vital it is to Moscow that Eastern Europe not be protected by American military installations). Even after the U.S. announced the new system, the cables reveal, American officials viewed the refurbished platform as usable against Russia, should that be needed—contrary to what they had been telling Moscow. *The Guardian* in the UK reported that a senior U.S. official told Poland that the new system could shield against rocket attacks from Iran or Syria but that it could also protect against "missiles coming from elsewhere"—in other words, Russia.[108]

The Russians didn't know at the time that the U.S. saw the missiles as weapons for potential use against Russia, but Moscow nonetheless had insisted all along that the U.S. make a promise to never use the system against them. The United States refused to do so, prompting Nikolai Makarov, the chief of the general staff of the Russian armed forces, to threaten a preemptive strike against the missile systems: "Taking into account a missile-defense system's destabilizing nature, that is, the creation of an illusion that a disarming strike can be launched with impunity, a decision on preemptive use of the attack weapons available will be made when the situation worsens."[109] In November 2012, shortly after the U.S. presidential election, Russia's deputy prime minister, Dmitri Rogozin, expressed the nervousness in Russia about American missile defense, saying: "We hope that now, after his reelection, President Obama will be more flexible on taking into account the opinions of Russia and other countries on the configuration of NATO missile defense."[110]

And "flexibility" is exactly what President Obama showed in early 2013, when he made the announcement that the U.S. would scrap the crucial fourth phase of its already-downgraded European missile-defense plan and move an additional 14 interceptors to the Pacific to protect against North Korea.[111] This fourth phase, as noted in Chapter 1, would have upgraded the SM-3s to make them at least theoretically viable against ICBMs. As it stands, the European shield is effectively neutered, but it has achieved "interim operability," which means Europe is currently protected against short- and intermediate-range ballistic missiles. In short: There is a NATO missile-defense shield in Europe; it is operable, but it is useless against the Russians because Obama has repeatedly given in to their demands.

What might future WikiLeaks cables tell us about these decisions?

An Inadequate, Ill-Conceived Defense

The administration's March 2013 announcement shifting missile-defense priorities from Europe to the Pacific was disturbing for two key reasons: First, as indicated earlier, it revealed utter strategic confusion. Nothing was happening on the European continent to indicate that it was wise to pull back from missile defense—quite the contrary. Our allies in Western Europe feel as threatened by the potential of an Iranian nuke—and the actuality of Russian ones—as they did before.

Second, the interceptor that was the defining piece of the fourth phase—the ICBM-capable interceptor now scrapped in Europe—is the only element of the system that provided the capacity to defend the U.S. homeland, according to Mike Rogers. "I fear there is now a choice between defending ourselves and defending our allies," he said. If the administration didn't push for a major new funding infusion into missile defense, he warned, we would be forced to tell our European allies—for the third time since 2009—that our plans for missile defense on the Continent had changed.[112]

And where do the administration's decisions leave the American people, in terms of missile defense? Unfortunately, they leave us protected by an incomplete and inadequate system. While some might be encouraged to learn that the United States has added 14 ground-based interceptors in Alaska to the 30 already deployed on the West Coast to defend the mainland, there is less here than meets the eye. For one thing, the interceptors, 44 in all, only get us back to the total number achieved under the Bush administration, which had eventually envisioned having 54.[113] Moreover, the new interceptors lack the technological improvements that the Bush administration had supported.[114]

The system today, John Kyl explains, could probably guard against the current threat from North Korea, but not against an attack from Russia or China, which have more advanced capabilities. "On missile defense, then," he says, "the U.S. is now stuck with numbers and technology capable of dealing only with low-level threats."[115] Meanwhile, just a month before our unsuccessful test at Vandenberg Air Force base, the Russian Strategic Missile Forces tested a prototype of a new ICBM. This was no ordinary missile. Deputy Premier Dmitri Rogozin called it "a missile-defense killer." He boasted: "Neither modern nor future American missile-defense means will be able to stop this missile from hitting its target directly."[116] The new missile has a range of 6,835 miles and is the most sophisticated and powerful weapon of its kind. It's also a major setback to our efforts to engage the Russians on nuclear reduction.

So for all their bluster against our missile-defense systems, the Russians are eagerly constructing their own. Russia has been rapidly upgrading radar and interceptor systems around St. Petersburg and in Russia's exclave in Kaliningrad.[117] These systems will probably include the forthcoming cutting-edge S-500 interceptor system, which is highly mobile and much more difficult to neutralize.[118] Putin had originally threatened that he would carry out these deployments if we completed the NATO missile shield. Obama backed down on European missile defense in early 2013, but Putin went ahead anyway with aggressive deployment of Russian missile-defense assets in Europe.[119]

Here's a perfect example of how Moscow talks one way for public consumption while acting in an entirely different way in pursuit of its interests. "It's one of those historical ironies that the Russians, who scream the loudest about our missile defenses, like to ignore, and like us to ignore, that they keep on building them," says Mike Rogers, noting that Moscow's expansion of its missile defenses included nuclear-armed interceptors around Moscow. And he quotes what a former defense secretary told him about treaties with Russia: "We build, they build. We stop, they build."[120]

Whatever the cause of U.S. missile-defense failures—Obama's disinterest, design flaws dating back to the Bush administration, or a combination of these, along with failure to modernize—the program's defects *must* be corrected, and soon. They need to be corrected before Iran's nuclear program is up and running or before Kim Jong Un decides that he isn't interested in talking anymore, and before our relations deteriorate further with Russia—a nation armed with missiles capable of hitting us today.

CONCLUSION

Despite our technological superiority and long history of providing whatever resources were necessary to protect our mainland, the United States has been continually scaling back its nuclear weaponry and nuclear defenses, even as every important adversarial regime is rapidly ramping up its own. Our nuclear stockpile and our missile-defense platform have been systematically downgraded at a time when Russia and China are aggressively modernizing their nuclear technology—and while rogue regimes, such as the ones we examined in Chapter 2, continue to build, stockpile, and proliferate these weapons and technologies.

In previous chapters, in discussing the inadequacy of American responses to the Axis, we have been careful not to lay the blame solely at the current administration's door. For the most part, these are complex developments, and responsibility can be broadly shared. But in the nuclear area, the Obama administration has been uniquely at fault.

The root of the problem is President Obama's much-touted desire to get to nuclear zero.

As we have noted before, the notion of nuclear zero is, in the abstract, a noble aspiration, one that no less a Cold Warrior than Ronald Reagan shared. But Reagan's plan to get to nuclear zero was the polar opposite of the current president's: Reagan believed, admittedly with some paradox, that the way to reduce arsenals was first to increase them, on the American side—applying so much pressure that the Russians would come to him and agree on serious reductions. In 1987, this strategy came to fruition with the landmark INF Treaty eliminating intermediate-range nuclear and conventional ballistic missiles. The number of nuclear weapons in the world has drastically fallen since Cold War days, demonstrating the wisdom and courage of President Reagan's approach.

Obama, however, apparently believes that he can reduce weaponry by doing what Reagan would never dream of: bargaining away America's nuclear deterrent, in the belief that our adversaries, inspired by our nobility, will follow suit. This kind of wishful thinking afflicted the leftists of Reagan's own era; they called for a unilateral nuclear freeze in the hopes that the Soviets would happily join us. Reagan was never tempted by such naiveté. Yet Obama, a generation later, seems to be reliving this liberal dream. He and his closest advisers must see by now that their approach is not working. Yet it is not clear that they have the political will—let alone the financial wherewithal—to reverse course.

As President Obama said at Berlin's Brandenburg Gate in 2013, "Peace with justice means pursuing the security of a world without nuclear weapons—no matter how distant that dream may be."[121] The dream remains distant for the world, but perhaps closer for the United States than anyone had previously imagined.

CHAPTER 6

The Economic Contest:
America on the Sidelines

"What's happening is a zero-sum game between China and the U.S. where their gain is our loss. It's about the fact that we don't make things any more, that we lost our manufacturing base, the 25 million people who can't find a decent job in this country, the zero wage growth. I want consumers to connect the dots, to go to any store and look at the label and connect the dots between buying cheap China products, which is better for the wallet, and all the other things we lose, like jobs."

—PETER NAVARRO, CO-AUTHOR OF *DEATH BY CHINA*[1]

"Energy supplies are important in the run-up to winter. I hope you won't freeze."

—RUSSIAN DEPUTY PREMIER DMITRI ROGOZIN, ADDRESSING MOLDOVANS CONSIDERING JOINING THE EU RATHER THAN RUSSIA'S CUSTOMS UNION[2]

"It will be the same old Smithfield, only better," Smithfield Foods CEO Larry Pope told a skeptical U.S. Agricultural Committee in July 2013.[3] Pope was trying to reassure skeptical senators that all would be well after China's Shuanghui International Holdings had paid $4.7 billion to acquire the iconic American company—the largest Chinese acquisition of a U.S. company in history.[4] The deal was the latest Chinese effort to acquire companies that could supply a resource needed back home—but this was the first one involving food. Business analysts saw the Smithfield purchase as a way for America to export more of Smithfield's products to China—the world's largest pork market. Many in Congress voiced concerns about the implications of the deal, but it seems to be a fait accompli and a shining example of China's tireless pursuit of economic advantage around the world—including right here in the U.S.

Along with a French private equity firm, a Chinese conglomerate has taken over the French resort company Club Med. China's state-owned companies control oil and gas pipelines from Turkmenistan to China and from South Sudan to the Red Sea, with more to come.[5] The catch phrase "American Made, Chinese Owned" was common parlance in the 2012 presidential election, and for good reason. Even Detroit, symbolic home of American auto might, at least before it declared bankruptcy in 2013, is slowly giving way: Chinese car companies are proliferating in number and expanding their reach in the distressed Motor City, which is in no shape to resist Chinese intrusion.

By now, even casual observers in America are familiar with the story on China: The Chinese are buying up the world, pursuing economic domination through the power of their apparently limitless cash and labor force. It's often called "China, Inc." Beijing's investment dollars have penetrated every continent, and its cheap labor has killed countless jobs in Europe and the United States. Operating without the democratic pressures that force Western companies to observe established norms and at least pay lip service to social responsibility, Chinese firms have had an open playing field, especially in the developing world, where many despotic governments, on the outs with Western governments over human-rights issues, have welcomed Beijing's cash. At the same time, the Chinese juggernaut faces mounting political and economic challenges: slowing growth, rampant inequality, massive corruption, environmental degradation, and widespread anger over human-rights abuses and lack of political freedom.

In Russia, too, the economic landscape has shifted over the last five years as the country's powerhouse energy industry has ran into tough new competition, and as Vladimir Putin has faced political criticism and opposition movements. Russia's economy has even more serious challenges ahead than China's. GDP growth has slowed almost to a halt, especially as the energy market has been transformed by the advent of shale gas and the expansion of liquefied natural gas, both of which are cutting into the profit margins of Russia's state-owned energy giant, Gazprom. While Putin has directed Gazprom's leaders to respond more creatively to these challenges, he is also looking for stability from other economic sources, such as gold. Putin made Russia the world's biggest gold buyer in 2013. "The more gold a country has, the more sovereignty it will have if there's a cataclysm with the dollar, the euro, the pound or any other reserve currency," said Evgeny Fedorov, a lawmaker in Putin's United Russia party.[6]

Where some American commentators take heart in Russia's recent economic struggles—and the American-led shale-gas boom is certainly worth celebrating—they often lose sight of the impact that economic adversity is having in Moscow. A difficult economic climate makes Russia a more, not less, provocative adversary. Declining economic growth provides an opening for critics of Putin's iron-fisted rule. To quell the critics, Putin has little choice but to recoup political clout in other areas—whether overseas, as in his cold-blooded stand-down against President Obama on Syria; at home, through the persecution of gays and political dissidents and the rallying of nationalist sentiment; or in the Russian "near abroad," as with his advance into Ukraine. It's not clear that he would feel the need for these drastic measures if Russia's GDP were still humming along at the pace it did from 2000 to 2008.

Facing major economic challenges and the political ramifications that go along with them, both China and Russia have responded in similar fashion: with more aggression and determination to counter the West economically and politically overseas, and with increased authoritarianism at home. For China, the way to keep the West off-balance and preserve Communist Party stability at home is to ramp economic growth back up to previous levels if possible; for Russia, the economic goal is to shore up its current energy arrangements and prevent the Americans and others from taking its customers and threatening Russia's already-endangered prosperity.

The United States, meanwhile, seems passive at best in its economic strategy, both at home and abroad. True, new trade agreements hold much potential, such as the Trans-Pacific Partnership (should the United States formally adopt it), a free-trade agreement that seeks to bolster North and South American trade with certain Pacific Rim nations. On the whole, however, Washington has been much more acquiescent economically, especially abroad, than has China or Russia.

As in the other areas we've covered in this book, China and Russia have disadvantages of their own to overcome, but they hold one key edge over the United States: They have no ambivalence about defining their national interests and no hesitation whatsoever in pursuing them with maximum force. Economic downturns, new challenges, and the occasional setback only make them redouble their efforts.

CHINA AND RUSSIA: ECONOMIC MUSCLE, POLITICAL VOLATILITY

Both Axis nations have flexed their economic muscles at home and abroad for years, and before the financial crisis of 2008, both enjoyed long runs of economic growth—robust, in Russia's case, meteoric, in China's. Since 2008, though, the playing field has shifted in multiple ways, some having to do with the international financial crisis and others with changing technological and macroeconomic trends. Both countries nonetheless remain bare-knuckled economic players at home and abroad.

The Chinese Economic Juggernaut

One key way that China has grown and keeps growing is through aggressive, sometimes ruthless, use of foreign direct investment (FDI), by which it often funds massive infrastructure projects. China's FDI is set to skyrocket in the coming years: It's projected to reach as much as $2 trillion by 2020, according to the Rhodium Group.[7] Indeed, China has surpassed other emerging economies because it encourages FDI so strongly—and not just in neighboring countries. China has extended its reach far beyond its natural regional sphere of influence and in the process has garnered tremendous power.

China has become one of the world's great builders of infrastructure. The U.S., long the leader in this area, seems a laggard by comparison. Already the Chinese have completed a massive oil pipeline from Siberia to northern China. Beijing will soon finish an Indian Ocean pipeline through Myanmar to Kunming, in China. China's infrastructure push also includes hydroelectric projects in Africa and Latin America: the Merowe Dam on the Nile in Sudan, for instance, and the $2.3 billion Coca Codo Sinclair Dam in Ecuador.[8] And China's FDI work is not confined to the developing world.

Beijing has flexed its economic muscles in Europe and the United States as well. China now invests about $10 billion annually in Europe—a tenfold increase just since 2008. One-third of China's FDI now goes to Europe. In the U.S., a similar spike has occurred: Chinese investment is now more than $6 billion annually. It had totaled just $1 billion as recently as 2008. Of course, that date is no coincidence; the financial crisis made European and American institutions all too eager for the seemingly limitless supply of Chinese cash.[9]

In Europe, recession-weary firms welcome that cash with open arms. The Chinese have acquired major European firms such as Volvo and the German parts manufacturer Putzmeister. "Chinese companies are looking for companies that, like Putzmeister, have a technological edge and have become world leaders in niche markets," write Heriberto Araújo and Juan Pablo Cardenal, authors of *China's Silent Army*. "Those takeovers also allow them to absorb Western know-how on branding, marketing, distribution, and customer relations."[10] The Europeans feel they have little choice but to accept Chinese investment dollars, and that means they check their other objections at the door. "We don't have any stick," one European official said. "We can just offer carrots and hope for the best."[11]

That same quid pro quo mentality regarding Chinese money has also taken hold in Canada. Thanks in part to President Obama's refusal to endorse the Keystone Pipeline—which, admittedly, might turn at any moment—the Canadians were eager to find an export partner for the country's crude oil. Prime Minister Stephen Harper signed an investment deal with the Chinese just as Beijing was securing its largest foreign takeover yet: a $15 billion deal for its state-owned oil company, CNOOC, to acquire Canadian energy firm Nexen. Since the deals were signed, the Harper administration, once a vocal critic of China's suppression of dissent, has clammed up—a "clear indication," Araújo and Cardenal write, "of how China's economic influence can push the political agenda to the sidelines, even in the West."[12]

Araújo and Cardenal argue that the loans Beijing extends around the world—including, among others, $40 billion to Venezuela and $8 billion to Turkmenistan—are even more significant in financial terms than FDI. These loans, they write, provide billions to "foreign countries to acquire Chinese goods; finance Chinese-built infrastructure; and start projects in the extractive and other industries." They achieve something else, too: buying the silence of these China clients on human rights, labor, and environmental issues. It's no accident that China tends to favor countries, such as Angola, Sudan, Iran, and others, that often run afoul of human-rights groups. While the West won't extend aid to countries that violate these international norms, China has no qualms. Beijing moves in with its money, strengthening Chinese investment and economic opportunity while also shoring up despotic regimes. Through only two state-controlled banks in 2009 and 2010, China has lent more money to developing countries than the World Bank has (although not all loans are made public).[13]

What's more, China uses its investments to promote the state's political agendas at home and overseas. A main vehicle for this is through policy banks, a scheme in which Chinese banks lend money with a mandate to further whatever Beijing sees as its national interests.[14] These policy banks help free up the flow of raw materials to China and open foreign markets for Chinese companies.

American-Made, China-Owned

China has been the fastest growing source of foreign investment in the U.S. In 2012, "Chinese companies bought 10 companies worth $10.5 billion," says Reuters. That's more than 20 percent of the 484 U.S. companies, worth a total of $43.6 billion, that foreign companies have bought this year, Reuters adds.[15] Indeed, America is the perfect place for China to invest—Beijing wants to be more competitive but lacks the management and technology expertise. By acquiring American companies, they gain access to both. For example, in 2012, Chinese movie chain Wanda bought American cinema chain AMC because "movie theaters are a growing industry in China," said Thilo Hanemann, a research director at the Rhodium Group. "That acquisition gave Wanda access to an established industry brand, and the technology and management expertise to help it grow the concept in China."[16]

Nowhere has Chinese investment—and takeover—been more prominent than in the U.S. auto industry. Dozens of companies have been putting down roots in Detroit. David E. Cole, the founder of the Center for Automotive Research in Ann Arbor, Michigan, argues that the Chinese "lack the know-how, and they're coming here to get it."[17] Chinese-owned companies are investing in American businesses and new vehicle technology. They are selling everything from seat belts to shock absorbers in retail stores. And they are hiring experienced engineers and designers in an effort to soak up the talent and expertise of domestic automakers and their suppliers.[18] But the Chinese are being stealthier about it than the Japanese were in the 1980s. Bill Vlasic wrote, in the *New York Times*: "In contrast to the Japanese, Chinese auto companies are assiduously avoiding the spotlight. Last year, the biggest carmaker in China, Shanghai Automotive Industries, opened new offices in suburban Detroit without any publicity, which is almost unheard-of in an industry that thrives on media coverage."[19] Shanghai Auto, China's largest carmaker, has major joint ventures with G.M. and Volkswagen. But when it opened a Detroit-area office in 2012, even G.M. was surprised.[20]

Chinese companies haven't managed to avoid the spotlight altogether. The Obama administration filed a complaint with the World Trade Organization in 2012 alleging that China's government was unfairly subsidizing the production of some parts being shipped to the U.S., putting American manufacturers at a disadvantage.[21] It was the administration's eighth complaint against China and the third in 2012, in a continuing series of intense trade standoffs between the two countries. In the slow-recovering American economy, the short-term benefits of Chinese investment are easy to see, but they come at a cost to our long-term competitiveness. We cannot afford to keep losing out to China's cheaper labor and manufacturing costs. As Peter Navarro and Greg Autry argue in *Death by China*, America's impotent response to Beijing's economic imperialism is a serious danger to our economic future. Rejecting the arguments of some critics that the U.S. and China can be economic partners, Navarro sees a "zero-sum game between China and the U.S. where their gain is our loss."[22]

A crucial aspect of China's race ahead is the willingness of ordinary Chinese to help one another here. "Wherever there is a Chinese person keen to set up a business," Juan Pablo Cardenal and Heriberto Araújo argue, "there will always be a compatriot ready to lend him or her money to provide help with getting a visa or a permit, whether out of family or racial ties."[23]

Flush with cash, the Chinese are buying up American real estate, too. Chinese buyers accounted for 18 percent of the $68.2 billion that foreigners spent on homes during the 12 months that ended in March 2013, according to the National Association of Realtors.[24] Unlike other foreign buyers, who spend an average of $276,000 on U.S. homes, the Chinese purchase more expensive homes with a median price of $425,000. Amazingly, almost 70 percent of these deals were made in cash.

A Chinese businessman in San Jose, Costa Rica, summed up a great deal of the challenge the Chinese model poses. "If a Chinese man were to set out to compete in a cycling competition like the Tour de France, he'd end up coming last. Do you know why? Because he'd spend the whole race looking around him at the villages and towns along the road, thinking to himself: Where would be a good place to set up a business?"[25]

To casual observers, then, the Chinese juggernaut seems only to keep rolling, amassing momentum and building dominance—both at home and abroad. But fundamental problems at the heart of the Chinese system threaten everything the regime has gained—and, if they are not solved satisfactorily, they might well push Xi Jinping in the future to become even more authoritarian in his efforts to obscure the dissatisfaction of hundreds of millions of Chinese citizens.

Clouds on the Chinese Economic Horizon

"Mothers with children wearing face-masks scurry past toward the Shanghai aquarium, mindful of the cars and motorcycles that try to exploit any gap in the traffic that may provide temporary respite from the grinding gridlock," wrote John Ivison from Shanghai. "No-one saunters; everyone wants to get inside away from the smog. Most suffer from the 'Beijing cough.' The whole city is like the inside of a smoker's lung."[26]

Ivison pointed out that the city of Ontario, Canada, declares a "smog day" if the air-quality index is 30 or higher; when Ivison was in Shanghai, the index hit 254. In Beijing, he said, it's even worse: 900, which counts as "beyond index." China's mounting pollution crisis—an outgrowth of its turbo-charged industrial output combined with minimal environmental standards—is only the most visible sign of the difficulties ahead.

As Ivison put it: "Half a billion people have been lifted out of poverty since Deng Xiaoping inaugurated reform in the mid-1970s but at a cost: The air is unbreathable; incomes are more unequal than in South Africa; and crony capitalism flourishes."[27] Shanghai, where Ivison wrote his reports for Canada's *National Post,* is one of the world's most expensive cities, but most ordinary Chinese cannot afford most items sold there, especially the luxury brands. Yet China's wealthy elites spend so freely that they accounted for 47 percent of global luxury consumption in 2013.[28] The country's economic growth has left hundreds of millions behind; they're no better off than they were before the Chinese market revolution. The business culture is steeped in bribery and corruption; many deals don't go through without the exchange of a "red bag"—an envelope stuffed with cash. Young Chinese, meanwhile, despair of getting good jobs—or any jobs at all—unless they know someone within the Communist Party hierarchy.

President Xi has suggested that he aims to address both the country's radically uneven distribution of wealth and its rampant corruption. "We must have the resolution to fight corruption at every level, punish every corrupt official and eradicate the soil that breeds corruption," he told a Communist Party audience.[29] But at the same time, Xi is charged with perpetuating the Party's rule and power. Pushing for reform will mean bumping up against the Party's institutional norms and its members' well-loved perks and privileges—which, so far, Xi has not proved he will do. At a much-ballyhooed senior meeting of Communist Party officials in November 2013, Xi disappointed reform advocates by resorting to jargon and generalities instead of tackling China's pressing policy needs. In the meantime, his challenge is cut out for him in the macroeconomic sense, as China's historic economic growth shows every sign of cooling down to a more moderate pace. This slowdown is partially a result of something that was always inevitable: the rise of labor costs (20 percent over the last four years) as competition for labor has forced companies to pay more for workers.[30] Some economists project that, along with rising labor costs, the cost of shipping goods from China and the rising value of the Chinese currency will combine to make China's manufacturing costs nearly on par with America's in the next four or five years.[31]

After China's second-quarter numbers were released in summer 2013, Barclays Capital revised its growth forecast downward, from close to 8 percent to 7.4 percent.[32] Indeed, China's growth rate had been slowing since the fourth quarter of 2010, with the exception of a robust fourth quarter in 2012.[33] While its growth remains the envy of most nations, it represents a comedown from the rates China had enjoyed for a generation: an average rate of 10 percent for the past 30 years.[34]

China's economic success has been powered by its transition from a highly centralized planned economy to a market economy, of course, just as the nation itself moved from being a mostly hermetic enclave to a major player on the international scene.[35] The reform and development of China's banking industry and financial markets were important catalysts for China's rapid economic expansion. The markets have been under pressure, however, from China's crackdown on rampant credit growth as well as from new proposals that aim to control state prices of energy and natural resources, encourage private business, and promote market competition.[36]

There is also new concern that China could be headed for a debt crisis. Beijing has tried to rein in undisciplined lending in the fastest-growing portion of China's financial industry, its "shadow banking" sector: the trust companies, insurance firms, leasing companies, pawnbrokers, and other lenders that take risks traditional banks won't, backing projects that might never pay off.[37] The shift in monetary policy from "quantity to quality," as China's official news agency Xinhua calls this push, aims to stave off a crisis like the one the U.S. experienced in 2008.[38] "The main concern is that 'hidden debt' will come flying out of the woodwork onto public balance sheets in a slowdown, ultimately leading to a problem" the government must absorb, says Harvard University economist Kenneth Rogoff, a former International Monetary Fund chief economist.[39] The shadow banking industry's future is now in the hands of Beijing's central bank.

China's trade data for June 2013 came in much weaker than expected: Exports fell 3.1 percent from the same period a year earlier, and imports decreased 0.7 percent. While things look shaky, then, across several fronts, the Chinese economy's prospects over the long term remain strong thanks to its high savings rate—another attribute of state capitalism. Chinese banks are flush with cash because the government forces the country's 1 billion depositors to accept below-market interest rates and prevents them from investing their money in more profitable investment vehicles.[40]

Whatever the Chinese economy's problems, most analysts still project that it will overtake the United States' sometime in the 2020s, and Beijing's state-capitalist policies remain one reason why. The state sponsorship that Chinese companies enjoy, often in the form of hidden subsidies and cheap financing, gives them an unfair advantage against competitors. These state-owned companies (often described as "national champions"), such as Sinopec or China Mobile, accounted for 43 percent of all business profits in 2011.[41] While President Xi has made noises about economic liberalization, it's highly unlikely that the nation's statist economic model will undergo major reform. The Chinese economic leadership remains highly technocratic, as evidenced by the huge $586 billion stimulus package that Beijing implemented to stave off the effects of the global financial crisis.

China will surely remain the dominant economic force in Asia. Its two closest competitors, India and Japan, each have GDPs far less than half of China's when adjusted for purchasing power. And after India and Japan, no other state in Asia even comes close to matching China's GDP: The latest figures put it at $8.23 trillion in 2012, a GDP representing 13.27 percent of the world economy.[42] So China's economic dominance is unlikely to ebb soon.

The real issue here is not China's economic might—but how the difficulties of maintaining and extending it, while dealing with restless citizens and political corruption, will push the regime not to further democratization but to greater authoritarian measures and antidemocratic alliances. This, in fact, is what we have been seeing from China, and it mirrors the response to adversity taken by a less potent though still formidable economic player: Russia.

State of the Russian Economy

"Our key challenge in the coming years is to remove many infrastructure constraints that literally stifle our country and prevent unlocking of entire regions," said Putin as he announced a decision to tap the country's pension reserves for a $43 billion loan. The Russian president would use the cash infusion to pay for infrastructure projects that he hoped would pump new life into Russia's flagging economy.[43] The plans included a superhighway in Moscow, a high-speed railway between Moscow and Kazan, and a modernization of the Trans-Siberian Railway. Critics questioned the move, suggesting that Putin's decision would endanger pension funds and lead to inflation, not economic growth—or at least not growth anywhere near what Putin has envisioned.[44]

Economically, Putin has made big promises to the Russian people. On returning to power in 2012, he pledged to deliver GDP growth of at least 6 percent annually to keep Russian living standards rising steadily.[45] But the IMF has cut projected Russia GDP growth to 2.5 percent in 2013 and 3.25 percent in 2014 because of "weak investment and poor external demand,"[46] and Economy Minister Andrey Belousov conceded that a recession might be on the way. The Russian economic boom of 2000 to 2008 has not revived; since 2010, the economy has lagged far below the annual GDP growth target of 5–6 percent that Putin had set. Russia is unlikely to meet those targets in the future. In August 2013, Moscow announced that GDP growth in the second quarter was a paltry 1.2 percent. Putin's critics pounced.

"I don't really think the economy is heading toward collapse, more likely long-term stagnation—a lost decade, if you will," said Vladimir Milov, a former deputy energy minister and now a leader in the political opposition. "This will not lead to an immediate surge in protests, but it will be very difficult for Mr. Putin to stage another successful election in 2018 should the economy be dead."[47]

Putin is doing everything he can to prove Milov wrong, and the Russian economy does retain some powerful advantages. Russia straddles two vastly different regions and has a different economic position relative to each. Per capita, Russia is about as wealthy as most of its central Asian, Eastern European, and Asian neighbors, but because of its size, it has a vastly higher GDP than any of these countries: over $2 trillion in 2011.[48] With no legitimate rival peers in the region, Russia enjoys huge economic leverage over its relatively weak neighbors. And Russia is trying to expand its economic trade in the Asia-Pacific region, currently about a quarter of its national total (the EU remains Russia's biggest trading partner). Russia's Asia-Pacific position is strong in two areas: It is the sole petroleum-exporting region in the trading bloc, and it possesses nuclear expertise unmatched by any other Asian Pacific Economic Cooperation (APEC) nation.[49]

Russia has pursued economic expansion through smart use of plentiful natural resources, predominately in oil and energy. Russia leads the world in natural-gas production, generating 20 percent of global output, and is one of the two largest oil producers in the world, generating 12 percent of global oil output.[50] Russia has used its growing oil and energy industry to increase state power and the country's political leverage. Especially during the 2000s, Moscow became expert at using its oil and gas supplies as a tool of geopolitical influence—and often of intimidation.

Meanwhile, privatized Russian oil companies, such as LUKOIL, began expanding internationally beginning in the 1990s.[51] Gazprom, Russia's state-owned gas giant, expanded into Europe to gain influence in Eastern Europe, especially over former Soviet republics. In June 2013, Gazprom signed an agreement to explore possibilities for extending the Nord Stream gas pipeline with GDF Suez. If the project goes through, two new pipelines will run through the Baltic Sea, and the extended arm would reach the UK. The capacity of the twin pipelines would be 55 billion cubic meters.[52]

And yet despite its potency, Russia's energy industry—and with it, its national economy—faces serious obstacles. A number of factors now work against Moscow's energy dominance, and these obstacles are contributing to Russian volatility, aggressiveness, and unpredict-ability on the world stage.

Energy: Russia's Trump Card and Potential Downfall

In 2007, at its annual corporate meeting, Gazprom served red and black caviar. Back then, the firm boasted a market value of $360 billion, and its chairman, Alexey Miller, promised that it would someday reach $1 trillion as it became the world's biggest company. The Russian economy was growing 7 percent year over year.[53] Gazprom played hardball with its customers in Eastern Europe, Ukraine, Bulgaria, and elsewhere, set-ting high prices, spurning negotiations, and even cutting off supplies when disputes could not be settled in timely fashion. Moscow shut off Ukraine's supplies in 2006 and 2009 during contract and payment disputes, and it has continued to exploit Ukraine's dependency on Rus-sian gas, pressuring it to pay down its $2.2 billion fuel debt.[54] Bulgaria fell victim to the 2009 shutoff as well. Moscow's hardball tactics left Bulgarians freezing in the dead of winter for days until a new agree-ment could be reached. Observers saw Gazprom as an instrument of Kremlin foreign policy; Vice President Dick Cheney even accused Russia of using gas for "intimidation or blackmail" in 2006.[55]

The landscape has changed radically since then. Gazprom has lost more than $280 billion since 2008.[56] Today, the energy giant is worth all of $94 billion—a 74 percent drop in six years.[57] The Russian economy has declined along with it, seeing its quarterly GDP growth plunge to 1.2 percent in the second quarter of 2013.

Three factors combined to halt the Russian gas-powered economic boom: the financial crisis, which wiped out trillions in wealth and wrought havoc on economies worldwide; the Russian overreliance on energy for economic growth; and the shale-gas revolution, especially in the United States. While the crisis itself has mostly passed, its effects are still being felt, and Russia and its energy economy, while still strong, have not regained the massive leverage they enjoyed before the crash, especially because oil prices have not approached the highs of those heady days. Still, though weakened, the energy industry remains the linchpin of the Russian economy.

Hydrocarbons drove more than half of Russia's GDP growth from 2000 to 2008.[58] But even since then, the country's reliance on energy has shown little sign of easing, despite efforts to stimulate a Russian technology industry and revive a once-powerful manufacturing sector. Even as late as 2012, oil and gas made up about 70 percent of the country's exports—17 percent of Russian GDP. Gazprom makes up almost 15 percent of the total capitalization of the Russian stock market. That dependence could spell future trouble for Russia, especially since the nation's reserves may sustain current production levels for only another 20 years. Shoring them up would require exploration of the untapped reserves in the Arctic and eastern Siberia, a massively expensive undertaking.[59]

Finally, the shale revolution threatens Russia's future economic prosperity and many of Putin's political goals. The advent of fracking—in which water, along with sand and chemicals, is injected into shale-rock formations to extract gas—has changed the energy economy dramatically. Gazprom head Miller dismissed fracking as "a myth" in 2010; more recently, he dismissed it as "a bubble that will burst very soon," adding: "We don't see any risks to us at all."[60] But Miller is way wrong: Fracking is the real deal. In the United States, it has transformed North Dakota into a boom state. A decade ago, the United States eyed the goal of "energy independence" as a pie-in-the-sky aspiration. Now, the United States has leapfrogged over Russia to become the world's top gas producer, and analysts project that the U.S. will achieve energy independence within 20 years, perhaps sooner.

Outside the United States, fracking is changing the international economy by cutting into Russia's share of the gas market in Europe.

Because America now supplies more of its own gas, the U.S. has been buying less liquefied natural gas (LNG) from Qatar, the world's largest LNG exporter. The Europeans have been buying more LNG from Qatar—and less from Russia and Gazprom, which supplies about 25 percent of Europe's gas. But in 2012, Gazprom's exports to Europe were down 8 percent, to their lowest level in a decade. Further, the abundance of American gas led U.S. companies to shift from coal to gas for their energy needs, freeing up more American coal for European markets. Between the LNG from Qatar and the coal from the U.S., the Europeans had more options. Not only can they buy less Russian gas; they can also bargain for what they pay for it. And countries within Gazprom's stronghold (Lithuania, Poland, Ukraine) are all developing shale-energy capabilities of their own.[61]

Gazprom, notorious for forcing brutal pricing agreements on its customers, has no choice but to back off. Already, it has given German and Italian firms retroactive price cuts, and it's under pressure from all sides to adopt more spot-market pricing instead of pegging its prices to the cost of oil. And the European Union is investigating the company for anticompetitive behavior and unfair pricing practices. Perhaps the best example of how much the climate has changed for Russian energy is this: Bulgaria, which had been left freezing in 2009, recently renegotiated its contract with Gazprom, securing a 20 percent pricing cut.[62] Putin's aggression against Ukraine gives the Europeans even more reason to look for alternatives to Russian gas, though it remains to be seen whether, when push comes to shove, Europe will really stand up to Russia in this way.

All of this puts pressure on Putin to modernize and reform the Russian economy and its political system, over which he exercises iron-fisted control. Russia may open up its gas industry to companies other than Gazprom to foster competition and efficiency. But ultimately the challenge facing Putin is twofold: to regain Russia's energy momentum while also finding a way to diversify the economy beyond energy. "The country needs to make huge infrastructure investments in the east and to expand non-energy sectors where Russia has real potential, such as information technology, airplanes, helicopters, engines, turbines, and industrial pumps and compressors," wrote Brian Bremner for *Bloomberg Businessweek*.[63] But political and economic reform may weaken Putin's grip on power.

The new climate has also motivated Putin to press aggressively to expand the Customs Union of Belarus, Kazakhstan, and Russia, an economic alliance launched in 2010 and intended by Moscow to rival the European Union. Putin wants the current grouping to expand into a new Eurasian Union, which would include Kyrgyzstan, Tajikistan, Armenia, and other nations. Further, this new union, as Putin conceives it, would operate exclusively; that is, no states could be co-members in the EU. When Armenia showed signs of wanting to sign up with the Europeans, Putin threatened them with increased arms shipments to its foe Azerbaijan—and the Armenians backed down and joined the Customs Union. Russia has applied similar pressure to Moldova, which has been considering whether to join the EU rather than the Customs Union. Moldova remains dependent on Russian gas, and Russian Deputy Premier Dmitri Rogozin reminded Moldovans of this after he met with Moldovan Prime Minister Iurie Leanca in September 2013: "Energy supplies are important in the run-up to winter," Rogozin said. "I hope you won't freeze."[64]

But the Moldovans have resisted the pressure so far, faring better than their Ukrainian neighbors. It's worth remembering how, before Ukraine was plunged into crisis, Putin used energy to strong-arm then-President Viktor Yanukovych, who once proudly proclaimed that "Ukraine's European aspirations are the main pillar of the country's development." But after Putin pulled out all the stops, threatening gas shutoffs and an end to the two nations' "special trading partnership," Yanukovych abandoned his European dream in favor of a place in the

Russian circle of influence.[65] Yanukovych's capitulation was quickly followed by the implementation of draconian laws that strip Ukrainians of their rights to free speech and assembly.[66] That, in turn, helped precipitate the street protests and political movement that led to his ouster—and Russia's subsequent move to seize Crimea.

Ruthless and antidemocratic as many of his efforts are, the picture that emerges of Putin is of a leader who recognizes Russia's challenges and is determined to shore up its weaknesses, economic and otherwise. Given Putin's approach to power and his nationalistic ambitions, economic adversity only increases Russian authoritarianism at home—as his clampdown against protests, persecution of gays, and other repressive measures have shown—and its belligerence internationally. The tough, provocative Russian leader that American leaders have confronted in recent years can be likened to the proverbial cornered bear: dangerous when wounded.

AXIS TOGETHER: RUSSIA AND CHINA'S STRATEGIC ECONOMIC PARTNERSHIP

Russia and China have also forged a growing economic partnership. China's need for Russia's oil and gas is almost a matter of national security; Russia needs to diversify its economy, especially toward the Asia-Pacific region, and thus welcomes Chinese investment in its Far East. At the same time, Russia makes a convenient and ideologically aligned trading partner for China. To this end, in February 2013, cash-strapped Russian oil company Rosneft, controlled by the Kremlin, turned to state-owned China National Petroleum Corporation (CNPC) and proposed to borrow up to $30 billion in exchange for doubling its oil supplies to Beijing.[67] The deal, completed in March, has Rosneft agreeing to increase oil deliveries to CNPC to 31 million tons a year, over 25 years, while obtaining $2 billion from China.[68] Rosneft, now the world's largest listed oil producer, already supplies 15 million tons a year to China based on a 2009 deal. The new deal came on the heels of the $800 million Russo-Chinese oil-for-loan agreement, signed in 2008, in which the two nations agreed to build a trans-Siberian pipeline. In that deal, Russia agreed to send China 300,000 barrels of oil per day for 15 years in exchange for a loan to help Rosneft acquire OAO Yukos, then the largest Russian oil company.[69]

"Oil and gas pipelines have become the veins connecting the two countries in a new century," Xi said during his March 2013 trip to Moscow, in which he made the case for stronger economic cooperation between the two nations.[70] Picking up the momentum from Rosneft's oil-for-loan deal, gas giant Gazprom entered into an understanding in March 2013 with CNPC to deliver natural gas to its neighbor via a new pipeline—in return for a loan that will make China the company's biggest customer by 2018. The deal stipulates that Gazprom will deliver 38 billion cubic meters a year to China via a new pipeline from Siberia starting in 2018. To put the dimensions of this deal in perspective: Germany, long the largest consumer of Russian gas, imported 33 billion cubic meters last year.[71]

Indeed, the geopolitical ramifications of these deals are immense: Beijing can lessen its dependence on oil coming through the Malacca and Hormuz Straits, two vulnerable shipping bottlenecks, while industrializing areas of the country left behind during its economic boom. At the same time, Russia receives a much-needed infusion of capital. Beyond the economic benefits, these enormous new business deals between Russia and China send a signal to the West that the Axis's deepening political alliance also has a robust economic component. This signal also extends to the broader world of international finance.

A New Banking Model? The Challenge of the BRICS

"Up until now, it has been a loose arrangement of five countries meeting once a year. It's going to be the first real institution we have seen."[72] So said Abdullah Verachia, director of the Frontier Advisory Group, in reaction to the news that the BRICS—Brazil, Russia, India, China, and South Africa—would form a new development bank, a direct challenge to the dominance of the World Bank and the International Monetary Fund. Meeting in Durban in March 2013, leaders from the five growing economic powers agreed that the new bank would focus on infrastructure and development in emerging markets and pool foreign reserves as a bulwark against currency crises.

"We have decided to enter formal negotiations to establish a BRICS-led new development bank based on our own considerable infrastructure needs, which amount to around $4.5 trillion over the next five years," said South African president Jacob Zuma, adding that the alternative bank planned to cooperate with other emerging markets and developing countries in the future.[73] The group's finance ministers have yet to settle on how much capital the bank would have—perhaps $50 billion—as well as its structure, the role of its shareholders, and its location. Yet there was a "great sense of urgency to establish the entity as soon as possible," according to Pravin Gordhan, South Africa's finance minister. "An observation that many of us would make as developing countries is that the roots of the IMF and World Bank still lie in the post–World War II environment," Gordhan said. "The reforms that have been undertaken so far . . . are inadequate in terms of reflecting current economic and other realities around the world."[74]

Putin suggested that he wanted to steer the BRICS toward "a full-scale strategic cooperation mechanism that will allow us to look for solutions to key issues of global politics together."[75] A common BRICS economic *and* foreign policy, in other words: a clear challenge to the United States and its Western allies.

As other critics have pointed out, the BRICS countries are not exactly a perfect match. They compete against one another, they have widely divergent economies and different forms of government, and China and India have a long history of reciprocal hostility. A United

Nations Conference on Trade and Development report showed that the BRIC countries, at least to date, barely invest in one another, instead opting for their neighbors and the developed world.[76] Perhaps this will change when the banking system and other arrangements are put more firmly in place.

Still, a new, rival development bank oriented along non-Western lines is as clear a sign as any, in the financial and economic realm, of Russian and Chinese intentions to forge new international models and institutions that counter Western and especially American dominance. "When Putin stressed that he does not see the BRICS as a 'geopolitical competitor' to the West, it was the clincher," writes Pepe Escobar in the *Asia Times*, "the official denial that confirms it's true."[77]

BEYOND MOSCOW AND BEIJING: RUSSIA AND CHINA'S ECONOMIC REACH

Moscow and Beijing's economic challenge to the United States has not only led to competition with, and direct investment in, Western enterprises. It has also taken full flight in the developing world, especially Africa and Latin America—regions that the European powers and the United States had traditionally seen as within their sphere of economic influence.

Africa

The African continent has long been a central site for Chinese investment and economic growth; Beijing made its earliest forays in the 1950s. By 2012, however, China had surpassed the U.S. and the EU to become the African continent's largest trading partner. Chinese investments have reached $15 billion, up from $500 million in 2002. At the start of 2012, some 2,000 Chinese companies were operating across Africa.[78]

Chinese trade with Africa is dominated by mineral and oil extraction; these industries constitute some 90 percent of bilateral trade. But the Chinese also pay for roads, schools, airports, hospitals, and ports, providing infrastructure improvements that Western companies have been unwilling to fund.[79] Indeed, as Zambian-born Dambisa Moyo, a former Goldman Sachs economist, argues, the U.S. and other Western countries have continually passed over investment opportunities in Africa in favor of giving foreign aid. This approach has helped sabotage African economies by encouraging corrupt governments to make wasteful decisions, while forestalling the necessity of developing sustainable growth. Chinese investment, by contrast, comes in the form of productive industry, rather than subsidized loans. Chinese aid comes quickly, decisively, and without strings attached.[80]

China's African involvement is certainly not universally praised. In a 2012 speech, Hillary Clinton condemned Beijing for engaging in resource exploitation: "The days of having outsiders come and extract the wealth of Africa for themselves, leaving nothing or very little behind, should be over in the 21st century."[81] Peter Eigan, writing for the Africa Progress Panel, an NGO chaired by Kofi Anan, identified five problems with China's economic strategy in Africa:

- China's investments and returns may be large and headline-grabbing, but they don't necessarily produce many jobs.
- Commodity booms distort local currencies, making it difficult for exporters to sell their goods in foreign markets.
- Mineral exports encourage corruption.
- China has not advocated for Africa on the world stage or helped African exporters sell goods in China.
- China has used its veto power in the United Nations Security Council to consistently limit human-rights protection, preventing action, for instance, on the Darfur crisis.[82]

Many ordinary Africans share Eigen's skepticism. "Ask any African ministry official or businessperson his or her views on Chinese companies and you tend to get the same response: horrible quality and broken promises," wrote Alexander Bernard in the *Christian Science Monitor* in August 2012. "Africa's business and government elite aren't the only ones taking note; the Chinese brand is often the object of ridicule even among average Africans. Photographs of a leaking ceiling in the new African Union headquarters in Addis Ababa, donated and built by Chinese contractors, made the rounds on Facebook last month, with a caption mocking the quality of Chinese construction."[83]

Indeed, President Xi was forced to defend China's economic stake in many African countries—and the often-noted similarities to colonialism—in a speech in Dar es Salaam, the seaside economic hub of Tanzania, in March 2013. "China frankly faces up to the new circumstances and new problems in Sino-African relations," Xi said. "China has and will continue to work alongside African countries to take the practical measures to appropriately solve problems in trade and economic cooperation so that African countries gain more from that cooperation."[84] In the same speech, Xi said that China would abide by his predecessor's promise to provide $20 billion in loans over three years for African infrastructure and development, farming, and businesses. He also announced a plan to provide training for 30,000 Africans over the next three years, including 18,000 scholarships to study abroad—apparently in China, though he did not say so explicitly.[85]

Some African countries—such as Niger, Gabon, and Chad—have been pushing back against Chinese contractual terms for oil deals, objecting to CNPC's high costs and unfair charges, and even, in at least one case, shutting down oil operations after learning that Chinese firms were dumping excess crude oil in ditches. All of these countries, poor economically but rich in resources, originally welcomed Chinese investment in their nations' oil fields and the economic development that they hoped investment would spur. But retrospectively, political leaders are realizing that they may be selling their most precious natural commodities without getting enough in return.

"This is all we've got," said Foumakoye Gado, Niger's oil minister. "If our natural resources are given away, we'll never get out of this."[86] China's African road may get bumpier. "The Chinese are genuinely unprepared for this degree of pushback," said Ricardo Soares de Oliveira, an Oxford professor and expert on African oil.[87]

Others see China's aid as necessary and welcome. At the July 2012 Forum on China-Africa Co-operation, President Zuma of South Africa expressed the welcoming attitude of most African leaders: "Africa's past economic experience with Europe dictates a need to be cautious when entering into partnerships with other economies. We are particularly pleased that in our relationship with China, we are equals and that agreements entered into are for mutual gain. This gathering indicates commitment to mutual respect and benefit. We certainly are convinced that China's intention is different to that of Europe, which to date continues to attempt to influence African countries for their sole benefit."[88]

*****

Russia is a latecomer to the African investment race, but its interests on the continent are growing fast. Already rich in oil and other strategic materials, Russia does not need Africa for the fossil fuels that interest China. Rather, it wants to use Africa as an export market for services, capital, and industrial products, as a partner for exporting raw materials, and as a source of certain rare materials that may be cheaper or more plentiful in Africa.[89]

Russian businessmen are concerned that China and the U.S. may have gained too much of a head start in investments and extractive industries. Mikhail Margelov, a Russian presidential representative at a Russia-Africa cooperation summit held in Addis Ababa in December

2011, said: "In the 1990s, Russia gave up practically all of its interests, freeing up the territory for the United States, the European Union, and China. In 1992, Russia closed nine embassies in Sub-Saharan Africa. The new economy led to strategic losses, and now we need to make up for them." Margelov stressed that Russia should enter into competition for raw-materials exports needed for construction infrastructure, including gas, as well as vanadium, chromium, cobalt, and uranium—materials that are rare in Russia but important to many industrial processes.[90]

To be sure, Russia faces heavy challenges from China in Africa. "It is useless to fight with the Chinese," one Russian diplomat said. "They give Africa colossal amounts of credit on very good terms, and at the end of an important contract, they always give a gift—free construction of schools and hospitals." While Russia may have business interests in Africa, it has neither China's investment track record nor its inexhaustibly deep pockets.[91]

But Russia's late start in Africa may work to Moscow's benefit. Chinese companies are often viewed as instruments of a "new colonialism" that brings shoddy work and overly aggressive tactics; Russia does not carry this kind of baggage.[92] Russia has a relatively clean slate in the region. In October 2012, the Russian government wrote off some $20 billion in African debt in order to improve its image and gain support for more investment opportunities.[93] That strategy may well pay off.

Latin America and the Caribbean

"[I am] a great admirer of Mao," said Hugo Chávez during a 2004 visit to Beijing.[94] "I think if Mao Zedong and [Simon] Bolivar had known each other, they would have been good friends because their thinking was similar."[95] For Latin America's leftist leaders, such as Chávez, Rafael Correa, and Evo Morales, partnerships with Communist China have been especially welcome. While commercial needs undoubtedly underlie these relationships, Chinese investment also appeals along ideological lines.

In February 2012, Chinese development banks displaced the World Bank and the Inter-American Development Bank in the value of their investments in Latin America. In fact, estimates show that since 2005, China made loan commitments of more than $75 billion to Latin American countries.[96] Most of this financing came in the form of commodity-backed loans, in which countries ship oil to China at pre-set rates to pay off their debts. The majority of loans went to non-creditworthy nations such as Argentina, Ecuador, Venezuela, and Brazil, mostly for mining, oil, and infrastructure projects. Between 2005 and 2011, Chinese banks provided more than $75 billion in loans; $46 billion of these were commodity-backed.[97]

Latin America is a unique region for Chinese investors in that it couples a fairly large market for exports with large resource reserves not being tapped by local companies—two key components in China's growth strategy.[98] What's more, China's model of combining authoritarianism with robust economic growth is appealing to traditional Latin American elites, as well as to populist strongmen who would like to retain their hold on power. Many view the Western model of free markets and democratization as a poor match for Latin America's problems. Traditional elites see the Chinese model as an efficient way to lift their people out of poverty without relinquishing their grip on power.[99] They believe China is a positive force, unlike the U.S., which they've long perceived as a meddler in Latin American affairs.

This is not to say that China is universally welcomed and beloved in Latin America. Many Latin American leaders and businessmen are becoming unhappy with Chinese growth in the region. Some accuse the Chinese of pursuing the same extractive strategy it has applied in Africa. In response, Chinese companies have begun to make more diversified investments in Latin America. The Chinese company Lenovo, for instance, acquired Brazilian consumer-electronics company CCE for $147 million; Chinese carmaker Foton Motors Co. is investing $300 million to build an auto plant in Brazil. In June 2012, the Chinese government proposed a $5 billion cooperation fund for infrastructure development in Latin America, along with a $10 billion credit line to support these projects.[100]

Russia, meanwhile, has a long history in Latin America. During the Cold War, the Soviet Union had extensive ties with Cuba, but these eroded with the fall of the USSR. In 2008, however, Dmitri Medvedev expressed Russia's desire to renew the faded partnership with Cuba. In 2009, Raul Castro visited Moscow and signed an agreement to promote bilateral development, including projects in energy, transport, civil aviation, biopharmaceuticals, and high-tech sectors.[101]

Vladimir Putin developed a close relationship with Hugo Chávez before the Venezuelan leader died in 2012. In October 2011, Russia and Venezuela signed a bilateral deal worth $8 billion, including a $4 billion loan for military training. The two countries are working together to develop production in the Orinoco oil field. Venezuela is by far Russia's most important ally in Latin America; Russia entered the Latin American arms market only with Chávez's help.[102]

From 2004 to 2010, Russia sold Venezuela a staggering $5.4 billion in weapons, from tanks to missiles to rifles. Chávez dubiously claimed that he had purchased anti-aircraft missiles to protect oil derricks from aerial assault. Venezuela's investments in Russian arms have troubled the Chilean, Colombian, and Brazilian governments, which fear that a heavily armed Venezuela could set off a continental arms race or enable Caracas to intimidate and coerce its neighbors.

Neighbors near and far also worry that Venezuela could provide high technology and weapons to sophisticated drug runners, such as the Colombian narco-terrorist group FARC. According to Stephen Blank of the U.S. Army War College, "Venezuela's arms purchases make no sense unless they are intended for purposes of helping the

FARC and other similar groups, fighting Colombia, projecting power throughout Latin America drug running with subs that are protected against air attacks, or providing a temporary base for Russian naval and air forces where they can be sheltered from attacks but threaten North or South America."[103] Chávez, for his part, simply asserted his right to do as he pleased as a sovereign leader. Speaking of the arms purchases, he said: "We can do it today because we are free. We could not have done this before, because we were dominated by Yankees, the World Bank, and the entire imperial economy and financial structure."[104]

The Axis's involvement in Latin America represents an encroachment on a territory the U.S. has considered its backyard ever since the Monroe Doctrine, a policy originally created to prevent former colonial powers from attempting to regain their holdings in Latin America. The U.S. maintained the policy successfully for almost a century and a half. In recent decades, however, foreign powers have greatly expanded their military and economic ties to Latin America.

To be sure, the United States remains by far the predominant military power in the region, a position it has recently bolstered by reestablishing the Fourth Naval Fleet in Latin American waters and by conducting extensive joint activities with several Latin American countries.[105] Latin America's links with the United States are long-standing and fundamental to the economies of North, Central, and South America; the United States remains the preferred business partner of most Latin American companies because of its deep understanding of the market and culture.[106] Yet the Chinese and Russian infiltration presents a serious challenge.

At the very least, China's presence in Latin America will mean a loss for American businesses, as cheap Chinese products edge out American exports. It's also possible that future engagement between Russia or China and such anti-American powers as Venezuela could form an anti-American axis in our own backyard, limiting access to resources or even destabilizing friendlier regimes.[107] American estimations of Chinese and Russian arms influence in the region might not even be fully reliable, because figures of arms sales do not provide a comprehensive picture. While China sells few weapons, it has made large donations of military equipment to Bolivia, for instance, since the election of Evo Morales—including missiles, logistical equipment, and non-weapons support gear. Military aid to Latin America achieves certain soft-power goals for Beijing; thus the precise depth and scope of China's involvement may not be apparent.[108]

The Chinese are also making major inroads into another traditional American enclave: the Caribbean. In June 2013, Beijing lavished $3 billion in development loans on a region whose economy is equivalent to that of the state of Kansas; the Chinese have doled out $6 billion over the last decade. Beijing now has "a major project in nearly every Caribbean country," Rush Doshi and David Walter wrote in a *Wall Street Journal* report, including the construction of a huge commercial port in Jamaica by the state-owned Chinese Communications Construction Company. Doshi and Walter see the Chinese posture in the Caribbean as less about traditional Chinese economic expansion—though the getting is good, to be sure—and more about mimicking the Soviet Union's Cold War strategy of using the region to contain the United States. They envision China eventually signing naval-access agreements with Caribbean countries and establishing surveillance posts. "In times of crisis," they write, "China could use the Caribbean to draw U.S. attention away from Asia and Beijing's own maritime backyard, the South China Sea."[109]

UNDERSTANDING THE AXIS'S ECONOMIC CHALLENGE

As President Xi has made clear, China and Russia support each other politically, militarily, and, as we have seen, also economically. To this end, regional trade agreements, investment, and development projects in nations across the globe have aided China and Russia in extending their global economic influence. Both countries are moving ahead with plans to expand their economies, investing at home and abroad, and working (sometimes together) on enormous infrastructure projects to transport natural resources. But their economic cooperation extends further than energy deals and trade agreements. It is also rooted in a mutual vision to counter the influence of the united States, in part by creating and formalizing alternative alliances and institutions that work independently of—and often directly against—American and Western interests.

Yet for all of their considerable success, both countries face serious economic challenges. China's meteoric economic growth is slowing; its banks are stagnant under heavy government involvement, and corruption throughout its quasi-private economy is endemic. Its lack of environmental standards causes pollution and health problems. Cronyism within the Communist elite has denied opportunity to millions. Russia, meanwhile, faces even more serious problems—none more so than its economic overreliance on energy. With the American shale-gas revolution, Russia's ability to call the tune in Europe and elsewhere may about to be drastically curtailed.

Here is an example, again, of the tragic absence of American leadership. As in the other areas we have covered in previous chapters, the Axis nations pose serious challenges, but they also exhibit clear weaknesses and limitations. The absence of an effective American policy response in the economic realm, as elsewhere, is as damaging as it is bewildering.

Without question, any effective American response must address, comprehensively, the area where China hits us the hardest: jobs. "China continues to acquire more and more of our industrial capacity," Greg Autry and Peter Navarro write. "We have less and less of an ability to produce the jobs we need for our economy and the weapons systems we need for national defense."[110] Elsewhere, Navarro argues that the United States must address its trade deficit with China and pursue a policy of balanced trade with Beijing by, say, 2020; crack down on China's many unfair trade practices; and re-link human rights with Chinese trade. He also urges American consumers to stop buying Chinese products or at least "think about their purchases."[111]

The United States has stood up to China occasionally; the Obama administration has made repeated complaints against Beijing's trade practices, and the president did raise the issue of cyber security (if none too successfully) with Xi at their summit in 2013. Yet, like our European neighbors, we in the United States must often feel as if we have only carrots, not sticks: It's difficult for hard-pressed American consumers to stop buying Chinese, or even to "think about their purchases," as Navarro urges, when incomes are stagnating and millions remain jobless. The blizzard of Chinese cash—as investment for U.S. businesses and as cheap products for U.S. consumers—is very difficult to resist in a troubled economy.

What is lacking here, as in other areas, is a comprehensive vision of how to proceed. How should the United States understand its economic policy in the face of the Chinese challenge? What policies do we need to pursue to regain our economic self-sufficiency and protect our own people against the exploitation that other nations have alleged against China and its ruthless fiscal and trade policies?

Given how successful the Chinese have been in using cheap labor to destroy jobs in the developed world, reviving the once-proud American manufacturing sector would certainly be a step in the right direction. Reforming and streamlining the tax code, providing stronger incentives for businesses to invest, and ensuring the stability and vitality of key American entitlement programs such as Social Security would also be crucial components of a comprehensive policy. As in other areas, there is no shortage of good ideas. What is lacking is a leader to adopt them with conviction and purpose, one who will articulate and sell them to the people, and pursue them with the kind of single-minded determination that we see on display daily from leaders in Moscow and Beijing.

In economics as in national security, it is not too late for the United States to retake the initiative, defend its interests, and slow the momentum of its adversaries. The United States does not lack the economic know-how; it possesses many built-in advantages, including rich natural resources, a creative and industrious people, and a heritage of free enterprise. What the United States lacks is leadership, and it's an absence all the more glaring when contrasted with the leadership of our Axis adversaries. They have it, we don't—at least for now.

CHAPTER 7

Intelligence Wars:
Stealing America's Secrets

"The public needs to decide whether these programs and policies are right or wrong. . . . This is the truth. This is what's happening. You should decide whether we need to be doing this."

—EDWARD SNOWDEN[1]

"Such a present for us for Christmas."

—VLADIMIR PUTIN, TALKING ABOUT EDWARD SNOWDEN[2]

"Stealing American secrets is not a crime in Russia."

—DIMITRI SIMES, HEAD OF THE CENTER FOR THE NATIONAL INTEREST[3]

"Don't ask me why there's a director of national intelligence and a director of central intelligence. Something to do with 9/11, after which the government decided it could use more intelligence. Instead it wound up with more directors of intelligence, which is the way it usually goes in Washington."

—MARK STEYN[4]

"Washington should come clean about its record first. It owes, too, an explanation to China and other countries it has allegedly spied on. It has to share with the world the range, extent, and intent of its clandestine hacking programs."

—XINHUA, STATE NEWS AGENCY OF CHINA[5]

He was the most famous international traveler ever to take up temporary residence in Moscow's Sheremetyevo Airport—a fugitive wanted by the most powerful country in the world for leaking national-security secrets. And not just any national-security secrets: "basically the instruction manual" for how America's National Security Agency operated. As Edward Snowden, formerly a technical contractor for the NSA and employee of the CIA, sat under the protective watch of the Russian government and Vladimir Putin, he had information that could cause more damage to the U.S. government than "anyone else has ever had in the history" of the country.[6]

What Snowden leaked, via left-wing *Guardian* journalist Glenn Greenwald, was huge volumes of information about top-secret United States and British mass-surveillance programs. The programs, called PRISM in the U.S. and Tempora in Britain, involved massive data collection of telephone and Internet metadata on hundreds of millions of people, via cooperative arrangements with telephone and Internet-service companies. Snowden's leaks also disclosed that the United States was spying aggressively and comprehensively on its allies in Europe. All told, what Snowden made public added up to one of the worst intelligence breaches in American history. (The heads of the House and Senate Intelligence Committees, a Republican and Democrat, would later charge that Snowden may have had earlier ties with Russian intelligence.[7])

And the Russians had no intention of turning him over to the United States, despite earnest American pleas. "We have returned seven prisoners to them in the last two years that they requested," Secretary of State John Kerry said of the Russians. "I think it's very important for them to adhere to the rule of law and respect the relationship."[8] But Kerry made no mention of consequences should the Russians refuse to cooperate, and his defeatist wording suggested there would be none.

Putin played the affair with the consummate skill of an old spy, making Kerry and President Obama seem like novices. His confidence showed when, giving a speech in Finland, he claimed—to much audience laughter—that Russia did not want Snowden to damage the United States. Amusing his listeners, Putin described how he had told Snowden that Russia would consider his application for asylum on the condition that he stop damaging "our American partners" by leaking documents.

"You are laughing, but I am serious," said Putin. "[Snowden] said, 'I want to continue my activities, I want to struggle for human rights, that the U.S. violated some international law, interference with privacy, and my goal is to struggle against this.' We said: 'Only, not with us. We have other things to struggle against.'"

Putin even insisted that the U.S. had forced his hand, trapping Snowden in Russia by persuading other countries not to accept him for asylum: "They themselves scared all other countries; no one wants to take him, and in this way they themselves in fact blocked him on our territory." It sounded plausible, but then Putin couldn't resist a gloat.[9] "Such a present for us for Christmas," he said. The audience laughed again.

(Putin has been more nuanced in other contexts. At a December 2013 news conference, he conceded that surveillance was "necessary to fight terrorism," though he also argued that it was "necessary to limit the appetite of special services with certain rules."[10] And in fact the Kremlin has beefed up its own efforts against cyber crime and hackers.)

Of course, what Putin didn't say was that he could have turned Snowden over to Obama himself, but this Putin was never going to do. Nor were the Chinese; before landing in Moscow, Snowden had taken refuge in Hong Kong. The White House's insistence that he be returned fell on deaf ears there, too, as Hong Kong government officials made a host of bureaucratic excuses for why they couldn't respond to the American request.

Meanwhile, Snowden had become a global cause célèbre. He met with human-rights organizations at the Russian airport, including Amnesty International, Human Rights Watch, and Transparency International. A Swedish sociology professor nominated him for a Nobel Prize, saying that honoring Snowden would make up for the Nobel Committee's error in giving the award to President Obama in 2009.

"Edward Snowden has—in a heroic effort at great personal cost—revealed the existence and extent of the surveillance the U.S. government devotes [to] electronic communications worldwide," wrote Stefan Svallfors. "By putting light on this monitoring program—conducted in contravention of national laws and international agreements—Edward Snowden has helped to make the world a little bit better and safer."[11]

U.S. adversaries enjoyed the spectacle from the sidelines. America did not have "the moral right to request the extradition of a young man who is only warning of the illegalities committed by the Pentagon and the CIA and the United States," said Venezuelan president Nicolás Maduro. "As head of state, I reject any request for extradition. They are simply disregarding bilateral agreements."[12]

Beijing, for its part, celebrated Snowden and damned the U.S. for its blatant hypocrisy: "These, along with previous allegations, are clearly troubling signs. They demonstrate that the United States, which has long been trying to play innocent as a victim of cyber attacks, has turned out to be the biggest villain in our age."[13]

The Edward Snowden affair was a devastating event for the United States national-security and intelligence communities, and it became even more so when Putin accepted Snowden's request for asylum in Russia, at least for a year, allowing the American to leave his airport sanctuary. Eventually, he took up residence in Russia and reentered the spotlight by asking Putin on a television program in 2014 whether Russia spied on its citizens the way America does. Certainly not, Putin assured him.[14]

Although it was a self-inflicted wound (Snowden decided to become a leaker on his own, without foreign assistance), it was difficult to miss the symbolism of Snowdon's choices for shelter—first China, then Russia—to say nothing of his requests for asylum from other nations with which America has poor relations—Venezuela, Ecuador, and Bolivia. Both Axis countries steadfastly refused to cooperate with Washington and used the event to their advantage, serene in their confidence that the Americans would do little to make them pay. A disgusted President Obama canceled a scheduled meeting in Moscow with Putin, but his gesture seemed more an admission of defeat than anything else. And as the debate continues to rage over whether Snowden deserves amnesty—a request National Security Adviser Susan Rice summarily shot down in a *60 Minutes* interview—the Obama administration continues to look outsmarted and outmaneuvered at every turn.[15]

Snowden's deeds were as much of a surprise to the Chinese and Russians as they were to us, but the Axis response to them, as in so many other areas we have chronicled, outlined a familiar picture: China and Russia playing the game for keeps, relentless in the pursuit of their interests; America confused, passive, and ineffective. It's a picture that unfortunately holds as true in the area of intelligence warfare as in the others we have discussed. China and Russia are far more aggressive and effective here than is commonly understood, while the U.S. does not counter their efforts. In part, this comes from a failure of vision and nerve. In part, it is due to post–Cold War transformations in how the intelligence game is played internationally. Our adversaries have adapted much more readily to these changes than we have, and, to some degree, the changing landscape has given them a built-in advantage.

THE OLD GAME IS OVER

On June 28, 2010, the FBI accused 11 people of acting as Russian spies. The accused spies' neighbors in New York, Boston, and Virginia were shocked by the news. As one neighbor put it: "They couldn't have been spies. Look what she did with the hydrangeas." Another neighbor referred to one of the couples as "suburbia personified."[16]

Suburbanites or no, according to the FBI, the accused were involved in the "Illegals Project," a spy ring dedicated to obtaining secrets about American nuclear weapons, CIA leadership, and Congressional politics, among other subjects. They used fake civilian identities, and their tactics included both old-fashioned espionage and high-tech devices: forged passports, stolen identities, invisible ink, and special computer software.[17] In a coded message, one couple disclosed the purpose of their trip: "You were sent to USA for long-term service trip . . . Your education, bank accounts, car, house, etc.—all these serve one goal: fulfill your main mission, i.e., to search and develop ties in policymaking circles and send intels [intelligence reports] to C[enter]."[18]

The FBI gathered information on the spies for more than seven years, with the help of Colonel Alexander Poteyev, a high-ranking Russian official who had penetrated the spy ring by appearing to administrate it—all the while feeding information back to the FBI.[19] The FBI's long investigation resulted in what seemed an intelligence coup: a broken-up spy ring that reminded some of the old Cold War days. Operation Ghost Stories, as the bureau called its investigation, played into a broader story about espionage and counter-espionage between the United States and Russia.

And yet, the spy ring itself was almost entirely ineffectual.

To be sure, the spies were good at fooling their suburban neighbors. But while they apparently cultivated relationships with certain academics, nuclear-weapons experts, and U.S. officials, no evidence indicated that they had actually retrieved anything beyond, as *The Economist* put it, what "could have been gleaned from reading the better papers." Indeed, the spies often had to justify their expenses and behavior to their superiors, who wondered what was taking them so long. None of the spies were charged with espionage—not because of a lack of intent, but because there was not enough evidence to warrant the charge.[20] They were exchanged for four Russians who'd been imprisoned in Russia for spying for the United States.

What the broken-up spy ring really showed was how outdated the Cold War model of human moles has become in 21st-century intelligence wars. The entire episode had the somewhat comical quality of a bad Cold War spy film. The last time anyone had a clear snapshot of the human face of espionage—that is, the struggle to gather information and deploy influence by hidden means—was during the Soviet era, a time of master spies, John Le Carré characters, and *The Manchurian Candidate.*

Human intelligence, boots on the ground, moles, and operatives played a crucial role during the Cold War. The game has changed. Deployed from afar, spying need not depend on undercover spooks. Agents of influence need not function in the shadows. They ply their trade in the open in the PR industry, in the media, working as Washington lobbyists or as top business executives who depend on profits from commerce with Russia and China.

The new playing field might be characterized as one of decentralized intelligence, with heightened surveillance. Eavesdropping, for instance—a staple of Cold War practice, not to mention a thousand spy novels—has changed radically since the days of bugged hotel rooms and men in raincoats watching from doorways. The human element is not nearly so necessary in an era when modern-day communications, from cellphones to emails, are so porous. As we discussed in our "Cyber Wars" chapter, the U.S. government fights a daily war to keep hackers from disrupting it websites and penetrating passwords and IDs. We don't worry about individual spies such as Robert Hansen; we worry about an entire technological spying apparatus, like the unit China runs in Shanghai, built and sustained and operated by countless hands.

The surveillance culture, then, has only intensified since the days of the Cold War, but with this difference: We take it for granted that we're on our own and that our government cannot protect us. During the Beijing Olympics, for instance, every taxi in Beijing carried an audio bug, and most carried video monitors.[21] The technology of spying has proliferated in quantum leaps, and both Russia and China can now monitor not only large swaths of their own population, but also ours—indeed, the world's.

So, while the Cold War spy model is obsolete, the intelligence wars themselves are very much alive, both around the world and in the U.S. Unfortunately, while our adversaries have adapted to the new terrain and seized the advantage, the U.S. has been slow to respond to the serious losses it is already suffering—first and foremost, in the area of national security.

MILITARY-INTELLIGENCE FAILURES

In recent years, the U.S. has shown more vulnerability than ever to old-fashioned military-intelligence failures. The public remains mostly uninformed as to how such things have happened and whether the leaks have been plugged.

In the old days, again, the individual human element was key: A mole would take microfilm photos of secret drawings and pass them on to a Soviet Embassy contact, who would smuggle them abroad.

These days, computer hacking can do this work via the Internet or through "trapdoors" inside computer parts largely manufactured in China. Hackers tend to have loose national loyalties, and computer experts can hail from different countries and move around the world.

The United States remains the highest-value target of such thieves, as we are the player with the greatest investments in high-tech, the most advanced equipment, the heaviest defense expenditures—and, alas, the biggest vulnerability to theft. Recent years have provided several alarming examples. As we discussed in our "Cyber Wars" chapter, the leaking of technological information about American stealth technology and specifically about the F-35 Joint Strike Fighter—the centerpiece of the Air Force and Navy's collaborative air arm—may well have given Beijing the know-how they needed to produce, years ahead of schedule, China's first stealth fighter. But that is not the only troubling incidence of recent years. Such lapses are occurring with greater frequency.

Iran and the Lost Drones

In December 2011, a CIA-operated drone landed in Iran and was recovered by the Revolutionary Guard. Using its sophisticated stealth technology to avoid radar detection, the drone, a Lockheed Martin RQ-170 Sentinel, was spying on Iranian nuclear facilities. American satellites have been spying on Iranian nuclear sites for years, but the RQ-170 captured an unprecedented degree of detail, using continuous video feeds and radioactive isotope-detection sensors, among other surveillance technologies. Up until the crash, the RQ-170's role in the spy program was undisclosed.[22]

A photograph quickly appeared on the Internet showing Iranian security forces inspecting the drone, a large white plane with bat-shaped wings. In December 2012, the Iranian government claimed that it had successfully hacked into the drone's computer system, commandeered it, and decoded all the data stored on its system.[23]

An Iranian engineer involved in the process of reverse-engineering the captured drone said that Iran used a series of sophisticated computer attacks to bring it down. Iranian engineers cut off communications between the drone and its remote pilot and then switched in a fake signal, which allowed them to take control of the plane. This signal tricked the onboard GPS system into thinking that its landing site in Iran was its base in Kandahar, Afghanistan. "The GPS navigation is the weakest point," the engineer later boasted. "By putting noise [jamming] on the communications, you force the bird into autopilot. This is where the bird loses its brain."[24]

The U.S. insisted that the drone had been brought down by a mechanical failure, not by anything the Iranians did. American officials claimed that the drone had broken into pieces upon landing and that the Iranians had reassembled them to make it look as though the drone had landed on its own power. The RQ-170 was painted gray, they said, but the Iranian video showed a white craft, indicating that it had been repainted, possibly to conceal damage.[25]

It is worth noting the legitimate doubts that some observers have raised about Iranian claims. "The weak point in the Iranian argument is how they detected the drone in the first place, which I find implausible given the existing quality of their air-defense system, which is not sufficiently sophisticated to detect it," said Dennis Gomley, a University of Pittsburgh expert on unmanned air systems. "Their air defenses are of a type that doesn't have the ability to detect a low-cross-section vehicle like the RQ-170."[26] Several other American and international experts have voiced similar doubts. They point out that Iran would have had to outperform U.S. estimations of Iranian capacity in several key areas at the same time. Their air defenses would have been hard-pressed to detect the American drone in the first place. Had they done so, jamming the GPS signal—at 50,000 feet—and substituting their own codes would have presented further challenges.[27]

So, with all of these obstacles, how could one truly believe that the Iranians were behind the downing of the drone?

Perhaps they had help—from the Russians or the Chinese.

From its experience in the Balkan Wars, Russia has some knowledge of the challenge of hijacking GPS systems. The Russians may have helped spot encryption vulnerabilities that allowed them to break into the control systems. It's commonly known that Russia spies on the U.S. Defense Department; the Russians may have learned about some of the planes' weak spots. There is also the matter of Russia's track record of helping the Iranians, particularly with Iran's nuclear program. Electronic warfare is a logical extension of that mission, and capturing technological information about the RQ-170 would be a feather in the Russians' cap.[28]

In December 2012, Iran claimed to have captured yet another American drone, this time a Boeing ScanEagle, using a similar GPS-related tactic, known as "spoofing." Iranian television displayed a picture of the ScanEagle in front of a map of the Persian Gulf, with a banner reading "We Will Trample on the United States."[29] Iranian sources again claimed that they had "extracted the drone's information."

Again, the U.S. denied that the drone had been captured. "The U.S. Navy has fully accounted for all unmanned air vehicles operating in the Middle East region," a Navy spokesman said. "Our operations in the gulf are confined to internationally recognized water and airspace. We have no record that we have lost any ScanEagles recently." The Navy suggested that the Iranians might be exhibiting a drone that had been lost at sea long before the incident, or that the drone might belong to another country.[30]

In the second drone case, the Iranian claims do seem weak. The first case is much more plausible, though not definitive. But taken together, and especially when considering the huge data thefts from the American stealth and Joint Strike Fighter systems, it is clear that the U.S. military is a primary target in the intelligence wars—and that it is not merely an aspirational target, either. While the costs of our losses remain undetermined, so far, it's clear that the attackers are getting through. This fact alone should arouse profound concern in Washington.

CIA FAILURES

"In spite of the deteriorating security situation in Benghazi and ample strategic warnings, the United States government simply did not do enough to prevent these attacks and ensure the safety of those serving in Benghazi," said Senator Saxby Chambliss, the ranking Republican on the Senate Intelligence Committee. With those words, Chambliss blamed the State Department, the FBI, and the CIA for the terrorist attack that killed four Americans at our consulate in Benghazi.[31] The Senate report was the latest black eye for the American intelligence community, whose failures—especially the CIA's—have become all too commonplace.

By now, few Americans would tell pollsters that they have strong confidence in the Central Intelligence Agency, the nation's leading intelligence-gathering arm. Although the agency still enjoys a romantic image in movies and novels, its recent history has been dominated by calamitous intelligence failures. A brief consideration of its track record makes clear that the U.S. faces serious performance issues in the crucial area of intelligence gathering.

In the ashes of 9/11, the question everyone in America wanted answered was: How did the CIA miss this? How did the CIA and other well-funded intelligence agencies, which together Harry Truman called a kind of "secret newspaper," fail to identify such a mortal threat?

Those were good questions, but they were applicable years before 9/11, because the CIA had also failed to predict the most significant global development of the second half of the 20th century: the collapse of the Soviet Union and its breakup into multiple states.

A few years after the Soviet Union's fall, Russ Travers of the Defense Intelligence Agency authored an insightful essay, "The Coming Intelligence Failure," which in effect predicted the disasters of the next decade and a half. What Travers saw was that the nation's intelligence apparatus had become "sufficiently dysfunctional that intelligence failure is guaranteed." In a chillingly prescient passage, he forecast the CIA's many failures:

> Failure may be of the traditional variety: We fail to predict the fall of a friendly government; we do not provide sufficient warning of a surprise attack against one of our allies or interests; we are completely surprised by a state-sponsored terrorist attack; or we fail to detect an unexpected country acquiring a weapon of mass destruction. Or it may take a more nontraditional form: We overstate numerous threats leading to tens of billions of dollars of unnecessary expenditures; database errors lead to a politically unacceptable number of casualties in a peace-enforcement operation; or an operation does not go well because the IC is not able to provide the incredibly specific data necessary to support a new generation of weapons.[32]

Americans have seen most of these scenarios come to pass since Travers wrote.

The CIA and other intelligence agencies defend themselves by suggesting that major historical events—Black Swans, as the writer Nasim Talib calls them—are generally beyond the predictive capacity of intelligence work. One might be more sympathetic to this argument about the caprices of history and human nature if the CIA were better at the job that it supposedly *can* do well: providing reliable and consistent assessment of the military and technological capabilities of its subjects. Yet in May 1998, the CIA and American policymakers were blindsided by India's first successful test of a nuclear weapon.[33] Even if the CIA can't predict a *political* atom bomb such as the end of the Cold War, surely it should be able to report on the detonation of an *actual* atom bomb. Between the Soviet collapse and the Indian nuke, the CIA proved in the 1990s that it was capable of total failure in a diverse array of high-profile and consequential intelligence-gathering operations.

In the wake of 9/11, the agency and other elements of the federal intelligence bureaucracy faced calls for reform. The national intelligence apparatus had devolved into a web of self-interested bureaucracies advancing their own agendas. "The agency, fearful above all else of dismemberment by politicians outraged by its appalling track record, has lied with pathological consistency to presidents and Congresses about its failed missions," wrote a reporter in *The Nation*.[34] Somehow, policymakers decided that the solution to the problem was even more bureaucracy: the creation of the Department of Homeland Security and the Office of National Intelligence.

It hasn't helped. By now, the CIA's utterly worthless intelligence on Iraqi WMDs is part of American political lore. Certainly the political leadership deserves some blame here: The influence of the Pentagon and White House inside the CIA peaked during the early- and mid-2000s, compromising the agency's ability to objectively present materials to the president and others. But had the intelligence community presented a unified and authoritative view of the situation in Iraq, such distortion would have been impossible.[35] One reason the intelligence community was so easily overcome by the political arm was that the extensive turf battles between the CIA and the NSA prevented the agencies from sharing the intelligence each had collected on the same targets. The agency heads tended to put protecting their bureaucratic brethren ahead of national security, so much so that the CIA inspector general's office finally accused the agency of "systemic failure."[36]

More recently, the CIA has been busy as the drone-directing wing of the American military, focusing increasingly on its counterterror operations in Afghanistan and Pakistan. In this capacity, the agency has seen many successes, especially the killing of al-Qaeda leadership through drone strikes. As its focus narrowed, though, the likelihood of another major intelligence failure increased. That failure came in early 2011, when the CIA was once again caught off guard by major global developments: the wave of unrest in the Middle East that would eventually become the Arab Spring.[37] Once again, echoing its excuses for failing to forecast the Soviet collapse, the CIA claimed that it was nearly impossible to predict the "triggering mechanism" that leads to unrest. Not everyone bought it.

"Was someone looking at what was going on, on the Internet?" Senate Intelligence Committee chair Diane Feinstein asked contemptuously during hearings on the matter. Some suggested that the agency's fixation on bin Laden and al-Qaeda had compromised its ability to conduct "long-term strategic analysis and prediction"—but just when was it that the agency excelled at such things, anyway?[38]

The CIA has been of almost no help with North Korea, either—admittedly a tough part of the world about which to get information. But the United States remained completely unaware that Syria was building a nuclear plant in North Korea until Mossad chief Meir Dagan "visited President George W. Bush's national-security adviser and dropped photographs of the reactor on his coffee table." The Israelis destroyed the plant in a 2007 air strike, but American satellite monitoring would later fail to detect the construction of uranium-enrichment facilities at the Yongbyon complex, North Korea's flagship nuclear installation. In 2012, Kim Jong Il's sudden death went completely undetected for 51 hours. Only when North Korean media announced the news did stunned Americans and South Koreans learn of it.[39]

It's not possible to do justice to the depth and scope of the CIA story here, but as this brief sketch should suggest, the agency and the U.S. intelligence community as a whole do not inspire confidence. Reforms have attempted to heal the bureaucratic sclerosis and the corruptions of careerism and turf loyalties, but for the most part, we have succeeded only in making the CIA's organizational flowchart even more complex. As Mark Steyn put it in *National Review*: "Don't ask me why there's a director of national intelligence and a director of central intelligence. Something to do with 9/11, after which the government decided it could use more intelligence. Instead it wound up with more directors of intelligence, which is the way it usually goes in Washington."[40]

We have capabilities, assets, and resources in abundance; what we do not have is an effective organizational approach to using them; nor do we have—most important—the political and strategic commitment to employ them in ways that benefit the national interest. The losses have been costly, and they are mounting.

HOW ECONOMIC TIES WEAKEN U.S. INTELLIGENCE LEVERAGE

A vital and underappreciated aspect of the intelligence situation is that the U.S., by virtue of its close economic and financial ties with China and Russia, is necessarily limited in how it can respond to transgressions. Too much is at stake in other realms for the U.S. to take forceful action.

This is especially true when it comes to China. Most Americans know by now that the federal government is essentially in hock to Beijing. The Chinese government owns about 8 percent of publicly held U.S. debt, making it the third-largest holder behind the Social

Security Trust Fund and the Federal Reserve.[41] China also holds slightly more than a fifth of America's foreign-held Treasury securities. It buys Treasuries at low rates, allowing the U.S. to keep its interest rates low and enabling U.S. companies to finance their operations affordably.[42] Although many feel it's unlikely, some worry about a scenario in which China would liquidate its holdings.

In an interview with the *Daily Telegraph*, two Chinese officials indicated that China could cause the U.S. dollar to collapse if it chose to do so, though they admitted that such an action would also hurt China and the global economy.[43] In a 2011 *China Daily* editorial, Ding Gang, a Communist Party mouthpiece, suggested that China should punish America for selling arms to Taiwan by refusing to buy U.S. Treasury bonds, or "massively reducing" how many it buys:

> Now is the time for China to use its "financial weapon" to teach the United States a lesson if it moves forward with a plan to sale [sic] arms to Taiwan.... some US Congress members hold a contemptuous attitude toward the core interests of China ... China–US relations will always be constrained by these people and will continue along a roller coaster pattern if China does not beat them until they feel the pain.[44]

If China decided to sharply reduce its investments, the results could be a catastrophic spike in American interest rates and a serious recession, if not a depression.[45] Of course, the Chinese also have a strong interest in U.S. economic health: They need us to pay our debts and consume their goods. One might call it a stalemate. But it also means that there is constant maneuvering on both sides of this equation, with each nation trying to gain advantage over the other.

Perhaps the greatest pressure leveled by the Chinese comes from the amount of Western, and in particular American, investment in their economy. In 2009, American investment in China reached $49 billion. American companies have flocked to China to capture business from its vast and expanding middle class, especially as growth in the developed world slows. American multinationals' investment commitment in China shows no sign of lessening. Starbucks, Coca-Cola, Ford, Pepsi, Volkswagen, Las Vegas Sands, and Wynn Resorts were all cited by *Forbes* in 2010 as top investors in China. GM sold more cars in China in 2010 than it did in the United States. In 2009, it closed 10 plants in the United States; since the turn of the century, the automaker has opened 15 plants in China. Yum Brands, the owner of KFC, Pizza Hut, and other fast-food staples, reported $1.2 billion in sales in China in the first quarter of 2010, eclipsing its U.S. sales for the first time.[46] Smaller and midsize companies have also been turning to China in recent years.[47]

To a lesser but still important extent, the U.S.–Russian economic relationship presents entanglements that make it difficult to implement a tougher intelligence policy. Russian commodities have become crucial to some American businesses. Russia exports many key industrial minerals to the United States. These include quartz crystal, thallium, diamonds, potash, cobalt, titanium, palladium, chromium, silicon, nickel, ammonia, ammonium, and magnesium—vital materials in the manufacturing of industrial or electronic components.[48] Russia also exports some industrial components crucial to American business. In 2007, the Russian company OAO VSMPO-Avisma, the world's largest maker of titanium products, signed a $1 billion contract with Boeing to produce titanium forgings for the Boeing 787 Dreamliner.[49]

American financial houses invest substantially in Russian banks, and they keep offices in Moscow that turn big profits for their companies. The Russians know that if Americans are heavily invested in the wealth derived from Moscow's dependent neo-colonies, then hard business sense will dictate caution in dealing with Moscow and its intelligence practices. Here is where the influence game, an important part of the intelligence wars, can be deployed in lieu of traditional espionage. With its open society and markets, the U.S. allows commercial considerations to influence its strategic decisions. This dynamic becomes more insidious when one recognizes how Russia and China have been willing to treat Western businessmen.

CAPITALISM FOR KEEPS: THE AXIS ATTACK ON WESTERN BUSINESSMEN

The global economy has brought great riches to businesses and individuals in the West, as well as in Russia and China. But what appeared to be, on the surface, a force for potential unity and increased comity—former adversaries united by their devotion to markets and economic activity—has had some unexpected results. An open exchange of goods and services has also brought with it easier access for espionage and all manner of secret operations. Whereas, in the Cold War, business relations between the West and the Communist world were strictly circumscribed, no clear boundaries obtain today. The globalization of commerce and finance has created interdependence between large portions of the U.S. economy and the economies of Russia and China.

In the Soviet era, the separation of East and West in all things actually made the intelligence wars easier. Now the battle lines have blurred, and Washington is pressured from multiple angles to soft-pedal its approach so as to protect business interests. Both Russia and China have learned to play the capitalist game, and they do it with a tough-minded focus on global power strategy; their aim is not to bring freedom and prosperity to their own people or to their allies but merely to bring legitimacy to arbitrary rule. They are playing for keeps, while we play for ideals.

The result is that the world of business has become an intelligence battleground. It's a field where, at least for now, the Axis nations have held the upper hand. Western businessmen are constantly followed, wiretapped, intimidated, and even killed—as several high-profile cases have shown.

Neil Heywood and Bo Xilai

Consider the case of British businessman Neil Heywood, an expatriate living in Beijing. The wealthy and well-connected Heywood spoke Mandarin and acted as an intermediary between Chinese and Western firms and the Chinese government. In 2011, he was found dead in a hotel room in Chonqing, allegedly from alcohol poisoning. Heywood's friends said that he was not a heavy drinker. His family was told that he had died of a heart attack. Heywood was cremated without an autopsy.[50]

In February 2012, Chongqing's chief of police, Wang Lijun, was demoted; four days later, he fled to the U.S. Consulate. There, he told a shocking story about Heywood's death and its connection to Bo Xilai, then a popular Chinese politician and party boss in Chongqing, and Bo's wife, Gu Kailai. Wang had worked with Bo to institute punitive police policies, including work camps for criminals.[51] Persuaded to leave the consulate, Wang was immediately arrested by Chinese authorities.[52] Reporters have never fully uncovered what Wang told the Americans at the consulate; the story emerged in fragmentary fashion over several months.

Bo was soon removed from his post as party chief because of his involvement in what had become known as the Wang Lijun Incident. Rumors suggested that Bo and Wang had had a falling out over an investigation into Bo's family on corruption charges. Others claimed that Bo had somehow been involved in Heywood's death. By the end of March, the British government demanded that China reexamine the businessman's death. Bo was eventually stripped of his Communist Party title and, along with his wife, placed under investigation for a possible role in Heywood's death.[53]

As the case unfolded, rumors flew. Some claimed that Heywood and Gu had had an affair; others suggested that Heywood had somehow been involved in illegal business dealings with Bo or Gu, or both. Others suggested that Gu had demanded that Heywood divorce his Chinese wife and commit to her. There was even the hint of a possible espionage component: It came out that Heywood had connections to a firm started by ex-MI6 agents.[54]

The increasingly sordid incident led to the downfall of almost every person involved. In August, Gu Kailai and her aide, Zhang Xiaojun, stood trial for the intentional murder of Heywood. She received a "suspended death penalty," or life in prison, for poisoning Heywood with cyanide.[55] By the end of September, Wang Lijun had also been tried and convicted—in his case for defection, power abuse, and taking bribes. Bo was charged with obstructing the investigation into Heywood's death, wiretapping other Party officials, and even engaging in illicit sexual relations with multiple women.[56]

We'll probably never know the truth about Neil Heywood's demise, though it seems clearly bound up with corruption, espionage, and international business. The scandal illustrates not only the shadowy relations between Chinese business and government but also the inability of foreign governments to protect their nationals. Heywood's alleged connections to the MI6, and the fact that his death took place against the backdrop of a massive power transition within the Communist Party, could suggest that he was a pawn of Communist Party machinations beyond his control.

The Hermitage Capital Scandal and the Death of Sergei Magnitsky

Hermitage Capital, an investment fund based in Guernsey, England, was once one of the largest foreign investors in Russia. Its CEO, William Browder, was a vocal champion of Russian investment. He tirelessly combated negative media stereotypes about the Russian government and Russian business.

Then, without warning, in 2005, while Browder was on a routine trip from London, Russian officials barred him from entering the country. Somehow, his name had found its way onto a list of individuals considered security threats to Russia. *Bloomberg Businessweek* speculated at the time that private interests had placed Browder's name on the list, given that he was an outspoken supporter of the Russian government's.[57] Browder discussed the issue with then–Deputy Prime Minister Dmitri Medvedev, but to no avail.[58]

In February 2007, Lieutenant Colonel Artem Kuznetsov of the Russian Interior Ministry contacted Hermitage. Kuznetsov claimed he could resolve Browder's visa problem in exchange for certain information, favors, or money. Four months later, he returned with 25 officers to raid Hermitage's offices. The offices of Firestone Duncan, Hermitage's lawyer, were also raided. Kuznetsov claimed to be investigating tax evasion by Kameya, a Hermitage company. Hermitage claimed that one of their lawyers had been severely beaten during the raid and needed hospitalization for two weeks. As it turned out, shortly before the raid, Russian tax authorities had issued a report indicating that Kamaya had committed no wrongdoing.[59]

Moreover, according to Hermitage, an obscure company called Pluton—if it even was a company—dispatched lawyers to surrender Hermitage assets under false premises.[60] Finally, fed up with the intimidation and cloak-and-dagger tactics, Hermitage instructed Sergei Magnitsky, a top Firestone Duncan lawyer, to investigate.

Magnitsky quickly determined that the charges against Hermitage were fraudulent. He also discovered what might be the greatest fraud scheme in Russian history. Evidence indicated that the Russian police had stolen documents, corporate seals, and other information about Hermitage's subsidiaries that allowed them to produce forgeries of important Hermitage documents. Magnitsky alleged that $260 million in taxes that Hermitage had paid to the Russian government had been stolen in a complex network of phantom claims, orchestrated with the compliance of judges, policemen, tax officials, and government agents.[61]

One of the policemen whom Magnitsky identified was then assigned to investigate him—and in short order, Magnitsky was himself accused of tax evasion and sent to jail. For more than a year, while awaiting trial, he was detained in a prison, denied family visits and even medical attention when he developed pancreatitis. In November 2009, Magnitsky was taken to the medical unit and placed in a straitjacket. He died shortly thereafter.[62]

This horrifying story—as heartbreaking as it is mysterious—led multiple agencies to investigate the Russian government's behavior. The Public Oversight Commission, a Moscow-based watchdog, interviewed doctors charged with Magnitsky's treatment.

"I did not consider Magnitsky sick," Ivan Prokopenko, the head of the detention center where Magnitsky was being held, told the commission. "Prisoners often try to pass themselves off as sick, in order to get better conditions. We are all sick."

However, having reviewed this testimony against those of the doctors and other officials, one of the commission's investigators, Zoya Svetova, stated: "I had the impression that Magnitsky died because of doctors' negligence, because they thought he had invented his illness. . . . Now I have the frightening feeling that it was not negligence but that it was, to some extent, as terrible as it is to say, a premeditated murder."[63]

Then–Prime Minister Medvedev launched a number of investigations. One found, not surprisingly, that the charges against Magnitsky were fabricated; another accused two doctors of criminal negligence. A sawmill foreman was convicted of involvement in the crime ring. Medvedev promised further investigations. "It is an incident that needs a very thorough investigation," he said. "First of all, what really happened and why he was taken into custody, who was behind that, what deals were clinched by both those he represented and by the other side. I have asked the prosecutor general and Ministry of Interior to work on that."[64] But to date, no investigations have been conducted on the eight most senior officials involved in the case.[65]

Hermitage CEO William Browder began lobbying Washington to take strong action against Russia. In December 2012, the U.S. House and Senate passed the Sergei Magnitsky Rule of Law Accountability Act, which condemned Russian human-rights abuses and barred individuals accused of such abuses—such as those in the Magnitsky affair—from traveling to the U.S., owning property here, or using U.S. banks.[66] (Unfortunately, barely more than a year after the Magnitsky Bill was signed, the Obama administration is already backing away from its promise to tighten the sanctions. In December 2013, Deputy National Security Adviser Ben Rhodes announced, "We are not anticipating adding new names to the [Magnitsky list]—certainly by the end of the year or in the near future, early next year."[67] As the *Wall Street Journal* pointed out, it's not as if Russia's human-rights record has miraculously improved in the meantime. In an interview, Rhodes provided a clue: He praised Moscow's role in making a deal with Syrian President Assad over his chemical-weapons stockpile.[68])

The 2012 passage of the Magnitsky Law set off a diplomatic row between the United States and Russia. The Russians, in turn, banned Americans accused of human-rights violations from entering Russia and also passed a law ending U.S. adoption of Russian children. "It is strange and savage to hear human-rights claims from politicians of the state that officially legalized torture and kidnappings all over the world in the 21st century," said the Russian Foreign Ministry.[69]

The ugliness of the case continues, as shown by the recent death of Alexander Perepilichny, a Russian whistleblower involved in it.

Perepilichny was found dead in Surrey, England, in November 2012. He was wearing running clothes and appeared to have died of a stroke, but he was 44 and healthy, and an autopsy proved inconclusive. He had approached Hermitage Capital with documents relating to the fraud that Magnitsky had uncovered. Perepilichny feared for his life and had sought refuge in Britain in 2009. At the time of his death, he was helping Swiss investigators research systematic fraud in the Russian tax system.[70]

This kind of intimidation is not confined to businessmen; it has also been used to silence adversaries in the intelligence wars. Particularly in Russia, the law of the jungle applies to spies who cross the Kremlin.

SECRECY AND LAWLESSNESS IN PUTIN'S RUSSIA

Alexander "Sasha" Litvinenko was an agent in the Russian Federal Security Service (FSB), the successor to the KGB. He worked in the divisions of counterterrorism and organized crime. In 1998, he was assigned to a special undercover unit tasked with clandestine assassinations of mob bosses and terrorist leaders. But he told Russian reporters that he learned the FSB unit was not in fact focused on catching criminals. Instead, his missions that year had included the assassination of whistleblowers, kidnapping and ransoming the brother of a billionaire hotel owner, and attempting to assassinate Boris Berezovsky, a powerful oligarch.[71]

Based on Litvinenko's statements, the FSB fired its top official and replaced him with a reformer named Vladimir Putin. Litvinenko tried to persuade Putin that the FSB had been penetrated by criminal elements, but he sensed that Putin wasn't interested. Litvinenko's wife, Marina, said that he came home one evening, after meeting with Putin, and said: "This new guy's not right. He has a limp handshake, he doesn't look me in the eye. He's so paranoid he's brought his own driver from St. Petersburg. He's not interested in clearing up corruption." Litvinenko's phone lines were bugged that very evening.[72]

Litvinenko was soon arrested, along with Alexander Gusak, his department chief. They were sent to Lefortovo prison, which Litvinenko described as "a place that crushed you spiritually."[73] No sooner were they cleared of one charge than another would emerge. Months later, Litvinenko was released, but he was forbidden from leaving Moscow. In August 2000, he managed to arrange for a "vacation" on the Black Sea with his wife and son. With the help of Berezovsky, whose life he had saved, Litvinenko managed to secure his escape. In November, he arrived at Heathrow Airport.[74]

The British provided aliases for Litvinenko and his family. He began to wage battle against the FSB, accusing the organization of transporting drugs, training terrorists, and perpetrating acts of terror that the government tried to pin on Chechen rebels. He published several books, although his evidence was circumstantial and widely dismissed. His timing was bad: After the September 11 attacks of 2001, the world—and especially the West—was not sympathetic to accusations against Putin, our ally in the War on Terror.[75]

In 2006, Litvinenko fell into the trap that would kill him, when he agreed to meet with Andrei Lugovoy, a former KGB director and prisoner of Lefortovo. Lugovoy offered some documents to Litvinenko, which he promised might be useful. The precise details of the two men's meetings in London remain unclear.[76]

On November 1, 2006, Litvinenko became desperately ill. He first came down with severe gastrointestinal symptoms; later, his hair fell out and his skin turned yellow. He was hospitalized and soon afterward suggested that he had been deliberately poisoned. Police tried fruitlessly to discover the cause of his illness. A few weeks later, Litvinenko died of what had turned out to be poisoning from Polonium-210—an extraordinarily rare radioactive isotope. Workers at a specialized lab at the Ministry of Defense had determined the cause of his illness just three hours before his death.[77] Two days before he died, Litvinenko composed a chilling note that later appeared in the media.

"You may succeed in silencing me, but that silence comes at a price," he wrote. "You have shown yourself to have no respect for life, liberty, or any civilised value. You may succeed in silencing one man. But a howl of protest from around the world will reverberate, Mr. Putin, in your ears for the rest of your life."[78]

A British investigation demonstrated that, before his death, Litvinenko had been a paid agent of MI6 and had been preparing to fly to Spain to assist in an investigation into KGB misdeeds. He was also working with the MI6's Spanish counterpart. Investigators tracked the Polonium-210 back to a hotel where Litvinenko had met Lugovoy, and even to a teacup from which Litvinenko drank. Litvinenko's associates alleged that the tea was laced with poison. The British government eventually agreed and accused Lugovoy of murdering Litvinenko.[79]

The Russian government and secret services denied any role in Litvinenko's death. The British demanded that Lugovoy be extradited to Britain for trial. Moscow refused. The Russians then promoted Lugovoy to a higher military rank and a parliamentary seat, making him immune to prosecution.[80]

Litvinenko's widow, Marina, has vocally demanded justice, yet, as time passes, relations between the two countries, badly bruised by the affair, show signs of easing.[81] The British government blocked the coroner's call for a public inquiry, saying that a public hearing would risk exposing sensitive national-security secrets. "Were they trying to protect the Russian state?" Marina asked. An inquest is ongoing, but it will not have the broad mandate that a public inquiry would have commanded.[82]

Not the least of the questions the case arouses is that of motive. If Litvinenko was working for MI6 or the Spanish government, was that involvement alone sufficient to earn him a deadly reprisal? Before his death, Litvinenko was preparing to travel to Spain, where he planned to present evidence to investigators of ties between the Russian mafia and the Kremlin. Was he silenced to prevent this information from coming to light? In 2012, testimony revealed a bizarre twist to the story. On his upcoming trip, Litvinenko was set to travel with none other than the man who presumably murdered him—Andrei Lugovoy.[83]

*****

In March 2012, as the Litvinenko case made its way through the British courts, Russian banker German Gorbuntsov became another high-profile target of a Russian assassination. Once again, the attack took place in London.

Gorbuntsov was a wealthy businessman who had owned a number of Russian and Moldovan banks. Near his home in London's Canary Wharf, he was sprayed with a semiautomatic machine gun and hit six times, collapsing on the scene. After being placed in a medically induced coma, amazingly, he survived and recovered.[84]

Gorbuntsov gave extensive interviews detailing what he believed had caused the attack. He had come to Britain, he said, in order to escape his former business associates, whom he believed were trying to kill him. He was shocked when Britain turned out to be almost as dangerous as Moscow: "I thought that in London you are safe, and this kind of thing can't happen here."[85] In his view, he was targeted because he was preparing to give evidence to Russian prosecutors about a failed assassination attempt on his former business partner, Alexander Antonov, who was shot in Moscow in 2009. Gorbuntsov claimed that common business partners had targeted him and Antonov. "I think it was because I was ready to give evidence," he said. "They decided that if there is no person, there's no problem."[86]

Gorbuntsov told reporters that several high-ranking Russian officials with ties to Putin had conspired to kill him. While this has not been proved, the case clearly is linked in some way with high-level Russian politics. One of the Chechen hit men who killed Ruslan Yamadayev, an enemy of Chechnya's pro-Kremlin president, allegedly also shot Antonov.[87] Moreover, a source revealed that in the week before Gorbuntsov was shot, Russian prosecutors were planning to fly to the UK to obtain testimony from him about the Yamadayev and Antonov cases. They cancelled the trip without explanation days before the shooting.[88]

In 2010, Gorbuntsov had claimed that criminal raiders forced him to sign over $1 billion in assets. The raiders boasted of their connections within the FSB as well as the mafia. His protests to the FSB and to police were ignored.[89] Russian prosecutors have still not spoken with him, probably because of the ties between his enemies and the Kremlin. "The evidence I have is enough to put them behind bars," he said. "Of course they have good connections, but I'd like to believe there is justice in Russia."[90]

The Gorbuntsov case is another clear illustration of how, under Vladimir Putin, the "new" Russia has retained many of the worst authoritarian and repressive tendencies of its Soviet predecessor. In fact, with the help of modern technologies, the new Russia has honed some of these repressive practices to a degree of sophistication not possible or conceivable in the old Soviet days.

CONCLUSION

For millions of Americans, victory in the Cold War seemed to augur the end not only of the dreaded specter of nuclear annihilation but also of the kind of spying and intelligence theft that the two adversaries had practiced against each other. But just as the Soviet Union's demise has not eradicated the challenge of nuclear security, it also has not brought an end to the spy game. Only its nature has changed.

The West's Cold War victory has opened up a more complex and more challenging, even more dangerous, intelligence landscape. We are in a new phase, for which we have yet to find a doctrinal response. Russian destabilization of Ukraine, for instance, relied heavily on what close observers considered classic KGB tactics, updated for contemporary circumstances. "What we're seeing are practices and capabilities that are inherent in the Russian intelligence system, but they have been brought back and reinvigorated with new funding and emphasis by Putin," says Nikolas Gvosdev, a specialist in Russian security affairs at the U.S. Naval War College. "Some of it goes back to Soviet times and Soviet intelligence, when there was a great deal of emphasis placed on how you organize front groups to disguise your intentions. Another important element is how you always organize things to give yourself 'plausible deniability.'"[91]

Assassinations, as we have seen in Putin's Russia, have become mere problems of law enforcement—problems with no outcome. Mysteries never quite get solved. The beneficiary, however, is always the Kremlin. In the Cold War era, we would have extended protection to regime critics, promising them a new life and the possibility of freedom and safety. Today, no survivors of such treatment testify before Congress or defect to the West while seeking asylum. Even if they did, they wouldn't necessarily expect to survive.

Along different lines, China has also embraced the age of global economics and information exchange for its own purposes. As we described in our "Cyber Wars" chapter, Beijing is the world's leading cyber thief, and its assault on Western, especially American, targets occurs daily. It is in the cyber arena that China is waging much of its intelligence warfare. China's intelligence efforts, however, have subtler aspects, intimately related to the global economy and to the U.S.–China trade relationship. Although the Communist Party remains in power,

China's embrace of global capitalism and technology has made it a much more decentralized adversary than in the days of Mao. Combined with its economic leverage—especially over the United States, its debtor—this new nimbleness serves the regime's purposes well.

During the Cold War, the Soviets would never have dared intrude into the communications of Americans at home and abroad. These days, American diplomats, employees of banks, news media, NGOs, oil companies, chemical companies, entertainment personnel, and numerous other professionals fully expect to be monitored wherever they are in Russia and China—as well as at home in the U.S. Thus we see an irony of the triumph of market capitalism: The free flow of information and labor across borders was supposed to soften the power of totalitarian governments. Instead, the Axis has successfully used the new freedoms to extend the reach of oppressive or coercive state behavior, which is now easier to engage in and harder to scrutinize. Decentralization, long touted as a positive force for spreading democracy, has turned out to be a mixed blessing. Now, instead of trying to identify the relevant spokes on one wheel, we are dealing with seemingly countless wheels.

Yet the challenge the United States faces in this area is ultimately one not of capacity but of will. We are certainly capable of taking a harder line against Putin's various depredations and human-rights abuses, and we can set in place firmer policies with regard to Beijing's economic coercion. But to respond more forcefully, we must first recognize that our adversaries do not bear us good will and are not susceptible to mere pleas. No resource should be spared to provide better protections for our military, technological, and private-sector secrets. At the same time, the U.S. must find a way to strengthen the performance of our intelligence community, which exacts a lavish price tag from taxpayers even though it underperforms, again and again, when it matters most.

If the Cold War terrain has changed, one fact hasn't: The same battle for global dominance across the continents continues, only under different names. Russia and China understand this; the United States and the West seem unwilling to acknowledge it. We do not participate in the intelligence game with the same intensity as Moscow or Beijing. They know what they're playing for and what they're willing to do to achieve their goals.

Can the same be said about the United States and its Western allies?

CHAPTER 8

Propaganda Wars: Losing Ground in the Battle for Hearts and Minds

"The core, the binding fabric of this unique civilization—is the Russian people, Russian culture."

—VLADIMIR PUTIN[1]

"To achieve the great revival of the Chinese nation, we must ensure there is unison between a prosperous country and strong military."

—XI JINPING[2]

"I believe in American exceptionalism, just as I suspect that the Brits believe in British exceptionalism and the Greeks believe in Greek exceptionalism."

—BARACK OBAMA[3]

"You're bandits. Democratic bandits. You've destroyed thousands, maybe millions of people [in Iraq and Afghanistan]. I'm living through being democratised with a truncheon on the head by the West every day. Who needs that kind of democracy?" Thus spoke Alexander Lukashenko of Belarus, in a rare interview.[4] Lukashenko is widely known as the "last dictator in Europe" owing to his obviously fixed elections and repression of dissent.

In the same interview, given to a London *Independent* reporter in 2012, he cited the chaos after the fall of the Soviet Union and argued that he had brought safety and security to his country. "These were terrible years of anarchy, and not only in Russia. I don't need your democracy! Belarusians don't need this democracy if there's no economy. If a man can't work in his own country and earn his living, if he can't take a piece of land, if he can't build a house, plant a tree, raise his children because he's scared to let them go outside."[5]

No one who lived through the Russia of the 1990s—with its endemic corruption, violence, massive unemployment, and spiraling social problems—wants to go back there. What the Belarus dictator offers instead is stability: "So Lukashenko is a bad guy! Go out on the street, look around—everything is clean, neat, normal people walking around. There's no way that the dictator can't take at least some credit for that."[6] More recently, Belarus's economy has faltered, but the dictator's argument has been persuasive to many—and he is one of Vladimir Putin's staunchest allies. During a May 2012 visit, Putin referred to "brotherly Belarus" and praised "the special nature of our relations."[7]

A few months later, in Beijing, more than 500 rural Chinese farmers paraded through the streets holding portraits of Mao. "Down with the Japanese imperialists!" they chanted. They had come to the capital from Heibei Province, a distance requiring a bus trip—the kind of transportation and logistics that suggested a government role. "How else could 500 farmers come from the provinces?" asked a Chinese blogger.[8]

The farmers were just one part of a broader national protest in September 2012. Huge crowds trashed Japanese-owned businesses—a Panasonic plant, a Toyota dealership, and 7-Eleven stores, among others. They torched Japanese model cars. Chinese police helped direct the protests, steering the demonstrators to proper areas. "I need to lead the crowd and guide them to march in an orderly fashion," a policeman wrote.[9]

September 18 is a traditional day of protest in China, commemorating the Japanese invasion of Manchuria. But at the same time, with the two nations mired in an intense dispute over a set of islands in the East China Sea, the protests had a contemporary feel. And their massive size and seamless coordination seemed to make clear that the Communist Party was directing the dissent toward a desired target—the Japanese—both to whip up nationalist sentiment and tamp down internal criticism of the regime's domestic policies. Nationalism has long served that function for governments.

Lukashenko's devotion to order and Beijing's appeal to nationalism are just two instances that illustrate the broader phenomenon of Axis and Axis-friendly countries rallying public support by appealing to fundamental, visceral impulses: the need for stability, the fear of chaos, anger at foreigners, and nationalist pride. All these elements, and others, form what has become an increasingly compelling Axis propaganda model—one that implicitly and explicitly rejects the Western democratic model of openness, untrammeled free markets, and a liberal, tolerant, multicultural society. For millions, these ideals, which Americans especially hold dear, are dangerous and threatening.

After the Soviet Union fell, many assumed that the Western model—individual liberty, democracy, and economic freedom—had been as responsible for the triumph as military might. Yet two decades later, we seem to be losing the argument. Why?

In large part, it's because the world has arrived at one of those cyclic stages where upheaval induces fatigue and fear. Electorates around the world are exhausted by the radical changes that globalism, free markets, and democracy have ushered in. They wish to slow down the rate of change, and they have elected dictators who promise them stability and protection; they have tolerated the abrogation of democratic freedoms for the sake of order. The Axis takes advantage of such fears. They make Americanization synonymous with a multitude of sins—especially chaos.

What we are seeing is a massive challenge to the Western worldview. Around the world, events have seemed to contradict our fundamental assumptions. Freedom has brought not wealth to millions, but dissolution of wealth—first in the post-Soviet years in the Warsaw Pact countries, then in South America, and finally in Europe and the U.S. after the financial crisis. Assessing the rivalry between India and China, the world saw better economic results for the less democratic model in China. The example of Iraq also weighed against the West. Who wants freedom if it leads to carnage?

Russia and China have used this new skepticism about freedom to develop appeals and arguments for their hybrid systems, which are far from democratic yet not as monolithic as the old Communist powers. This hybrid quality, in fact, is the key to their appeal: Russia and China promise economic prosperity and national security, but they also make clear that the American promise of individual rights is not part of the package. Millions in Russia, China, and elsewhere have embraced these alternative models.

For all the concern we have expressed over military and nuclear strength, about cyber-war tactics and economic competition, the war over ideas and values is every bit as important. It is this field of conflict that could determine the outcome of the struggle. America and the West offer the same set of compelling values to the world as we always have, and these values remain humanity's best hope. But we are failing to convince the world of this as we once did (and it's hard not to wonder if we're failing because we doubt these values ourselves). Faced with rapid and often frightening change across the globe, we are not offering a clear road map to the future.

Russia and China do, and they busily make their case, in word and deed.

THE AXIS VALUE PROPOSITION

At first glance, except for their unifying anti-Americanism, there could be no more disparate countries than Russia and China. Ethnically, culturally, and geographically, they inhabit largely different worlds. One might describe Russia as a once-socialist, pseudo-democratic oligopoly and China as a pseudo-socialist, market-oriented, one-party state. But, in fact, they share fundamental political and economic flaws.

Both suffer from deep and widespread corruption. Both operate a barely disguised kleptocracy from the top down. Both are run by elites terrified of the instability inherent in the system's inequities. Simmering ethnic issues trouble both countries with no apparent solution on the horizon other than intimidation and repression, while the majority ethnic group equates the nation's cultural identity with its own. And, of course, lack of transparency in government goes hand in hand with rule by cliques, closed networks, and mafias.

Add up these elements and you get strong clues to why Western social and political principles pose an active threat to the Axis nations. You also get a definitive explanation for the kind of messages the Axis feeds to its citizens at home and allies abroad: a tacit ideology heavy with pressure to conform. Axis propaganda derives directly from the systemic weaknesses in Russia and China, and from the need to hide them while offering compensatory illusions.

One such illusion is nostalgia for national greatness—in a word, nationalism, which Axis elites use more and more frequently to rally their domestic populations. The purpose and the effect of this dangerous tool we all know from historical precedents.

The notion of national greatness is part of a broader illusion involving a theme of conservatism at home and abroad—a pivotal development that the West has yet to notice or address. Meanwhile, the true activating principle of the state is continuity in power, with all the methods of modern surveillance and control deployed to head off trouble wherever it might arise. Shutting down untrammeled free speech by controlling the media, the Internet, and foreign NGOs fits into the strategy, along with mysterious assassinations that rub out vocal dissidents and whistleblowers.

Even more troublingly, the Axis has had great success in exporting its formula actively and by example. More and more countries now seem to prefer the Axis model of curbing opposition by invoking national exigencies, even when individual countries profess a closer allegiance to the West. Large swaths of the globe now desire stability above all, and they are thus more receptive to Axis propaganda, which promises exactly that. Across Eastern Europe, from Hungary through Belarus to Ukraine and Georgia, from Turkey to Egypt across the Middle East and Central Asia, the Putinist example has become the norm: jailing journalists and opponents, suborning the judiciary, censoring websites, and controlling media ownership while amassing executive power. The great wave of democratic movements championed by the U.S. during the post-Soviet era has hit a wall. Many states now operate from a fear of internal weakness. The West has failed to anticipate the wave of conservatism overtaking the globe; the Axis is deeply tuned in to it.

In contrast to the sometimes vague aspirational principles that America espouses, China and Russia focus on promoting things people need—food and jobs—or, failing that, things that people feel passionately about, such as national identity, religion, or culture. China achieves this by implicitly bribing its populace: In exchange for political docility, it enriches its citizens. The message is clear to potential allies such as Sudan or Zimbabwe: China can use the same methods to help keep other regimes in power. Russia offers a different method: appeals to culture, religion, morality, Russian pride, and anti-Americanism.

A closer look at both models makes clear how compelling they are for troubled populations, especially when compared with the muddled, amorphous American message. Two case studies—one Russian, one Chinese—illustrate the tenacity of the Axis nations in putting their models into practice. They succeed not only through their ruthlessness but also through the clarity of their vision. This was never more apparent than in the Georgian elections of 2012.

What Happened in Georgia, and Why It Matters

On October 1, 2012, the pro-American, former Soviet Republic of Georgia held a national parliamentary election. The winning party would nominate its leader as prime minister. The prime minister would work closely with President Mikheil Saakashvili, perhaps the most vocal anti-Kremlin head of state still in power around Russia's periphery. Georgia was invaded by Russian tanks in 2008. Large chunks of Georgian territory had been occupied, including regions held by separatists, which were then effectively integrated into the Russian Federation. Moscow had ripped away and swallowed pieces of Georgia—this after centuries of Czarist and Soviet domination. Anti-Russian feeling in Georgia was centuries old. Yet in the 2012 election, the opposition party, Georgian Dream—what many called the pro-Moscow party—won the election.

How was this possible in a country that had virtually defined its post-Soviet identity through its refusal to kowtow to Russia, in a country that had escaped from Russian domination despite massive pressure? What happened to the Georgian people that they would elect a leader so clearly linked to their mortal enemies in the Kremlin? How was the electorate persuaded to vote against the incumbent party that had delivered modernization, growth, transparency, and dynamism—even through a global recession—at a rate unprecedented in Georgian history?

Propaganda, that's how.

Bidzina Ivanishvili, a 56-year-old Georgian oligarch, headed up Georgian Dream. It was no secret that Ivanishvili's money came from Moscow, where he had lived until 2003. In an attempt to de-emphasize his Moscow connections, the oligarch made a show of selling his Russian properties in the months preceding the election. Behind the smoke and mirrors of the media blitz, nobody knew exactly what Ivanishvili owned, how much of it he had sold, and how much he was able to take out of Russia—especially at a time when Putin had signed a decree forcing oligarchs to repatriate funds they had stashed abroad. It was public knowledge that Ivanishvili could not sell his shares in Gazprom and Lukoil without special permission from the Kremlin. It doesn't take a conspiracy theorist to conclude that Moscow permitted him to withdraw tens of millions—by some estimates, more than $100 million—in order to influence the elections.

Some 10 days before the vote, Georgia's opposition TV stations began showing grainy black-and-white videos of prison abuse apparently secretly taped in Georgian prisons. The images were lurid, including scenes of a man being sodomized with a broomstick. The videos had an instant, electrifying effect on the mood of the country. The international media picked up the videos, and political pressure intensified. Saakashvili and his party found themselves on the defensive, taking heat from all sides. He fired several key officials, including the interior minister and the head of prisons, while arresting others and promising a full-scale investigation. Meanwhile, the opposition exhorted its supporters to hit the streets and demonstrate against government corruption and secrecy.

The videos came at the end of a long, behind-the-scenes battle for leverage over the election process. Saakashvili's government faced a clandestine, hydra-headed campaign to corrupt the political process in myriad ways, beginning almost a year before the election, when Ivanishvili first declared his intention to enter the race and unite the fragmented opposition. According to authorities, his brother, who owned a large satellite-dish company, bought people's votes by giving them free dishes.[10]

Meanwhile, Ivanishvili, who had given money to the Georgian Church for years, exploited his connections for maximum political impact, and "in some localities priests and bishops actively campaigned against the government."[11] Any attempt to move against the church in a country as religious as Georgia would be disastrous.

Ivanishvili threatened to bring a million people onto the streets if Georgian Dream lost.[12] Apparently it never occurred to him that he could lose legitimately. Indeed, with such threats, he merely aped the spontaneous processes that had marked the so-called Color Revolutions of the 2000s, in which the populace in regions of the former Soviet Union, the Balkans, and elsewhere rose up, in each case, against stolen elections. But Ivanishvili's threats contained more sinister undercurrents than the generally nonviolent approach of the earlier revolutionaries in places such as Ukraine in 2004 and Kyrgyzstan in 2005.

What terrified the Saakashvili administration most was a scenario in which Ivanishvili's mobs would reject a negative election outcome and take to the streets (with robust financial support), causing such sustained paralysis that the government would have to fight street battles to oust them. This would offer the Russians an excuse to intervene militarily "to restore peace and stability"—the old excuse, one that they'd used to invade Georgia in 2008. The pressure applied not only to the post-election period but also to the election itself, because the opposition also threatened to send mobs to voting centers to "protect the vote" and ensure fairness.

In effect, the planners of Georgian Dream's campaign had neatly trapped the Saakashvili administration in a political checkmate even before the people expressed their preference. The public quietly concluded that the most peaceful way forward lay in voting for the challenger, Ivanishvili. For its part, if it wished to avoid a possible destruction of the country, Saakashvili's ruling party simply could not afford to win.

And so, on Election Day, Ivanishvili prevailed with 55 percent of the vote. Within a month of taking office as prime minister, he began arresting and prosecuting leaders of Saakashvili's pro-Western party, many of whom had vocally criticized the Kremlin in previous years. The message was clear: Georgians could say good-bye to Western-style democratic processes of the sort they had enjoyed under President Saakashvili.

The 2012 Georgian elections offer a glimpse of how the Axis is winning the global propaganda struggle. Here is a country that astonishingly voted against its interests, even its emotions, and chose to realign itself with its centuries-long oppressor. The outcome of the elections should act as a huge slap in the face for all those who believe in American values and Western leadership as the best hope for humanity. We should all wake up to a new reality, one in which our principles are not self-evident and do not automatically generate support.

We are facing a highly effective antidotal force—not only from Moscow but also from Beijing. It is illustrative to take a look at how the Chinese government orchestrated political protests against Japan to shore up support for the Communist Party and galvanize nationalistic sentiment.

Protest, Beijing-Style

"Just skip to the main course and drop an atomic bomb," the state-run *Beijing Evening News* declared. "Simpler."[13] The newspaper made this startling pronouncement in September 2012 in reference to Japan, which had just purchased from a private landholder part of the Senkaku Islands—known as the Diaoyu Islands in China—an archipelago that has long been disputed between the two nations (as discussed in Chapter 4). Tokyo's purchase seemed to push official organs of the Chinese government and media establishment over the edge. A few days after the sale, the Chinese navy sent six surveillance vessels to the islands' shores, prompting a protest by the Japanese government.

"Is Japan prepared for the consequences of its odious acts?" asked the *People's Daily*. Ten Chinese generals, quoted in Hong Kong's *South China Morning Post*, declared that the People's Liberation Army was "ready to take Japan on."[14] Meanwhile, around Beijing and across the country, massive anti-Japan protests were under way. They coincided with the 81st anniversary of Japan's invasion of Manchuria on September 18, a day of annual commemoration in China. But under the influence of the Senkaku dispute, the historical observances transformed into exhibits of intense nationalist frenzy. Soon enough, the demonstrations became destructive and violent.

Popular outrage was widespread. A hot bowl of noodle soup was thrown in the face of a Japanese man in Shanghai; the scene, also in Shanghai, of a Japanese car burning in front of anti-Japan banners in the background was photographed and circulated online.[15] Protests took place across China. The demonstrations of several hundred outside the Japanese Embassy in Beijing were relatively orderly, though the crowd angrily demanded that China assert its control over the islands. The rallies in more than 50 other cities from Shanghai to Guangzhou to Qingdao were more raucous and occasionally violent.[16] In Qingdao, locals looted a Toyota dealership and set fire to a factory owned by Panasonic.

In a country that prizes order above all other things, one might expect that such mass unrest—even if directed against another country—

would make the political and media establishments uneasy. Not this time. The *People's Daily* praised the protests as an apt symbol of Chinese patriotism and suggested that anything less energetic would paint the Chinese as a weak people: "No one would doubt the pulses of patriotic fervor when the motherland is bullied," the paper wrote in an editorial. "No one would fail to understand the compatriots' hatred and fights when the country is provoked; because a people that has no guts and courage is doomed to be bullied, and a country that always hides low and bides its time will always come under attack."[17] The protests even reached Japan's shores. "New scores and old scores will be settled together," read a cardboard sign carried by Chinese men protesting in Tokyo.[18]

All told, the anti-Japan demonstrations were of a size and energy not seen in China, perhaps, since the Tiananmen protests of 1989. But the 2012 protests differed from the 1989 demonstrations in two crucial respects: First, the people's target was not the Communist Party leadership in Beijing but another country; second, the government wholeheartedly endorsed the protests. In fact, there is a good case to be made that the government orchestrated them. Conspicuous signs of government direction include the aforementioned 500 rural farmers, who could not have traveled to Beijing without government transport. Most of these protestors didn't speak the local language and didn't have rail passes.

It's also undeniable that the state-run media incited the protests; it practically begged people to act up. Tapping into long-held resentment against the Japanese for their historical abuses in Manchuria, the media skillfully fostered a climate of anger.

Chinese police played a crucial collaborative role as well. After protests became particularly heated, the Chinese government sent large numbers of police to oversee the demonstrations—for example, ensuring that protestors in front of the Japanese Embassy in Beijing didn't get out of hand. Each group of protestors was brought by the police to the embassy, given some time to throw government-supplied water bottles and express their feelings, and then whisked off to make room for the next group. During the rally outside the embassy, a police station played a recording telling the protestors that the government shared their concerns and supported their vocal, patriotic protest, but the recording also asked people to remain orderly and follow instructions. Plainclothes officers outside the embassy directed two journalists, whom they had misidentified as protesters, to a location where they could join the demonstration.[19]

One longtime foreign resident in China was convinced that "the whole thing was a fake." The resident, who spoke to *The Economist*, suggested that "every single person with their fist in the air" was a member of either the Chinese army or police force who had been "assigned to compulsory duty to fake the protest."[20] While that may be an exaggeration, given that anti-Japanese feeling in China is genuine and has been around a long time, it's likely that the government played a substantial role in ginning up protest fever, channeling it in the proper direction, and then bringing it to a satisfactory conclusion.

"The party is skilled a manipulating such public opinion . . . and the signs that these demonstrations were organized by the government is very high," said Liu Junning, a Chinese political analyst. "The protests come when the leaders need one to come, and the protests will stop when they want them to stop."[21]

Sure enough, the state-run media began to change its tone after several days of demonstrations, signaling that Beijing was ready to wind them down. The mood in the media shifted rapidly as the state decided that the protests had run their course. Though statewide news agencies had supported the protests earlier and even tacitly approved of the use of violence in those protests, the New China News Agency suddenly removed anti-Japanese content and then ran new editorials urging restraint.

"Irrational, violent anti-Japanese protests should be avoided," wrote a Communist Party newspaper, the *Global Times*.[22] And they were. Soon, Beijing's streets were quiet again. The protests had served their purpose, and Beijing had given the world a lesson in a seamlessly managed, 21st-century propaganda campaign.

THE MUDDLED AMERICAN MESSAGE VS. THE NEW CONSERVATISM

When compared with determined political and communications operations like the ones just described, America's model seems very ill-fitted to the current tasks. We have prevailed before against ruthless adversaries, and there is no reason we cannot do so again. But we face a new and more complex set of conditions and circumstances that require a creative response and determined rethinking. For a country so well versed in the arts of marketing, we have become surprisingly reluctant to market ourselves, and when we do make PR efforts, we're incompetent. Our approach, we all believe, is better for many reasons—for happiness, for freedom, for liberation of talent, for equal rights. But we cannot win that argument if we don't understand the arguments against it—they are not the same as they were during the Cold War.

Unfortunately, our approach remains naive. We tell ourselves that in our system, freedom stands supreme and that the open friction of ideas ultimately produces the best outcomes. Too often, the result is that the U.S. serves up a babble of contradictory messages, emanating from numerous sources, from different ethnic groups to bizarre pop-culture niches to civic groups with single-issue agendas. What less diverse populations in less sophisticated cultures see is not a rich kaleidoscope but a state with no crafted image, no unified voice or message. Many would argue that this is the very strength of our tradition: Democracy is messy, and we wouldn't have it any other way. To a good portion of the rest of the world, though, it seems more threatening than liberating.

Neither Vladimir Putin nor the Chinese leadership has formulated a fully articulated ideological alternative to the American vision; again, this is not the Cold War. But they do tacitly offer a worldview, one that begins with the simple advantage of being clear about *who* they are. The Russians are Russians. The Chinese are visibly Chinese. Who are the Americans?

We believe that American culture is now world culture and vice versa, not least because the world shares the same media technology through which that culture inexorably flows. But the world is now perfectly capable of cherry-picking among elements of Western culture, and, more and more often, citizens in other countries are rejecting vital segments, especially those that might unleash the uncontrolled centrifugal forces that can accompany Westernization. Consider the effects of our ethics scandals on the increasingly religious politics of the Islamic world as it democratizes. They accept our political machinery but reject the content that comes with it. They use Western liberal methods to impose illiberal policies, and they often do so because they do not wish to arrive at the same place. Conservative societies, indeed most societies, have no desire to embrace the brash, loud, unabashed freedoms of our society.

We in America do not set any limits on diversity, nor do we offer an answer to the question of how other countries faced with minority or ethnic conflicts might set limits. Perhaps this allows us to feel more virtuous and humane than everyone else, but it does not constitute a winning formula in the battle of ideas.

"At least the Russians will not force our men to marry men." That was one of the slogans Georgian Dream used in the 2012 election to appeal to pro-Russian, conservative sentiments in the electorate. Others spoke darkly of the capital Tbilisi's being full of "Chinese and Jews," implicitly criticizing President Saakashvili's party for overwhelming Georgian identity with multicultural elements.

In East Asia and the rest of the China sphere, similar conservative values prevail in the culture. You won't find much sympathy for immigrant rights or a welcoming attitude, in the name of global meritocracy, toward a continuous influx of outsiders. In Egypt—or indeed anywhere in Africa—it would not be wise to ask for official recognition of gay or lesbian rights. In Afghanistan, the surest way to ensure Taliban victory would be to demand that women have the right to wear makeup on the street in Kandahar or Jalalabad.

The problem is that we are not dealing merely with social prejudices and inflexible customs. We are also dealing with a world full of countries insecure in their statehood and threatened by contradictory pressures from within and without, and we are asking them to take on board our postmodern notions of diversity when they are wrestling with total fragmentation, if not dissolution. These countries are not accustomed to democracy. They are afraid, or have become afraid, of liberation without order.

Let us not forget the devastating critique leveled by the great author and dissident Alexander Solzhenitsyn against the Soviet system: It was impersonal, secular, and dehumanized, he charged. He believed in Holy Mother Russia, in the Russian Orthodox Church, in Russian culture and humanism. In short, he asserted the primacy of Russia's site-specific culture—its soul. That is one dimension of the appeal of the new Russian conservatism: It furnishes a tacit excuse for racism and xenophobia and homophobia, as seen in June 2013, when Russia passed its notorious anti-gay bill banning "propaganda of nontraditional sexual relations."[23] (The American response was typically weak: President Obama decried the law and sent openly gay athletes Billie Jean King and Caitlin Cahow to join the U.S. delegation to the Winter Olympic Games in Sochi, while the president himself, Joe Biden, and Michelle Obama stayed home—the first time since 2000 that a U.S. delegation has not included a president, vice president, or first lady.[24])

Most post-Soviet countries are not ready for what they see as the utopian dream of open borders, open sexuality, religion devoid of national identity, and the like. In fact, outside the West, most countries associate their religion with the place they're born. The globalized principle of portable identities began mainly in the U.S., with its founding myth of a nation of immigrants. The utopian ideal of choice in everything, including sexuality, goes against the grain of most of the earth's non-immigrant inhabitants, who are wedded to the framework of their *patria*. America's current liberation ethos terrifies them.

This is something we simply don't understand in the West. Such countries look at us and see an impersonal system, one with a diffuse identity of many component parts but no central core. They look at the Russians and Chinese, and they know what they're looking at—countries that have a coherent national identity, not least because the Axis forcibly imposes identity on its population.

Ethnic Russians, for instance, have no doubt that their own traditions take precedence in the Russian Federation. The multiculturalism practiced and exported by the old Soviet Union no longer holds sway in the Russian Federation. The KGB is known to be largely of Russian stock, and the power hierarchy gradates downward from there. Citizens, even politicians, who don't look ethnically Russian are attacked on Moscow's streets with some frequency by Russian supremacists. Putin has articulated an explicit policy of protecting Russians wherever they may be in the world, especially the "near abroad" former Soviet Republics where Russians live in large enough numbers that Moscow can use them as an excuse to intervene.

Beijing, meanwhile, has transferred millions of Han Chinese into the troubled regions of Tibet and Xinjiang as a way of outnumbering the locals and thus subjugating them. China has also supported the ethnic Burmese generals for years in their war against minority provinces.

The Axis conveys a coherent policy: They have continuity at the top of their leadership, and they have unified nationalist policies. They attract partners around the world with the promise of sharing their muscular approach to unity and coherence. It is an approach that, allowing for national differences, can transfer across borders and even cultures. Its prevailing principle is protection against the destabilizing revolutions of American democracy, such that family and ethnic stability, and cultural and economic continuity, are ensured.

In short, both Axis nations offer a kind of conservatism.

Chinese Conservatism: National Pride and Self-Interest

The Chinese propaganda model relies on two conservative arguments: First, it makes an increasingly aggressive and even crude appeal to nationalism; second, and most vitally, it promises prosperity and peace in exchange for restricted individual liberties and unquestioning loyalty to China's Communist leadership.

The nationalist variant of propaganda, compellingly demonstrated by the orchestrated anti-Japanese protests, might predominate in the future, especially if China's economy cools down, as many forecasters predict it will. If that happens, loyalty to Beijing in exchange for an illusory economic prosperity might prove less marketable and the appeal to Chinese glory, à la Putin's appeal to Russian pride, could become more important.

"The last thing for the party to grab on to ... might be nationalism," said Michael Hayden in 2012, referring to China's current leadership.[25] Hayden, a retired four-star general and former director of both the NSA and the CIA, surely knows that the last recourse of corrupt regimes for a century or more has been to appeal to nationalism as an excuse for cracking down on internal dissent. In this light, we can see the anti-Japan protests as a rehearsal on Beijing's part, should it need to call more urgently on such forces in the future.

The Chinese leadership has also sought to use nationalism to rally support for the Communist Party and dissuade Chinese citizens from pushing for Western-style reforms, especially the ideas of constitutionalism and human rights. Xi himself made this abundantly clear in August 2013, when the Communist Party with his approval issued Document No. 9 to its members. As the *New York Times* described it:

> Communist Party cadres have filled meeting halls around China to hear a somber, secretive warning issued by senior leaders. Power could escape their grip, they have been told, unless the party eradicates seven subversive currents coursing through Chinese society.
>
> These seven perils were enumerated in a memo, referred to as Document No. 9, that bears the unmistakable imprimatur of Xi Jinping, China's new top leader. The first was "Western constitutional democracy"; others included promoting "universal values" of human rights, Western-inspired notions of media independence and civic participation, ardently pro-market "neo-liberalism," and "nihilist" criticisms of the party's traumatic past.[26]

Document No. 9 is part of Xi's broader "rectification" campaign aimed at reinforcing ideological discipline, an effort that has included vigorous defenses of Mao's legacy. Under Xi's guidance, the Communist Party is issuing messages through what the *Times* called "a series of compulsory study sessions" throughout the country. The theme of anti-Westernism is sounded regularly. "Promotion of Western constitutional democracy is an attempt to negate the party's leadership," said deputy head of propaganda Cheng Xinping, who also warned that human-rights advocates want "ultimately to form a force for political confrontation." Another propaganda official, Zhang Guangdong, said, "Western anti-China forces led by the United States have joined in one after the other, and colluded with dissidents within the country to make slanderous attacks on us in the name of so-called press freedom and constitutional democracy." The *People's Daily* chimed in: "Constitutionalism belongs only to capitalism," read one commentary, while another held that constitutionalism was merely "a weapon for information and psychological warfare used by the magnates of American monopoly capitalism and their proxies in China to subvert China's socialist system."[27]

The vigor with which the Communist Party is pursuing this nationalistic and ideological strategy suggests that its leaders feel vulnerable, perhaps because of the Chinese economy's less-robust performance of late, at least in comparison with its high standard. And yet, China's economic growth continues to outpace the world's, despite its recent problems. Beijing's economic might is, in itself, a powerful propaganda tool, one that it has used skillfully to build alliances around the world, especially with nations that share its skepticism about Western democracy.

China's implicit message is that everyone should play along with Beijing's suppression of freedoms and periodic crackdowns on dissenters, because China has found the secret to wealth creation, and ultimately all will benefit: Keep quiet, keep your head down, and leave the political decisions to us, and you'll grow rich. That's the Chinese message to its own citizens, and it explains why Beijing props up despotic regimes abroad. Too much freedom equals chaos; chaos hurts the bottom line. In contrast with America, which equates freedom with prosperity, China urges a surrender of freedom in exchange for prosperity.

It isn't the American approach, which holds that democratic freedoms entail and can weather occasional political upheaval, and that markets work better when free. Rather, China operates by dirigisme applied to all things moral, political, social, and religious. If you do business with China, you will get rich, the message goes. You will hold on to your political power, whether you're a private individual or an African statesman, whether you are corrupt or choose to close your eyes to the corruption of others. Beijing promises prosperity with order. Radical change will bring only suffering and hardship.

Of course, America has always emphasized wealth; it's part of our system's appeal, as embodied by mega-wealthy industrialists and by shoppers prone to conspicuous consumption. But America emphasizes equally the freedoms that allow the enjoyment of wealth through self-expression and individual rights. China's counter to this is simple: American-style freedoms destroy stability in other countries, and in the U.S., they have led to immense debt and the banking collapse. China's approach is superior, it claims, as evident in its ever-increasing wealth.

The Chinese pitch to potential allies goes something like this: We will not tell you how to run your country, your morals, or your culture. Those are indigenous, idiosyncratic phenomena. Only America tells you your faults and forces you to become more like America. China will collaborate with you to keep your system going, whether you're North Korea, Zimbabwe, Burma, or an American company. There is only one catch: China needs more room to grow, and its claims on world resources will only increase.

Events around the world in recent years have seemed to confirm this Chinese thesis that people can have either wealth creation or chaos, but not both. The regime is confident that its people will continue to opt for the model that says: stability now, freedom later (or never). And Beijing is in a position to demand that the rest of the world respect the smooth functioning of Chinese procedures as well, because, more and more, the world's wealth depends on it. China is now the world's top consumer of luxury goods, and alliances with other countries underpin

Chinese wealth. In short, China is too big to fail. If we don't want the global economy to collapse, we must acquiesce in Chinese power.

Thus, Beijing is inexorably corrupting the political principles in countries across the globe in exchange for the affluence China disseminates—and this applies also, sadly, to American investors in China, including top computer companies and our largest banks and car manufacturers. We are all complicit in human-rights abuses in China, because China purchases our debt.

It's important to note that this message—conveyed by political speeches, controlled media, censored Internet content, foreign-language broadcasts, and the like—is not aimed only at domestic audiences. The audience is global. A threat to China Inc.'s smooth functioning constitutes a threat to the world. Everybody must invest in the Communist Party's continuity. And every regime can take a version of that message and apply it internally—if only the version that equates the U.S. with revolutions and chaos.

And disturbingly, the message seems to be persuasive.

Russia's New Conservatism and the Appeal to Stability

Ironically, it's precisely the cultural depredations issuing from the global economy that Russia exploits as it seeks to regain control over former satellites that had strayed toward the West. A quiet new ideology now emanates from Russia that can be disseminated in virtually every country, much as Moscow once deployed Marxism, to subvert pro-Western systems and ideas. It is a new, reactionary brand of conservatism that stands squarely against the Western model of personal freedom, multiculturalism, and social and economic dynamism.

Here's what it's about: In espousing the rather foggy notion of "stability," Russia along with China presents an us-versus-them, polarized worldview in which America represents political disintegration and social fragmentation. This is convincing in part because the U.S., as lone world leader and champion of democracy, can be associated, one way or another, with the problems of every failed country in the world. And no doubt the us-versus-them belief draws strength from the Western media's tendency to blame the U.S. for everything from genocides in Africa to the debacle in Assad's Syria. If we didn't cause the problem—any problem—we should at least have done more to stop or alleviate it.

Our adversaries can point to a string of instances where the U.S. helped topple a presiding order and then bugged out, leaving the outcome to chance; where, on the other hand, we stayed with the task, we're blamed for all the ensuing problems. So, for example, we are held responsible for the wholesale collapse of socialist regimes in South America during the post-Soviet 1990s and the economic strife that followed. That blame game helped fuel the anti-American dogma of Hugo Chávez and other neo-socialist leaders in Latin America. Russians also remember the Wild West, post-Soviet conditions of the Warsaw Pact zone, in which untrammeled free markets displaced regional economies and gave Mafia oligarchs control of national assets. Then came the Iraq War, the Color Revolutions, and finally, the Arab Spring.

All these events serve as exhibits in the argument against a fundamental American assumption: that freedom trumps all the other values holding these societies together. On the contrary, many around the world believe that order is a higher good than freedom. Chaos is the overriding enemy, and chaos is American.

Consider how the new conservatism played into Georgian Dream's appeal. The party attracted a significant following from a broad swath of society that felt the president's reforms had ushered in a color-blind, ethnically impartial, sexually liberated, global system of meritocracy that styled itself as a revolution—and, indeed, it was. Recall that around this time, in Russia, the Putin government prosecuted and jailed the Russian female punk band Pussy Riot. (The last two jailed members were released in December 2013 on an amnesty measure, widely regarded as a "cosmetic measure" ahead of the Sochi Olympic Games.[28]) The young women were punished not for political crimes but for trumped-up offenses against religious and social sensitivities. The prosecution was mere cover for the Kremlin to rid itself of figures who might've galvanized the opposition; the case stirred up countervailing popular support for Putin.

All the while, Putin had been making highly public overtures to the Russian Orthodox Church, cracking down on gay activism in the country while extolling, by example, the virtues of manliness and the nationalist traditions of Russia's religious institutions. Putin has been building an alliance with the church for years, turning it into a de facto official religion and cracking down against rival Protestant denominations given to more liberal attitudes. He built a public alliance with the church's leader, Patriarch Aleksei II, frequently appearing with him on Kremlin-controlled television networks. The two men share a commitment to Russian nationalism and a dedication to restoring Russia's lost glory.[29]

Some perspective is in order here: As a young KGB agent, Vladimir Putin lived through the last years of Soviet power, when the Russian Orthodox Church became a formidable force against the state. A devoted child of the Soviet system, Putin witnessed how the West allied itself with Russian religious institutions by smuggling Bibles and funds to believers, helping them undermine the Soviet state. That was a lesson Putin could scarcely forget. Indeed, as he once famously said, the collapse of the Soviet system was the greatest catastrophe of the 20th century—and certainly the defining disaster of his life. It shaped his worldview, and it will always be associated, in his mind, with the collapse of order.

Then, in an era when post-Soviet Russia was relatively weak—before the Iraq War spiked oil prices and pumped new blood into the Russian economy—Putin watched as pro-Western democratic revolutions overtook former Soviet republics, one by one. The Orange Revolution brought anti-Russian politicians to power in Ukraine. The Rose Revolution in Georgia ushered in the Saakashvili era. It is widely known that Putin regarded the Color Revolutions as artificial political events deliberately engineered by Western intelligence forces. Western funds came in from abroad to help protestors sustain their weeks-long occupation of central squares. Computers and Internet communications played a vital role; the way Putin saw it, these technologies were also supplied by the West for such purposes. His worldview can never credit popular feeling as genuine; dark forces must always be at work. Power, rather than ideals, drives human events.

The irony here is that, a mere generation ago, it was Russia and China espousing revolutionary systems that overturned traditions and forced people to abandon their long-held values. Now, the reality is reversed: The Axis nations have forged a new conservative ideology to counter the West's radical values and ideas. The various forms of conservatism converge in rejecting America's globalized immigrant state—that is, the multicultural, multi-ethnic, change-driven meritocratic system open to all comers from around the world.

The new conservative message resonates across national and cultural borders. In August 2012, Moscow even encouraged oligarchs to set up and fund a lobby in Britain called Conservative Friends of Russia. The lobby quickly set to work criticizing Pussy Riot. British people, however, felt much sympathy for the band's predicament and admired the women's courage; and, as the country that invented punk rock, England certainly didn't support the Kremlin's repression. Next, the website of the conservative lobby posted a picture of a Putin critic—a gay Briton who was a member of the European

Parliament—in underpants. Perhaps the lobby thought it could influence British politics by destroying regime critics through scandal. It miscalculated, though, and dissolved in a flurry of embarrassment in November 2012 after a number of prominent Conservative members of Parliament who had joined the lobby reconsidered and jumped ship. The lobby reconstituted itself as the Westminster Russia Forum.

Despite its quick flameout, the lobby speaks volumes about the Russian attempt to make common cause with conservatism abroad. Moscow may have overreached in this case, but we shouldn't dismiss the audacity and scope of its plan. Social conservatism can bind diverse cultures in common cause against the affluence-producing but destabilizing system of free markets and free speech. Nowhere has Russia demonstrated that fact more powerfully than in its massive internal and external propaganda campaign against Ukraine. It is an effort fueled, says one journalist, by "a cocktail of chauvinism, patriotism, and imperialism," and it exploits deep-seated feelings in the Russian public—from nostalgia for Soviet power to resentment of the West, from nationalistic and ethnic pride to a desire for order and authority. As *The Economist* put it: "The public seems intoxicated by victory in a war that was begun, conducted, and won largely through propaganda."[30]

Any propaganda system that can achieve something like that is formidable. Indeed, the Russian propaganda model is fierce, committed, and cogent. The Western model has none of these qualities.

CONCLUSION

A central attribute of the Western ethos has always been the ability to look at issues squarely, to discuss them openly. Openness has practical benefits; it allows debate that produces solutions. Yet the huge amplification of voices produced by proliferating media in recent years—from cable TV to satellite to the Internet—has paradoxically *weakened* our advantages. Our debates have grown louder and ever more politicized and polarized, leaving leaders unable to resolve a host of major questions.

Ruling from the top down, making unilateral decisions after only minimum debate, our rivals can address questions on a range of issues: immigration, abortion, ethnic integration, curbs on globalization, the gender wars, the aging population, the contradiction between savings and consumerism, among many other vexing challenges. Despite the constant blizzard of media coming out of the United States daily, we offer fewer and fewer coherent answers to the world's questions— especially compared with the Cold War days, when we embodied and articulated clear pathways for others to follow.

Our incoherence in the face of global challenges is also partly due to our reluctance since the Cold War to conduct ourselves as a public example to the world. The discipline imposed by those years gave way to a kind of post-triumph relaxation. We felt that our way of life had won. It spoke for itself. We no longer needed to be aware that the world was watching our every move. We didn't need to defend our societal choices or bear ourselves consciously as role models with a stake in our own respectability.

The dislocations of the global economy, perhaps more than any other development, intervened. A long-held equation in the West, and especially in America, between freedom and prosperity broke down. Free markets in Eastern Europe and post-Soviet Russia brought wildly divergent results and made substantial numbers of people worse off than they had been before—or at least convinced that they were. The terrorist attacks of 9/11 set the United States on an incredibly ambitious global mission to stamp out terrorism—a mission that brought us into conflict after conflict around the world and convinced many that the U.S. was not an unambiguous force for liberty or even human rights. The last two decades, in short, have weakened American and

Western arguments that our form of government and political economy, wherever it is tried, is a sure bet to peace, freedom, and prosperity. Millions are now telling us: *Thanks, but no thanks. We'll take the pieces we like and leave the rest. It isn't doing so well for you, anyway.*

We need to recognize that the democratic revolutions of the last generation have also sparked a conservative backlash—one that sees America's devotion to democracy as irresponsible, even reckless. We in America believe in the integrity of the process without guaranteeing the outcome. We are apparently willing to see hundreds of thousands of our own jobs go abroad because it's only fair that harder-working populations elsewhere benefit from free-market forces. And we are willing to import millions of immigrants because they wish to work hard, pay taxes, and generate economic wealth. We believe that the free flow of capital is a crucial kind of freedom that generally benefits the most industrious and virtuous. Believing in the integrity of this process—or ideology, some would say—we are willing to sacrifice social traditions, demographic and ethnic balance, and perhaps the nation-state itself. At least, that's how it looks to many watching from afar.

These anti-Western arguments are, of course, caricatures—but they result from a massive, decades-long communications failure. Perhaps as important as our failure to take our message to Russia and China is our failure to provide arguments to those countries that would resist the influence of Moscow and Beijing if they could. Eastern Europe and Central Asia remain within Russia's power orbit. Some of Eastern Europe is now free from Moscow's shadow, via European influence (and Ukraine was on the verge of making its break until Putin lured the Ukrainians back in with his $15 billion sweetener). But many parts are not—indeed, huge swaths from Belarus through Moldavia, Ukraine, and Georgia. We must give them the intellectual ammunition to resist Moscow's overtures. People in those societies have been through a historical cycle in which they saw the collapse of totalitarian systems and the horrors that followed. They identify these horrors as the consequence of too much freedom—which, as the Axis nations continually remind them, is an American evil.

We have not allayed these fears. Thus freedom appears in a problematic light around the world. We need to acknowledge these dislocations—which, after all, we are experiencing ourselves—while also renewing our defense of individual liberty, free markets, rule of law, and human dignity. These virtues may seem self-evident to most Americans, but around the world, as we have seen, many question them.

Our task is complex and nuanced, since what we defend is somewhat amorphous—freedom, liberty, and other abstract goods are not as immediate as blood and soil—and also because the system we espouse has had, in many respects, a rough 20 years. Compared with the eloquent, if simplistic, appeals of Russia and China, ours seems a harder sell. This is especially true because we believe in a kind of progress that derives directly from our Constitution—ever and greater freedoms and liberty to ever and greater numbers of people—and we believe that other cultures will inevitably arrive at the same outcomes. This belief is our own guiding principle, a very American one.

And yet, we've been down this road before—not just during the Cold War, but in World War II as well. Then as now, America faced the task of getting across its message without the benefit of a state-sanctioned media apparatus designed to do the government's bidding, and with a message so overarching that it risked dissolution, especially in the face of crude and emotional appeals on the other side. Then as now, the American ethos of liberty and opportunity had to compete with nationalistic, ethnic, ideological appeals that spoke directly to people's fears and resentments. At its best, America does not appeal to those instincts but rather to hope and aspiration.

We can hardly fail to do less now. But we need to sharpen our tools and our arguments, as well as our understanding of our adversaries—and why we oppose them.

CHAPTER 9

Countermoves:
Some Thoughts on Fighting Back

"The problem with words is that the administration is very good with them. Words aren't the problem here. The problem is the sizeable gap that has opened up between rhetoric and action."

—AARON DAVID MILLER [1]

"President Putin and his associates . . . don't respect your dignity or accept your authority over them. They punish dissent and imprison opponents. They rig your elections. They control your media. They harass, threaten, and banish organizations that defend your right to self-governance. To perpetuate their power, they foster rampant corruption in your courts and your economy and terrorize and even assassinate journalists who try to expose their corruption."

—JOHN MCCAIN [2]

"U.S. leadership in advancing freedom is neither an easy sell at home nor a simple undertaking abroad. But it is essential to reverse the current decline of freedom globally and turn the international order more toward U.S. values and interests."

—DANIEL CALINGAERT, FREEDOM HOUSE [3]

"United States . . . credibility is at [an] all-time low," Syrian president Bashar al-Assad told Charlie Rose in September 2013. [4] One can reject the messenger while recognizing the validity of the message: The reputation of the United States internationally has suffered a precipitous decline. An ongoing series of blundering, even humiliating, missteps by the Obama administration on Syria makes this plain to see.

Currently, the United States does not comport itself as the "indispensable nation" that former Secretary of State Madeleine Albright once described.[5] "The real problem is this: After the Islamist wars, the United States has, as happened before, sought to minimize its presence in the world and while enjoying the benefits of being the world's leading economy, not pay any political or military price for it," global intelligence specialist George Friedman writes. "It is a strategy that is impossible to maintain, as the United States learned after World War I, Vietnam, and Desert Storm. It is a seductive vision but a fantasy. The world comes visiting."[6]

The Obama administration seems reluctant, even now, to acknowledge this lesson. As Obama's paralysis demonstrates—from his backpedaling on Syria to his failure to stop Putin in Ukraine—the United States has wilted under shoddy leadership. Our economy at home has begun to recover, but our ability to achieve strategic goals abroad remains crippled. Our current international weakness is a result first and foremost of our departure from the mindset that guided American foreign policy through a century of World Wars, a Cold War, imperialism and decolonization, and historic technological leaps. For a century, the United States stood for an uncompromising commitment to liberal democracy, free markets, and human rights. In defense and pursuit of these goals, successive administrations, Republican and Democrat, were willing to apply, forcefully if judiciously, America's military and economic might. Some administrations were more successful than others, some more or less staunch in their commitment to these ideas. But we submit that no administration has walked back from them as far as the Obama administration has, with the escalating consequences around the world that we have been seeing. Few today would regard President Obama's foreign policy as a success. On the contrary, his approach has failed strategically, militarily, in terms of nuclear strategy, and in its lack of any coherent philosophy. As David Keyes, the founder of Advancing Human Rights has noted, Obama's approach to growing global challenges has been "to dither and appease."[7] The failure is rooted in an unwillingness to embrace America's role in the world and conduct foreign policy vigorously and with an unrelenting devotion to our national interest, our allies, and our values.

A vigorous American foreign policy in the service of our ideals would actively advocate our values, deter states from violating norms, and punish those that do. A focused doctrine of coercive diplomacy would restore the dignity and vibrancy of American policy abroad. In order to fully leverage its strength on the international stage, the United States must demonstrate again that America's friendship is worth courting and maintaining. Our alliances emerged from shared values and a shared vision of a peaceful, prosperous, and free world. We must show our troubled allies that America still cares about this vision by containing and confronting the international provocateurs in Beijing, Moscow, Tehran, and elsewhere.

America no longer needs to prepare for a ground war in Europe, but we must retain a robust and diverse set of capabilities to support our objectives, particularly in the Middle East and East Asia. Many of our allies have found ways to slim down their militaries without compromising effectiveness, but American policymakers who also wish to pare down the military must begin by examining which systems we no longer need—not by setting arbitrary and potentially catastrophic budget targets, as we have been doing for years and are now doing even more aggressively thanks to the destructive budget sequester. As Russia, China, and their allies field new systems with an eye to conflict with the United States, we cannot compromise the ability of our military to project power and provide our diplomats with the blunt martial instrument they sometimes need to succeed.

In previous chapters, we have attempted to chronicle how serious the situation has become vis à vis Russia and China across multiple vital areas—whether military or nuclear security, the economy, or intelligence and communications. Yet we have also tried to remind readers that, for all of our setbacks, we continue to hold powerful advantages of our own. And we still have time—not nearly so much as we'd like, but time yet, to reverse the negative trends and take the struggle to our adversaries. In this chapter, we offer some thoughts on how to shore up our weaknesses and prevail in this new cold war. Underpinning our analysis is the fundamental need to understand the nature of the conflict. Until we do, we cannot hope to formulate the necessary responses.

THE IMPORTANCE OF COERCIVE DIPLOMACY

In September 2013 as the Obama administration tried to rally support for military strikes on Syria, Secretary of State John Kerry gave a press conference in London. Describing the strikes, he said, "That is exactly what we're talking about doing—an unbelievably small, limited kind of effort."[8] His words caused confusion and were met with widespread derision. Senator John McCain tweeted, "Kerry says #Syria strike would be 'unbelievably small'—that is unbelievably unhelpful."[9] President Obama didn't do any better. Throughout the Syrian crisis, he was consistently lackluster, deficient in conviction, strategic clarity, and political will. No wonder Bill Clinton, who has been a staunch defender of the president's, warned months before that Obama risked looking like a "wuss" on Syria. At a McCain Institute event in June 2013, the former president discussed how "lame" it would have been if he hadn't gone into Kosovo because "the House of Representatives voted 75 percent against it."[10]

The contrast with his adversary in Moscow is stark. At the height of the Syrian crisis in September 2013, Vladimir Putin authored an op-ed in the *New York Times*. The piece ran the morning after Obama delivered a speech on Syria from the East Room of the White House. Putin wrote:

> From the outset, Russia has advocated peaceful dialogue enabling Syrians to develop a compromise plan for their own future. We are not protecting the Syrian government, but international law. We need to use the United Nations Security Council and believe that preserving law and order in today's complex and turbulent world is one of the few ways to keep international relations from sliding into chaos. The law is still the law, and we must follow it whether we like it or not. Under current international law, force is permitted only in self-defense or by the decision of the Security Council. Anything else is unacceptable under the United Nations Charter and would constitute an act of aggression.[11]

In response to Putin's management of the Syria crisis, Ian Bremmer, president of the Eurasia Group, said on September 11, "Putin probably had his best day as president in years yesterday."[12] Despite being Assad's strongest and most powerful ally, Putin seemed to transform himself into the voice of reason. Suddenly, he appeared as an international peacekeeper whose deep opposition to a U.S. military strike made him seem more rational than all the rest. Of course, this couldn't be further from the truth. Even as Putin was authoring his op-ed, Assad's elite military team, Unit 450, was in the process of scattering its chemical weapons to as many as 50 sites, making them more difficult for international inspectors to track.[13]

In reaction to Putin's op-ed, Senator Bob Menendez said, "I almost wanted to vomit." And Senate Majority Leader Harry Reid joked, "I think he's just looking for a chance to show off his Super Bowl ring," referring to an accusation that Putin had stolen a Super Bowl ring from

New England Patriots owner Robert Kraft.[14] Unsurprisingly, McCain had the most spirited reply: an op-ed in the Russian Web newspaper *Pravda.ru* entitled "Russians Deserve Better Than Putin." McCain argued that Putin was not pro-Russian; he was more interested in preserving his power. He did not respect human dignity or the right to self-determination, because, worst of all, he didn't believe in his own people. Addressing his words to ordinary Russians, McCain wrote:

> I believe you should live according to the dictates of your conscience, not your government. I believe you deserve the opportunity to improve your lives in an economy that is built to last and benefits the many, not just the powerful few. You should be governed by a rule of law that is clear, consistently and impartially enforced and just. I make that claim because I believe the Russian people, no less than Americans, are endowed by our Creator with inalienable rights to life, liberty, and the pursuit of happiness.
>
> A Russian citizen could not publish a testament like the one I just offered. President Putin and his associates do not believe in these values. They don't respect your dignity or accept your authority over them. They punish dissent and imprison opponents. They rig your elections. They control your media. They harass, threaten, and banish organizations that defend your right to self-governance. To perpetuate their power they foster rampant corruption in your courts and your economy and terrorize and even assassinate journalists who try to expose their corruption.[15]

If only these words had come from the White House. McCain's impassioned defense of liberty and democracy made a stark contrast with the Obama administration's mealy-mouthed, indecisive pronouncements. Many Obama critics have written over the years that the president's vaunted eloquence fails him when it comes American exceptionalism, human rights, and the promotion of democracy abroad—among other principles. Critics have cited his failure to promote these principles as proof that Obama does not believe in them. Rather than try to enter into the president's head, though, we'd offer a more modest, if equally damning, critique.

At minimum, what the Obama administration's treatment of the Syria and Ukraine crises—and this applies to its foreign policy generally—lacks is a mastery of coercive diplomacy, which combines the threat of force with strong diplomatic and bargaining efforts. To be sure, the president did threaten to use force against Assad, and, as several commentators pointed out, it was only the credible threat of force in Syria that brought any progress at all. But that threat came only after years of standing on the sidelines, and even then it came in tandem with a series of breathtaking missteps that made even the administration's defenders questions its competence. Obama delayed addressing the Syrian situation until almost the very last moment; put himself out on a limb with his "red line" comments in 2012; began mobilizing the military for action even as it became clear that he had little public or congressional support; and all along promised, with John Kerry, to conduct such a limited operation that even supporters of force were left wondering how the strikes could possibly achieve anything. No wonder Julia Ioffe wrote in the *New Republic*: "Obama Got Played by Putin and Assad."[16]

If anything, Obama's response in Ukraine was even more lackluster, with no serious discussion of military aid for Kiev. America had pledged to support Ukraine's sovereignty in the 1994 Budapest Memorandum. Leslie Gelb, president emeritus of the Council on Foreign Relations, said, "The United States cannot simply walk away from the plain meaning of the Budapest Memorandum and leave Ukraine in the lurch." Yet as this book went to press, it seems that we will wind up doing exactly that. No wonder James Bruno wrote in a *Politico* headline, "Russian Diplomats Are Eating America's Lunch."[17]

Ironically, one of coercive diplomacy's champions was once a member of the Obama cabinet: former Secretary of State Hillary Clinton. Throughout her tenure in the administration, Hillary consistently took a harder line than her boss. Unlike the president, she has an appreciation for coercive diplomacy, and she is willing to defend the principle, even retrospectively, in cases where her judgment didn't work out as well as she had hoped. During a 2008 primary debate in California, for instance, Clinton defended her vote in favor of the Iraq War:

> I did an enormous amount of investigation and due diligence to try to determine what if any threat could flow from the history of Saddam being both an owner of and a seeker of WMD. The idea of putting inspectors back in was a credible idea. I believe in coercive diplomacy. You try to figure out how to move bad actors in a direction that you prefer in order to avoid more dire consequences. If you took it on the face of it and if you took it on the basis of what we hoped would happen with the inspectors going in, that in and of itself was a policy that we've used before. We have used the threat of force to try to make somebody change their behavior.[18]

Indeed, Clinton has called her Iraq vote one for coercive diplomacy, not for war. As she argued, coercive diplomacy is a tool presidents must have in their arsenal. Obama uses it so poorly that one wonders whether he genuinely understands it.

American foreign policy is in retreat around the world; our security is endangered by Edward Snowden's intelligence leaks; U.S.–Russian ties fall far short of the much-touted "reset" goals; and we consistently lose ground, economically and otherwise, to the Chinese. American rhetoric no longer carries much weight. As cited in the epigraph to this chapter, former Middle East peace negotiator Aaron David Miller analyzed the Obama failings this way: "The problem with words is that the administration is very good with them. Words aren't the problem here. The problem is the sizeable gap that has opened up between rhetoric and action."[19]

Miller's assessment applies not only to the situation in Syria and Ukraine but also to the growing threats in Iran and North Korea, and indeed across the many other areas where the United States seems to be on the defensive as its adversaries move aggressively to pursue their interests.

ROGUES AND NUKES

"Our program is transparent, but we can take more steps to make it clear to the world that our nuclear program is within intl regulations," the new Iranian president, Hassan Rouhani, tweeted in August 2013.[20] With a growing threat from Hezbollah in the region—and specifically in Iran—the United States rightly regarded with caution Rouhani's pledge not to develop nuclear weapons. President Obama sent Rouhani a letter in September 2013, urging him to "cooperate with the international community, keep your commitments and remove ambiguities" about the Iranian nuclear program; in exchange, the president suggested, the Iranians might get some relief from economic sanctions.[21] Iran clearly wanted that relief badly, along with a lessening of its international isolation, and the six-month deal brokered with Secretary of State John Kerry sent some conciliatory signals in pursuit of these goals. But even though the ink hasn't had time to dry on the deal, Tehran has made it clear that it can be undone in less than a day. Their program can be up and running again in just 24 hours. Experts assess that it might be barely a year, or perhaps a year and a half, before Iran has the bomb. Tehran might already have a device capable of delivering one by the time this book is published. What's more, despite Rouhani's rhetoric, Tehran continues to enrich uranium.[22] The Iranian–American nuclear standoff is nearing a climax despite this apparent diplomatic solution.

Time will tell how the new deal plays out, but the United States must also actively pursue international consensus for military action against Iran should it fail. We could, for example, use a series of air strikes on chemical-weapons depots and other game-changing weapons systems. Many critics warn that any military action against Iran would have catastrophic consequences in the Middle East, perhaps leading to a wider regional war. But in 2013, when the Israelis conducted airstrikes against Syria to remove some Russian-supplied missiles, no serious retaliation resulted.[23] As noted Jewish journalist and historian Abraham Rabinovich argued in the *Washington Times* in May 2013, after Israeli airstrikes in Syria: "Israel's airstrikes served as a reminder, particularly to Iran, that the Jewish state has intelligence capable of silently keeping track of its enemies, operational capabilities to execute complex missions, and the national will to do so if necessary. The strikes also showed Washington that effective operations in murky circumstances can be carried out without the sky falling in."[24] Andrew Brookes, of the Royal United Services Institute, also argues in favor of airstrikes, which he sees as the only feasible military option regarding Iran. Ground troops, he believes, would fare poorly in a country where weapons facilities are hidden and buried everywhere. "The only credible military option is an air attack," he writes. This is especially true with American military exhaustion and troop pullbacks in the Middle East.[25]

The U.S. should continue to work toward formalizing the 4+1 defense pact, in which Israel would join up with several moderate Arab states—Turkey, Jordan, Saudi Arabia, and the United Arab Emirates— to prevent Iran from reaching nuclear capability.[26] By encouraging the Israelis to share anti-ballistic missile technology in exchange for access to early-warning radar in Arab states, we will create a buffer of American-aligned states against continued Iranian expansionism. The *Times of Israel* reported: "The so-called 4+1 plan is being brokered by Washington, and would mark a sharp shift in stated policy for the White House, which has insisted the U.S. is not interested in containing Iran but rather stopping it before it reaches nuclear weapon capability. The Sunni states of Saudi Arabia, UAE, and Jordan are all opposed to Tehran shifting the regional power balance. Though Turkey maintains strong trade ties with Iran, it has found itself opposed to Tehran over the issue of Syria."[27] Building such an alliance focused on the more modest goal of containment makes good practical sense as a hedge against our potential failure to prevent Iran from developing nukes.

*****

Twice in 2013, North Korea offered to enter into talks with the United States, but the U.S. wisely held off, insisting that North Korea make meaningful concessions before we begin any serious diplomatic discussions. Where there is room for some nuance and complexity regarding the Iranian nuclear negotiations, the North Korean situation presents no such complexity. The outlaw regime is simply too unstable, too ruthless, and too dangerous to be approached with anything other than unbending resolve and the military and political tools that reinforce it.

At the top of that list of tools is defense: missile defense primarily, but also the military and naval assets in the region that are necessary to maintain a decisive force posture. As we discussed in our "Nuclear Security" chapter, the United States' retreat from missile defense is highly disturbing. Regarding North Korea, though, we probably retain sufficient means to defend ourselves—at least under current conditions. We should also work closely with our allies in South Korea to enhance defense systems in Seoul.

We've been consistently critical of the Obama administration, but here we can offer some praise: The administration's response to Pyongyang's provocations in March 2013 was effective and shrewd. The military sent a B-52 bomber from Guam along with a pair of B-2s—flown from Missouri—close to the North Korean border to send an unmistakable message of American power to the regime. "The U.S. wants to let the North Koreans know," wrote White House press corps reporter Paul Brandus, "that in addition to the 28,500 U.S. troops in South Korea, and the 35,000 in Japan (including the Navy's Seventh Fleet), the U.S. can strike in many ways, and from many places."[28]

This is precisely the way we need to proceed with Pyongyang—not toward deliberate provocation, but with the will and determination to defend ourselves and our allies. We must make clear to North Korea that there will be real-world consequences for its deeds, not just angry words. The next time the North Koreans take out a South Korean vessel, we might answer by "taking out North Korean naval assets," suggests American Enterprise Institute scholar Nicholas Eberstadt.[29] The point is to let the regime know at every turn that its provocations and brutalities have a serious price.

Toughness should be the operative word in the economic realm as well. We should pursue tighter sanctions on North Korean elites to rein in banking, travel, and criminal activity such as drug running and counterfeiting. We did this effectively in 2007, when we blacklisted Banco Delta from doing business in United States dollars. We must remember that the North Korean regime is dangerous in part because it is weak—economically especially—and that our failure to use our power will only delay the day when the North Korean people can be liberated. As Brandus puts it, "Clarity, conviction, and a stealth bomber or two: That's the way to deal with North Korea."[30]

We cannot solve the North Korean problem alone, of course, and where we can work with the Chinese—where, that is, we have reason to trust that China may actually work constructively—we should do so. There is no question that Beijing has begun to acknowledge North Korea's destabilizing role in East Asia and has started to play ball on sanctions. China's primary concern is that North Korea might collapse under the crippling weight of economic sanctions.[31] If America makes clear that North Korea's nuclear disarmament and military drawdown are the preconditions for sanctions relief, the Chinese will have no excuse for opposing a new round of talks. Likewise, the United States should make it publically embarrassing and politically costly for China to continue behavior such as its stonewalling of the UN's comprehensive human-rights report on North Korea.

Beijing, after all, has a vested interest in stabilizing the Korean Peninsula. "China really, really doesn't want North Korea to collapse," Matt Schiavenza writes in *The Atlantic*. "For one thing, the trickle of North Koreans currently crossing the border would turn into a flood, leaving China with a messy humanitarian situation on its hands. Secondly, a North Korean collapse would no doubt foster the creation of a unified, pro-U.S. Korea on China's northeastern flank, depriving Beijing of a valuable buffer against American interest. For these reasons, China needs North Korea to stay afloat—and North Korea knows it."[32] Thus we should continue to encourage Chinese economic sanctions on North Korea to help cripple Pyongyang's nuclear-arms program, which Chinese diplomats have publicly condemned.

Additionally, we should push Seoul to tie its Chinese trade to progress on North Korean issues. The United States should accept South Korea's request that America retain wartime command of Seoul's forces beyond 2015, the date when transfer of authority was to take place. The North's recent provocations have changed that calculus, and South Korea wants the Americans to keep the reins for now.[33] We should send every signal that the United States remains highly invested in the security of the Korean Peninsula.

MILITARY PREPAREDNESS

The event of the last several years—wherein both Russia and China have vigorously beefed up their military capabilities, directly threatened, bullied, and even invaded their neighbors; and begun holding joint military and naval exercises—should have made clear to the Obama administration that America's extensive defense drawdown is ill-suited to the world we face today. We have already cut the Pentagon budget far too steeply, and more cuts are to come. The sequestration cuts are expected to trim $52 billion, or roughly 10 percent, from the Pentagon budget request in fiscal year 2013, with the largest percentage of reductions coming from weapons programs.[34] The cuts have already taken a toll. Our scaling back in the South China Sea has left U.S. interests increasingly vulnerable and forced us to rely more on our alliances in the region—alliances, which, in several cases, have become strained. (In December 2013, for instance, Prime Minister Shinzo Abe of Japan, visited a shrine associated with his country's militarist history; the visit enflamed relations with China and South Korea, and also drew criticism from Washington.[35])

Certainly the issue of Pentagon costs is a legitimate one, but we're going to have to find savings in ways other than slashing the capabilities that ensure our national security. We could tackle the sensitive issue, say, of how to incentivize and compensate our troops. High-cost benefits such as pensions and health care could be rolled back to 2001 levels, saving $10 billion annually.[36] We also need to find better ways to persuade tech-savvy people to pursue military careers.[37]

Our entire system of military bases in East Asia can be made less costly financially and less controversial politically (especially in Okinawa) by moving the Marines now in East Asia to bases in California and Guam and flying them to forward-based ships during a crisis, an option the Pentagon has already begun to explore. Building a runway at Okinawa's civilian airport, and making it available to the U.S. for military purposes, would be a similarly pragmatic arrangement.[38] Keeping American soldiers and assets mobile within a broader region would be more affordable than basing them in specific sites permanently.[39] Our cooperation with Australia[40] and, more recently, the Philippines[41] to create facilities for temporary forward deployments is instructive.[42]

Finally, the Pentagon needs to change its procurement system and culture. As in any healthy free-enterprise system, program managers who save taxpayer money should be rewarded. Pentagon procurement is inefficient and wasteful. Experiments with online bidding for defense contracts yielded a 12 percent savings with no loss in hard-power capabilities. We should waste no time in implementing better procurement practices. At the same time, a review body should be established to find ways to improve the process.[43]

Finally, as Hugh White argues in his book *The China Choice: Why America Should Share Power*, and as he repeated at a meeting at the Council on Foreign Relations in October 2013: "Everybody in Asia fears living under China—everyone wants the U.S. to find a way to stay in Asia. . . . The U.S. needs to show intent and commitment to stay, but also a willingness to work with China. Nothing less than a fundamental change in the relationship will do."[44] We agree.

NUCLEAR SECURITY

Further cuts to the American nuclear arsenal, even if matched by Russia, are deeply unwise and will erode our strategic advantage to a degree that endangers our national security. Paul Nitze's Cold War–era nuclear logic continues to hold true: "The greater the margin (and the more clearly the Communists understand that we have a margin), the less likely it is that nuclear war will ever occur."[45] More recently, extensive research by Georgetown's Matthew Kroenig has borne out the truth of Nitze's words and exploded the myths cherished by denuclearization advocates. Kroenig conducted a comprehensive historical review of the relationship between national security and the size of a nation's nuclear arsenal. His findings, dating back to the beginning of the atomic age, make clear that nukes remain central to any great power's defenses:

> In a statistical analysis of all nuclear-armed countries from 1945 to 2001, I found that the state with more warheads was only one-third as likely to be challenged militarily by other countries and more than 10 times more likely to prevail in a crisis—that is, to achieve its basic political goals—when it was challenged. Moreover, I found that the size of this advantage increased along with the margin of superiority. States with vastly more nukes (95 percent of the two countries' total warheads) were more than 17 times more likely to win. These findings held even after accounting for disparities in conventional military power, political stakes, geographical proximity, type of political system, population, territorial size, history of past disputes, and other factors that could have influenced the outcomes.[46]

Kroenig goes on to point out that when the U.S. stood at the peak of its nuclear armaments in the middle of the Cold War, it significantly deterred Soviet adventurism. For instance, the U.S. succeeded in stopping the Soviets from constructing a nuclear-submarine base in Cuba in 1970 and forced the Russians to limit their support for the Arab countries that opposed Israel during the 1967 and 1973 wars.

Today, more of America's geopolitical foes, including Iran and North Korea, have some nuclear component. The contentious relationship between India and Pakistan is shadowed by the two rivals' nuclear capabilities. We are living in an unprecedented period of nuclear proliferation, but we're the only nation scaling back. With fewer nukes, we won't have enough weapons to cover military targets in Russia, China, and elsewhere.[47] To preserve our nuclear advantage—as well as our general military advantage—we have to look at making cuts elsewhere and raising revenue from other sources. None of this means that there aren't useful and cost-efficient changes that we can make to our nuclear program. For instance, the Department of Energy's Lawrence Livermore National Laboratory could cease its nuclear activities entirely and focus on other areas of research. The work at the Los Alamos lab is sufficient to support the American nuclear effort and maintain our state-of-the-art capabilities. Planned upgrades for weapons such as the B61 nuclear bomb could be scaled back while the D5 missile could be terminated, saving billions without harming capabilities.[48]

Recent Obama-induced setbacks in the missile-interceptor program do not belie the immense strategic importance of that program. It will probably require the arrival of a new president, but the U.S. should retract its cancellation of Phase IV of the NATO defense shield in Eastern Europe. Basing interceptors in Poland and radar in the Czech Republic was always a sensible response to Russian radars and interceptors in St. Petersburg, southern Russia, and, most worryingly, in Kaliningrad.[49] Continued Russian cooperation with Iran's nuclear program and Russia's advances in Ukraine make clear that Moscow intends to keep the pressure on; it's hardly the time for the United States to be making such dangerous cuts.

Meanwhile, the United States' recent augmentation of missile defenses on the West Coast should be mirrored on the East Coast, precisely because Obama has retreated on NATO's European missile shield. An East Coast missile-defense site could be operable before 2020.[50] We should make sure that it is.

ALLIANCES

The weakened state of the American-centered alliance system is clear evidence that the way we approach foreign relations needs to change, and soon. Look no further than David Cameron's fiasco before the British Parliament, in which the lawmakers denied his request for authorization to join the U.S. effort against Assad. Of the Western European allies, only France was prepared to stand with the U.S.—a truly remarkable turn of events. In the Middle East, defenders of Israel have worried for years that the U.S. is far too restrained in its support for its ally, especially as regards the ongoing standoff with Iran.

Everywhere we look, America can and should be doing more to support its allies and formulate more cohesive regional strategies. We should fast-track the proposed Transatlantic Free Trade Area between the United States and European Union. Should Ukraine survive Russia's purposeful destabilization, America and the EU must be prepared to integrate it into Western institutions, just as we did former Warsaw Pact states in the 1990s. Even former Soviet states such as Azerbaijan are open to a better relationship with Washington. Yet many of these East European states are unconvinced that Western Europe is willing or able to protect them from Russian aggression. The 2008 Georgian war and the 2014 Ukraine crisis only confirmed this instinct. We should offer them a real opportunity to participate in the global democratic project. Embracing the dynamism of New Europe means following through on missile defense, expanding military cooperation, and letting the Eastern Europeans know that we are committed to a genuine partnership.

We must commit especially to those countries that identify with the West or are seeking to become more Westernized. The fight to once again liberate Eastern Europe must return as a U.S. priority. Moscow is taking back its former empire in parts of Central and Eastern Europe. As the U.S. and Europe have an increasingly unfocused sense of cultural identity, the West's unity—our sense of belonging to an age-old, distinct, and coherent civilization—diminishes. And Moscow is winning the war of ideas. Country after country in the old Eastern Bloc has opted to reject the West in order to remain more distinctly themselves. We must meet this challenge, not only by allowing countries such as Georgia and Moldova to join the EU and NATO more quickly but also by showing that we support their national identities.

We must, above all, reinforce our commitments to those countries we consider closest to our own traditions, even at the risk of inciting cries of elitism, racism, and the like. The UK and Europe were part of America's genesis and the source of the West's deepest values and beliefs. If we cannot unify and save that once-coherent tradition, we certainly cannot offer any message of salvation to countries in the Middle East, Africa, or Asia. We must begin with what we can win.

Our Pacific allies need more reassurance that America remains capable of advancing its strategic agenda in the region; and here, at least, there are some positive signs. Washington has gotten behind Shinzo Abe's push to rearm Japan and assume more responsibility in East Asia.[51] In October 2013, the U.S. and Japan signed an agreement broadening their security alliance. Under the agreement's terms, surveillance drones would be introduced in Japan, buttressing American efforts to contain Chinese and North Korean challenges. Japan and the United States, the agreement said, would be ready to respond to "coercive and destabilizing behaviors." To that end, the drones would be augmented by Navy reconnaissance planes being stationed outside the U.S. for the first time; in tandem, the drones and planes would patrol regional waters, including those around the island chain that has caused tension between China and Japan in recent years.[52]

The U.S. should continue to strengthen its ties with Japan while seeking to build as large a coalition as possible to counteract China's influence. (We have diplomatic work to do in ensuring that South Korea, the Philippines, and other Pacific allies are not threatened by Japan's new role in the region.) Up to now, Washington's halfhearted and underfunded "pivot" to Asia has not done nearly enough to position America favorably for the "Pacific Century." Furthermore, the U.S. should work to encourage countries bordering the South China Sea to settle their maritime disputes. In August, Chinese Foreign Minister Wang Yi said China would be willing to discuss a code of conduct to help nations peacefully address competing claims. But he also suggested that China was in no hurry to have this happen—another delaying tactic.

In each region, including Eastern Europe, the U.S. should pick a linchpin partner to empower, a true believer in the struggle for democracy and openness, one that will export the democratic message and set an example. That country need not always have a fully developed economy such as that of Japan or Germany or even Australia, strong allies during the Cold War years and today. Rather, we should look toward aspirational up-and-comers that have a potential for growth and development, such as Poland in the West or the Philippines or Thailand in the East. The U.S. should encourage its more established allies to collaborate in the strengthening of that country economically and militarily. Countries such as India, South Korea, and Japan are essential partners in their regions, but their influence has limits. We need newer strategic partners with fresh ambitions.

REAFFIRMING AMERICAN VALUES

"Sergei Magnitsky wasn't a human-rights activist," wrote John McCain in his *Pravda.ru* op-ed. "He was an accountant at a Moscow law firm. He was an ordinary Russian who did an extraordinary thing. He exposed one of the largest state thefts of private assets in Russian history. He cared about the rule of law and believed no one should be above it. For his beliefs and his courage, he was held in Butyrka prison without trial, where he was beaten, became ill, and died. After his death, he was given a show trial reminiscent of the Stalin era and was, of course, found guilty. That wasn't only a crime against Sergei Magnitsky. It was a crime against the Russian people and your right to an honest government—a government worthy of Sergei Magnitsky and of you."[53]

McCain's words strike at the heart of what the Magnitsky Bill is about. As we noted in our "Intelligence Wars" chapter, Congress passed the Magnitsky Rule of Law Accountability Act in 2012 to punish Russian officials thought to be responsible for Magnitsky's death; the bill prohibited these individuals from traveling to the U.S., owning property here, or using U.S. banks. This was a deft use of policy to support American values and punish regimes that fail to honor human rights. Directing policy in this way can make clear that abuse of human rights and basic liberties will not go unpunished, even when we have no jurisdiction in the regions where such abuse takes place. But we have to hold firm on these policies, not backslide like we already have on Magnitsky. The stakes are too high. The U.S. must lead the way on human rights regularly, not just occasionally.

Even while a broad spirit of decline grips the West, it remains true that to be excluded from the Western world carries an enormous stigma. We still represent the respectable half of the globe. Well-intentioned oligarchs (and those not so well-intentioned), foreign mafia chiefs, and political bosses all send their children to the West to be educated because that is where strong ideals and the rule of law abide. Understandably, when it comes to the younger generation of the Axis elite, we prefer to expose as many of them as possible to our way of life, hoping that they will go home and spread enlightenment around them. But we can be more selective in bestowing the privilege of access to the West's benefits.

At present, our approach seems amoral, to say the least. The right of Bo Xilai's son to study and live in the West was never questioned, even while his mother was prosecuted for the murder of a British businessman and while his father, a top Politburo member, was facing trial for corrupting entire regions of China. No one could have believed that it was clean money that their son spent to attend Harvard College and Cambridge University—and Bo Guagua was well known for his extravagant international lifestyle. It is time to get unsentimental on this issue. Money and power should not overcome all other criteria. The exclusion of entry, the refusal of a visa: These are among the simplest, cheapest, and most effective tools in our arsenal, and often the least utilized.

More broadly, democracy promotion should be a priority for every American presidential administration. It draws sharp lines between the U.S. system and despotic governments; it offers support for our allies and the populations of undemocratic countries striving to gain liberty; and it clarifies and reinforces our own mission at home and abroad. Many liberals and some conservatives blanche at the concept of energetic democracy promotion. Conservatives associate it with misguided foreign adventures à la Woodrow Wilson; leftists link it with George W. Bush's Bush Doctrine, a mandate its critics saw as limitless. The truth is that democracy promotion often does not involve explicit military force. We must increase American support for civil-society organizations—NGOs, charities, environmental organizations, foundations, independent political parties, nonprofits, cultural groups—that will help foster democracy and diversification in countries like China and North Korea, but also in countries with poorly functioning democracies, such as Russia and Iran.

We need to challenge more forcefully China's blocking of human-rights protections in North Korea. While the United States cannot intervene everywhere, recent years have given us stark reminders that democracy and human rights are under constant assault worldwide: the massacres and atrocities across Africa and the Middle East; the election rigging, corruption, and violence by government forces against civilians in Venezuela, torture of prisoners in Brazil, and authoritarian control of media in Bolivia, among other problems in Latin America.[54] These crimes demand a coherent and vigorous response from Washington—rhetorically, diplomatically, and otherwise. There are many tools short of military force that we don't use adequately—visa restrictions for high-ranking officials, for example. We can be more aggressive in freezing international bank accounts for elite adversaries and imposing tighter economic limitations on cooperation (up to and including sanctions) with repressive governments.

Above all, we can no longer afford to "lead from behind," and in fact we never could. Even the Obama administration must recognize this by now; its destructive dithering on Syria, for instance, only allowed an open field for the Assad regime to commit more atrocities while weakening the democratic opposition. The Syrian experience ought to remind us that the United States must stand at the forefront in the defense of democracy around the world. But to do so requires leaders who embrace America's governing ideals without ambivalence—something that the

Obama administration seems unwilling or unable to do. If we are not committed to our own values, we cannot expect to defend them, let alone spread them.

SHAPING A PRO-WESTERN, PRO-DEMOCRATIC MESSAGE

For decades, it was the United States that acted as its own best commercial for democracy, with high living standards and individual freedom unknown to most of the world. And we had a government and a popular culture that championed these virtues. By contrast, the Communist Bloc was staid, gloomy, and authoritarian; its economy was stagnant, its people depressed, and its government propaganda organs transparently dishonest and unsophisticated.

Today, that's all changed. Both Moscow and Beijing have caught up in the communications game, and they have become skilled in disseminating a new and highly effective conservative message. Ukrainian or Georgian patriots, instinctively anti-Russian, turn anti-American instead when the Kremlin's propaganda machine tells them that their national grid will be owned by Turks or their military run by gays if they sign on to Western globalism. Russian propaganda has been decisive in Ukraine, where pro-Russian militias are egged on by the insistence of the Kremlin-controlled media that the government in Kiev is fascist, anti-Semitic, and intent on repressing Ukraine's sizeable Russian-speaking population.[55] China's already-infamous Document No. 9, as mentioned in the previous chapter, enumerates "seven subversive currents" that party cadres must reject—among them "Western constitutional democracy," "neo-liberalism," and "universal values" such as human rights and media freedom.[56] Meanwhile, Western media spin from one crisis to the next—from Edward Snowden's revelations about NSA snooping to events in Syria or Egypt, with nothing resembling a national consensus or common framework of understanding. Indeed, the Axis itself can hijack Western media cycles in order to cover up their machinations. For example, Snowden's revelations came on the heels of widespread reports of Chinese cyber attacks against Western companies.

Shocking though this may sound to the liberal mindset, the U.S. must revamp its propaganda voice to the levels of the Cold War. The fact is, we are in a full-blown Cold War, but we are the only ones not fully engaged. We prevailed against Communism not merely because President Reagan outspent the Soviets in defense or because our pop culture became universal, but because we sent a coherent message abroad about our ideas and their benefits. We did this by exporting entertainment, as we do now, but also by openly using organs of propaganda—Radio Liberty and the like—to get our point across. We took other countries and their ideas seriously enough to argue with them on matters of substance. Today, we lack a coherent message and seem nearly paralyzed by indecision and self-doubt. But the power of our pop culture to convert people to the American way has had its full effect; history is now at the next stage. Millions around the world have fully absorbed the principles of consumerism and entertainment. They look to America for the next step in ideas. They have evolved economically to a stage where they are asking serious questions about what comes next, including questions about our claims to global leadership. We no longer have the powerful official-broadcast platforms that we once had for engaging in that debate.

Consider it from a different angle: If the U.S. could openly broadcast debates about non-Islamist forms of Islam to Muslims around the world, in the appropriate languages, no doubt they would be greeted with great hostility at first—as similar messages were greeted by the Communist countries. But over time, the opening of debate had its effect on the Cold War. Let us apply this principle again, openly, formally, around the world and disseminate unashamed propaganda for the ideas we espouse. Some form of official or semi-official government media organ, along the lines of Radio Free Europe but built to have the reach and sophistication of the new communications age, is needed here.

We need this much more robust voice not only to tout our own virtues but also to highlight the many depredations on the other side. When Hillary Clinton or John Kerry denounces Axis conduct at various public forums, much of the world literally doesn't see or hear it. In many countries, media outlets remain either state-controlled or controlled by oligarchs friendly to the state, and many governing regimes do not wish to alienate the Axis. Their publics don't hear about Moscow's machinations or China's exploitation of African resources or the inhumane conditions in Chinese mines abroad. Thousands demonstrate against U.S. corporations that are exploiting natural resources in foreign lands, but no such demonstrations erupt against Chinese companies. In no Arab countries have we seen mass demonstrations against Moscow's support for Assad. It is time to hold the Axis nations publicly accountable, on a global scale, for their outrageous conduct.

THE POWER WE HOLD OURSELVES

Ultimately, the battle begins at home—in awakening the hearts and minds of Americans. We believe the threat is equal in scope and complexity (if not in imminent danger) to what we faced during the Soviet era. We propose a federal response modeled on the War on Terror, starting with a task force to deal specifically with the Axis threat. Task-force members should have cabinet-level access and work closely with Russian and Chinese policy experts. In the manner of the Department of Homeland Security, the Axis task force should coordinate expert contributions in a holistic approach, from intelligence gathering and military planning to diplomacy and propaganda.

When President Reagan referred to the Soviet Union as the Evil Empire, he was loudly ridiculed for his brashness. When President George W. Bush spoke of the Axis of Evil, he, too, was roundly mocked. Bush promptly gave comfort to his critics by blundering unprepared into two wars. Sadly, we are now loath to identify enemy states explicitly as enemies, except perhaps North Korea. The fraying of borders, the globalization of money and citizenship, and the diffusion of national identity make it increasingly difficult to draw clear lines between us and them, especially since the Bush Doctrine of being either for us or against us caused such confusion. Nevertheless, no country can survive for long without a clear definition of friends and opponents. This is not a form of simplistic, know-nothing yahooism. This is how states have conducted their business from the beginning of civilization. We have come to the point where any such explicit iteration is met with protest from some vocal corner of our fragmented societies.

Here, then, is a modest proposal: The U.S. should officially and publicly tabulate a hierarchy of foreign states from the friendliest to the least friendly. Something comparable already exists in the form of NATO and the EU: Those blocs of allies show the world, in the clearest way, who's in and who's not. But there is no demonstrable way for countries outside these well-known alliances to position themselves advantageously, although most-favored-nation treatment, whereby countries agree to reciprocal bilateral relations, is a minor gesture in that direction. We can imagine, say, three categories, with the EU states and Great Britain, Canada, Japan, South Korea, Israel, and Australia in the top division—all are NATO or "major non-NATO" allies. Intensifying our cooperation with them and making these alliances more explicit will reassure our partners. Middling countries such as Georgia, Mexico, and certain Middle Eastern countries might occupy a middle division, and so on down. Privileges such as immigration and trade quotas, student visas, investment facilitation, family unification, and numerous other considerations would ride on such positioning. Those countries that allow Axis power to dominate their affairs would be clearly identified; they would suffer economically and otherwise, and their citizens would know why. It is time to get serious about favoring our allies and punishing our adversaries, who have, for some time now, been punishing us with near impunity. During the Cold War, such differentiations existed concretely; every state knew the consequences of its actions. Such simple categorical distinctions may not be achievable in our multipolar world, but the effort to make them so would be clarifying for national security and strategic rigor.

It bears repeating: We are in a new Cold War, and we are the only ones not fighting.

Why America Must Wake Up

"What we have been witnessing in Ukraine, with protests that began in November and have gained a volatile intensity in recent days, is the first geopolitical revolution of the 21st century."

—MIKHEIL SAAKASHVILI, FORMER PRESIDENT OF GEORGIA[1]

When we started writing this book, our first concern was to raise the alarm about the threat Russia and China posed to the West and to the well-being of the world at large. It was a matter of heightening awareness about an enormous challenge that had escaped the notice of most Americans. But in the interim, the problem we sought to bring to greater attention brought notice to itself, as developments around the world made Russia and China's behavior page-one international news, nearly every day. The world watched in horror as an intransigent Moscow blocked U.S. and European efforts to forestall the carnage in Syria for years. The West had to face the prospect of a kind of world war if it dared to intervene in Syria, with the Axis backing a bloc of powers—from the mullahs in Iran to Hezbollah in Lebanon—that thwarted all attempts to remove Bashar al-Assad.

Russia's aggression in Ukraine was backed by similar threats to escalate tensions with the West if it dared to intervene. Ukrainians found themselves effectively abandoned by the West and left to Moscow's mercies. Saying little, as always, the Chinese ran diplomatic interference at the United Nations, joining with Moscow to thwart a Security Council resolution upholding Ukraine's sovereignty.

The Edward Snowden affair became an international sensation, with Russia and China playing leading roles. And it became impossible to ignore massive cyber hacking by both countries directed against the United States and other Western nations and their businesses.

So today, many Americans are probably more aware than they were a year ago about the role Russia and China are playing around the world to counter American influence. But the full dimensions of the Axis challenge are still not well known. Here is what Americans need to understand.

The United States is a nation in crisis. Ongoing partisan warfare has left our government nearly impotent in its effort to address our most pressing domestic and foreign-policy needs. While we are hobbled, Russia and China are resurgent on the international stage. Thinking on the challenges each Axis nation presents, we can reach some broad conclusions. First, America's influence around the world is receding: our military and diplomatic power; our political influence; economic might; and, perhaps most dangerously, the power and appeal of our ideas. Second, in these same areas, the influence of Russia and China is increasing. To be sure, there are huge differences between Russia and China in terms of their economic strength and position, their prospects for the future, and their place in the global political economy. But as we have tried to show, the similarities and shared interests are far more important than the differences.

Russia and China are increasingly expansionist, whatever the short-term weaknesses of their economies. Beyond its incursions into Ukraine, Russia is gaining power in parts of the former Soviet Union, through the Customs Union and its expanded successor, the proposed Eurasian Union, an alternative to the European Union. Russian influence is also growing in Central Asia. China is becoming more economically dominant in the South and East China Sea and in Asia generally.

Both Russia and China have increased their military budgets substantially while the United States is dramatically scaling back its military expenditures. Whether in spite of or because of their recently troubled economies, Russia and China have become increasingly nationalistic and aggressive, while America, worn down by a decade-plus of wars, has become inner-directed, even isolationist. Russia and China are pursuing systematic plans to upgrade their militaries and expand their conventional forces; the United States is slashing its defense budget and reducing the size of its conventional forces. Moreover, under President Obama's often rudderless leadership, the United States not only lacks a clear strategy but also has been forced to implement a series of additional automatic cuts, mandated by the budget sequester, that experts across the board—including the last two defense secretaries, Republican Robert Gates and Democrat Leon Panetta—agree will be profoundly damaging.

The same story is playing out in the nuclear area. Again, we see the United States reducing its arsenal sharply—and President Obama contemplates doing so even more dramatically—while the Russians and Chinese have, if anything, taken advantage of arms-control agreements and their own technological advances to upgrade their arsenals and expand their capabilities. The U.S. retreat from the nuclear playing field is not just apparent in offensive capabilities; the American missile-defense shield that protects both our homeland and our European allies is gravely deficient as well, as we have described. And our allies don't even buy missile-defense technology from us anymore: Turkey, a NATO member, purchased its $3 billion missile-defense system from Beijing.[58]

Recent reports of Chinese hackers stealing drone technology to use for offensive weapons and also to globally export underscore the degree to which cyber crime remains a huge challenge—especially from China, but also from Russia. Despite our apparent success in disabling the Iranian nuclear facility at Natanz through the Stuxnet virus, the U.S. shows no sign of having formulated an effective policy that would discourage the Chinese (and the Russians, to some extent) from their huge and ongoing cyber war against us. Put another way, our cyber defenses are not nearly as sophisticated or broad-ranging as the NSA's capabilities for monitoring and collecting data on our own citizens.

Economically, America's decades-long advantage is wearing away. Experts predict that sometime in the next decade, China's economy will surpass ours as the world's largest; some suggest that China will take the lead as early as 2016. Domestically, the American economy shows signs of recovery, although it has been a largely jobless recovery thus far. We might be saved yet by an energy boom from horizontal drilling: We must continue production of domestic oil and energy sources, in particular through fracking, which in a short time has brought tremendous hope to the U.S. economy and begun to transform the global energy market (much to Russia's detriment, if trends hold). An all-out commitment to fracking is critical if we are to break the hold of foreign oil on our domestic economy and compete with Russia and especially China.

American economic success overseas pales beside the influence the Chinese have been able to gain in the last decade. China has put its incredible cash power to work around the world, with Chinese companies investing directly in myriad foreign entities. Whether pursuing private equity in Western companies or investing in Africa's vast natural-resources boom, China is energetically buying into other nations' economies and taking a share in future development. The Russians, while no match for the economically mighty Chinese, have also pursued their interests with renewed vigor, especially as their gas dominance is threatened by American fracking and other challenges. The Russians have been applying bare-knuckled political pressure to persuade their former Soviet neighbors to join the Customs Union rather than the EU, as many have been contemplating. These efforts have already borne fruit with Armenia, which was set to join the EU; when Russia started to sell arms to Azerbaijan, Armenia's bitter enemy, Armenia reversed course and sided with the Russians. Moscow is bullying Moldova and Ukraine in similar fashion and has apparently proved successful in the latter case.

And there's still more. Rogue nations such as Syria, Iran, and North Korea, and terrorist organizations such as Hamas and Hezbollah all have directly benefited from the patronage—both direct and indirect—of the Russians and the Chinese. Much of the assistance is covert or indirect, but it is also the case that increasingly, Iran and North Korea have expanded their nuclear programs with the economic and arguably the technological assistance of the Russians and Chinese. There is room for disagreement about the precise degree to which the Russians have aided the Iranians; and the Chinese, the North Koreans. We will probably never uncover all the facts. But we've learned enough to point unmistakably to deep-seated ties and substantial, critical support. Moreover, Russian and Chinese intentions in this area are evident in both nations' intransigence at the UN and elsewhere when they're asked to rein in the behavior of their rogue allies.

As this book went to press, it had become clear to most observers that American influence in the Middle East has declined precipitously. Russia is rebuilding its influence there to levels not seen since the height of the Cold War. We cannot directly blame the Russians for Bashar al-Assad's use of chemical weapons, but it's crucial to understand that Russian patronage of Syria—from steadfast political support for Assad to economic and military assistance—made it possible for the dictator to use chemical weapons and then to engage in a negotiating process that prevented a U.S. strike against Syria. Assad has an excellent chance of staying in power indefinitely, despite the so-called red line that President Obama drew in August 2012. The president's stupefying walk-back from that red line, as well as his retreat from his earlier public position that Assad had to go, have sent an unmistakable message of American weakness to our foes. We spy on our own and spy on foreign leaders with impunity but have been far less successful influencing events positively and proactively in the countries of the former Soviet Union, the Middle East, Africa, or Asia. In fact, our impotence has been obvious, apparent, and clear for a number of years now even to our allies; countries such as Saudi Arabia and Japan increasingly pursue their own policies and interests with much less deference to American interests and concerns. Indeed, Egypt has now recently moved closer to Russia politically and economically. Even Israel, our oldest ally in the Middle East, has increasingly demonstrated its independence, with its leaders distancing themselves from Secretary of State John Kerry and making energy deals with India and other countries—deals the U.S. views with suspicion and concern.

We wrote this book as a warning about the threat America faces. Others have made many of these individual arguments elsewhere. But as we examined each of the disparate issues we have joined together here, it became clear to us that American influence across the board is waning, while the Russians and Chinese have grown economically, politically, and militarily more formidable. Beyond the discouraging trend in all these areas is a less tangible but more fundamental sign of American retreat: the decline in the power and appeal of the American idea. We do not defend and argue for the principles of freedom, liberty, and democracy as we once did. As a result, these ideals lack a global champion in an era of great social and economic dislocation, political violence, and technological change. In the meantime, the Chinese and Russians have put forward compelling alternative models—authoritarian, nationalistic, antidemocratic, and socially conservative—that have resonated with millions. They also challenge the American role in the world. Putin calls loudly for "non-interference" and state sovereignty, while the Chinese amorally push a promise of never-ending economic growth and consumerism as a justification for their authoritarian rule and human-rights abuses. The United States, meanwhile, largely stays silent, conceding the rhetorical and even moral high ground to these despotic, antidemocratic regimes.

In the previous chapter, we outlined a number of key recommendations: Advance American principles of freedom and liberty; support free trade around the world; recommit ourselves to a defense budget suited to the challenges we face; reach consensus on the need for a more robust global presence; reverse the tendency toward a restricted and limited nuclear arsenal; do everything within our power to counter conventional and unconventional use of technology by our adversaries. If we do not take these steps, we will face a grimmer and more challenging future.

Others around the world see the same stakes. Writing about the bloody confrontations between police and citizens in the streets of Kiev in Ukraine, Mikheil Saakashvili, former president of Georgia, called the impending struggle nothing less than "the first geopolitical revolution of the 21st century." What he meant was that the two sides in Kiev (those who supported "independent, Western democracy" versus those who backed "Vladimir Putin's Russia") were waging a battle relevant to the rest of the world: a conflict between Western-oriented democracy and a reinvigorated authoritarianism. If the protesters were defeated, it would mean "a huge rollback of European influence and values," Saakashvili wrote. "The credibility of the U.S., already eroding in the region, would vanish. Mr. Putin knows it. Brave citizens of Ukraine know it."[59]

We wish we could say that we're optimistic about what the future holds, at least under our present leadership. As believers in American exceptionalism, it is hard for us not to be hopeful, even now. But we believe that it's more prudent to conclude with a warning than with a Pollyannaish assurance that everything will be OK, especially because the future prospects, at least in the short term, are not encouraging. We hope these arguments will serve as a wake-up call for Americans—and especially for America's somnambulistic, negligent political leaders.

While our weaknesses have many causes, from economic malaise to international developments over which we have limited control, our struggle is fundamentally about how we see ourselves. As a nation, we have lost the shared conviction that the American way is worth celebrating and defending, that democracy is the best form of government, and that America is rightly engaged with the world in defense of others who share these convictions. We must articulate this uniquely American vision again, both for our own sake and for the benefit of those around the world who look to America for leadership. Standing up to Russia and China and countering the corrosive impact of their antidemocratic message is central to regaining our national strength— and vital to the peace and security of the world.

RUSSIA

- The United States and Europe must work with the new government of Ukraine to develop economic, political, and military partnerships that will guarantee Ukraine's continued independence from Russia.
- Western leaders must make clear that any further disruption of democracy in Ukraine, the Baltics, or elsewhere in Europe will be met with stiff sanctions against the Russian energy sector. If Putin refuses to engage democratically elected leaders in Eastern Europe, the West should increase its material support for pro-democracy activists in Russia.[1]
- The United States should initiate sweeping sanctions against companies with ties to the Russian state that operate in America, and we should consider cutting trade ties entirely. Additionally, there must be serious consideration of the "nuclear option" of sanctions: cutting Russian financial institutions off from the SWIFT international transactions system.[2] This step, currently in use against Iran, would cut Russia off from global financial markets and devastate its economy.
- All European states should reduce their dependence on Russian energy sources, preferably by supplanting them with American liquefied natural gas (LNG).
- America should ease restrictions on special-issue visas—such as the O-1A and the EB-5—that would let Russians emigrate more easily. This would allow any Russian with a clean criminal

record and either a doctorate or $5 million deposited in the U.S. to get a visa and come here. The results for Putin would be disastrous.[3]

- NATO must return to its original purpose: collective defense against interstate violence in Europe. NATO should focus on enhanced internal security, homeland security, training, intelligence, early warning, cybersecurity, and public-diplomacy capacities.[4]

- America and Europe should continue to support the sovereignty and independence of states that have stood up to Putin, such as Georgia and Moldova. This means fast-tracking trade deals, continuing and increasing military cooperation and support, as well as cultural and governmental exchanges, including visits by high-profile Western politicians and dignitaries.

- The United States must put a halt to its dependence on Russian technology for space travel and launching spy satellites. Moscow's announcement that it will deny American access to the International Space Station starting in 2020, and bar export of rocket engines to the United States, is simply an outrageous provocation—and the United States must answer it in kind.

- As Putin's censorship of the Russian Internet grows, the West must step in to provide alternate venues for expression and discussion, such as Voice of America and Radio Free Europe. The West should boost funding for these organizations and promote the creation of new venues for Russia's pro-democracy activists.

WHAT TO DO

CHINA

- China's southern neighbors need a coordinated response to Beijing's aggression that puts an end to China's habit of redrawing borders by force. This would mean taking steps to reinforce the defensive capacities of allies and partners as they guard against Chinese coercion. We must firmly uphold international maritime law and strengthen the Association of Southeast Asian Nations (ASEAN) as a force for positive consensus and cooperation among allies. We should also facilitate cooperation, where possible, between our allies and China.[1]

- The United States must ratify the United Nations Convention on the Law of the Sea. Being one of the few UN member states not to do so diminishes our ability to protect our Pacific allies and balance China in the South China Sea. Taking this step will give the U.S. and our allies a stronger legal claim if we must use force in future confrontations.[2]

- In the East China Sea, the United States must remain credible in its treaty obligations to defend Japanese territory, including the disputed Senkaku Islands. America should forcefully discourage Chinese aggression but also encourage responsibility and level-headedness—reassuring Beijing that a prosperous and secure China is in the world's best interest.[3]

- Western sanctions against Chinese companies and banks could turn the tide against China's neocolonial agenda in the developing world. Chinese companies abroad, especially in developing-world countries, have exported the poor labor conditions, human-rights abuses, and corporate irresponsibility that typify so much of China's economy. The mining and other resource-extraction operations that Chinese state banks finance, particularly in Africa, are the subject of much local protest that rarely translates into any improvement in circumstances.[4]

- The Chinese must be persuaded either of the wisdom of withdrawing support from North Korea or the cost of failing to do so. Without Chinese cooperation, American and European efforts to isolate North Korea are unlikely to succeed.

- American and European leaders should take a more public stance against China's mistreatment of its own citizens. China's human-rights record is one of the worst in the world, with thousands executed every year, hundreds of thousands imprisoned without trial, and nearly all of China's 1.4 billion citizens denied basic freedom of expression.[5]

- Some Chinese companies benefit from child labor and slave-like work conditions, as do the Chinese banks that fund these heinous practices.[6] When Chinese companies and financial institutions violate basic concepts of human dignity, they should face serious consequences—including loss of access to Western consumer and capital markets.

- Most Chinese have access only to heavily censored state-run media. Free news sources, such as Voice of America and Radio Free Asia, battle to overcome jamming and blocking by China's state censors. They make a huge impact on an approximately $700 million annual budget; increasing that budget by \$100–\$200 million would help them continue to promote a free society and independent media in China.[7]

- In May, the FBI charged five members of China's elite cyber-espionage military unit with spying. This should be only a start, however. In addition to charging more of China's cyber spies, the U.S. should release the names of Chinese companies that hired this military unit to conduct corporate espionage, and the U.S. should issue sanctions against these companies.[8]

THE NEW AXIS

- The New Axis is emboldened by declining American military might. Rebuilding our armed forces sends a strong message that, whether in Eastern Europe or the East China Sea, America's military capabilities remain unequalled in the world.
- International election monitors from organizations such as the Organization for Security and Cooperation in Europe (OSCE) and the National Endowment for Democracy (NED) should receive increased funding and support—OSCE by its member states, NED by USAID. Their services should be made readily available to Ukraine and other fledgling democracies. In addition, America should push the United Nations to develop a new standard for monitoring and certifying elections, so that autocrats like Putin can no longer falsely claim democratic legitimacy.
- The West should redouble its efforts to support embattled journalists in China, Russia, Iran, and elsewhere. Just as the Magnitsky Act punishes Russian officials who engage in corrupt and criminal activity, politicians who are complicit in the persecution or silencing of journalists should be barred from traveling to the West, and their access to Western financial, cultural, and political institutions severely limited. China and Russia have signed a historic $400 billion dollar gas deal that will deepen their economic partnership; but for now, China does far more business with the West than with Russia. We

must make clear that if China continues to make deals with Putin while he threatens his neighbors, Western governments will discourage investment in and trade with China's increasingly rickety economy—while promoting other investment destinations such as the Philippines, Malaysia, and India.

- Russia continues to provide diplomatic cover for Bashar al-Assad's use of chemical weapons against civilians in Syria. As the situation in Syria continues to deteriorate, the United States must consider hard-power options to prevent further chemical attacks.

- Buying Iranian oil directly or in bartered swaps, Russia and China supply Tehran with critical equipment and goods, and they thus help Iran circumvent UN sanctions.[1] Wherever possible, illegal Russian and Chinese deals with Iran should be met with offsetting sanctions and penalties against companies linked to the regimes of these countries.

- In light of recent IAEA revelations involving Iran's potential violations of the nuclear deal it struck with the U.S. in 2013, the United States should postpone any further compliance with the terms and conditions of the deal until a comprehensive investigation can determine whether Iran is following the agreement.[2]

- Since 2008, the United States has made unilateral moves to shrink our nuclear arsenal and weaken the nuclear triad of bombers, submarines, and land-based missiles that protected us during the Cold War. Meanwhile Russia, China, North Korea, and Iran are rapidly expanding their nuclear capabilities. There is no strategic logic to current American nuclear policy, and we must return to a level of readiness commensurate with the dangerous nuclear landscape we face.

Rebuilding Alliances

- The U.S. and E.U. should complete negotiations on the Transatlantic Trade and Investment Partnership, creating a U.S.-E.U. free-trade zone. In light of stunning anti-E.U. and anti-Atlanticist victories in European elections, a Transatlantic free-trade zone would reaffirm the common values and vision that unite the West, and reassure Europe that America remains committed to a close and mutually prosperous relationship.
- The U.S. should push NATO member states to strengthen their military presence in continental Europe and other NATO territory—perhaps on a rotational basis—to act as a deterrent against aggressors and enhance the security of all European member states.[1]
- Strong U.S. action on Syria, such as improving efforts to intercept Iranian arms shipments to Assad, will reassure embattled American allies such as Turkey and Saudi Arabia. We need to prove to these increasingly skeptical Sunni countries that America can lead in the Middle East and prevent Iran from dominating the region.
- The U.S. should encourage Japan to take steps toward responsible remilitarization while we continue to support our Asian allies with a strong American military presence.[2]
- Japan and South Korea have a common interest in ensuring that their territorial waters are respected by a fast-growing Chinese navy that has little regard for internationally recog-

nized borders. The United States should serve as a facilitator for Japan and South Korea to coordinate naval strategy, and endeavor to build trust between the two countries until they are comfortable cooperating with each other bilaterally.[3]

- Japan and South Korea also have a common interest in protecting against North Korean aggression. As Pyongyang plans its fourth nuclear test, the U.S. should allow Japan and South Korea to develop their own joint missile-defense system to complement the existing system run by the United States. This step would help the two American allies, still leery of each other, to devise joint strategic goals and increase intelligence sharing.[4]

- The U.S. should install cutting-edge THAAD missile-defense systems in South Korea. This will not only deter further North Korean aggression; it will also have the added benefit of balancing against Chinese military power while Beijing continues to improve its own nuclear and missile capabilities.[5]

Endnotes

FOREWORD

1. "'Russia-China Ties at Highest Level in History'—Putin," RT, May 18, 2014, http://rt.com/news/159804-putin-china-visit-interview/.

2. Charles Krauthammer, "Who Made the Pivot to Asia? Putin," *Washington Post*, May 22, 2014, http://www.washingtonpost.com/opinions/charles-krauthammer-who-made-the-pivot-to-asia-putin/2014/05/22/091a48ee-e1e3-11e3-9743-bb9b59cde7b9_story.html.

3. Jane Perlez, "China and Russia Reach 30-Year Gas Deal," *New York Times*, May 21, 2014, http://www.nytimes.com/2014/05/22/world/asia/china-russia-gas-deal.html.

4. "The New Non-Aggression Pact: The Russia-China Gas Deal Has Strategic Benefits for Both Sides," editorial, *Wall Street Journal*, May 23, 2014, http://online.wsj.com/news/articles/SB10001424052702303480304579576052453731102.

5. John Bolton, "Doubling Down on a Muddled Foreign Policy," *Wall Street Journal*, May 28, 2014, http://online.wsj.com/articles/john-bolton-doubling-down-on-a-muddled-foreign-policy-1401317355.

6. Brian Spegele, Wayne Ma, and Gregory L. White, "Russia and China Agree on Long-Sought Natural-Gas Supply Contract." *Wall Street Journal,* May 21, 2014, http://online.wsj.com/news/articles/SB10001424052702303749904579575820607872000.

7. Neil MacFarquhar and David M. Hersenzhorn, "Ukraine Crisis Pushing Putin Toward China," *New York Times*, May 19, 2014, http://www.nytimes.com/2014/05/20/world/europe/ukraine-crisis-pushing-putin-toward-china.html.

8. "'Russia-China Ties at Highest Level in History'–Putin."

9. Ibid.

10. Ibid.

11. Brian Spegele and Wayne Ma, "Putin's China Visit Highlights Shifting Power Balance," *Wall Street Journal*, May 15, 2014, http://online.wsj.com/news/articles/SB1 0001424052702304908304579563930004679204.

12. Ariel Zirulnick, "China Warns It Cannot Be Contained as U.S. Defense Secretary Visits," *Christian Science Monitor*, April 8, 2014, http://www.csmonitor. com/World/Security-Watch/terrorism-security/2014/0408/China-warns-it-cannot-be-contained-as-US-defense-secretary-visits-video.

13. Krauthammer, "Who made the pivot to Asia? Putin."

14. Kirit Radia, "Putin on Obama: 'Who made Him a Judge?'" ABC News, May 23, 2014, http://abcnews.go.com/blogs/headlines/2014/05/putin-on-obama-who-made-him-a-judge/.

15. Neil MacFarquhar, "From Crimea, Putin Trumpets Mother Russia," *New York Times*, May 9, 2014, http://www.nytimes.com/2014/05/10/world/europe/russia-celebrates-victory-day.html.

16. Ibid.

17. "Ukraine Crisis: Vladimir Putin Visits Annexed Crimea," BBC News, May 9, 2014, http://www.bbc.com/news/world-europe-27344029.

18. Paul Sonne, "Putin Arrives in Crimea on First Official Visit Since Russian Annexation," *Wall Street Journal*, May 9, 2014, http://online.wsj.com/news/articles/ SB10001424052702304655304579551310539881766.

19. Radina Gigova, Lena Kashkarova, and Victoria Butenko, "Ukraine's Donetsk Region Asking to Join Russia, Separatist Leader Says," CNN, May 12, 2014, http:// www.cnn.com/2014/05/12/world/europe/ukraine-crisis/.

20. "China Answers Obama" editorial, *Wall Street Journal*. May 8, 2014, http:// online.wsj.com/news/articles/SB10001424052702304431104579549783890027084.

21. Jane Perlez, "China and Vietnam Point Fingers After Clash in South China Sea," *New York Times*, May 27, 2014, http://www.nytimes.com/2014/05/28/world/ asia/vietnam.html.

22. "The South China Sea: Not the Usual Drill," *The Economist*, May 10, 2014, http://www.economist.com/news/asia/21601879-tensions-mount-dangerously-contested-waters-not-usual-drill.

23. Martin Fackler, "Chinese Flybys Alarm Japan as Tensions Escalate," *New York Times*, May 25, 2014, http://www.nytimes.com/2014/05/26/world/asia/japan-east-china-sea.html.

24. Bill Gertz, "Tensions Mount in South China Sea Dispute Over Chinese Oil Drilling," *Washington Free Beacon*, May 14, 2014, http://freebeacon.com/national-security/tensions-mount-in-south-china-sea-dispute-over-chinese-oil-drilling/.

25. Trefor Moss, "China Begins Construction in Spratly Islands," *Wall Street Journal*, May 14, 2014, http://online.wsj.com/news/articles/SB1000142405270230 49083045795611232911666730.

26. "China Answers Obama."

27. David Pilling, "China Is Stealing a Strategic March on the U.S.," *Financial Times*, May 28, 2014, http://www.ft.com/intl/cms/s/0/98f43524-e5ad-11e3-aeef-00144feabdc0.html#axzz33OCPo8qq.

28. Helene Cooper and Jane Perlez, "U.S. Sway in Asia Is Imperiled as China Changes Allegiances," *New York Times*, May 30, 2014, http://www.nytimes.com/2014/05/31/world/asia/us-sway-in-asia-is-imperiled-as-china-challenges-alliances.html.

29. Mark Landler, "Obama to Detail a Broader Foreign Policy Agenda, *New York Times*, May 24, 2014, http://www.nytimes.com/2014/05/25/world/obama-to-detail-a-broader-foreign-policy-agenda.html.

30. Mark Landler, "In Obama's Speeches, a Shifting Tone on Terror," *New York Times*, May 31, 2014, http://www.nytimes.com/2014/06/01/world/americas/in-obamas-speeches-a-shifting-tone-on-terror.html.

31. Ken Dilanian and Deb Reichmann, "Questions Loom Over Bergdahl-Taliban Swap," AP, June 3, 2014, http://bigstory.ap.org/article/us-soldier-released-after-5-years-captivity.

32. Mark Landler, "Obama Warns U.S. Faces Diffuse Terrorism Threat," *New York Times*, May 28, 2014, http://www.nytimes.com/2014/05/29/us/politics/obama-foreign-policy-west-point-speech.html.

33. Leon Wieseltier, "The Inconvenience of History: Obama Abandons Another Country to Its Fate," *New Republic*, April 23, 2014, http://www.newrepublic.com/article/117491/obama-and-inconvenience-history-abandoning-ukraine.

34. Ibid.

35. Council on Foreign Relations event, New York City, April 23, 2014.

36. Leon Panetta, "Playing Politics With Military Readiness in a Dangerous World," *Wall Street Journal*, April 30, 2014, http://online.wsj.com/news/articles/SB1 00014240527023039394045795303632670544646.

37. Alexander Panin, "Russia Prioritizes Military Buildup as Nato Cuts Back," *Moscow Times*, February 3, 2014, http://www.themoscowtimes.com/news/article/russia-prioritizes-military-buildup-as-nato-cuts-back/493828.html.

38. Nikolas Gvosdev, "Russia's Military Is Back," *National Interest*, October 4, 2013, http://nationalinterest.org/commentary/russias-military-back-9181.

39. Bill Gertz, "4 Russian Bombers Flew Within 50 Miles of the California Coast," *Washington Free Beacon*, June 11, 2014, http://www.businessinsider.com/russian-bombers-california-2014-6.

40. Panin, "Russia Prioritizes Military Buildup as Nato Cuts Back."

41. "China's Military Spending: At the Double," *The Economist*, March 15, 2014, http://www.economist.com/news/china/21599046-chinas-fast-growing-defence-budget-worries-its-neighbours-not-every-trend-its-favour.

42. David League, "China's Hawks Take the Offensive," Reuters, January 17, 2014, http://www.reuters.com/investigates/china-military/.

43. Andrew Brown, "Beijing Moves Boldly, Calculates Carefully," *Wall Street Journal*, June 3, 2014, http://online.wsj.com/articles/chinas-world-beijing-moves-boldly-calculates-carefully-1401781794.

44. Cooper and Perlez, "U.S. Sway in Asia Is Imperiled."

45. Chun Han Wong and Julian Barnes, "China Military Official Blasts U.S. 'Hegemony' at Shangri-La Conference," *Wall Street Journal*, June 1, 2014, http://online.wsj.com/articles/china-military-official-blasts-u-s-hegemony-at-shangri-la-security-conference-1401648136.

46. Jonah Goldberg, "Jonah Goldberg: Obama's Lame Sock Hop With Putin," *New Hampshire Union Leader*, April 21, 2014, http://www.unionleader.com/article/20140421/OPINION02/140429800/0/FRONTPAGE.

47. William J. Broad, "In Taking Crimea, Putin Gains a Sea of Fuel Reserves," *New York Times*, May 17, 2014, http://www.nytimes.com/2014/05/18/world/europe/in-taking-crimea-putin-gains-a-sea-of-fuel-reserves.html.

48. Freedom House, "Nations in Transit 2014," http://www.freedomhouse.org/report/nations-transit/nations-transit-2014.

49. Erin McClam, "Putin Jabs Obama: 'Who Is He to Judge, Seriously?'" NBC News, May 23, 2014, http://www.nbcnews.com/storyline/ukraine-crisis/putin-jabs-obama-who-he-judge-seriously-n112806.

50. Thom Shanker and Lauren D'Avolio, "Former Defense Secretaries Criticize Obama on Syria," *New York Times*, http://www.nytimes.com/2013/09/19/world/middleeast/gates-and-panetta-critical-of-obama-on-syria.html.

51. Bob Woodward, "Robert Gates, Former Defense Secretary, Offers Harsh Critique of Obama's Leadership in 'Duty,'" *Washington Post*, January 7, 2014, http://www.washingtonpost.com/world/national-security/robert-gates-former-defense-secretary-offers-harsh-critique-of-obamas-leadership-in-duty/2014/01/07/6a6915b2-77cb-11e3-b1c5-739e63e9c9a7_story.html.

52. Evan McMurray, "*New Yorker*'s Remnick on Obama: 'The World Seems to Disappoint Him,'" Mediaite, May 6, 2014, http://www.mediaite.com/tv/new-yorkers-remnick-on-obama-the-world-seems-to-disappoint-him/.

53. David Ignatius, "Obama Tends to Create His Own Foreign-Policy Headaches," *Washington Post*, May 6, 2014, http://www.washingtonpost.com/opinions/david-ignatius-damage-to-obamas-foreign-policy-has-been-largely-self-inflicted/2014/05/06/d3e7665a-d550-11e3-aae8-c2d44bd79778_story.html.

54. David Rothkopf, "The Blind Squirrel Gambit: Has Obama Stumbled Into a Solution for Syria?" *Foreign Policy*, September 11, 2013, http://www.foreignpolicy.com/articles/2013/09/11/the_blind_squirrel_gambit_obama_syria.

55. "Saudi Arabia Turns Down UN Security Council Seat," BBC News, October 18, 2013, http://www.bbc.com/news/world-middle-east-24580767.

56. Ariel Ben Solomon, "Russia to Conduct Joint Army Drills Amid Bid to Regain Regional Hold," *Jerusalem Post*, May 11, 2014, http://www.jpost.com/Middle-East/Russian-military-delegation-leaves-Egyptplans-joint-military-exercises-for-early-next-year-351934.

57. Elizabeth Dickinson, "Turkey-U.S. Tension Risks Complicated Business Ties," *Monitor Global Outlook*, May 5, 2014, http://monitorglobaloutlook.com/turkey-us-tension-risks-complicating-business-ties/.

58. Emma Graham-Harrison, "Afghan President Hamid Karzai Backs Russia's Annexation of Crimea," *The Guardian*, March 24, 2014, http://www.theguardian.com/world/2014/mar/24/afghan-president-hamid-karzai-backs-russia-annexation-crimea.

59. Ibid.

60. Ahmed Rashee, "Exclusive: Iraq Signs Deal to Buy Arms, Ammunition From Iran—documents," Reuters, February 24, 2014, http://www.reuters.com/article/2014/02/24/us-iraq-iran-arms-idUSBREA1N10D20140224.

61. Farnaz Fassihi, "Iran Pays Afghans to Fight for Assad," *Wall Street Journal*, May 22, 2014, http://online.wsj.com/news/articles/SB10001424052702304908304579564161508613846.

62. Jay Solomon, "U.S. Data Suggests Syria Used Chlorine," *Wall Street Journal*, May 15, 2014, http://online.wsj.com/news/articles/SB10001424052702303409004579564343207404138.

63. Nick Cumming-Bruce, "U.N. Panel Finds Crimes Against Humanity in North Korea," *New York Times*, February 15, 2014, http://www.nytimes.com/2014/02/16/world/asia/un-panel-finds-crimes-against-humanity-in-north-korea.html.

64. Andrew Brown, "North Korea Holds Key to a China Nightmare," *Wall Street Journal*, May 6, 2014, http://online.wsj.com/news/articles/SB1000142405270230483130457954477191697410.

65. Benny Avni, "Iranian Nukes? Sorry About That, Chief" *New York Post,* May 15, 2014, http://nypost.com/2014/05/15/iranian-nukes-sorry-about-that-chief/.

66. Emily Rauhala, "Obama Ends Asia Tour in China's Long Shadow," *Time,* April 29, 2014, http://time.com/80500/obama-asia-tour-china-philippines/.

67. Jim Acosta, "Obama Leaves Japan After Defending Foreign Policy," *PoliticalTicker* (blog), CNN, April 24, 2014, http://politicalticker.blogs.cnn.com/2014/04/24/obama-leaves-japan-after-defending-foreign-policy/.

68. Gerard Baker, "Abe's Strategy: Rearrange Region's Power Balance," *Wall Street Journal,* May 26, 2014, http://online.wsj.com/news/articles/SB10001424052702304811904579585702903470312.

69. Tsuyoshi Inajima and Emi Urabe Emi, "Japanese Lawmakers Lobby Abe for Russian Gas Pipeline," Bloomberg News, May 27, 2014, http://www.bloomberg.com/news/2014-05-27/japanese-lawmakers-to-push-abe-on-russia-natural-gas-pipeline.html.

70. Baker, "Abe's Strategy."

71. "Putin's European Enablers," editorial, *Wall Street Journal,* May 18, 2014, http://online.wsj.com/news/articles/SB10001424052702303908804579564140684929388.

72. "Why France Still Sells Warships to Putin," *Chronicle Herald,* May 16, 2014, http://thechronicleherald.ca/world/1208004-why-france-still-sells-warships-to-putin.

73. Stacey Meichtry, "France Moves to Defy Allies on Sale of Warship to Russia," *Wall Street Journal,* June 4, 2014, http://online.wsj.com/articles/france-moves-to-defy-allies-on-sale-of-warship-to-russia-1401877000.

74. Andrew Higgins, "Far-Right Fever for a Europe Tied to Russia," *New York Times,* http://mobile.nytimes.com/2014/05/21/world/europe/europes-far-right-looks-to-russia-as-a-guiding-force.html.

75. John Vinocur, "Vladimir Putin's Woman in Paris," *Wall Street Journal,* May 26, 2014, http://online.wsj.com/news/articles/SB1000142405270230390330457958579206384568.

76. "President Obama Misses a Chance on Foreign Affairs," editorial, *New York Times,* May 28, 2014, http://www.nytimes.com/2014/05/29/opinion/president-obama-misses-a-chance-on-foreign-affairs.html.

77. "Doubts and Obama's Diplomacy," editorial, *Financial Times,* May 28, 2014, http://www.ft.com/intl/cms/s/0/3dc73d02-e66d-11e3-9a20-00144feabdc0.html#axzz33OCPo8qq.

78. John Bolton, "Doubling Down on a Muddled Foreign Policy," *Wall Street Journal,* May 28, 2014, http://online.wsj.com/articles/john-bolton-doubling-down-on-a-muddled-foreign-policy-1401317355.

79. Thomas Erdbrink, "Iran's Leader Says Obama Has Removed Military Option," *New York Times*, June 4, 2014, http://www.nytimes.com/2014/06/05/world/middleeast/ayatollah-ali-khamenei-sees-change-in-west-point-speech.html.

80. "What Would America Fight For?" *The Economist*, May 3, 2014, http://www.economist.com/news/leaders/21601508-nagging-doubt-eating-away-world-orderand-superpower-largely-ignoring-it-what.

81. Mike Dorning, "Obama as Reluctant Warrior Backed by Combat-Weary Voters," Bloomberg News, May 16, 2014, http://www.bloomberg.com/news/2014-05-16/obama-as-reluctant-warrior-backed-by-combat-weary-voters.html.

82. Robert Kagan, "Superpowers Don't Get to Retire," *New Republic*, May 26, 2014, http://www.newrepublic.com/article/117859/allure-normalcy-what-america-still-owes-world.

UPDATED FORWORD, 2015

1. Paul Sonne and James Marson, "Putin Hails Russia-China Ties While Rosneft Does Deals With West," *Wall Street Journal*, June 19, 2015, http://www.wsj.com/articles/putin-hails-russia-china-ties-while-rosneft-does-deals-with-west-1434751773.

2. Michael Weiss and James Miller, "New Putin Invasion Coming This Summer," *Daily Beast*, May 17, 2015, http://www.thedailybeast.com/articles/2015/05/17/new-putin-invasion-coming-this-summer.html.

3. "More Russian Troops and Weapons Enter East Ukraine War Zone," *Kyiv Post*, April 12, 2015, http://www.kyivpost.com/content/ukraine/more-russian-troops-and-weapons-enter-east-ukraine-war-zone-386004.html.

4. Robert Hackett, "Russian Cyberwar Advances Military Interests in Ukraine, Report Says," *Fortune*, April 29, 2015, http://fortune.com/2015/04/29/russian-cyberwar-ukraine.

5. "The Russians Are Coming, Again," editorial, *Wall Street Journal*, May 28, 2015, http://www.wsj.com/articles/the-russians-are-coming-again-1432853799.

6. Andrew E. Kramer and Michael R. Gordon, "Russia Sent Tanks to Separatists in Ukraine, U.S. Says," *New York Times*, June 13, 2014, http://www.nytimes.com/2014/06/14/world/europe/ukraine-claims-full-control-of-port-city-of-mariupol.html. See also Neil MacFarquhar and Michael R. Gordon, "Ukraine Leader Says 'Huge Loads of Arms' Pour In From Russia," *New York Times*, August 28, 2014, http://www.nytimes.com/2014/08/29/world/europe/ukraine-conflict.html.

7. Paul Roderick Gregory, "New Study on the Shooting Down of MH17 Points to Russian Forces," *Forbes*, January 12, 2015, http://www.forbes.com/sites/paulroderickgregory/2015/01/12/new-study-on-the-shooting-down-of-mh17-points-to-russian-forces.

8. "Putin Reveals Secrets of Russia's Crimea Takeover Plot," BBC News, March 9, 2015, http://www.bbc.com/news/world-europe-31796226.

9. Laura Smith-Spark, Alla Eshchenko, and Emma Burrows, "Russia Was Ready to Put Nuclear Forces on Alert Over Crimea, Putin Says," CNN, March 16, 2015, http://www.cnn.com/2015/03/16/europe/russia-putin-crimea-nuclear.

10. Graham Allison and Dimitri K. Simes, "Russia and America: Stumbling to War," *National Interest*, April 20, 2015, http://nationalinterest.org/feature/russia-america-stumbling-war-12662.

11. Helle Dale, "Putin Sets His Sights on the Baltic States," *Newsweek*, July 14, 2015, http://www.newsweek.com/putin-sets-his-sights-baltic-states-353682.

12. "China's Maritime Disputes," Council on Foreign Relations InfoGuide Presentation, accessed May 11, 2015, http://www.cfr.org/asia-and-pacific/chinas-maritime-disputes/p31345#!.

13. Jane Perlez, "China Building Aircraft Runway in Disputed Spratly Islands," *New York Times*, April 16, 2015, http://www.nytimes.com/2015/04/17/world/asia/china-building-airstrip-in-disputed-spratly-islands-satellite-images-show.html.

14. Josh Rogin, "U.S. Misses Real Threat of China's Fake Islands," *Bloomberg View*, April 2, 2015, http://www.bloombergview.com/articles/2015-04-02/u-s-misses-real-threat-of-china-s-fake-islands.

15. Ted Galen Carpenter, "Is America About to Make a Fatal Mistake in the South China Sea?" *National Interest*, May 18, 2015, http://nationalinterest.org/feature/america-about-make-fatal-mistake-the-south-china-sea-12905.

16. John Blosser, "China Warns War May Be Coming With US," *Newsmax*, May 26, 2015, http://www.newsmax.com/Newsfront/china-united-states-south-china-sea-navy/2015/05/26/id/646828/#ixzz3n6AD9HMG.

17. Ibid.

18. "Kaiser Xi's Navy," editorial, *Wall Street Journal*, May 29, 2015, http://www.wsj.com/articles/kaiser-xis-navy-1432939293.

19. Andrew Browne, "Stuck on a Reef, a Bilateral Relationship Founders," *Wall Street Journal*, May 19, 2015, http://www.wsj.com/articles/stuck-on-a-reef-a-bilateral-relationship-founders-1432017372.

20. Bill Gertz, "Verifying Iran Nuclear Deal Not Possible, Experts Say," *Washington Free Beacon*, April 6, 2015, http://freebeacon.com/national-security/verifying-iran-nuclear-deal-not-possible-experts-say.

21. Ray Takeyh, "How Iran Can Game the Deal," *Politico*, April 3, 2015, http://www.politico.com/magazine/story/2015/04/iran-deal-flaws-116655.

22. Noah Browning and David Alexander, "Iranian Revolutionary Guards Seize Cargo Ship in Gulf," Reuters, April 28, 2015, http://www.reuters.com/article/2015/04/28/us-iran-usa-ship-guards-idUSKBN0NJ27R20150428.

23. Louisa Loveluck and David Lawler, "Iran 'Seizes Cargo Ship' in What US Calls a 'Provocative Act' in the Gulf," *The Telegraph*, April 28, 2015, http://www.telegraph.co.uk/news/worldnews/middleeast/iran/11568724/Iranian-force-seizes-US-cargo-ship.

24. Eliott C. McLaughlin, "Iran's Supreme Leader: There Will Be No Such Thing as Israel in 25 Years," CNN, September 11, 2015, http://www.cnn.com/2015/09/10/middleeast/iran-khamenei-israel-will-not-exist-25-years.

25. Tzvi Kahn, "FPI Bulletin: China-Iran Strategic Partnership Undermines Nuclear Talks," Foreign Policy Initiative, April 27, 2015, http://www.foreignpolicy.org/content/fpi-bulletin-china-iran-strategic-partnership-undermines-nuclear-talks.

26. "Iran's Navy Commander in China to Discuss Wider Military Cooperation," Fars News Agency, October 9, 2014, http://english.farsnews.com/newstext.aspx?nn=13930727000256.

27. Sydney J. Freedberg Jr., "Navy Strains to Handle Both China and Iran at Once," *Breaking Defense*, May 21, 2012, http://breakingdefense.com/2012/05/navy-strains-to-handle-both-china-and-iran-at-once.

28. Armin Rose, "Russia and Iran Just Showed How 'They Can Do Whatever They Like' Right Now," *Business Insider*, April 13, 2015, http://www.businessinsider.com/russia-is-selling-a-game-changing-missile-system-to-iran-2015-4#ixzz3acPMutbQ.

29. Amir Taheri, "An Iran-Russia Axis," *New York Post*, December 7, 2014, http://nypost.com/2014/12/07/an-iran-russia-axis.

30. Kathrin Hille and John Reed, "Russia to Deploy 2,000 in Syria Air Base Mission's 'First Phase,'" *Financial Times*, September 21, 2015, http://www.ft.com/intl/cms/s/0/95971a4e-607d-11e5-a28b-50226830d644.html#axzz3mgDIAs2e.

31. Jethro Mullen, "Is Russia Preparing to Move Troops to 2 New Syria Bases?" CNN, September 23, 2015, http://www.cnn.com/2015/09/23/middleeast/syria-russia-military-buildup.

32. Dion Nissenbaum and Carol E. Lee, "Russia Expands Military Presence in Syria, Satellite Photos Show," *Wall Street Journal*, September 22, 2015, http://www.wsj.com/articles/russia-expands-military-its-presence-in-syria-satellite-photos-show-1442937150.

33. Michael Weiss, "Russia Is Sending Jihadis to Join ISIS," *Daily Beast*, August 23, 2015, http://www.thedailybeast.com/articles/2015/08/23/russia-s-playing-a-double-game-with-islamic-terror0.html.

34. Deb Riechmann and Lolita C. Baldor, "Top General: Only a Handful of US-Trained Syrian Fighters Remain in Battle Against ISIS," Associated Press, September 16, 2015, http://www.usnews.com/news/politics/articles/2015/09/16/general-only-handful-of-syrian-fighters-remain-in-battle.

35. Doug Bandow, "Friends With Benefits: Russia and North Korea's Twisted Tango," *National Interest*, March 6, 2015, http://nationalinterest.org/feature/friends-benefits-russia-north-koreas-twisted-tango-12369.

36. Jeremy Page and Jay Solomon, "China Warns North Korean Nuclear Threat Is Rising," *Wall Street Journal*, April 22, 2015, http://www.wsj.com/articles/china-warns-north-korean-nuclear-threat-is-rising-1429745706.

37. Ibid.

38. Tom Burgis, "North Korea: The Secrets of Office 39," *Financial Times*, June 24, 2015, http://www.ft.com/intl/cms/s/0/4164dfe6-09d5-11e5-b6bd-00144feabdc0.html#axzz3e7Y2VwsA.

39. David E. Sanger and Julie Hirschfeld Davis, "Hacking Linked to China Exposes Millions of U.S. Workers," *New York Times*, June 4, 2015, http://www.nytimes.com/2015/06/05/us/breach-in-a-federal-computer-system-exposes-personnel-data.html.

40. Michael S. Schmidt and David E. Sanger, "Russian Hackers Read Obama's Unclassified Emails, Officials Say," *New York Times*, April 25, 2015, http://www.nytimes.com/2015/04/26/us/russian-hackers-read-obamas-unclassified-emails-officials-say.html.

41. Courtney Kube and Jim Miklaszewski, "Russia Hacks Pentagon Computers: NBC, Citing Sources," CNBC, August 6, 2015, http://www.cnbc.com/2015/08/06/russia-hacks-pentagon-computers-nbc-citing-sources.html.

42. Daniel Halper, "Top Spy: Hillary's Emails 'Likely' Hacked by China, Russia, Iran," *Weekly Standard*, April 7, 2015, http://www.weeklystandard.com/blogs/top-spy-hillarys-emails-likely-hacked-china-russia-iran_911707.html. Also see "Ex-Obama Intel Head: 'Very Likely' China, Russia Hacked Hillary's Private Email Account," *Breitbart News*, April 7, 2015, http://www.breitbart.com/big-government/2015/04/07/ex-obama-intel-head-very-likely-china-russia-hacked-hillarys-private-email-account.

43. Jeffrey Scott Shapiro, "Stealth B-2s Buzz Europe as Russian Bombers Skirt U.S. Airspace," *Washington Times*, June 9, 2015, http://www.washingtontimes.com/news/2015/jun/9/stealth-b-2s-buzz-europe-russian-bombers-skirt-us-.

44. Gleb Bryanski, "Russia's Putin Calls for Stalin-Style 'Leap forward,'" Reuters, August 31, 2012, http://www.reuters.com/article/2012/08/31/us-russia-putin-stalin-idUSBRE87U16420120831.

45. James M. Inhofe, "It's Time to Stop Putin's Nuclear Arms Buildup," *Foreign Policy*, September 8, 2014, http://foreignpolicy.com/2014/09/08/its-time-to-stop-putins-nuclear-arms-buildup.

46. David E. Sanger and William J. Broad, "China Making Some Missiles More Powerful," *New York Times*, May 16, 2015, http://www.nytimes.com/2015/05/17/world/asia/china-making-some-missiles-more-powerful.html.

47. Andrew Jacobs, "China, Updating Military Strategy, Puts Focus on Projecting Naval Power," *New York Times*, May 26, 2015, http://www.nytimes.com/2015/05/27/world/asia/china-updating-military-strategy-puts-focus-on-projecting-naval-power.html.

48. Ibid.

49. Hannah Beech, "How China Sees the World," *Time*, June 17, 2013, http://www.time.com/time/magazine/article/0,9171,2145062,00.html.

50. Kevin P. Gallagher, "Latin America Needs China to Help Close Infrastructure Gap," *Beyond Brics* (blog), *Financial Times*, May 19, 2015, http://blogs.ft.com/beyond-brics/2015/05/19/latin-america-needs-china-to-help-close-infrastructure-gap.

51. Andrew O' Reilly, "Russia's Growing Presence in Latin America Is Cause of Worry for U.S. And Its Allies," Fox News Latino, March 25, 2015, http://latino.foxnews.com/latino/news/2015/03/25/russia-growing-presence-in-latin-america-is-cause-worry-for-us-and-its-allies.

52. Ibid.

53. Dmitri Trenin, "Putin's Latin America Trip Aims to Show Russia Is More Than Just Regional Power," *The Guardian*, July 15, 2014, http://www.theguardian.com/world/2014/jul/15/putin-latin-america-russia-power.

54. "China–Latin America Finance Database," Inter-American Dialogue, accessed September 29, 2015.
http://thedialogue.org/map_list.

55. Jacob M. Schlesinger, Mitsuru Obe, and Mark Magnier, "TPP: Momentum on Trade Deal Bolsters U.S., Japan Efforts to Counter China," *Wall Street Journal*, April 17, 2105, http://www.wsj.com/articles/tpp-momentum-on-trade-deal-bolsters-u-s-japan-efforts-to-counter-china-1429249448.

INTRODUCTION: WHILE AMERICA SLEPT

1. David. M. Herszenhorn and Chris Buckley, "China's New Leader, Visiting Russia, Promotes Nations' Economic and Military Ties," *New York Times*, March 22, 2013, http://www.nytimes.com/2013/03/23/world/asia/xi-jinping-visits-russia-on-first-trip-abroad.html.

2. Ibid.

3. "Russia Putin Meets With New Chinese Leader," Radio Free Europe/ Radio Liberty, November 19, 2013, http://www.rferl.org/content/russi-china-xi-jinping-/24935553.html.

4. Herszenhorn and Buckley, "China's New Leader."

5. Ibid.

6. Ibid.

7. Ibid.

8. Joshua Kurlantzick, "A New Axis of Autonomy," *Wall Street Journal*, March 29, 2013, http://online.wsj.com/article/SB100014241278873246851045783885503 46881268.html.

9. Bill Chappel, "Russia Vetoes U.N. Security Council Resolution on Crimea," NPR, March 15, 2014, http://www.npr.org/blogs/thetwo-way/2014/ 03/15/290404691/russia-vetoes-u-n-security-council-resolution-on-crimea.

10. Richard Weiss, "Superpower Symbiosis: The Russia-China Axis," *World Affairs*, November/December 2012, http://www.worldaffairsjournal.org/article/superpower-symbiosis-russia-china-axis.

11. Luke Harding, "Syria Misses Chemical Weapons Deadline," *The Guardian*, December 31, 2013, http://www.theguardian.com/world/2013/dec/31/syria-misses-chemical-weapons-deadline.

12. Ibid.

13. Carol Howard, "Forbes' List of the World's Most Powerful People, 2013 Edition," *Daily Finance*, October 30, 2013, http://www.dailyfinance.com/2013/10/30/ worlds-most-powerful-people-2013-forbes/.

14. Josh Rogin, "U.S. Rations, Promised for Ukraine, Are Missing in Action," *Daily Beast*, March 19, 2014, http://www.thedailybeast.com/articles/2014/03/19/u-s-rations-promised-for-ukraine-missing-in-action.html.

15. Anne Applebaum, "Ukraine Shows the 'Color Revolution' Model Is Dead," *Washington Post*, January 24, 2013, http://www.washingtonpost.com/opinions/ anne-applebaum-ukraine-shows-the-color-revolution-model-is-dead/2014/01/24/ c77d3ab0-8524-11e3-8099-9181471f7aaf_story.html.

16. Michael R. Gordon, "U.S. Says Russia Tested Missile, Despite Treaty," *New York Times*, January 14, 2014, http://www.nytimes.com/2014/01/30/world/europe/ us-says-russia-tested-missile-despite-treaty.html.

17. Puppets Maidan, February 4, 2014, https://www.youtube.com/watch?v=MSxaa-67yGM#t=89.

18. Alison Smale, "Leaked Recordings Lay Bare E.U. and U.S. Divisions in Goals for Ukraine," *New York Times*, February 7, 2014, http://www.nytimes.com/2014/02/08/world/europe/ukraine.html.

19. Ibid.

CHAPTER 1: THE NEW TERRAIN

1. Jeremy Page, "For Xi, a 'China Dream' of Military Power," *Wall Street Journal*, March 13, 2013, http://online.wsj.com/article/SB100014241278873241285045783 48774040546346.html.

2. Megan K. Stack, "Russia's Putin Talks Tough on U.S. Missile Shield," *Los Angeles Times*, December 30, 2009, http://articles.latimes.com/2009/dec/30/world/la-fg-russia-nukes30-2009dec30.

3. "Romney Chides Obama for 'Open Mic' Slip With Russia's Medvedev," Fox News, October 23, 2012, http://www.foxnews.com/politics/2012/10/23/flashback-romney-chides-obama-for-open-mic-slip-with-russia-medvedev/.

4. David K. Schneider, "The Shanghai Cooperation Organization," *American Diplomacy*, September 2008, http://www.unc.edu/depts/diplomat/item/2008/0709/comm/schneider_shanghai.html#_edn2.

5. Joshua Kucera, "Turkey Makes It Official With SCO," *EurasiaNet*, April 28, 2013, http://www.eurasianet.org/node/66896.

6. Andrew Scheineson, "The Shanghai Cooperation Organization," Council on Foreign Relations, March 24, 2009, http://www.cfr.org/international-peace-and-security/shanghai-cooperation-organization/p10883.

7. Ralph A. Cossa, "A Mild Chinese-Russian Affair," *New York Times*, January 14, 1997, http://www.nytimes.com/1997/01/14/opinion/14iht-edralph.t.html.

8. Gregory L. White and Paul Sonne, "As the Winter Olympics Open, Putin Showcases a Defiant Russia," *Wall Street Journal*, February 7, 2014, http://online.wsj.com/news/articles/SB10001424052702304450904579364991108125598.

9. William C. Martel, "An Authoritarian Axis Rising?" *The Diplomat*, June 29, 2012, http://thediplomat.com/2012/06/29/an-authoritarian-axis-rising/.

10. Sergei Lavrov, "Lavrov Outlines the Way Forward for Relations," *China Daily*, April 4, 2014, http://www.chinadaily.com.cn/world/2014-04/14/content_17433463.htm.

11. SIPRI Arms Transfers Database, "TIV of Arms Exports From the Top 10 Largest Exporters, 1991–2011" (generated June 14, 2012). The database can be accessed at http://www.sipri.org/databases/armstransfers. Dollar values are in constant 1990 USD.

12. George L. Simpson Jr., "Iranian Reform and Stagnation: Russian and Chinese Support for Tehran," *Middle East Quarterly* (Spring 2010): 65–66.

13. John Bolton, "Abject Surrender by the United States," *Weekly Standard*, November 24, 2013, http://www.weeklystandard.com/print/blogs/abject-surrender-united-states_768140.html.

14. Jennifer Rubin, "Obama vs. America on Iran," *Right Turn* (blog), *Washington Post*, January 28, 2014, http://www.washingtonpost.com/blogs/right-turn/wp/2014/01/28/obama-vs-america-on-iran/.

15. Jay Solomon, Carol E. Lee, and Laurence Norman, "Iranian Nuclear Accord Advances," *Wall Street Journal*, January 12, 2014, http://online.wsj.com/news/articles/SB10001424052702304549504579316643349109898.

16. Claudia Rosett, "The Iran–North Korea Axis of Proliferation," *Forbes*, March 9, 2013, http://www.forbes.com/sites/claudiarosett/2013/03/09/the-iran-north-korea-axis-of-proliferation/.

17. Liz Sodoti, "McCain Favors a 'League of Democracies,'" *Washington Post*, April 30, 2007, http://www.washingtonpost.com/wp-dyn/content/article/2007/04/30/AR2007043001402.html.

18. Vladimir A. Putin, "A Plea for Caution From Russia," *New York Times*, September 11, 2013, http://www.nytimes.com/2013/09/12/opinion/putin-plea-for-caution-from-russia-on-syria.html.

19. "West Using UN Probe in Syria Chemical Attack to Oust Assad: Russia," Press TV, December 5, 2013, http://www.presstv.ir/detail/2013/03/26/295228/west-using-syria-probe-to-topple-assad/.

20. Andre de Nesnera, "Russia Defends Arms Sales to Syria, Blasts US," Voice of America, June 13, 2012, http://www.voanews.com/content/russia_defends_arms_sale_to_syria_blasts_us/1210542.html.

21. Michael Martina, Sui-Lee Wee, and Ben Blanchard, "Syrian Opposition Group to Visit China Next Week," Reuters, September 14, 2012, http://www.reuters.com/article/2012/09/14/us-syria-crisis-china-idUSBRE88D09720120914.

22. James Clapper, "Unclassified Statement for the Record on the Worldwide Threat Assessment of the US Intelligence Community for the Senate Select Committee on Intelligence," January 31, 2012, http://www.intelligence.senate.gov/120131/clapper.pdf.

23. Julian E. Barnes and Siobhan Gorman, "U.S. Says Iran Hacked Navy Computers," *Wall Street Journal*, September 27, 2013, http://online.wsj.com/article/SB10001424052702304526204579101602356751772.html.

24. Stack, "Russia's Putin Talks Tough on U.S. Missile Shield."

25. Jon Kyl, "America's Nuclear Deterrent—and Defenses—Are Eroding Fast," *Wall Street Journal*, March 21, 2013, http://online.wsj.com/news/articles/SB10001424127887323415304578370783312615740.

26. Stephen Harner, "The Xi-Putin Summit, China-Russian Strategic Partnership, and the Folly of Obama's 'Asian Pivot,'" *Forbes*, March 24, 2013, http://www.forbes.com/sites/stephenharner/2013/03/24/the-xi-putin-summit-china-russian-strategic-partnership-and-the-failure-of-obamas-asian-pivot/.

27. All arms-transfer data is from the SIPRI Arms Transfers Database.

28. David Lague, "Special Report: China's Military Hawks Take the Offensive," *Reuters*, January 17, 2013, http://www.reuters.com/article/2013/01/17/us-china-hawks-idUSBRE90G00C20130117.

29. Peter. W. Singer, "Inside China's Secret Arsenal," *Popular Science*, December 20, 2102, http://www.popsci.com/technology/article/2012-12/inside-chinas-secret-arsenal.

30. "China Warns Australia Against Military Pact With US," *Economic Times*, November 17, 2011, http://articles.economictimes.indiatimes.com/2011-11-17/news/30410218_1_defence-pact-china-and-india-canberra.

31. Robert D. Kaplan, *Asia's Cauldron: The South China Sea and the End of a Stable Pacific* (New York: Random House, 2014), 35.

32. Jane Perlez, "China and Russia, in a Display of Unity, Hold Naval Exercises," *New York Times*, July 10, 2013, http://www.nytimes.com/2013/07/11/world/asia/china-and-russia-in-a-display-of-unity-hold-naval-exercises.html.

33. Jeremy Page, "For Xi, a 'China Dream' of Military Power," *Wall Street Journal*, March 13, 2013, http://online.wsj.com/article/SB10001424127887324128504578348774040546346.html.

34. Ibid.

35. Vladimir Putin, interview with Kevin Owen, "Putin: Using al-Qaeda in Syria Like Sending Gitmo Inmates to Fight," RT, September 6, 2012, http://rt.com/news/vladimir-putin-exclusive-interview-481/.

36. Eliot Cohen, "American Withdrawal and Global Disorder," *Wall Street Journal*, March 19, 2013, http://online.wsj.com/article/SB1000142412788732419620457830026245493952.html.

37. Jay Solomon, Carol E. Lee, and Laurence Norman, "Iranian Nuclear Accord Advances," *Wall Street Journal*, January 13, 2014, http://online.wsj.com/news/articles/SB10001424052702304549504579316643349109898.

38. Lydia Polgreen, "Group of Emerging Nations Plans to Form Development Bank," *New York Times*, March 26, 2013, http://www.nytimes.com/2013/03/27/world/africa/brics-to-form-development-bank.html.

39. Vladimir Soldatkin, "In Moscow, New Chinese Leader Xi Warns Against Meddling," *Chicago Tribune*, March 23, 2013, http://articles.chicagotribune.com/2013-03-23/news/sns-rt-us-china-russia-moscowbre92m02f-20130323_1_russia-and-china-xi-russian-students.

40. Stephen Harner, "Xi-Putin Summit," *Forbes*, March 24, 2013, http://www.forbes.com/sites/stephenharner/2013/03/24/the-xi-putin-summit-china-russian-strategic-partnership-and-the-failure-of-obamas-asian-pivot/.

41. John McCain on *Face the Nation*, April 7, 2013, http://www.cbsnews.com/news/face-the-nation-transcripts-april-7-2013-schumer-mccain-albright/.

42. "Bank of China Cuts Off N. Korea Bank Accused of Weapons Dealing," Bloomberg News, May 7, 2013, http://www.bloomberg.com/news/2013-05-07/bank-of-china-cuts-off-n-korea-bank-accused-of-weapons-dealing.html.

43. Elizabeth Dwoskin, "Hillary Clinton's Business Legacy at the State Department," *Bloomberg Businessweek*, January 10, 2013, http://www.businessweek.com/articles/2013-01-10/hillary-clintons-business-legacy-at-the-state-department.

44. Aaron L Friedberg, *The Contest for Supremacy* (New York: W.W. Norton, 2011), 131.

45. William R. Hawkins, "'U.S. Hegemony Ends,'" FrontPageMag.com, March 9, 2009, http://archive.frontpagemag.com/readArticle.aspx?ARTID=34262.

46. Caroline Wyatt, "Bush and Putin: Best of Friends," BBC News, June 16, 2001, http://news.bbc.co.uk/2/hi/1392791.stm.

47. Steve Holland and Margaret Chadbourne, "Obama Describes Putin as 'Like a Bored Kid,'" Reuters, August 9, 2013, http://www.reuters.com/article/2013/08/09/us-usa-russia-obama-idUSBRE9780XS20130809.

CHAPTER 2: ROGUE REGIMES

1. Josh Rogan, "Exclusive: John McCain Slips Across Border Into Syria, Meets With Rebels," *Daily Beast*, May 27, 2013, http://www.thedailybeast.com/articles/2013/05/27/exclusive-john-mccain-slips-across-border-into-syria-meets-with-rebels.html.

2. Stephen Yates, "Name and Shame China Over North Korea Launch," *Global Public Square* (blog), CNN, December 13, 2012, http://globalpublicsquare.blogs.cnn.com/2012/12/13/name-and-shame-china-over-north-korea-launch/.

3. Ariel Cohen and Stephen Blank, "Reset Regret: Russian Global Strategy Undermines American Interests" (WebMemo #3333, Heritage Foundation, August 3, 2011), http://www.heritage.org/research/reports/2011/08/reset-regret-russian-global-strategy-undermines-us-interests.

4. Gordon G. Chang, "North Korea to Launch Missile for Iran?" *World Affairs*, December 5, 2012, http://www.worldaffairsjournal.org/blog/gordon-g-chang/north-korea-launch-missile-iran.

5. David Hearst, "Putin: We Have Lost Russia's Trust," *The Guardian*, November 11, 2011, http://www.guardian.co.uk/world/2011/nov/12/putin-russia-lost-trust.

6. David Cohen, "Putin Wins China Peace Prize," *The Diplomat*, November 16, 2011, http://thediplomat.com/china-power/putin-wins-china-peace-prize/.

7. Jane Perlez, "Chinese President to Seek New Relationship With U.S. in Talks," *New York Times*, May 28, 2013, http://www.nytimes.com/2013/05/29/world/asia/china-to-seek-more-equal-footing-with-us-in-talks.html.

8. Gordon G. Chang, "Policy Implications of China–North Korea Relations," *International Journal of Korean Studies* 16, no. 1 (Spring/Summer 2012): 24, http://www.icks.org/publication/pdf/2012-SPRING-SUMMER/3.pdf.

9. Christine Kim and Joyce Lee, "North Korea Warns Foreigners to Leave South Amid New Threats of War," Reuters, April 9, 2013, http://www.reuters.com/article/2013/04/09/us-korea-north-idUSBRE93408020130409.

10. Laura Smith-Spark, "Report: North Korea Launches Fourth Short-Range Missile," CNN, May 19, 2013, http://www.cnn.com/2013/05/19/world/asia/north-korea-missiles/index.html.

11. Rick Gladstone and David E. Sanger, "New Sanctions on North Korea Pass in Unified U.N. Vote," *New York Times*, March 7, 2013, http://www.nytimes.com/2013/03/08/world/asia/north-korea-warns-of-pre-emptive-nuclear-attack.html.

12. Flavia Krause-Jackson, "China Agrees to Join U.S. to End N. Korea Weapons Pursuit," Bloomberg News, April 13, 2013, http://www.bloomberg.com/news/2013-04-12/kerry-to-press-china-to-crack-down-on-north-korea-regime.html.

13. Jane Perlez, "China Bluntly Tells North Korea to Enter Nuclear Talks," *New York Times*, May 24, 2013, http://www.nytimes.com/2013/05/25/world/asia/china-tells-north-korea-to-return-to-nuclear-talks.html.

14. Ibid.

15. Keith Bradsher and Nick Cumming-Bruce, "China Cuts Ties With Key North Korean Bank," *New York Times*, May 7, 2013, http://www.nytimes.com/2013/05/08/world/asia/china-cuts-ties-with-north-korean-bank.html.

16. Alexander Martin, "North Korea Doubles Down on China Ties," *Wall Street Journal*, April 30, 2013, http://online.wsj.com/article/SB10001424127887324763404578432633025779640.html.

17. Malcolm Moore, "China Breaking UN Sanctions to Support North Korea," *The Telegraph*, April 13, 2013, http://www.telegraph.co.uk/news/worldnews/asia/northkorea/9991907/China-breaking-UN-sanctions-to-support-North-Korea.html.

18. Ibid.

19. Ibid.

20. Ibid.

21. Jane Perlez, "China Ban on Items for Nuclear Use to North Korea May Stall Arms Bid," *New York Times*, September 29, 2013, http://www.nytimes.com/2013/09/30/world/asia/china-ban-on-items-for-nuclear-use-to-north-korea-may-stall-arms-bid.html.

22. Choe Sang-Hun, "Activity Seen at North Korean Nuclear Plant," *New York Times*, December 14, 2013, http://www.nytimes.com/2013/12/25/world/asia/experts-say-north-korea-may-be-producing-fuel-for-nuclear-reactor.html.

23. Gordon G. Chang, "How China Enables North Korea's Mischief," *New York Daily News*, April 3, 2013, http://www.nydailynews.com/opinion/china-enables-north-korea-mischief-article-1.1305864#ixzz2UPfyAEbk.

24. Ibid.

25. Ibid.

26. Donald Kirk, "UN Blast Against North Korea Faces Chinese Rebuke, NK Rage," *Forbes*, February 17, 2014, http://www.forbes.com/sites/donaldkirk/2014/02/17/un-blast-against-north-korea-faces-chinese-rebuke-north-korean-rage/.

27. Andrei Lankov, "Why Does China Continue to Support North Korea?" *East Asia Forum*, March 4, 2010, http://www.eastasiaforum.org/2010/05/14/why-does-china-continue-to-support-north-korea/.

28. Robert Windrem, "North Korean Progress on Nuclear Arms, Long-Range Missiles Rattles US and Allies," NBC News, December 13, 2012, http://openchannel.nbcnews.com/_news/2012/12/13/15875261-north-korean-progress-on-nuclear-arms-long-range-missiles-rattles-us-and-allies.

29. Michael J. Totten, "What If North Korea Is Serious?" *World Affairs*, April 11, 2013, http://www.worldaffairsjournal.org/blog/michael-j-totten/what-if-north-korea-serious.

30. Steven Pifer and Michael O'Hanlon, "The Opportunity: Next Steps in Reducing Nuclear Arms," Brookings.edu, October 12, 2012, http://www.brookings.edu/research/books/2012/theopportunity#ref-id=20121015_pifer.

31. Julia Ioffe, "The Cold War Heats Up in Syria: Why Russia Won't Allow an Intervention," *New Republic*, May 21, 2013, http://www.newrepublic.com/article/113255/syria-why-russia-and-united-states-cant-agree.

32. George L. Simpson Jr., "Iranian Reform and Stagnation: Russian and Chinese Support for Tehran," *Middle East Quarterly* (Spring 2010): 65–66.

33. Stephen Blank, "Nonproliferation, Russian Style," *Journal of International Security Affairs* no. 19 (Fall/Winter 2010), http://www.securityaffairs.org/issues/2010/19/blank.php#footnotes.

34. Ali Akbar Dareini, "Iran Nuclear Reactor at Bushehr Power Plant B egins Fueling With Help From Russia," *Huffington Post*, August 21, 2010, http://

www.huffingtonpost.com/2010/08/21/iran-nuclear-reactor-bushehr_n_689911. html.

35. "Update on the Arak Reactor in Iran," Institute for Science and International Security, August 25, 2009, http://isis-online.org/uploads/isis-reports/documents/ Arak_Update_25_August2009.pdf.

36. "US Calls Iran's Nuclear Reactor Plans 'Deeply Troubling,'" Voice of America News, June 5, 2013, http://www.voanews.com/content/us-calls-iran-nuclear-reactor-plans-for-heavy-water-reactor-arak/1676038.html.

37. Mark N. Katz, "Why Russia Won't Play Ball on Iran," *The Diplomat*, June 23, 2012, http://thediplomat.com/2012/06/why-russia-wont-play-ball-on-iran/.

38. "Iran President Hassan Rouhani: No Nation Should Possess Nuclear Weapons," *The Telegraph*, September 26, 2013, http://www.telegraph.co.uk/news/worldnews/ middleeast/iran/10338155/Iran-President-Hassan-Rouhani-no-nation-should-possess-nuclear-weapons.html.

39. "Israel PM Netanyahu Criticises Iran 'Deal of the Century,'" BBC News, November 8, 2013, http://www.bbc.co.uk/news/world-middle-east-24866004.

40. Jay Solomon, Carol E. Lee, and Laurence Norman, "Iranian Nuclear Accord Advances," *Wall Street Journal*, January 12, 2014, http://online.wsj.com/news/articles/ SB10001424052702304549504579316643349109898.

41. Blank, "Nonproliferation, Russian Style."

42. Fred Weir, "Russia Worried About a Nuclear Iran, but Leery of U.S. Sanctions," *Christian Science Monitor*, January 11, 2012, http://www.csmonitor.com/World/Europe/ 2012/0111/Russia-worried-about-a-nuclear-Iran-but-leery-of-US-sanctions.

43. Blank, "Nonproliferation, Russian Style."

44. Amir Taheri, "The New Cold War," *New York Post*, April 15, 2013, http:// nypost.com/2013/04/15/the-new-cold-war/#axzz2TxXegdyi.

45. Ibid.

46. Scott Peterson, "Russian Nuclear Support for Iran Limited by Distrust," *Christian Science Monitor*, September 6, 2012, http://www.csmonitor.com/World/ Middle-East/2012/0906/Russian-nuclear-support-for-Iran-limited-by-distrust.

47. "Iran Begins Loading Bushehr Nuclear Reactor," BBC News, August 21, 2010, http://www.bbc.co.uk/news/world-middle-east-11045537.

48. "Iran, Russia Ink Final Deal on Building New Nuclear Plants," *AzerNews*, April 22, 2014, http://www.azernews.az/region/66326.html.

49. Paul Richter, "Russia Pushing Back on Tougher Sanctions Against Iran," *Los Angeles Times*, September 24, 2010, http://articles.latimes.com/2010/sep/24/world/ la-fg-russia-sanctions-20100925.

50. Weir, "Russia Worried About a Nuclear Iran."

51. Ibid.

52. Rick Gladstone, "Russia Hints at Using Iran Talks as Leverage," *New York Times*, March 20, 2014, http://www.nytimes.com/2014/03/21/world/middleeast/russia-hints-at-using-iran-talks-as-leverage.html.

53. "China Must Protect Iran Even With WWIII," Press TV, December 4, 2011, http://www.presstv.ir/detail/213760.html.

54. Reza Kahlili, "China Is Helping to Arm Iran and Sidestep Sanctions Thanks to an Assist From North Korea," Fox News, December 14, 2011, http://www.foxnews.com/opinion/2011/12/14/china-is-helping-to-arm-iran-and-sidestep-sanctions-thanks-to-assist-from-north/.

55. Jamal Afridi and Jayshree Bajoria, "China-Pakistan Relations," Council on Foreign Relations, July 6, 2010, http://www.cfr.org/china/china-pakistan-relations/p10070#p2.

56. Joseph Farah, "China at Odds With U.S. on Iran Arms Sale," *WND*, March 25, 2012, http://www.wnd.com/2012/03/china-at-odds-with-u-s-on-iran-arms-sales/.

57. Ibid.

58. Brian Spegele and Wayne Ma, "Asia Summit to Debate Nuclear Iran," *Wall Street Journal*, June 5, 2012, http://online.wsj.com/article/SB100014240527023038 30204577447932029699456.html.

59. Brandon Fite, "U.S. and Iranian Strategic Competition: The Impact of China and Russia" (report, Center for Strategic and International Studies, March 2012), http://csis.org/files/publication/REPORT_Iran_Chapter_X_China_and_Russia_Final_Revision2212.pdf.

60. Yeganeh Torbati and Christopher Johnson, "Factbox—Top Importers of Iranian Crude Oil," Reuters, February 6, 2012, http://af.reuters.com/article/commoditiesNews/idAFL3E8C529I20120206.

61. Simon Webb, "Iran Buys July Gasoline From Turkey, Chinese Sellers," Reuters, July 8, 2010, http://af.reuters.com/article/energyOilNews/idAFLDE6671KD20100708.

62. Najmah Bozorgmehr and Geoff Dyer, "China Overtakes EU as Iran's Top Trade Partner," *Financial Times*, February 8, 2010, http://www.ft.com/cms/s/0/f220dfac-14d4-11df-8f1d-00144feab49a.html.

63. Barbara Slavin, "Iran Turns to China, Barter to Survive Sanctions" (report, Atlantic Council, November 2011), http://www.atlanticcouncil.org/images/files/publication_pdfs/403/111011_ACUS_IranChina.PDF.

64. Scott Harold and Alireza Nader, "China and Iran: Economic, Political, and Military Relations" (report, Rand Corporation, Center for Middle East Public Policy,

2012), http://www.rand.org/content/dam/rand/pubs/occasional_papers/2012/RAND_OP351.pdf.

65. Perlez, "China Ban on Items for Nuclear Use."

66. Claudia Rosett, "The Iran–North Korea Axis of Proliferation," *Forbes*, March 9, 2013, http://www.forbes.com/sites/claudiarosett/2013/03/09/the-iran-north-korea-axis-of-proliferation/.

67. Donald Kirk, "Why Iranian Engineers Attended North Korea's Failed Rocket Launch," *Christian Science Monitor*, April 8, 2012, http://www.csmonitor.com/World/Asia-Pacific/2012/0418/Why-Iranian-engineers-attended-North-Korea-s-failed-rocket-launch.

68. Chang, "North Korea to Launch Missile for Iran?"

69. David E. Sanger and Choe Sang-Hun, "North Korea Confirms It Conducted 3rd Nuclear Test," *New York Times*, February 11, 2013, http://www.nytimes.com/2013/02/12/world/asia/north-korea-nuclear-test.html.

70. "Iran, N. Korea 'Trading Missile Technology,'" Al Jazeera, May 14, 2011, http://www.aljazeera.com/news/middleeast/2011/05/2011514223248385833.html.

71. John S. Park, "What's Behind New Iran and North Korea Pact?" PBS, September 8, 2012, http://www.pbs.org/wgbh/pages/frontline/tehranbureau/2012/09/comment-whats-behind-new-iran-and-north-korea-pact.html.

72. Rosett, "Iran–North Korea Axis of Proliferation."

73. Ibid.

74. Ibid.

75. Ibid.

76. Christina Y. Lin, "China, Iran, North Korea: a Triangular Strategic Alliance," Gloria Center, March 5, 2010, http://www.gloria-center.org/2010/03/lin-2010-03-05/.

77. Bertil Lintner, "Tunnels, Guns, and Kimchi: North Korea's Quest for Dollars, Part I," Yale Global Online, June 9, 2009, http://yaleglobal.yale.edu/content/NK-quest-for-dollars-part1.

78. Jonathan Saul, "Exclusive: Russia Steps Up Military Lifeline to Syria's Assad—Sources," Reuters, January 17. 2014, http://www.reuters.com/article/2014/01/17/us-syria-russia-arms-idUSBREA0G0MN20140117.

79. Shaun Walker, "Vladimir Putin Expresses Doubts over Syria's Disposal of Chemical Weapons," *The Guardian*, September 19, 2013, http://www.theguardian.com/world/2013/sep/19/vladimir-putin-doubts-syria-plan-weapons.

80. Ibid.

81. "Russia warns UK on Arming Syrian Rebels," BBC News, March 13, 2013, http://www.bbc.co.uk/news/uk-politics-21772658.

82. Maayan Lubell, "Israel Warns Against Russian Arms Supply to Syria," Reuters, May 18, 2013, http://www.reuters.com/article/2013/05/18/us-israel-syria-idUSBRE94H0BO20130518.

83. "Syria Unlikely to Use Chemical Weapons—FM Lavrov," RIA Novosti, December 24, 2012, http://en.ria.ru/world/20121224/178361278.html.

84. David Jolly, "Russia Urges Syria to Cooperate in Chemical Weapons Inquiry," *New York Times*, August 23, 2013, http://www.nytimes.com/2013/08/24/world/middleeast/syria-chemical-attack.html.

85. Ibid.

86. Robert Mackey, "Confused by How YouTube Assigns Dates, Russians Cite False Claim on Syria Videos," *The Lede* (blog), *New York Times*, August 23, 2013, http://thelede.blogs.nytimes.com/2013/08/23/confused-by-how-youtube-assigns-dates-russians-cite-false-claim-on-syria-videos/.

87. "Russia Warns Against Military Intervention in Syria," Tasnim News Agency, August 26, 2013, http://www.tasnimnews.com/English/Home/Single/126306.

88. Thomas Grove, "Russia Says Iran Must Take Part in Proposed Syria Talks," Reuters, May 16, 2013, http://www.reuters.com/article/2013/05/16/us-syria-crisis-russia-idUSBRE94F0UJ20130516.

89. Adam Entous, Julian E. Barnes, and Gregory White, "Russia Raises Stakes in Syria," *Wall Street Journal*, May 16, 2013, http://online.wsj.com/news/articles/SB10001424127887323398204578487333332405720.

90. Michael R. Gordon and Eric Schmitt, "Russia Sends More Advanced Missiles to Aid Assad in Syria," *New York Times*, May 16, 2013, http://www.nytimes.com/2013/05/17/world/middleeast/russia-provides-syria-with-advanced-missiles.html.

91. Ibid.

92. Jean Aziz, "Hezbollah's Russian Connection," *Al-Monitor*, May 12, 2013, http://www.al-monitor.com/pulse/originals/2013/05/nasrallah-tries-to-reassure-popular-base.html#ixzz2W3Y6zQOV.

93. Entous, Barnes, and White, "Russia Raises Stakes."

94. Adam Entous and Julian E. Barnes, "U.S. Weighs Syria Response," *Wall Street Journal*, April 28, 2013, http://online.wsj.com/article/SB10001424127887323798104578450863284390292.html.

95. Cohen and Blank, "Reset Regret: Russian Global Strategy Undermines American Interests."

96. Ruslan Pukhov, "Why Russia Is Backing Syria," *New York Times*, July 6, 2012, http://www.nytimes.com/2012/07/07/opinion/why-russia-supports-syria.html.

97. Tamsin Carlisle, "Qaddafi Offers Russia, China, and India a Stake in Libyan Oil Industry," *The National*, March 15, 2011, http://www.thenational.ae/

business/energy/qaddafi-offers-russia-china-and-india-a-stake-in-libyan-oil-industry#ixzz2CX40JZVG.

98. Daniel Treisman, "Why Russia Protects Syria's Assad," CNN, February 3, 2012, http://www.cnn.com/2012/02/02/opinion/treisman-russia-syria/index.html.

99. Igor Latunsky, "Why Didn't Russia Use Veto Right on Libya?" *Pravda*, November 7, 2012, http://english.pravda.ru/world/asia/11-07-2012/121625-libya-0/.

100. Pukhov, "Why Russia Is Backing Syria."

101. Ioffe, "The Cold War Heats Up."

102. Pukhov, "Why Russia Is Backing Syria."

103. Abed al-Toraifi, "Does China Truly Support Bashar al-Assad?" Al Arabiya, February 16, 2012, http://www.alarabiya.net/views/2012/02/16/194981.html.

104. Daniel Wallis, "Venezuela's Post-Chavez Oil Policy to Focus on China, Russia," Reuters, March 15, 2013, http://www.reuters.com/article/2013/03/15/venezuela-election-oil-idUSL1N0C69N220130315.

105. Roger Noriega, "Is There a Chavez Terror Network on America's Doorstep?" *Washington Post*, March 20, 2011, http://articles.washingtonpost.com/2011-03-20/opinions/35207542_1_venezuelan-counterpart-rangel-silva-venezuelan-embassy.

106. "Venezuela Ranked Top Importer of Russian Arms," RIA Novosti, December 27, 2011, http://www.globalsecurity.org/military/library/news/2011/12/mil-111227-rianovosti01.htm.

107. "Putin Hopes for Continuity in Russian-Venezuelan Relations," RIA Novosti, March 7, 2013, http://en.rian.ru/russia/20130307/179878459.html.

108. "Venezuela, China Sign $6 Billion Oil Deals." Yahoo! Singapore Finance, November 25, 2011, http://sg.finance.yahoo.com/news/Venezuela-China-sign-6-afpsg-3543804459.html.

109. "Venezuela-China Relations Grow Following VP's Visit," *Correo del Orinoco International*, May 17, 2013, http://venezuelanalysis.com/news/9380.

110. Mitchell B. Reiss and Ray Takeyh, "Don't Get Suckered by Iran," *Foreign Affairs*, January 2, 2014, http://www.foreignaffairs.com/articles/140620/mitchell-b-reiss-and-ray-takeyh/dont-get-suckered-by-iran.

111. Maddy Fry, "Putin Wishes Egypt Army Chief 'Success' in Presidential Campaign," *Time*, February 13, 2014 http://world.time.com/2014/02/13/putin-wishes-egypt-army-chief-success-in-presidential-campaign/.

CHAPTER 3: CYBER SECURITY

1. Mike W. Thomas, "Air Force Looking to Hire 1,000 Cybersecurity Professionals," *San Antonio Business Journal*, January 31, 2013. http://www.bizjournals.com/sanantonio/blog/2013/01/air-force-looking-to-hire-1000.html.

2. Shane Harris, "China's Cyber-Militia," *National Journal*, March 31, 2008, http://www.nationaljournal.com/magazine/china-s-cyber-militia-20080531.

3. Josh Rogin, "The Top 10 Chinese Cyber Attacks (That We Know Of)," *Foreign Policy*, January 22, 2010, http://thecable.foreignpolicy.com/posts/2010/01/22/the_top_10_chinese_cyber_attacks_that_we_know_of.

4. Bill Gertz, "Cyber Threat Looms," *Washington Free Beacon*, January 24, 2013, http://freebeacon.com/cyber-threat-looms/.

5. Max Fisher, "Eric Schmidt, in New Book: China Could Contribute to Fracturing the Internet Into Pieces," *Worldviews* (blog), *Washington Post*, February 3, 2013, http://www.washingtonpost.com/blogs/worldviews/wp/2013/02/03/eric-schmidt-in-new-book-china-could-contribute-to-fracturing-the-internet-into-pieces/.

6. Philip Rucker, "At U.S.-China Shirt-Sleeves Summit, Formalities and Suspicions Were on Display," *Washington Post*, June 9, 2013, http://articles.washingtonpost.com/2013-06-09/politics/39856581_1_president-obama-obama-and-xi-donilon.

7. Glenn Greenwald, "NSA Prism Program Taps In to User Data of Apple, Google, and Others," *The Guardian*, June 6, 2013, http://www.guardian.co.uk/world/2013/jun/06/us-tech-giants-nsa-data.

8. Philip Rucker, "Obama Warns Xi that Continued Cybertheft Would Damage Relations, U.S. Officials Said," *Washington Post*, June 8, 2013, http://www.washingtonpost.com/politics/obama-warns-xi-that-continued-cybertheft-would-damage-relations-us-officials-said/2013/06/08/04843edc-d075-11e2-8845-d970ccb04497_story.html.

9. Michael Riley et al., "Missed Alarms and 40 Million Stolen Credit Card Numbers: How Target Blew It," *Bloomberg Businessweek*, March 13, 2014, http://www.businessweek.com/articles/2014-03-13/target-missed-alarms-in-epic-hack-of-credit-card-data.

10. Richard A. Clarke and Robert Knake, *Cyber War: The Next Threat to National Security and What to Do About It* (New York: HarperCollins, 2010), 67–68.

11. Ibid., 68.

12. "U.S. Should Prepare for a Cyber Attack That Will Ruin the Country in Just 15 MINUTES, Expert Warns," *Daily Mail*, May 7, 2010, http://www.dailymail.co.uk/news/article-1275001/U-S-prepare-cyber-attack-ruin-country-just-15-MINUTES-expert-warns.html.

13. "Text of Speech by Defense U.S. Secretary Leon Panetta," *Defense News*, October12, 2012, http://www.defensenews.com/article/20121012/DEFREG02/310120001/Text-Speech-by-Defense-U-S-Secretary-Leon-Panetta.

14. Ibid.

15. James Clapper, "Unclassified Statement for the Record on the Worldwide Threat Assessment of the US Intelligence Community for the Senate Select Committee on Intelligence," January 31, 2012, http://www.intelligence.senate.gov/120131/clapper.pdf.

16. Bill Gertz, "Cyber Threat Looms."

17. Tania Branigan, "US Calls on Chinese Government to Crack Down on Hacking," *The Guardian*, March 12, 2103, http://www.theguardian.com/world/2013/mar/12/us-chinese-government-hacking.

18. Mark Clayton, "Alerts Say Major Cyber Attack Aimed at Gas Pipeline Industry," *Christian Science Monitor*, May 5, 2012, http://www.csmonitor.com/USA/2012/0505/Alert-Major-cyber-attack-aimed-at-natural-gas-pipeline-companies.

19. Bill Gertz, "Cyber Breach," *Washington Free Beacon*, February 4, 2013, http://freebeacon.com/cyber-breach/.

20. Ibid.

21. Colonel Jayson M. Spade, "China's Cyber Power and America's National Security," U.S. Army War College, May 2012, http://www.carlisle.army.mil/dime/documents/China's Cyber Power and America's National Security Web Version.pdf.

22. Gertz, "Cyber Threat Looms."

23. Spade, "China's Cyber Power."

24. "Target Data Breach Cost for Banks Tops $200M," NBC News, February 18, 2014, http://www.nbcnews.com/business/business-news/target-data-breach-cost-banks-tops-200m-n33156.

25. "More Well-Known US Retailers Victims of Cyberattacks: Sources," Reuters, January 12, 2014, http://www.cnbc.com/id/101328744.

26. Ellen Messmer, "Cyberattacks in U.S. Cost an Average $8.9 Million Annually to Clean Up, Study Says," *Network World*, October 8, 2012, http://www.networkworld.com/news/2012/100812-ponemon-cyberattacks-263113.html.

27. Michael A. Riley and Ashlee Vance, "Chinese Hackers Knock the Wind out of US Companies," *Bloomberg Businessweek*, March 15 2012, http://www.businessweek.com/news/2012-03-15/china-corporate-espionage-boom-knocks-wind-out-of-u-dot-s-dot-companies.

28. "Foreign Spies Stealing US Economic Secrets in Cyberspace: Report to Congress on Foreign Economic Collection and Industrial Espionage 2009–2011," Office of the National Counterintelligence Executive, October 2011, http://www.ncix.gov/publications/reports/fecie_all/Foreign_Economic_Collection_2011.pdf.

29. Edward Wong, "Hackers Find China Is Land of Opportunity," *New York Times*, May 22, 2013, http://www.nytimes.com/2013/05/23/world/asia/in-china-hacking-has-widespread-acceptance.html.

30. Jeremy Page and Julian E. Barnes, "China Shows Its Growing Might," *Wall Street Journal*, January 12, 2011, http://online.wsj.com/article/SB100014240527487 04428004576075042571461586.html.

31. Terril Yue Jones, Bill Trott, and Rob Taylor, "Chinese Hackers Steal U.S. Weapons Systems Designs, Report Says," NBC News, May 28, 2013, http://usnews. nbcnews.com/_news/2013/05/28/18556787-chinese-hackers-steal-us-weapons-systems-designs-report-says.

32. Rogin, "The Top 10 Chinese Cyber Attacks."

33. Dave Mujumdar, "Chengdu J-20 Could Enter Service by 2018," *Flightglobal*, May 18, 2012, http://www.flightglobal.com/news/articles/chengdu-j-20-could-enter-service-by-2018-372082/.

34. Eddie Wrenn, "Is This the Biggest Chinese Rip-Off Ever? People's Republic Unveils Stealth Fighter . . . but It Looks Remarkably Similar to US Jet," *Daily Mail*, May 18, 2012, http://www.dailymail.co.uk/sciencetech/article-2146283/Chinas-stealth-jet-goes-strength-strength-U-S-air-technology-falters-just-Chinese-rip-off. html.

35. Peter Foster, "China Stealth Fighter a 'Masterpiece' of Homegrown Technology," *The Telegraph*, January 25, 2011, http://www.telegraph.co.uk/news/worldnews/asia/ china/8280707/China-stealth-fighter-a-masterpiece-of-homegrown-technology.html.

36. Dave Mujumdar, "J-20 a 'Wake-Up Call,' Former Intel Chief Says," *Air Force Times*, February 13, 2011, http://www.airforcetimes.com/news/2011/02/air-force-deptula-calls-j20-a-wake-up-call-021311w/.

37. Sibhan Gorman, August Cole, and Yochi Dreazen, "Computer Spies Breach Fighter-Jet Project," *Wall Street Journal*, April 21, 2009, http://online.wsj.com/article/ SB124027491029837401.html.

38. Ibid.

39. Ann Scott Tyson and Dana Hedgpeth, "Officials Say Hackers Didn't Steal Critical Data About New Fighter Jet," *Washington Post*, April 22, 2009, http://www. washingtonpost.com/wp-dyn/content/article/2009/04/21/AR2009042103938.html.

40. Gorman, Cole, and Dreazen, "Computer Spies."

41. "Security Experts Admit China Stole Secret Fighter Jet Plans," *The Australian*, May 12, 2012, http://www.theaustralian.com.au/news/world/security-experts-admit-china-stole-secret-fighter-jet-plans/story-fnb64oi6-1226296400154.

42. Edward Wong, "Hacking U.S. Secrets, China Pushes for Drones," *New York Times*, September 20, 2013, http://www.nytimes.com/2013/09/21/world/asia/ hacking-us-secrets-china-pushes-for-drones.html.

43. Ibid.

44. Ibid.

45. Rogin, "The Top 10 Chinese Cyber Attacks."

46. Ariana Eunjung Cha and Ellen Nakashima, "Google Attack Part of Vast Campaign," *Washington Post*, January 14, 2010, http://articles.washingtonpost. com/2010-01-14/news/36876544_1_cyber-intrusion-that-google-attributes-computer-attacks-china.

47. David E. Sanger and Nicole Perlroth, "Hackers From China Resume Attacks on U.S. Targets," *New York Times*, May 19, 2013, http://www.nytimes.com/2013/05/20/ world/asia/chinese-hackers-resume-attacks-on-us-targets.html.

48. Nicole Perlroth, "Hackers in China Attacked The Times for Last 4 Months," *New York Times*, January 30, 2013, http://www.nytimes.com/2013/01/31/technology/ chinese-hackers-infiltrate-new-york-times-computers.html.

49. David Barboza, "Billions in Hidden Riches for Family of Chinese Leader," *New York Times*, October 25, 2012, http://www.nytimes.com/2012/10/26/business/ global/family-of-wen-jiabao-holds-a-hidden-fortune-in-china.html.

50. Perlroth, "Hackers in China Attacked The Times."

51. Andrew Wong, "US and China Accuse Each Other of Cyber Warfare," RT, February 20, 2013, http://rt.com/usa/cyber-china-war-unit-604/.

52. David E. Sanger, David Barboza, and Nicole Perlroth, "Chinese Army Unit Is Seen as Tied to Hacking Against U.S.," *New York Times*, February 18, 2013, http:// www.nytimes.com/2013/02/19/technology/chinas-army-is-seen-as-tied-to-hacking-against-us.html.

53. Sanger and Perlroth, "Hackers From China Resume Attacks."

54. Fred Kaplan, "The Art of Cyber War," *Slate*, February 20, 2013, http:// www.slate.com/articles/news_and_politics/war_stories/2013/02/chinese_military_ cyberwarfare_how_would_beijing_threaten_the_united_states.single.html.

55. Adam Rawnsley, "Fishy Chips: Spies Want to Hack-Proof Circuits," *Wired*, June 24, 2011, http://www.wired.com/dangerroom/2011/06/chips-oy-spies-want-to-hack-proof-circuits/#more-49990.

56. Stephen Northcutt, "Security Laboratory: Methods of Attack Series: Logic Bombs, Trojan Horses, and Trap Doors," SANS Technology Institute, May 2, 2007, http://www.sans.edu/research/security-laboratory/article/log-bmb-trp-door.

57. Sebastian Anthony, "Rakshasa: The Hardware Backdoor That China Could Embed in Every Computer," *ExtremeTech*, August 1, 2012, http://www.extremetech. com/computing/133773-rakshasa-the-hardware-backdoor-that-china-could-embed-in-every-computer.

58. Steven Musil, "Experts Dispute the Threat Posed by Backdoor Found in Chinese Chip," CNET, May 29, 2012, http://news.cnet.com/8301-1009_3-57443293-83/experts-dispute-threat-posed-by-backdoor-found-in-chinese-chip/.

59. Mike Rodger and Dutch Ruppersberger, "Investigative Report on the U.S. National Security Issues Posed by Chinese Telecommunications Companies Huawei and ZTE," U.S. House of Representatives, October 8, 2012, http://goo.gl/1ECJrn.

60. "The Company That Spooked the World," *The Economist*, August 2, 2012, http://www.economist.com/node/21559929.

61. Ibid.

62. F. Michael Maloof, "China Tech Company Brags: We Hacked U.S. Telecoms," *WND*, June 14, 2012, http://www.wnd.com/2012/06/china-tech-company-admits-hacking-u-s-telecoms/.

63. Naomi Rovnick, "Are China's Economic Ambitions the Reason Why Cyber-Attacks From China Are Rising?" Yahoo! Finance, January 24, 2013, http://finance.yahoo.com/news/china-economic-ambitions-reason-why-054722424.html.

64. Clarke and Knake, *Cyber War*, 183.

65. Ron Rosenbaum, "Richard Clarke on Who Was Behind the Stuxnet Attack," *Smithsonian*, April 2012, http://www.smithsonianmag.com/history/richard-clarke-on-who-was-behind-the-stuxnet-attack-160630516/.

66. Michael J. de la Merced, "Accusations of Chinese Hacking in Coke's Failed Big Deal," *New York Times/Dealbook*, February 19, 2013, http://dealbook.nytimes.com/2013/02/19/accusations-of-hacking-in-cokes-failed-big-deal/.

67. Sanger, Barboza, and Perlroth, "Chinese Army Is Seen as Tied to Hacking."

68. Liat Clark, "Eric Schmidt: Chinese Hacking Culture Will Leave US Disadvantaged Economically," *Wired*, February 4, 2013, http://www.wired.co.uk/news/archive/2013-02/04/schmidt-china-hacking.

69. Cha and Nakashima, "Google Attack Part of Vast Campaign."

70. David Goldman, "Google Stops Censoring in China," CNN Money, March 22, 2010, http://money.cnn.com/2010/03/22/technology/google_china/index.htm.

71. David Goldman, "Massive Gmail Phishing Attack Hits Top U.S. Officials," CNN Money, June 2, 2011, http://money.cnn.com/2011/06/01/technology/gmail_hack/.

72. Hibah Yousef, "Google May Leave China After Cyber Attack," CNN Money, January 13, 2010, http://money.cnn.com/2010/01/12/technology/Google_China/index.htm.

73. Rogin, "The Top 10 Chinese Cyber Attacks."

74. Steven Lee Myers, "Cyberattack on Estonia Stirs Fear of 'Virtual War,'" *New York Times*, May 18, 2007, http://www.nytimes.com/2007/05/18/world/europe/18iht-estonia.4.5774234.html.

75. Ibid.

76. Ibid.

77. John Markoff, "Before the Gunfire, Cyberattacks," *New York Times*, August 12, 2008, http://www.nytimes.com/2008/08/13/technology/13cyber.html.

78. Matthew J. Schwartz, "Operation Red October Attackers Wielded Spear Phishing," *Information Week*, January 18, 2013, http://www.informationweek.com/attacks/operation-red-october-attackers-wielded-spear-phishing/d/d-id/1108272.

79. Ibid.

80. Ibid.

81. John Reed, "Hunting Red October: Who Done It?" *Foreign Policy*, January 17, 2013, http://killerapps.foreignpolicy.com/posts/2013/01/17/hunting_red_october_who_done_it.

82. Mark Clayton, "'Project Blitzkrieg': Are Russian Cybercriminals About to Invade US Banks?" *Christian Science Monitor*, December 13, 2012, http://www.csmonitor.com/USA/2012/1213/Project-Blitzkrieg-Are-Russian-cybercriminals-about-to-invade-US-banks.

83. Pam Benson, "Looming Cyber Attack Threatens Major Banks," *Security Clearance* (blog), CNN, December 13, 2012, http://security.blogs.cnn.com/2012/12/13/firm-cyberattack-threatens-major-banks/.

84. Clayton, "'Project Blitzkrieg.'"

85. Ibid.

86. "International Collegiate Programming Contest, Results 2013," http://icpc.baylor.edu/worldfinals/results.

87. "U.S. Defense Secrets Stolen in Cyber Attacks," *Washington Post*, Post TV, July 14, 2011, http://www.washingtonpost.com/national/national-security/us-defense-secrets-stolen-in-cyber-attacks/2011/07/14/gIQAgjV2EI_video.html.

88. Clarke and Knake, *Cyber War*, 43.

89. Ibid.

90. Loren Thompson, "U.S. Headed for Cyberwar Showdown With China in 2012," *Forbes*, December 22, 2011, http://www.forbes.com/sites/lorenthompson/2011/12/22/u-s-headed-for-cyberwar-showdown-with-china-in-2012/.

91. Markoff, "Before the Gunfire, Cyberattacks."

92. Kaplan, "The Art of Cyber War."

93. David E. Sanger, "In Cyberspace, New Cold War," *New York Times*, February 24, 2013, http://www.nytimes.com/2013/02/25/world/asia/us-confronts-cyber-cold-war-with-china.html.

CHAPTER 4: MILITARY SUPREMACY

1. Hannah Beech, "How China Sees the World," *Time*, June 17, 2013, http://www.time.com/time/magazine/article/0,9171,2145062,00.html.

2. Vladimir Putin, opening speech at a meeting with the command personnel of the Russian Armed Forces, October 2, 2003, via Isabelle Falcon, "The Modernization of the Russian Military: The Ambitions & Ambiguities of Vladimir Putin" (paper, Conflict Studies Research Center, August 2005), http://www.da.mod.uk/colleges/arag/document-listings/russian/05(19E)-IF.pdf/view.

3. Alan Caruba, "A Military in Decline," *Warning Signs* (blog), August 3, 2013, http://factsnotfantasy.blogspot.com/2013/08/a-military-in-decline.html.

4. Newt Gingrich, "Losing the War," Gingrich Productions, August 4, 2013, http://www.gingrichproductions.com/2013/08/losing-the-war-2/.

5. Jane Perlez, "China and Russia, in a Display of Unity, Hold Naval Exercises," *New York Times*, July 10, 2013, http://www.nytimes.com/2013/07/11/world/asia/china-and-russia-in-a-display-of-unity-hold-naval-exercises.html.

6. "China, Russia Conclude Joint Naval Drills," Xinhua, July 11, 2013, http://news.xinhuanet.com/english/china/2013-07/11/c_132533183.htm.

7. Perlez, "China and Russia, in a Display of Unity."

8. Ibid.

9. Ibid.

10. Ibid.

11. Ronald O'Rourke, "China Naval Modernization: Implications for U.S. Navy Capabilities—Background and Issues for Congress" (report for Congress, Congressional Research Service, September 5, 2013), http://www.fas.org/sgp/crs/row/RL33153.pdf.

12. Kimberly A. Strassel, "The Obama Jobs Sequester," *Wall Street Journal*, August 2, 2012, http://online.wsj.com/article/SB100008723963904443207045775654831900017286.html.

13. "Hagel Warns Congress to Stop Defense Budget Cuts," *U.S. News and World Report*, July 10, 2013, http://www.usnews.com/news/politics/articles/2013/07/10/hagel-warns-congress-to-stop-defense-budget-cuts.

14. "Bearing the Burden of Global Leadership: Does U.S. Leadership Have a Future?" Council on Foreign Relations panel, April 23, 2014, http://www.cfr.org/united-states/does-us-leadership-have-future/p32854.

15. Christopher J. Griffin, "FPI Analysis: No Way to Run the Defense Department" (report, Foreign Policy Initiative, August 1, 2013), http://www.foreignpolicyi.org/content/fpi-analysis-no-way-run-defense-department.

16. Jacob Siegel, "The Government Shutdown's Hidden Cost to the U.S. Military," *Daily Beast*, October 7, 2013, http://www.thedailybeast.com/the-hero-project/articles/2013/10/07/the-government-shutdown-s-hidden-cost-to-the-u-s-military.html.

17. Keith B. Richburg, "China Military Spending to Top $100 Billion, Alarming Neighbors," *Washington Post*, March 4, 2012, http://www.washingtonpost.com/world/china-military-spending-to-top-100-billion-this-year/2012/03/04/gIQAJRnypR_story.html.

18. "Annual Report to Congress: Military and Security Developments Involving the People's Republic of China 2012" (report, U.S. Department of Defense, Office of the Secretary of Defense, May 2012), 6, http://www.defense.gov/pubs/pdfs/2012_CMPR_Final.pdf.

19. Ibid.

20. O'Rourke, "China Naval Modernization."

21. "Annual Report to Congress, Military and Security Developments Involving the People's Republic of China 2010" (report, U.S. Department of Defense, Office of the Secretary of Defense, May 2010), 42, http://www.defense.gov/pubs/pdfs/2010_cmpr_final.pdf.

22. Figures from the SIPRI Military Expenditure Database, the Stockholm International Peace Research Institute, http://www.sipri.org/research/armaments/milex/milex_database.

23. Bill Gertz, "China Conducts First Test of New Ultra-High-Speed Missile Vehicle," *Washington Free Beacon*, January 13, 2014, http://freebeacon.com/china-conducts-first-test-of-new-ultra-high-speed-missile-vehicle/.

24. O'Rourke, "China Naval Modernization."

25. "Annual Report to Congress: Military and Security Developments Involving the People's Republic of China 2011" (report, U.S. Department of Defense, Office of the Secretary of Defense, May 2011), 46, http://www.defense.gov/pubs/pdfs/2011_cmpr_final.pdf.

26. Robert Kaplan, "Election 2012: The Pacific Century" (lecture, Center for a New American Security, April 18, 2012), http://www.cnas.org/media-and-events/audio-and-video/video-election-2012-the-pacific-century.

27. "The People's Liberation Army Navy: A Modern Navy With Chinese Characteristics" (report, Office of Naval Intelligence, August 2009), https://www.fas.org/irp/agency/oni/pla-navy.pdf.

28. Beech, "How China Sees the World."

29. Gopal Ratnam and Neil Western, "Hagel to Meet Xi as China Vows No Compromising on Sea Disputes," *Bloomberg Businessweek,* April 9, 2014, http://www.businessweek.com/news/2014-04-08/china-says-it-can-t-be-contained-as-hagel-seeks-more-cooperation.

30. Figures from O'Rourke, "China Naval Modernization," 18, 29, 31; chart original.

31. Daniel Michaels, "Russian Air Power Makes a Splash at Paris Air Show," *Wall Street Journal*, June 20, 2013, http://online.wsj.com/article/SB1000142412788 7323300004578557371399157236.html.

32. Ibid.

33. Vladimir Radyuhin, "Fifth Generation Fighter Crosses Milestone," *The Hindu*, April 10, 2013, http://www.thehindu.com/news/international/fifth-generation-fighter-crosses-milestone/article4602836.ece.

34. Michaels, "Russian Air Power Makes a Splash."

35. Charles Clover, "Russia: A Return to Arms," *Financial Times*, October 1, 2013, http://www.ft.com/intl/cms/s/0/82d3917e-2a80-11e3-8fb8-00144feab7de.html#axzz2gttUkQRU.

36. Ira Iosebashvili, "Putin, Citing NATO Shield, Vows More Defense Spending," *Wall Street Journal*, February 21, 2012, http://online.wsj.com/news/articles/SB30001 424052970203358704577234960796991408.

37. Gleb Bryanski, "Russia's Putin Calls for Stalin-Style 'Leap Forward,'" Reuters, August 31, 2012, http://www.reuters.com/article/2012/08/31/us-russia-putin-stalin-idUSBRE87U16420120831.

38. Richard Norton-Taylor, "Russia Overtakes UK and France in Global Arms Spending League Table," *The Guardian*, April 16, 2012, http://www.guardian.co.uk/world/2012/apr/17/russia-overtakes-uk-france-arms.

39. Data from SIPRI Military Expenditure Project, http://portal.sipri.org/publications/pages/expenditures/splash-expenditures; chart original.

40. Figures from the SIPRI Military Expenditure Database, Stockholm International Peace Research Institute, http://milexdata.sipri.org/result.php4.

41. Military expenditures as a percentage of GDP, Google Public Data, http://goo.gl/89oKdG.

42. Military expenditures as a percentage of central-government expenditure, Google Public Data, http://goo.gl/9jiEal.

43. Jim Nichol, "Russian Military Reform and Defense Policy" (report for Congress, Congressional Research Service, August 24, 2011), http://www.fas.org/sgp/crs/row/R42006.pdf.

44. Dale R. Herspring, "Russian Nuclear and Conventional Weapons: The Broken Relationship," in *Russian Nuclear Weapons: Past, Present, and Future*, ed. Stephen J. Blank (Carlisle, PA: Strategic Studies Institute, U.S. Army War College, 2011), 2–6.

45. Ibid., 6–8.

46. Ibid., 9–10.

47. Ibid., 22–23.

48. Roger N. McDermott, "Russia's Conventional Armed Forces: Reform and Nuclear Posture to 2020," in *Russian Nuclear Weapons*, ed. Blank, 35.

49. Pavel K. Baev, "Russian Military Perestroika" (paper, Center on the United States and Europe at Brookings, April 29, 2010), http://goo.gl/J4qLFZ.

50. McDermott, 36.

51. Ibid.

52. Corey Flintoff, "Remaking Russia's Military: Big Plans, Few Results," NPR, March 7, 2012, http://www.npr.org/2012/03/07/147595521/remaking-russias-military-big-plans-few-results.

53. Nichol, "Russian Military Reform and Defense Policy."

54. Ibid.

55. Michael R. Gordon, "Russia Displays a New Military Prowess in Ukraine's East," *New York Times*, April 21, 2014, http://www.nytimes.com/2014/04/22/world/europe/new-prowess-for-russians.html.

56. Mark Mazzetti, Eric Schmitt, and David. D. Kirkpatrick, "Benghazi Attack Called Avoidable in Senate Report," January 15, 2014, http://www.nytimes.com/2014/01/16/world/middleeast/senate-report-finds-benghazi-attack-was-preventable.html.

57. Mark Helprin, "Benghazi's Portent and the Decline of U.S. Military Strength," *Wall Street Journal*, April 9, 2013, http://online.wsj.com/article/SB10001424127887324100904578401083677703420.html.

58. Caruba, "A Military in Decline."

59. Philip Ewing, "Chuck Hagel Warns: Troops Are Close to the 'Breaking Point,'" *Politico*, July 23, 2013, http://www.politico.com/story/2013/07/chuck-hagel-troops-close-breaking-point-94584.html#ixzz2bVSmYin8.

60. "Panetta Warns of 'Disaster' From Defense Cuts," Fox News, June 13, 2012, http://www.foxnews.com/us/2012/06/13/panetta-warns-disaster-from-defense-cuts/.

61. O'Rourke, "China Naval Modernization."

62. Christine A. Cleary, "Culture, Strategy, and Security," in *China's Nuclear Future*, ed. Paul Bolt and Albert Willner (London: Lynne Rienner, 2006), 14.

63. "Annual Report to Congress, Military and Security Developments Involving the People's Republic of China 2012."

64. Patrick M. Cronin, "Cooperation From Strength: The United States, China, and the South China Sea" (report, Center for a New American Security, January 2012), http://www.cnas.org/files/documents/publications/CNAS_CooperationFromStrength_Cronin_1.pdf.

65. Spencer Swartz and Shai Oster, "China Tops U.S. in Energy Use," *Wall Street Journal*, July 18, 2010, http://online.wsj.com/article/SB10001424052748703720504575376712353150310.html.

66. Ibid.

67. "US-China Spat Over South China Sea Military Exercises," BBC News, July 11, 2011, http://www.bbc.co.uk/news/world-asia-pacific-14097503. See also Mark Landler, "Obama Expresses Support for Philippines in China Rift," *New York Times*, June 8, 2012, http://www.nytimes.com/2012/06/09/world/asia/obama-shows-support-for-philippines-in-china-standoff.html.

68. "Annual Report to Congress, Military and Security Developments Involving the People's Republic of China 2012."

69. Zhao Shengnan and Cai Hong, "Japan's New Helicopter Ship Called 'Military Buildup,'" *China Daily USA*, July 7, 2013, http://usa.chinadaily.com.cn/epaper/2013-08/07/content_16877272.htm.

70. Private communication with Professor Hugh White, October 28, 2013.

71. Robert Kaplan, "Election 2012: The Pacific Century" (lecture).

72. Ibid.

73. "Russia's First Mistral-Class Ship Stern Launched," RT, June 26, 2013, http://rt.com/news/mistral-ship-stern-russia-261/.

74. David Pugliese, "France Backtracks on Threat to Cancel Mistral-Class Ship Deal With Russia," *Defence Watch* (blog), *Ottawa Citizen*, March 20, 2014, http://blogs.ottawacitizen.com/2014/03/20/france-backtracks-on-threat-to-cancel-mistral-class-ship-deal-with-russia/.

75. "Arctic Map Shows Dispute Hotspots," BBC News, August 5, 2008, http://news.bbc.co.uk/2/hi/staging_site/in_depth/the_green_room/7543837.stm.

76. Andrew E. Kramer, "Warming Revives Dream of Sea Route in Russian Arctic," *New York Times*, October 7, 2011, http://www.nytimes.com/2011/10/18/business/global/warming-revives-old-dream-of-sea-route-in-russian-arctic.html.

77. Katia Moskvitch, "Glonass: Has Russia's Sat-Nav System Come of Age?" BBC News, April 2, 2010, http://news.bbc.co.uk/2/hi/8595704.stm.

78. Richard Halloran, "AirSea Battle," *AirForce Magazine*, August 2010, http://www.airforcemag.com/MagazineArchive/Pages/2010/August 2010/0810battle.aspx.

79. Kate Brannen and Dave Majumdar, "Pentagon Outlines 2013 Budget Cuts," *Defense News*, January 26, 2012, http://www.defensenews.com/article/20120126/DEFREG02/301260008/Pentagon-Outlines-2013-Budget-Cuts.

80. David Alexander, "U.S. Rebalance to Asia-Pacific Gaining Steam, Pentagon Chief Says," Reuters, June 1, 2013, http://www.reuters.com/article/2013/06/01/us-security-asia-usa-idUSBRE95002820130601.

81. Sydney J. Freedberg Jr., "'Is China Enemy No. 1?' Debate Erupts at Marine War Game," *Breaking Defense*, March 5, 2012, http://breakingdefense.com/2012/03/05/marines-debate-is-china-enemy-no-1/.

82. Ira Iosebashvili, "Putin, Citing NATO Shield, Vows More Defense Spending."

83. John Roberts, "Exclusive: Drones Vulnerable to Terrorist Hijacking, Researchers Say," Fox News, June 25, 2012, http://www.foxnews.com/tech/2012/06/25/drones-vulnerable-to-terrorist-hijacking-researchers-say/.

84. Carlo Kopp, "The Impact of Russian High Technology Weapons: Transforming the Strategic Balance in Asia," *Air Power Australia*, December 12, 2008, http://www.ausairpower.net/APA-2008-09.html.

85. Amnon Barzilai, "Defense Establishment Favors Rafael Tank Protection System," *Globes*, August 30, 2006, http://www.globes.co.il/serveen/globes/docview.asp?did=1000127813.

86. Isabel Kershner, "Israel Says It Seized Iranian Shipment of Rockets Headed for Gaza," *New York Times*, March 5, 2014, http://www.nytimes.com/2014/03/06/world/middleeast/israel-says-it-seized-iranian-shipment-of-rockets-headed-for-gaza.html.

87. Dominic Perry, "Syria Confirms Shooting Down of Turkish F-4 Phantom," *Flightglobal*, June 23, 2012, http://www.flightglobal.com/news/articles/syria-confirms-shooting-down-of-turkish-f-4-phantom-373342/.

88. Chris Buckley, "As Rover Lands, China Joins Moon Club," *New York Times*, December 14, 2013, http://www.nytimes.com/2013/12/15/world/asia/china-lands-probe-on-the-moon-report-says.html

89. Ibid.

90. "Satellite Test Sparks Overblow Worries," *Global Times*, January 6, 2013, http://www.globaltimes.cn/content/753925.shtml.

91. Yousaf Butt, "Satellite Laser Ranging in China" (technical working paper, Union of Concerned Scientists, January 8, 2007), http://www.ucsusa.org/nuclear_weapons_and_global_security/space_weapons/technical_issues/chinese-lasers-and-us.html.

92. Marc Kaufman and Dafra Linzer, "China Criticized for Anti-Satellite Missile Test," *Washington Post*, January 19, 2007, http://www.washingtonpost.com/wp-dyn/content/article/2007/01/18/AR2007011801029.html.

93. Ibid.

94. Bill Gertz, "China Launches Three ASAT Satellites," *Washington Free Beacon*, August 26, 2013, http://freebeacon.com/china-launches-three-asat-satellites/.

95. Kaufman and Linzer, "China Criticized for Anti-Satellite Missile Test."

96. Ewan MacAskill, "Western Protests Flood In Over Chinese Satellite Killer," *The Guardian*, January 19, 2007, http://www.guardian.co.uk/science/2007/jan/20/spaceexploration.china1.

97. Ian Easton, "The Great Game in Space" (paper, Project 2049 Institute, June 24, 2009), http://project2049.net/documents/china_asat_weapons_the_great_game_in_space.pdf.

98. Gingrich, "Losing the War."

99. Ibid.

100. Helprin, "Benghazi's Portent and the Decline of U.S. Military Strength."

CHAPTER 5: NUCLEAR SECURITY

1. Bill Gertz, "Russia Conducts Test of New ICBM Designed to Defeat U.S. Defenses," *Washington Free Beacon*, June 7, 2013, http://freebeacon.com/russia-conducts-test-of-new-icbm-designed-to-defeat-u-s-defenses/.

2. Helprin, "Benghazi's Portent and the Decline of U.S. Military Strength."

3. David Keyes, "How Iran, Putin, and Assad Outwitted America," *Daily Beast*, January 16, 2014, http://www.thedailybeast.com/articles/2014/01/16/how-iran-putin-and-assad-outwitted-america.html.

4. Bill Gertz, "Armed Services Subcommittee Chair: Missile Defense Modernization Needed," *Washington Free Beacon*, August 13, 2013, http://freebeacon.com/armed-services-subcommittee-chair-missile-defense-modernization-needed/.

5. "North Korea Vows Nuclear Attack on US, Saying Washington Will Be 'Engulfed in a Sea of Fire,'" Fox News, March 7, 2013, http://www.foxnews.com/world/2013/03/07/north-korea-vows-nuclear-attack-on-us-ahead-un-sanctions-vote/#ixzz2dOCtiMCt.

6. Tom Miles, "North Korea Threatens 'Final Destruction' of South Korea in UN Debate," NBC News, February 19, 2013, http://worldnews.nbcnews.com/_news/2013/02/19/17016501-north-korea-threatens-final-destruction-of-south-korea-in-un-debate?lite.

7. Chris Lawrence, "U.S. to Beef Up Missile Defense Against North Korea, Iran," CNN, March 16, 2013, http://www.cnn.com/2013/03/15/us/north-korea-missile-defense.

8. "US Drops Key European Missile Defense Component," RT, March 16, 2013, http://rt.com/news/us-cancels-missile-interceptors-350/.

9. David E. Sanger and Peter Baker, "Obama Limits When U.S. Would Use Nuclear Arms," *New York Times*, April 5, 2010, http://www.nytimes.com/2010/04/06/world/06arms.html.

10. Bill Gertz, "Obama to Announce Major US Nuclear Force Cuts Soon," *Newsmax*, December 12, 2013, http://www.newsmax.com/Newsfront/obama-nuclear-arsenal-cuts/2013/05/15/id/504736

11. Larry Bell, "Indefensible Policies: Our Commander-in-Chief Retreats as Putin's Missile Programs Advance," *Forbes*, July 14, 2013, http://www.forbes.com/sites/larrybell/2013/07/14/indefensible-policies-our-commander-in-chief-retreats-as-putins-missile-programs-advance/.

12. Ibid.

13. Mark W. Davis, "Why President Obama's Nuclear Weapons Policy Is Dangerous," *US News & World Report, April 27, 2012,* http://www.usnews.com/opinion/blogs/mark-davis/2012/04/27/why-president-obamas-nuclear-weapons-policy-is-dangerous.

14. Sanger and Baker, "Obama Limits When U.S. Would Use Nuclear Arms."

15. Ibid.

16. Trent Franks, "New START Treaty Fails America," press release, December 2, 2011, http://franks.house.gov/press-release/new-start-treaty-fails-america.

17. "Russia: Putin Praises Arms Treaty," Reuters, December 29, 2010, http://www.nytimes.com/2010/12/30/world/europe/30briefs-Russiabrf.html.

18. Andrew E. Kramer, "Russia Approves Arms Treaty, *New York Times*, January 26, 2011, http://www.nytimes.com/2011/01/27/world/europe/27start.html.

19. Steven Pifer, "The Russian Arms Control Agenda After New START," in *Russia and the Current State of Arms Control*, ed. Stephen J. Blank (Carlisle, PA: Strategic Studies Institute, U.S. Army War College, 2012), 66–80.

20. Ed Fueulner, "Stop the New START," *Washington Times*, June 9, 2010, http://www.washingtontimes.com/news/2010/jun/9/stop-the-new-start/.

21. Walter Pincus, "Russian Tactical Nuclear Weapons Still an Issue After START Treaty Ratification," *Washington Post*, December 27, 2010, http://www.washingtonpost.com/wp-dyn/content/article/2010/12/27/AR2010122702931.html.

22. Carla Garrison, "New START Treaty: Victory for Russia, Bad Strategy for U.S.," *Truth Be Told* (blog), *Washington Times*, January 26, 2011, http://communities.washingtontimes.com/neighborhood/truth-be-told/2011/jan/6/new-start-treaty-victory-russia-bad-strategy-us/.

23. Michael R. Gordon, "U.S. Says Russia Tested Missile, Despite Treaty," *New York Times*, January 29, 2014, http://www.nytimes.com/2014/01/30/world/europe/us-says-russia-tested-missile-despite-treaty.html.

24. Michaela Dodge, "Despite Arms Reduction Treaty, Russia Is Increasing Its Nuclear Capability," *The Foundry* (blog), Heritage Foundation, October 10, 2012, http://

blog.heritage.org/2012/10/10/despite-arms-reduction-treaty-russia-is-increasing-its-nuclear-capability/.

25. Adam Entous and Julian E. Barnes, "U.S. to Propose New Phase in Nuclear-Arms Cuts," *Wall Street Journal*, June 19, 2013, http://online.wsj.com/news/articles/SB10001424127887324520904578554010643116452.

26. "Transcript of Obama's Speech in Berlin," *Wall Street Journal*, June 19, 2103, http://blogs.wsj.com/washwire/2013/06/19/transcript-of-obamas-speech-in-berlin/.

27. Raf Sanchez, "Barack Obama Weighs Major Cuts to US Nuclear Arsenal," *The Telegraph*, February 14, 2012, http://www.telegraph.co.uk/news/worldnews/barackobama/9083148/Barack-Obama-weighs-major-cuts-to-US-nuclear-arsenal.html.

28. Daniel Wasserbly, "Hagel: US Nuclear Triad, Modernisation Would Continue amid Reductions," *IHS Jane's Defence Weekly*, June 19, 2013, http://www.janes.com/article/23436/hagel-us-nuclear-triad-modernisation-would-continue-amid-reductions.

29. Gertz, "Obama to Announce Major US Nuclear Force Cuts Soon."

30. Jon Kyl, "America's Nuclear Deterrent—and Defenses—Are Eroding Fast," *Wall Street Journal*, March 21, 2013, http://online.wsj.com/article/SB10001424127887323415304578370783312615740.html.

31. Entous and Barnes, "U.S. to Propose New Phase in Nuclear-Arms Cuts."

32. "Obama in Berlin, Calls for Huge Cuts in Nuclear Arsenal," Associated Press, June 19, 2013, http://www.newsmax.com/Newsfront/obama-nuclear-arsenalcuts/2013/06/19/id/510646.

33. Paul McLeary, "Obama Sparks New Fight in Seeking Huge Nuke Reductions, Defense News," *Defense News*, June 19, 2013, http://www.defensenews.com/article/20130619/DEFREG02/306190023/Obama-Sparks-New-Fight-Seeking-Huge-Nuke-Reductions.

34. John R. Bolton and Paula A. Desutter, "Russian Roulette," *Foreign Policy*, August 6, 2013, http://www.foreignpolicy.com/articles/2013/06/21/russian_roulette_obama_nukes_john_bolton.

35. Ibid.

36. Letter to President Obama from the Center for Security Policy, February 22, 2013, http://www.centerforsecuritypolicy.org/wp-content/uploads/2013/03/Letter-to-Obama-on-Nuclear-Cuts-22213.pdf.

37. Matthew Kroenig, "The Case for Overkill," *Foreign Policy*, June 20, 2013, http://www.foreignpolicy.com/articles/2013/06/19/the_case_for_overkill. See also Matthew Kroenig, "Nuclear Superiority and the Balance of Resolve: Explaining

Nuclear Crisis Outcomes" (paper, International Organization, August 21, 2011), http://www.matthewkroenig.com/resources/Publications/Nuclear-Superiority.pdf.

38. Charles Clover and Geoff Dyer, "Russia Turns Up the Nuclear Rhetoric," *Financial Times*, May 24, 2012, http://www.ft.com/cms/s/2/698334c8-a4d9-11e1-9908-00144feabdc0.html#axzz1vv2qAfyr.

39. Bell, "Indefensible Policies: Our Commander-in-Chief Retreats."

40. Bettina Renz and Rod Thornton, "Russian Military Modernization: Cause, Course, and Consequence," *Problems of Post-Communism*, January/February 2012, http://www.academia.edu/1473381/Russian_Military_Modernization_Cause_Course_and_Consequences.

41. "Russia to Upgrade Nuclear Systems," BBC News, September 26, 2008, http://news.bbc.co.uk/2/hi/europe/7638356.stm.

42. "Russia Speeds Up Upgrading Strategic Nuclear Forces," Xinhua, November 20, 2012, http://www.globaltimes.cn/content/745459.shtml.

43. Bill Gertz, "Russia Launched Massive Nuclear Drill, Pentagon Alarmed," *Washington Times*, March 5, 2013, http://www.washingtontimes.com/news/2013/mar/5/russians-launched-massive-nuclear-drill-sounded-al.

44. Bill Gertz, "Inside the Ring: Russia Builds Up, U.S. Down," *Washington Times*, May 1, 2013, http://www.washingtontimes.com/news/2013/may/1/inside-the-ring-russia-builds-up-us-down/.

45. Ibid.

46. Baker Spring and Michaela Bendikova, "The United States Must Not Concede the Russia Position on Tactical Nuclear Weapons" (WebMemo #3491, Heritage Foundation, February 8, 2012), http://www.heritage.org/research/reports/2012/02/us-strategy-on-russias-tactical-nuclear-weapons#_ftn2.

47. Jacob Kipp, "Russian Doctrine on Tactical Nuclear Weapons: Contexts, Prisms, and Connections," in *Tactical Nuclear Weapons and NATO*, ed. Tom Nichols, Douglas Stuart, and Jeffrey D. McCausland (Carlisle, PA: Strategic Studies Institute, U.S. Army War College, 2012), 121, http://www.strategicstudiesinstitute.army.mil/pdffiles/PUB1103.pdf.

48. Leonid Polyakov, "Aspects of the Current Russian Perspective on Tactical Nuclear Weapons," in Nichols, Stuart, and McCausland, *Tactical Nuclear Weapons and NATO*, 162.

49. Joshua Keating, "So Much for the Budapest Memorandum," *Slate*, March 19, 2014, http://www.slate.com/blogs/the_world_/2014/03/19/the_budapest_memorandum_in_1994_russia_agreed_to_respect_ukraine_s_borders.html.

50. "Sichuan Earthquake," *New York Times*, May 6, 2009, http://topics.nytimes.com/top/news/science/topics/earthquakes/sichuan_province_china/index.html.

51. Wu Weilin, "Nuclear Explosion Occurred Near Epicenter of the Sichuan Earthquake, Expert Says," *Epoch Times*, June 3, 2008, http://www.theepochtimes.com/news/8-6-3/71353.html.

52. Phillip A. Karber, "Strategic Implications of China's Underground Great Wall" (paper, Georgetown University, September 26, 2011), http://www.fas.org/nuke/guide/china/Karber_UndergroundFacilities-Full_2011_reduced.pdf.

53. Viktor Yesin, "Third After the U.S. and Russia," VPK News, May 2, 2012, http://vpk-news.ru/articles/8838.

54. Ibid.

55. Michael Richardson, "China's Nuclear Program Still Shrouded in Secrecy," *Japan Times*, May 23, 2013, http://www.japantimes.co.jp/opinion/2013/05/23/commentary/chinas-nuclear-program-still-shrouded-in-secrecy/.

56. Ibid.

57. "China Builds Underground 'Great Wall' Against Nuke Attack," *Chosun Ilbo*, December 14, 2009, http://english.chosun.com/site/data/html_dir/2009/12/14/2009121400292.html.

58. Richardson, "China's Nuclear program Still Shrouded in Secrecy."

59. Ibid.

60. Ibid.

61. Bell, "Indefensible Policies: Our Commander-in-Chief Retreats."

62. Jessica Elgot, "Israel's Benjamin Netanyahu Draws Cartoon Bomb at UN General Assembly to Illustrate Iran Nuclear Threat (PICTURES)," *Huffington Post UK*, August 28, 2012, http://www.huffingtonpost.co.uk/2012/09/27/israel-benjamin-netanyahu-bomb-cartoon-un-iran_n_1920495.html.

63. Ibid.

64. "Iran FM Says Construction Will Continue at Contested Arak Nuclear Reactor Site, Testing Limits of Deal," CBS News, November 27, 2013, http://www.cbsnews.com/news/iran-says-work-to-continue-at-arak-nuclear-reactor-site/.

65 Tom Cohen, "Iranian Official on Nuke Deal: 'We Did Not Agree to Dismantle Anything,'" CNN, http://www.cnn.com/2014/01/22/politics/iran-us-nuclear/.

66. "Report: Israel, Saudis Working on Iran Strike Plans," UPI, November 17, 2013, http://www.upi.com/Top_News/World-News/2013/11/17/Report-Israel-Saudis-working-on-Iran-strike-plans/UPI-63251384690743/.

67. Matthew Kroenig, "Iran Diplomatic Window Rapidly Closing: Another View," *USA Today*, June 17, 2013, http://www.usatoday.com/story/opinion/2013/06/17/iran-election-matthew-kroenig-editorials-debates/2432961/.

68. Gertz, "Armed Services Subcommittee Chair: Missile Defense Modernization Needed."

69. "Rouhani Says Netanyahu Threats Over Nuclear Program Are Laughable," *Jerusalem Post*, July 17, 2013, http://www.jpost.com/Middle-East/Irans-Rouhani-bids-support-of-Syrian-Hezbollah-efforts-against-Israel-320100.

70. Kroenig, "Iran Diplomatic Window Rapidly Closing: Another View."

71. Paul K. Kerr and Mary Beth Nikitin, "Pakistan's Nuclear Weapons: Proliferation and Security Issues" (report for Congress, Congressional Research Service, March 19, 2013), http://www.fas.org/sgp/crs/nuke/RL34248.pdf.

72. Bill Gertz, "China, Pakistan Reach Secret Nuclear Reactor Deal for Pakistan," *Washington Free Beacon*, March 21, 2013, http://www.washingtontimes.com/news/2013/mar/21/china-pakistan-reach-secret-reactor-deal-pakistan/#ixzz2d057SmEe.

73. Gordon G. Chang, "Iran Tried to Buy the Pakistani Bomb. What Was China's Role?" Fox News, March 17, 2010, http://www.foxnews.com/opinion/2010/03/17/gordon-g-chang-iran-pakistan-china-dr-khan/.

74. Siddharth Ramana, "China-Pakistan Nuclear Alliance" (paper, Institute of Peace and Conflict Studies, August 2011), 5, 11.

75. Kroenig, Matthew, "Exporting the Bomb: Why States Provide Sensitive Nuclear Assistance," *American Political Science Review* 103, no. 1 (February 2009): 129. Corroborated by Khan, as reported in Ramana, "China-Pakistan Nuclear Alliance."

76. Gertz, "China, Pakistan Reach Secret Nuclear Reactor Deal for Pakistan."

77. "Chinese Firm in Illegal Nuclear Exports to Pakistan," BBC News, December 3, 2012, http://www.bbc.co.uk/news/business-20590136.

78. "Profile: Nawaz Sharif," BBC News, September 24, 2013, http://www.bbc.co.uk/news/world-asia-22167511.

79. "Pakistan: Navy Plans to Design Own Nuclear-Powered Submarine," *Naval Today*, February 16, 2012, http://navaltoday.com/2012/02/16/pakistan-navy-plans-to-design-own-nuclear-powered-submarine/.

80. Shaun Gregory, "The Terrorist Threat to Nuclear Weapons in Pakistan," European Leadership Network, June 4, 2013, http://www.europeanleadershipnetwork.org/the-terrorist-threat-to-nuclear-weapons-in-pakistan_613.html.

81. David E. Sanger and Choe Sang-Hun, "North Korea Confirms It Conducted 3rd Nuclear Test," *New York Times*, February 11, 2013, http://www.nytimes.com/2013/02/12/world/asia/north-korea-nuclear-test.html.

82. Duyeon Kim, "Fact Sheet: North Korea's Nuclear and Ballistic Missile Programs" (fact sheet, Center for Arms Control and Non-Proliferation, July 2013), http://armscontrolcenter.org/publications/factsheets/fact_sheet_north_korea_nuclear_and_missile_programs/.

83. Bell, "Indefensible Policies: Our Commander-in-Chief Retreats."

84. "North Korea: Overview" (profile, Nuclear Threat Initiative, updated December 2013), http://www.nti.org/country-profiles/north-korea/.

85. Kim, "Fact Sheet: North Korea's Nuclear and Ballistic Missile Programs."

86. "North Korea's Nuclear Work Is Beyond Sanctions' Ability to Constrain: Experts," Yahoo! News, September 25, 2013, http://news.yahoo.com/north-koreas-nuclear-beyond-sanctions-ability-constrain-experts-110203903--politics.html.

87. "In Focus: North Korea's Nuclear Threats," *New York Times*, updated April 16, 2013, http://www.nytimes.com/interactive/2013/04/12/world/asia/north-korea-questions.html.

88. Bell, "Indefensible Policies: Our Commander-in-Chief Retreats."

89. Chuck Hagel, "Missile Defense Announcement," March 15, 2013, http://www.defense.gov/speeches/speech.aspx?speechid=1759.

90. "A Failure to Intercept," editorial, *New York Times*, July 24, 2013, http://www.nytimes.com/2013/07/25/opinion/a-failure-to-intercept.html.

91. Ibid.

92. Thom Shanker, "Missile Defense Interceptor Misses Target in Test," *New York Times*, July 5, 2013, http://www.nytimes.com/2013/07/06/us/missile-defense-interceptor-misses-target-in-test.html.

93. Gertz, "Armed Services Subcommittee Chair: Missile Defense Modernization Needed."

94. Ibid.

95. Michael R. Gordon, "U.S. Is Proposing European Shield for Iran Missiles," *New York Times*, May 22, 2006, http://www.nytimes.com/2006/05/22/world/middleeast/22missiles.html.

96. Nikolai Sokov, "A Second Sighting of Russian Tactical Nukes in Kaliningrad," Center for Nonproliferation Studies, February 15, 2011, http://cns.miis.edu/stories/110215_kaliningrad_tnw.htm#fn2.

97. Adrian Bloomfield, "Russia Piles Pressure on EU Over Missile Shield," *The Telegraph*, December 15, 2013, http://www.telegraph.co.uk/news/worldnews/1569495/Russia-piles-pressure-on-EU-over-missile-shield.html.

98. "Kaliningrad: European Fears Over Russian Missiles," BBC News, December 16, 2013, http://www.bbc.co.uk/news/world-europe-25407284.

99. "Putin Says NSA Surveillance 'Necessary' to Fight Terrorism," Fox News, December 19, 2013, http://www.foxnews.com/world/2013/12/19/putin-says-nsa-surveillance-necessary-but-should-be-limited/.

100. Peter Baker, "White House Scraps Bush's Approach to Missile Shield," *New York Times*, September 17, 2009, http://www.nytimes.com/2009/09/18/world/europe/18shield.html.

101. Ibid.

102. Ibid.

103. Benjamin Weinthal, "How Obama Lost Poland," *Foreign Policy*, August 2, 2012, http://www.foreignpolicy.com/articles/2012/07/30/how_obama_lost_poland.

104. Julian E. Barnes and Megan K. Stack, "Russia's Putin Praises Obama's Missile Defense Decision," *Los Angeles Times*, September 19, 2009, http://articles.latimes.com/2009/sep/19/world/fg-missile-defense19.

105. Stephen J. Flanagan, "No, Obama Did Not Abandon Poland," *Foreign Policy*, October 31, 2012, http://www.foreignpolicy.com/articles/2012/10/31/no_obama_did_not_abandon_poland.

106. Marcin Sobczyk, "WikiLeaks Helps Poland Get Clarity on U.S. Relations," *Emerging Europe* (blog), *Wall Street Journal*, December 1, 2010, http://blogs.wsj.com/emergingeurope/2010/12/01/wikileaks-helps-poland-get-clarity-on-us-relations/.

107. "New Arms Race? Poland to Spend Fortune on Missile Defense," RT, October 19, 2012, http://rt.com/politics/poland-missile-defense-invest-791/.

108. Ian Traynor, "WikiLeaks Cables: Poland Wants Missile Shield to Protect Against Russia," *The Guardian*, December 6, 2010, http://www.guardian.co.uk/world/2010/dec/06/wikileaks-cables-poland-russia-shield.

109. Andrew E. Kramer, "Russian General Makes Threat on Missile-Defense Sites," *New York Times*, May 3, 2012, http://www.nytimes.com/2012/05/04/world/europe/russian-general-threatens-pre-emptive-attacks-on-missile-defense-sites.html.

110. "Russia Expects Missile Shield 'Flexibility' From Reelected Obama," RIA Novosti, August 11, 2012, http://en.rian.ru/world/20121108/177294455.html.

111. David M. Herszenhorn and Michael R. Gordon, "U.S. Cancels Part of Missile Defense That Russia Opposed," *New York Times*, March 16, 2013, http://www.nytimes.com/2013/03/17/world/europe/with-eye-on-north-korea-us-cancels-missile-defense-russia-opposed.html.

112. Gertz, "Armed Services Subcommittee Chair: Missile Defense Modernization Needed."

113. Bell, "Indefensible Policies: Our Commander-in-Chief Retreats."

114. Kyl, "America's Nuclear Deterrent—and Defenses—Are Eroding Fast."

115. Ibid.

116. Gertz, "Russia Conducts Test of New ICBM Designed to Defeat U.S. Defenses."

117. Bell, "Indefensible Policies: Our Commander-in-Chief Retreats."

118. "S-500 Prometheus," Missile Threat Project of the George C. Marshall and Claremont Institutes, April 26, 2013, http://missilethreat.com/defense-systems/s-500/.

119. Bill Gertz, "Russian Defense Radar, Missiles Worry U.S. Officials," *Washington Free Beacon*, July 3, 2013, http://freebeacon.com/russian-defense-radar-missiles-worry-u-s-officials/.

120. Gertz, "Armed Services Subcommittee Chair: Missile Defense Modernization Needed."

121. Julie Pace, "Obama Berlin Speech Renews Calls for Nuclear Reductions," *Huffington Post*, June 19, 2013, http://www.huffingtonpost.com/2013/06/19/obama-berlin-speech_n_3466264.html.

CHAPTER 6: THE ECONOMIC CONTEST

1. Vanessa Wong, "Q&A: Peter Navarro on America's Death by China," *Bloomberg Businessweek*, August 22, 2012, http://www.businessweek.com/articles/2012-08-22/q-and-a-peter-navarro-on-americas-death-by-china.

2. Alexander Tanas, "Russia Warns Moldova Over Its Pro-Europe Push," Reuters, September 3, 2013, http://www.reuters.com/article/2013/09/03/us-moldova-russia-idUSBRE9820VI20130903.

3. Marilyn Geewax, "Smithfield Says Pork Won't Change, but Some Aren't Buying It," NPR, July 10, 2013, http://www.npr.org/2013/07/09/200393587/smithfield-says-pork-won-t-change-but-some-aren-t-buying-it.

4. Dana Mattioli, Dana Cimillucca, and David Kesmodel, "China Makes Biggest U.S. Play," *Wall Street Journal*, May 30, 2013, http://online.wsj.com/article/SB10001424127887324412604578512722044165756.html.

5. Heriberto Araújo and Juan Pablo Cardenal, "China's Economic Empire," *New York Times*, June 1, 2013, http://www.nytimes.com/2013/06/02/opinion/sunday/chinas-economic-empire.html.

6. Scott Rose and Olga Tanas, "Putin Turns Black Gold to Bullion as Russia Outbuys World," Bloomberg News, February 11, 2013, http://www.bloomberg.com/news/2013-02-10/putin-turns-black-gold-into-bullion-as-russia-out-buys-world.html.

7. Araújo and Cardenal, "China's Economic Empire."

8. Ibid.

9. Ibid.

10. Ibid.

11. Ibid.

12. Ibid.

13. Chris Hogg, "China Banks Lend More Than World Bank—Report," BBC News, January 18, 2011, http://www.bbc.co.uk/news/world-asia-pacific-12212936.

14. Ibid.

15. Matt Krantz and Elizabeth Weise, "China Continues to Target U.S. Companies," *USA Today*, May 29, 2013, http://www.usatoday.com/story/money/business/2013/05/29/china-shuanghui-smithfield/2369565/.

16. Parija Kavilanz, "China's Expensive Love Affair With Pork," CNN Money, May 29, 2013, http://money.cnn.com/2013/05/29/news/companies/smithfield-foods.

17. Bill Vlasic, "Chinese Creating New Auto Niche Within Detroit," *New York Times*, May 12, 2013, http://www.nytimes.com/2013/05/13/business/global/chinese-automakers-quietly-build-a-detroit-presence.html.

18. Ibid.

19. Ibid.

20. Ibid.

21. Carol E. Lee and Damian Paletta, "U.S. to File WTO Charges on China," *Wall Street Journal*, September 17, 2012, http://online.wsj.com/article/SB10000872396390443995604578001062038754322.html.

22. Wong, "Q&A: Peter Navarro on America's Death by China."

23. Juan Pablo Cardenal and Heriberto Araújo, *China's Silent Army: The Pioneers, Traders, Fixers and Workers Who Are Remaking the World in Beijing's Image* (New York: Random House, 2013), 33.

24. Les Christie, "Chinese Buyers Flood U.S. Housing Market," CNN Money, July 8, 2013, http://money.cnn.com/2013/07/08/real_estate/chinese-homebuyers/index.html.

25. Cardenal and Araújo, *China's Silent Army*, 15.

26. John Iveson, "The Success of China's Retail Revolution Threatens to Be the Regime's Undoing," *National Post*, January 2, 2013, http://fullcomment.nationalpost.com/2013/02/01/john-ivison-the-success-of-chinas-retail-revolution-threatens-to-be-the-regimes-undoing/.

27. Ibid.

28. "Chinese Consumers Account for 47 Percent of the World's Luxury Goods Market," *Chinascope*, updated November 18, 2013, http://chinascope.org/main/content/view/5936/107/.

29. Ibid.

30. Ibid.

31. Philip LeBeau, "New Study Finds China Manufacturing Costs Rising to US Level," CNBC, April 18, 2013, http://www.cnbc.com/id/100651692.

32. Kenneth Rapoza, "China's Economy Firing Blanks: Second Quarter Seen Worst Than First," *Forbes*, June 29, 2013, http://www.forbes.com/sites/kenrapoza/2013/06/09/chinas-economy-firing-blanks-second-quarter-seen-worse-than-first/.

33. Ramy Inocencio, "China's Economy Grows 7.8% for 2012, Better Than Expected," CNN, January 18, 2013, http://edition.cnn.com/2013/01/17/business/china-gdp-2012.

34. Ibid.

35. "China's Socialist Market Economic Reform and Its Strong Theoretical Consciousness and Confidence," *People's Daily Online*, October 17, 2012, http://english.peopledaily.com.cn/100668/102793/7980397.html.

36. Lingling Wei and William Kazer, "China Stocks Slide on Cash Crunch," *Wall Street Journal*, June 24, 2013, http://online.wsj.com/article/SB1000142412788 7324637504578564910240873572.html.

37. Lingling Wei and Bob Davis, "China's 'Shadow Banks' Fan Debt-Bubble Fears," *Wall Street Journal*, June 25, 2013, http://online.wsj.com/article/SB10001424 127887324637504578563570021019506.html.

38. Ibid.

39. Ibid.

40. Araújo and Cardenal, "China's Economic Empire."

41. Keith Bradser, "China's Grip on Economy Will Test New Leaders," *New York Times*, November 9, 2012, http://www.nytimes.com/2012/11/10/world/asia/state-enterprises-pose-test-for-chinas-new-leaders.html.

42. "China GDP," Trading Economics, http://www.tradingeconomics.com/china/gdp.

43. David M. Herszenhorn and Andrew E. Kramer, "Putin Puts Pensions at Risk in $43 Billion Bid to Jolt Economy," *New York Times*, June 21, 2013, http://www.nytimes.com/2013/06/22/world/europe/russia-to-tap-reserve-funds-for-infrastructure-projects.html.

44. Ibid.

45. Lukas I. Alpert and Andrey Ostroukh, "Russia Looks to Weaker Ruble for Revival," *Wall Street Journal*, June 18, 2013, http://online.wsj.com/article/SB100014 24127887324021104578553343831156974.html.

46. Ibid.

47. David M. Herszenhorn and Andrew E. Kramer, "Oil Wealth Ebbing, Russia Needs to Lure Foreign Capital," *New York Times*, June 20, 2013, http://www.nytimes.com/2013/06/21/world/europe/oil-wealth-reduced-russia-needs-to-lure-foreign-capital.html.

48. "Russia GDP," Trading Economics, http://www.tradingeconomics.com/russia/gdp.

49. "Russia's APEC Integration 'Just Beginning'—Experts," RIA Novosti, September 2, 2012, http://en.rian.ru/analysis/20120902/175545911.html.

50. Daniel Wiser, "U.S. Fracking Threatens Russia's Energy Dominance," *Washington Free Beacon*, August 14, 2013, http://freebeacon.com/u-s-fracking-threatens-russias-energy-dominance/.

51. Nina Poussenkova, "Rethinking Russia: The Global Expansion of Russia's Energy Giants," *Journal of International Affairs* 63, no. 2 (Spring/Summer 2010): 103–124, http://jia.sipa.columbia.edu/global-expansion-russia's-energy-giants.

52. "Gazprom, GDF Suez to Mull Possible Extension of Nord Stream," Itar-Tass, June 21, 2013, http://www.itar-tass.com/en/c32/780271.html.

53. Brian Bremner, "Why Is Vladimir Putin Acting So Crazy?" *Bloomberg Businessweek*, April 29, 2013, http://www.businessweek.com/printer/articles/147824-why-is-vladimir-putin-acting-so-crazy

54. Elena Mazneva and Olga Tanas, "Russia Pressures Ukraine on Gas as Biden Pledges Support," *Bloomberg Businessweek,* April 22, 2014, http://www.businessweek.com/news/2014-04-22/russia-pressures-ukraine-on-gas-as-biden-pledges-energy-support.

55. James Marson and Joe Parkinson, "In Reversal, Neighbors Squeeze Russia's Gazprom Over Natural-Gas Prices," *Wall Street Journal,* May 1, 2013, http://online.wsj.com/article/SB10001424127887324240804578414912310902382.html.

56. Wiser, "U.S. Fracking Threatens Russia's Energy Dominance."

57. Bremner, "Why Is Vladimir Putin Acting So Crazy?"

58. Wiser, "U.S. Fracking Threatens Russia's Energy Dominance."

59. Bremner, "Why Is Vladimir Putin Acting So Crazy?"

60. Marson and Parkinson, "In Reversal, Neighbors Squeeze Russia's Gazprom."

61. Bremner, "Why Is Vladimir Putin Acting So Crazy?"

62. Marson and Parkinson, "In Reversal, Neighbors Squeeze Russia's Gazprom."

63. Bremner, "Why Is Vladimir Putin Acting So Crazy?"

64. Tanas, "Russia Warns Moldova Over Its Pro-Europe Push."

65. François Lenoir, "Between Two Stools: Ukraine Says EU Trade Deal Certain, Russia-Led Union Also an Option," RT, September 25, 2013, http://rt.com/business/russia-ukraine-customs-eu-319/.

66. Will England, "Ukraine Enacts Harsh Laws Against Protests," *Washington Post,* January 17, 2014, http://www.washingtonpost.com/world/europe/ukraine-enacts-harsh-laws-against-protests/2014/01/17/365f377a-7fae-11e3-93c1-0e888170b723_story.html.

67. Dmitry Zhdannikov and Vladimir Soldatkin, "Exclusive: Russia plans $25–$30 Billion Oil-for-Loans Deal With China," Reuters, February 13, 2013, http://www.reuters.com/article/2013/02/13/us-rosneft-china-idUSBRE91C0TB20130213.

68. Isabel Gorst, "China-Russia: A Whole Lot of Energy Deals," *Beyondbrics* (blog) *Financial Times*, March 22, 2013, http://blogs.ft.com/beyond-brics/2013/03/22/china-russia-a-whole-lot-of-energy-deals/#axzz2OKGi1NWL.

69. Mike Obel, "Russia, China in Oil-for-Loan Talks That Could Be Worth $30B to the Kremlin," *International Business Times*, February 13, 2013, http://www.ibtimes.com/russia-china-oil-loan-talks-could-be-worth-30b-kremlin-report-1083230.

70. David M. Herszenhorn and Chris Buckley, "China's Leader Argues for Cooperation With Russia," *New York Times*, March 23, 2013, http://www.nytimes.com/2013/03/24/world/europe/chinas-leader-argues-for-cooperation-with-russia.html.

71. Isabel Gorst, "China-Russia: A Whole Lot of Energy Deals."

72. Lydia Polgreen, "Group of Emerging Nations Plans to Form Development Bank," *New York Times*, March 26, 2013, http://www.nytimes.com/2013/03/27/world/africa/brics-to-form-development-bank.html.

73. Andrew England, "Brics Agree to Create Development Bank," *Beyondbrics* (blog), *Financial Times*, March 27, 2013, http://www.ft.com/cms/s/0/2bcbd6e0-96e5-11e2-a77c-00144feabdc0.html#axzz2Olig1jJj.

74. Ibid.

75. Pepe Escobar, "BRICS Go Over the Qall," *Asia Times Online*, March 26, 2013, http://www.atimes.com/atimes/World/WOR-01-260313.html.

76. "The Rise of BRICS FDA and Africa," Global Investment Trend Monitor, UN Conference on Trade and Development, March 25, 2013, http://unctad.org/en/PublicationsLibrary/webdiaeia2013d6_en.pdf.

77. Escobar, "BRICS Go Over the Wall."

78. Wang Wei, "China Becomes Africa's Largest Trading Partner," CRI English, December 22, 2012, http://english.cri.cn/7146/2012/12/22/2361s739833.htm.

79. Peter Eigan, "Is China Good or Bad for Africa?" *Global Public Square* (blog) CNN, October 29, 2012, http://globalpublicsquare.blogs.cnn.com/2012/10/29/is-china-good-or-bad-for-africa/.

80. Dambisa Moyo, luncheon, The Common Good, September 13, 2012, New York City.

81. Eigan, "Is China Good or Bad for Africa?"

82. Ibid.

83. Alexander Bernard, "How the US Can Out-Invest China in Africa," *Christian Science Monitor,* August 30, 2012, http://www.csmonitor.com/Commentary/Opinion/2012/0830/How-the-US-can-out-invest-China-in-Africa.

84. Chris Buckley, "China's Leader Tries to Calm African Fears of His Country's Economic Power," *New York Times,* March 25, 2013, http://www.nytimes.com/2013/03/26/world/asia/chinese-leader-xi-jinping-offers-africa-assurance-and-aid.html.

85. Ibid.

86. Adam Nossitor, "China Finds Resistance to Oil Deals in Africa," *New York Times,* September 17, 2013, http://www.nytimes.com/2013/09/18/world/africa/china-finds-resistance-to-oil-deals-in-africa.html.

87. Ibid.

88. David Smith, "China Offers $20bn of Loans to African Nations," *The Guardian,* July 19, 2012, http://www.guardian.co.uk/world/2012/jul/19/china-offers-loans-african-nations.

89. "Russia Writes Off $20 Billion for African Countries," *Pravda,* October 19, 2012, http://english.pravda.ru/russia/economics/19-10-2012/122511-russia_africa-0/.

90. "Russia in Africa: An Alternative to China's Investment Monopoly?" *Worldcrunch,* December 20, 2011, http://goo.gl/0sTUIi.

91. Ibid.

92. Ibid.

93. Ibid.

94. R. Evan Ellis, "Chinese Soft Power in Latin America: A Case Study," National Defense University, *Joint Force Quarterly* 60 (1st Quarter, January 2011), http://www.ndu.edu/press/lib/images/jfq-60/JFQ60_85-91_Ellis.pdf.

95. "Mao and Bolivar Would Have Been Mates, says Chavez," *Daily Times,* December 25, 2004, http://archives.dailytimes.com.pk/foreign/25-Dec-2004/mao-and-bolivar-would-have-been-mates-says-chavez.

96. Kevin Gallagher, Amos Irwin, and Katherine Koleski, "The New Banks in Town: Chinese Finance in Latin America" (report, Inter-American Dialogue, February 2012), http://ase.tufts.edu/gdae/Pubs/rp/Gallagher ChineseFinanceLatinAmerica.pdf.

97. Kevin Gallagher, "Forget the Received Wisdom: Chinese Finance in Latin America Is a Win-Win," *Poverty Matters* (blog), *The Guardian,* March 16, 2012, http://www.guardian.co.uk/global-development/poverty-matters/2012/mar/16/chinese-finance-latin-america-win-win.

98. Shasta Darlington, "China-Latam Economic Ties Tightening," CNN, November 19, 2012, http://edition.cnn.com/2012/11/18/business/china-latam-ties/index.html.

99. Ibid.

100. Colum Murphy, "China Steps Up Push Into Latin America," *Wall Street Journal*, September 12, 2012, http://online.wsj.com/article/SB10000872396390443 696604577647102203290514.html.

101. Yuri Paniev, "Russia Turning on Latin America," *Austral: Brazilian Journal of Strategy & International Relations* 1, no. 1 (January–June 2012): 47, http://seer.ufrgs.br/index.php/austral/article/view/27991/18008.

102. Tatyana Rusakova, "Russia Might Lose Key Ally in Latin America," *Russia & India Report*, January 16, 2013, http://indrus.in/articles/2013/01/16/russia_might_lose_key_ally_in_latin_america_21653.html.

103. Stephen J. Blank, "Russia and Latin America: Motives and Consequences" (report, Center for Hemispheric Policy, Challenges to Security in the Hemisphere Task Force, April 13, 2010), https://umshare.miami.edu/web/wda/hemisphericpolicy/Blank_miamirussia_04-13-10.pdf.

104. Paniev, "Russia Turning on Latin America," 45.

105. Lauren Paverman and W. Alex Sanchez, "China and the End of the Monroe Doctrine," *Foreign Policy in Focus*, December 1, 2011, http://www.fpif.org/articles/china_and_the_end_of_the_monroe_doctrine.

106. Ellis, "Chinese Soft Power in Latin America."

107. Daniel P. Erikson, "Requiem for the Monroe Doctrine," *Current History* 107 (February 2008): 58–64, http://www.thedialogue.org/PublicationFiles/Erikson_Monroe Doctrine_Feb 2008.pdf.

108. Loro Horta, "China on the March in Latin America," *Deep Journal*, June 28, 2007, http://www.deepjournal.com/p/7/a/en/814.html.

109. Rush Doshi and David Walter, "China's Rising Tide in the Caribbean," *Wall Street Journal*, September 30, 2013, http://online.wsj.com/article/SB1000142412788 7324576304579072750474072912.html.

110. Peter Navarro and Greg Autry, "Just Say No to Chinese Acquisitions of American Assets," *Huffington Post*, December 12, 2012, http://www.huffingtonpost.com/peter-navarro-and-greg-autry/china-battery-company_b_2273127.html.

111. Wong, "Q&A: Peter Navarro on America's Death by China."

CHAPTER 7: INTELLIGENCE WARS

1. Gabriel Rodriguez, "Edward Snowden Interview Transcript," *Policy Mic*, June 9, 2013, http://www.policymic.com/articles/47355/edward-snowden-interview-

transcript-full-text-read-the-guardian-s-entire-interview-with-the-man-who-leaked-prism.

2. David M. Herszenhorn, "Putin Says U.S. Trapped Snowden in Russia," *New York Times*, July 16, 2013, http://www.bostonglobe.com/news/world/2013/07/15/putin-says-has-effectively-trapped-snowden/ARfIcpfJEHBmuwnSJpaWTI/story.html.

3. Peter Muhly, "For Edward Snowden, Why Russia?" CBS News, June 24, 2013, http://www.cbsnews.com/8301-202_162-57590837/for-edward-snowden-why-russia/.

4. Mark Steyn, "Failures of Intelligence," *National Review*, November 23, 2012, http://www.nationalreview.com/articles/333928/failures-intelligence-mark-steyn.

5. Ming Jinwei, "Commentary: Washington Owes World Explanations Over Troubling Spy Accusations," Xinhua, June 23, 2013, http://news.xinhuanet.com/english/indepth/2013-06/23/c_132478464.htm.

6. Maria Antonova, "Snowden to Stay in Moscow Airport for Now: Lawyer," Fox News, July 16, 2013,http://www.foxnews.com/world/2013/07/16/snowden-to-stay-in-moscow-airport-for-now-lawyer/.

7. Eric Schmitt and David E. Sanger, "Congressional Leaders Suggest Earlier Snowden Link to Russia," *New York Times*, January 19, 2014, http://www.nytimes.com/2014/01/20/us/politics/congressional-leaders-suggest-snowden-was-working-for-russia.html.

8. Muhly, "For Edward Snowden, Why Russia?"

9. Herszenhorn, "Putin Says U.S. Trapped Snowden in Russia."

10. "Putin Says NSA Surveillance 'Necessary' to Fight Terrorism," Fox News, December 19, 2013, http://www.foxnews.com/world/2013/12/19/putin-says-nsa-surveillance-necessary-but-should-be-limited/.

11. Tal Kopan, "Edward Snowden Nominated for Nobel Peace Prize," *Politico*, July 15, 2013, http://www.politico.com/story/2013/07/edward-snowden-nobel-peace-prize-94158.html#ixzz2ZEtVexWg.

12. "Venezuela, Nicaragua Offer Asylum to Snowden," WL Central, July 6, 2013, http://wlcentral.org/node/2844.

13. Jinwei, "Washington Owes World Explanations Over Troubling Spy Accusations."

14. Eli Lake, "Sorry, Snowden: Putin Lied to You About His Surveillance State—And Made You a Pawn of It," *The Daily Beast*, April 18, 2014, http://www.thedailybeast.com/articles/2014/04/17/sorry-snowden-putin-lied-to-you-about-his-surveillance-state-and-made-you-a-pawn-of-it.html.

15. Courtney Subramanian, "Obama Adviser Cool to Snowden Amnesty," *Swampland* (blog), *Time*, December 23, 2013, http://swampland.time.com/2013/12/23/obama-adviser-edward-snowden-doesnt-deserve-amnesty/.

16. Scott Shane and Charlie Savage, "In Ordinary Lives, U.S. Sees the Work of Russian Agents," *New York Times,* June 28, 2010, http://www.nytimes.com/2010/06/29/world/europe/29spy.html.

17. Ibid.

18. Ibid.

19. "FBI Releases Russian Spy Ring Papers, Video," Fox News, http://www.foxnews.com/us/2011/10/31/fbi-releases-russian-spy-ring-papers-video/.

20. "Spies Like Us," *The Economist,* July 1, 2010, http://www.economist.com/node/16486569.

21. Shai Oster and Gordon Fairclough, "Beijing Taxis Are Rigged for Eavesdropping," *Wall Street Journal,* August 6, 2008, http://online.wsj.com/news/articles/SB121795982193713959.

22. Scott Shane and David E. Sanger, "Drone Crash in Iran Reveals Secret U.S. Surveillence Effort," *New York Times* December 7, 2011, http://www.nytimes.com/2011/12/08/world/middleeast/drone-crash-in-iran-reveals-secret-us-surveillance-bid.html.

23. Lee Ferran, "Iran: We Stole All Secrets From US Drone," ABC News, December 10, 2012, http://abcnews.go.com/Blotter/iran-stole-secrets-us-rq-170-drone/story?id=17925395.

24. Scott Peterson, "Exclusive: Iran Hijacked U.S. Drone, Says Iranian Engineer," *Christian Science Monitor,* December 15, 2011, http://www.csmonitor.com/World/Middle-East/2011/1215/Exclusive-Iran-hijacked-US-drone-says-Iranian-engineer-Video.

25. Siobhan Gorman and Adam Entous, "U.S. Says Drone Crashed, Refuting Iran's Claim," *Wall Street Journal,* December 16, 2011, http://online.wsj.com/news/articles/SB10001424052970203733304577102504272876554.

26. Mark Clayton, "Did Iran Hijack the 'Beast'? US Experts Caution About Bold Claims," *Christian Science Monitor,* December 16, 2011, http://www.csmonitor.com/USA/Military/2011/1216/Did-Iran-hijack-the-beast-US-experts-cautious-about-bold-claims.-Video.

27. Ibid.

28. Ibid.

29. Whitney Eulich, "Did Iran Just Down a U.S. Drone by 'Spoofing'?" *The Christian Science Monitor,* December 4, 2012, http://www.csmonitor.com/World/terrorism-security/2012/1204/Did-Iran-just-down-a-US-drone-by-spoofing-video.

30. Thomas Erdbrink, "U.S. Navy Denies Iran's Claim to Have Captured Drone," *New York Times* December 4, 2012, http://www.nytimes.com/2012/12/05/world/middleeast/iran-says-it-seized-another-american-drone.html.

31. Adam Goldman and Anne Gearan, "Senate Report: Attacks on U.S. Compounds in Benghazi Could Have Been Prevented," *Washington Post*, January 15, 2013, http://www.washingtonpost.com/world/national-security/senate-report-attack-on-us-compound-in-benghazi-could-have-been-prevented/2014/01/15/5e197224-7de9-11e3-95c6-0a7aa80874bc_story.html.

32. Russ Travers, "The Coming Intelligence Failure: A Blueprint for Survival," Central Intelligence Agency, *Studies in Intelligence*, Semiannual Edition, no. 1, 1997, https://www.cia.gov/library/center-for-the-study-of-intelligence/csi-publications/csi-studies/studies/97unclass/failure.html.

33. Uri Friedman, "The Ten Biggest American Intelligence Failures," *Foreign Policy*, January 2, 2012, http://www.foreignpolicy.com/articles/2012/1/3/the_ten_biggest_american_intelligence_failures.

34. Spencer Ackerman, "The CIA's Failures," *The Nation*, July 14, 2008, http://www.thenation.com/article/cias-failures.

35. Ibid.

36. Mark Mazzetti, "C.I.A. Lays Out Errors It Made Before Sept. 11," *New York Times*, August 22, 2007, http://www.nytimes.com/2007/08/22/washington/22cia.html.

37. Marcu Baram, "CIA's Mideast Surprise Recalls History of Intelligence Failures," *Huffington Post*, February 11, 2011, http://www.huffingtonpost.com/2011/02/11/cias-mideast-surprise-history-of-failures_n_822183.html.

38. Ibid.

39. Mark Landler and Choe Sang-Hun, "In Kim's Undetected Death, Sign of Nation's Opacity," *New York Times*, December 19, 2011, http://www.nytimes.com/2011/12/20/world/asia/in-detecting-kim-jong-il-death-a-gobal-intelligence-failure.html.

40. Mark Steyn, "Failures of Intelligence."

41. Tom Murse, "How Much U.S. Debt Does China Really Own?" About.com, accessed May 15, 2014, http://usgovinfo.about.com/od/moneymatters/ss/How-Much-US-Debt-Does-China-Own.htm.

42. Wayne M. Morrison and Marc Labonte, "China's Holdings of U.S. Securities: Implications for the U.S. Economy" (report for Congress, Congressional Research Service, August, 2013), http://www.fas.org/sgp/crs/row/RL34314.pdf.

43. Ibid.

44. Ding Gang, "China Must Punish US for Taiwan Arms Sales With 'Financial Weapon,'" *China Daily*, August 8, 2008, http://www.chinadaily.com.cn/opinion/2011-08/08/content_13069554.htm.

45. Morrison and Labonte, "China's Holdings of U.S. Securities."

46. Chris Isidore, "U.S. Companies Dump Billions Into China," CNN Money, January 20, 2011, http://money.cnn.com/2011/01/20/news/international/us_business_chinese_investment_boom/index.htm.

47. Gary Epstein and Robyn Meredith, "U.S. Companies That Invest Big in China," *Forbes*, July 5, 2010, http://www.forbes.com/2010/07/05/us-investments-china-markets-emerging-markets-fdi.html.

48. "Minerals Imported by the United States," Mineral Information Institute, accessed December 21, 2013, http://www.mii.org/pdfs/imports.pdf.

49. "Russian Company Will Supply Components for Boeing 787," *USA Today*, December 27, 2007, http://usatoday30.usatoday.com/money/industries/travel/2007-12-27-boeing-russian-parts_N.htm.

50. Mamta Badkar, "The Strange Story of Neil Heywood, the British Businessman Who May Have Been Killed by the Wife of a Chinese Communist Party Boss," *Business Insider*, April 10, 2012, *http://www.businessinsider.com/china-who-was-neil-haywood-2012-4*

51. "Times Topics: Bo Xilai," *New York Times*, accessed July 18, 2014, http://topics.nytimes.com/top/reference/timestopics/people/b/bo_xilai/index.html.

52. Austin Ramzy, "Wang Lijun, Police Boss Who Triggered Bo Xilai Scandal, Sentenced to 15 Years," *Time*, September 24, 2012, http://world.time.com/2012/09/24/wang-lijun-police-boss-who-triggered-bo-xilai-scandal-sentenced-to-15-years/.

53. "Bo Xilai Scandal: Timeline," BBC News, November 11, 2013, http://www.bbc.co.uk/news/world-asia-china-17673505.

54. Badkar, "The Strange Story."

55. Ramzy, "Wang Lijun."

56. "Times Topics: Bo Xilai."

57. Jason Bush, "Knocking on Russia's Door," *Bloomberg Businessweek*, March 29, 2006, http://www.businessweek.com/stories/2006-03-29/knocking-on-russias-door.

58. Jason Bush, "Hijacking the Hermitage Fund," *Bloomberg Businessweek*, April 4, 2008, http://www.businessweek.com/stories/2008-04-04/hijacking-the-hermitage-fundbusinessweek-business-news-stock-market-and-financial-advice.

59. Ibid.

60. Ibid.

61. Philip Aldrick, "Who Was Sergei Magnitsky?" *The Telegraph*, January 21, 2011, http://www.telegraph.co.uk/finance/newsbysector/banksandfinance/8272606/Who-was-Sergei-Magnitsky.html.

62. Ibid.

63. Ellen Barry, "Scathing Report Issued on Russian Lawyer's Death," *New York Times*, December 28, 2009, http://www.nytimes.com/2009/12/29/world/europe/29russia.html.

64. Philip Aldrick, "Hermitage Capital Calls for Russian Inquiry into $330 Million 'Tax Frauds' Discovered by Sergei Magnitsky," *The Telegraph*, June 20, 2011, http://www.telegraph.co.uk/finance/financial-crime/8587718/Hermitage-Capital-calls-for-Russian-inquiry-into-330m-tax-frauds-uncovered-by-Sergei-Magnitsky.html.

65. Simon Shuster, "One (Rich) American vs. Moscow: The Quest of William Browder," *Time*, December 3, 2011, http://www.time.com/time/world/article/0,8599,2100298-2,00.html.

66. Kathy Lally and Will Englund, "Russia Fumes as U.S. Senate Passes Magnitsky Law Aimed at Human Rights," *Washington Post*, December 6, 2012, http://articles.washingtonpost.com/2012-12-06/world/35649594_1_magnitsky-law-magnitsky-act-law-accountability-act.

67. "Obama's Magnitsky Walkback," editorial, *Wall Street Journal*, January 5, 2014, http://online.wsj.com/news/articles/SB1000142405270230459160457929088074874 5144.

68. Ibid.

69. Kathy Lally, "Magnitsky Law Sets Off Human Rights Fight Between Russia and U.S. Politicians," *Washington Post*, December 7, 2012, http://articles.washingtonpost.com/2012-12-07/world/35673849_1_law-accountability-act-sergei-magnitsky-rule-hermitage-capital-management.

70. Natalie Huet and Maria Golovnina, "Russian Mafia Whistleblower, 44, Found Dead in UK," Reuters, November 28, 2012, http://uk.reuters.com/article/2012/11/28/uk-britain-russia-death-idUKBRE8AR0OM20121128.

71. Peter Pomerantsev, "The Ballroom Dancer and the KGB," *Newsweek*, January 4, 2013, http://www.newsweek.com/ballroom-dancer-and-kgb-63125.

72. Ibid.

73. Boris Volodarsky, "Alexander Litvinenko: A Very Russian Poisoning," *The Telegraph*, December 2, 2009, http://www.telegraph.co.uk/news/worldnews/europe/russia/6615872/Alexander-Litvinenko-A-very-Russian-poisoning.html.

74. Ibid.

75. Pomerantsev, "The Ballroom Dancer."

76. Volodarsky, "Alexander Litvinenko."

77. Ibid.

78. Ibid.

79. Alan Cowell, "Evidence of Russian State Role Seen in Death of Poisoned Spy," *New York Times*, December 13, 2012, http://www.nytimes.com/2012/12/14/world/europe/russian-state-role-seen-in-death-of-poisoned-spy.html .

80. Pomerantsev, "The Ballroom Dancer."

81. Ibid.

82. Jane Croft and Neal Buckley, "UK Turns Down Request for Litvinenko Public Inquiry," *Financial Times*, July 12, 2013, http://www.ft.com/intl/cms/s/0/5cf19446-eadf-11e2-9fcc-00144feabdc0.html#axzz2Z8rqf3fv.

83. Alan Cowell, "Hearing Reveals Details of Spy's Life, but Motive for Death Is Still a Mystery," *New York Times*, December 17, 2012, http://www.nytimes.com/2012/12/18/world/europe/hearing-into-litvinenkos-death-still-leaves-motive-a-mystery.html.

84. Will Stewart, Rebecca Chamber, and Damien Gayle, "Exiled Russian Banker Left in Coma by Submachine Gun 'Assassination Bid' Put Under Armed Guard in Hospital Over Fears of Further Attempts on His Life," *Daily Mail*, March 23, 2012, http://www.dailymail.co.uk/news/article-2119384/Canary-Wharf-shooting-Russian-banker-German-Gorbuntsov-gunned-assassination-attempt.html.

85. Shaun Walker, "Exclusive Interview: German Gorbuntsov—the Banker Shot Six Times in London," *The Independent*, June 8, 2012, http://www.independent.co.uk/news/people/profiles/exclusive-interview-german-gorbuntsov--the-banker-shot-six-times-in-london-7827996.html.

86. Ibid.

87. Natalya Krainova, "2 Jailed in Ruslan Yamadayev's Killing," *Moscow Times*, October 19, 2010, http://www.themoscowtimes.com/news/article/2-jailed-in-ruslan-yamadayevs-killing/420522.html.

88. Luke Harding and Miriam Elder, "Attack on Russian Banker Leaves Trail of Clues Back to Moscow," *The Guardian*, March 30, 2012, http://www.guardian.co.uk/world/2012/mar/30/russian-banker-london-clues-moscow.

89. Ibid.

90. Walker, "Exclusive Interview: German Gorbuntsov."

91. Howard LaFranchi, "Ukraine Standoff: For Some, Russia's Tactics Hark back to Soviet Practices (+video)," *Christian Science Monitor*, April 23, 2014, http://www.csmonitor.com/USA/Foreign-Policy/2014/0423/Ukraine-standoff-For-some-Russia-s-tactics-hark-back-to-Soviet-practices-video.

CHAPTER 8: PROPAGANDA WARD

1. Robert Bridge, "Putin Trumpets Russia's 'Cultural Dominance,'" RT, January 23, 2012, http://rt.com/politics/putin-immigration-manifest-article-421/.

2. Jeremy Page, "For Xi, a 'China Dream' of Military Power," *Wall Street Journal*, March 13, 2013, http://online.wsj.com/article/SB100014241278873241285045783 48774040546346.html.

3. President Obama, news conference, April 4, 2009, "http://www.whitehouse.gov/the-press-office/news-conference-president-obama-4042009."

4. Evgeny Lebedev, "What's So Good About Democracy Anyway? An Audience With the Last Dictator in Europe," *The Independent*, October 19, 2012, http://www.independent.co.uk/news/world/europe/whats-so-good-about-democracy-anyway-an-audience-with-the-last-dictator-in-europe-8218912.html.

5. Ibid.

6. Ibid.

7. "Putin, Lukashenko Hail Relations," *New Europe*, June 3, 2012, http://www.neurope.eu/article/putin-lukashenko-hail-relations.

8. Barbara Demick and Julie Makinen, "China Government's Hand Seen in Anti-Japan Protests," *Los Angeles Times*, September 20, 2012, http://articles.latimes.com/print/2012/sep/20/world/la-fg-china-japan-protests-20120921.

9. Ibid.

10. Andrew Roth, "Georgia: Satellite Dishes Seized," *New York Times*, June 21, 2012, http://www.nytimes.com/2012/06/22/world/europe/georgia-satellite-dishes-seized.html.

11. Ellen Barry, "Church's Muscle Aided Win of President's Rivals in Georgia," *New York Times*, October 13, 2012, http://www.nytimes.com/2012/10/14/world/europe/churchs-muscle-aided-win-of-presidents-rivals-in-georgia.html.

12. Jennifer Rubin, "Putin Ally Lines Up Washington Insiders," *Right Turn* (blog), *Washington Post*, September 17, 2012, http://www.washingtonpost.com/blogs/right-turn/post/putin-ally-lines-up-washington-insiders/2012/09/17/f0c0f1b4-0113-11e2-b257-e1c2b3548a4a_blog.html

13. Didi Kirsten Tatlow, "Rising Tension—and Stakes—in Japan–China Island Dispute," *Rendezvouz* (blog), *International Herald Tribune*, September 14, 2012, http://rendezvous.blogs.nytimes.com/2012/09/14/rising-tension-and-stakes-in-japan-china-island-dispute.

14. Ibid.

15. Ibid.

16. Ian Johnson and Thom Shanker, "Beijing Mixes Messages Over Anti-Japan Protests," *New York Times*, September 16, 2012, http://www.nytimes.com/2012/09/17/world/asia/anti-japanese-protests-over-disputed-islands-continue-in-china.html.

17. Ibid.

18. Tatlow, "Rising Tension—and Stakes—in Japan–China Island Dispute."

19. William Wan, "Chinese Government Both Encourages and Reins In Anti-Japan Protests, Analysts Say," *Washington Post*, September 19, 2012, http://www.washingtonpost.com/world/chinese-government-both-encourages-and-reins-in-anti-japan-protests-analysts-say/2012/09/17/53144ff0-00d8-11e2-b260-32f4a8db9b7e_story.html.

20. "Of Useful Idiots and True Believers," *Analects* (blog), *The Economist*, September 18, 2012, http://www.economist.com/blogs/analects/2012/09/protests-real-and-fake.

21. William Wan, "Chinese Government Both Encourages and Reins In Anti-Japan Protests."

22. Demick and Makinen, "China Government's Hand Seen in Anti-Japan Protests."

23. "Russian Anti-Gay Bill Passes, Protesters Detained," CBS News, June 11, 2013, http://www.cbsnews.com/news/russian-anti-gay-bill-passes-protesters-detained/.

24. Cindy Boren, "Obama Names Openly Gay Athletes to Sochi Olympic Delegation," *Washington Post*, December 18, 2013, http://www.washingtonpost.com/blogs/early-lead/wp/2013/12/18/obama-names-openly-gay-athletes-to-sochi-olympic-delegation/.

25. Jim Meyers, "LIGNET: China's Coming Crash Threatens U.S. Economy, Security," *Newsmax*, December 3, 2012, http://www.newsmax.com/Newsfront/lignet-china-briefing-huntsman/2012/12/03/id/466242.

26. Chris Buckley, "China Takes Aim at Western Ideas," *New York Times*, August 19, 2013, http://www.nytimes.com/2013/08/20/world/asia/chinas-new-leadership-takes-hard-line-in-secret-memo.html.

27. Ibid.

28. Alexander Roslyakov and Nataliya Vasilyeva, "2 Pussy Riot Members Released From Prison," Yahoo! News, December 23, 2103, http://news.yahoo.com/2-pussy-riot-members-released-prison-104718932.html.

29. Clifford J. Levy, "At Expense of All Others, Putin Picks a Church," *New York Times*, April 24, 2008, http://www.nytimes.com/2008/04/24/world/europe/24church.html.

30. "1984 in 2014," *The Economist*, March 29, 2014, http://www.economist.com/news/europe/21599829-new-propaganda-war-underpins-kremlins-clash-west-1984-2014.

CHAPTER 9: COUNTERMOVES

1. Reid J. Epstein, "White House Can't Sway Assad—So It Aims for Putin," *Politico*, August 26, 2013, http://www.politico.com/story/2013/08/syria-vladimir-putin-barack-obama-95923.html.

2. John McCain, "Senator John McCain: Russians Deserve Better Than Putin," *Pravda*, September 19, 2013, http://english.pravda.ru/opinion/19-09-2013/125705-McCain_for_pravda_ru-0/.

3. Daniel Calingaert, "As Democratic Freedoms Decline Globally, the US Must Do More," *GlobalPost*, January 24. 2014, http://www.globalpost.com/dispatches/

globalpost-blogs/commentary/US-leadership-must-advance-global-freedom-in-decline.

4. "Assad Says Any U.S. Strike on Syria 'Is Going to Support al Qaeda,'" CBC News, September 19, 2013, http://www.cbsnews.com/news/assad-says-any-us-strike-on-syria-is-going-to-support-al-qaeda/.

5. Madeleine Albright, "Transcript: Albright Interview on NBC TV February 19," Federation of American Scientists, February 19, 1998, http://www.fas.org/news/iraq/1998/02/19/98021907_tpo.html.

6. George Friedman, "Obama's Tightrope Walk," *Stratfor Geopolitical Weekly*, September 13, 2013, http://www.stratfor.com/weekly/obamas-tightrope-walk.

7. David Keyes, "How Iran, Putin, and Assad Outwitted America," *Daily Beast*, January 16, 2014, http://www.thedailybeast.com/articles/2014/01/16/how-iran-putin-and-assad-outwitted-america.html.

8. Tal Kopan, "John Kerry Under Fire for 'Unbelievably Small' Comment," *Politico*, September 9, 2013, http://www.politico.com/story/2013/09/syria-john-kerry-unbelievably-small-comment-96461.html.

9. Ibid.

10. Josh Rogin, "Bill Clinton: Obama May Look Like a 'Wuss' Over Syria," *Daily Beast*, June 13, 2013, http://www.thedailybeast.com/articles/2013/06/13/bill-clinton-obama-may-look-like-a-wuss-over-syria.html.

11. Vladimir Putin, "A Plea for Caution From Russia," *New York Times*, September 11, 2013, http://www.nytimes.com/2013/09/12/opinion/putin-plea-for-caution-from-russia-on-syria.html.

12. Steven Lee Meyers, "As Obama Pauses Action, Putin Takes Center Stage," *New York Times*, September 11, 2013, http://www.nytimes.com/2013/09/12/world/europe/as-obama-pauses-action-putin-takes-center-stage.html.

13. "Elite Syrian Unit Scatters Chemical Arms Stockpile," *Daily Alert*, Jerusalem Center for Public Affairs, September 13, 2013, http://www.dailyalert.org/rss/Mainissues.php?id=49586.

14. Michael McAuliffe, "John Boehner on Putin Op-Ed: 'I Was Insulted' (VIDEO)," *Huffington Post*, September 12, 2013, http://www.huffingtonpost.com/2013/09/12/john-boehner-putin_n_3914708.html.

15. McCain, "Russians Deserve Better Than Putin."

16. Julia Ioffe, "The Syria Solution: Obama Got Played by Putin and Assad," *New Republic*, September 10, 2013, http://www.newrepublic.com/article/114655/obama-syria-policy-octopus-fighting-itself.

17. James Bruno, "Russian Diplomats Are Eating America's Lunch," *Politico*, April 16, 2014, http://www.politico.com/magazine/story/2014/04/russias-diplomats-are-better-than-ours-105773.html.

18. "Transcript of Thursday's Democratic Presidential Debate," CNN, January 31, 2008, http://www.cnn.com/2008/POLITICS/01/31/dem.debate.transcript.

19. Epstein, "White House Can't Sway Assad—So It Aims for Putin."

20. "Reading Tweets From Iran," *New York Times*, editorial, August 25, 2013, http://www.nytimes.com/2013/08/26/opinion/reading-tweets-from-iran.html.

21. Thomas Erdbrink and Mark Landler, "Iran Said to Seek a Nuclear Accord to End Sanctions," *New York Times*, September 19, 2013, http://www.nytimes.com/2013/09/20/world/middleeast/iran-said-to-seek-a-nuclear-accord-to-end-sanctions.html.

22. Rachelle Younglai and Paul Carrel, "Lawmakers Target ECB to Stop Iran From Using Euros," Reuters, February 21, 2013, http://www.reuters.com/article/2013/02/21/us-ecb-iran-idUSBRE91K0V420130221.

23. Ben Hartman, "US officials: Israel Is Responsible for Syrian Missile Depot Attack," *Jerusalem Post*, July 13, 2013, http://www.jpost.com/Middle-East/US-officials-Israel-is-responsible-for-Syrian-missile-depot-attack-319688.

24. Abraham Rabinovich, "Analysis: Israel's Airstrikes on Syria Give Notice to Iran, U.S.," *Washington Times*, May 10, 2013, http://www.washingtontimes.com/news/2013/may/10/israel-airstrikes-syria-give-notice-iran-us/.

25. Andrew Brookes, "What Would an Air Attack on Iran Look Like?" Royal United Service Institute, March 30, 2012, http://www.rusi.org/analysis/commentary/ref:C4F7572130F2E4/#.Ug0SFNLMAmE.

26. "Israel May Join Defense Pact With Saudi Arabia, UAE," *Times of Israel*, May 5, 2013, http://www.timesofisrael.com/israel-reportedly-may-join-defense-pact-with-saudi-arabia-uae/.

27. Ibid.

28. Paul Brandus, "How the U.S. Should Deal With North Korea," *The Week*, April 4, 2013, http://theweek.com/article/index/242316/how-the-us-should-deal-with-north-korea.

29. Nicholas Eberstadt, "A Route to Reining in North Korea," *Wall Street Journal*, May 5, 2103, http://online.wsj.com/article/SB10001424127887324482504578453451317183488.html.

30. Brandus, "How the U.S. Should Deal With North Korea."

31. Gi-Wook Shin, Thomas Fingar, and David Straub, "A Chance to Defuse North Korea," *New York Times*, June 5, 2013, http://www.nytimes.com/2013/06/06/opinion/global/a-chance-to-defuse-north-korea.html.

32. Matt Schiavenza, "Can China Stop North Korea?" *Atlantic*, April 3, 2013, http://www.theatlantic.com/china/archive/2013/04/can-china-stop-north-korea/274626/.

33. Jeyup S. Kwaak, "Seoul Asks U.S. to Delay Transfer of Military Command," *Wall Street Journal*, July 17, 2013, http://online.wsj.com/article/SB10001424127887 3244481045786111172058809496.html.

34. Loren Thompson, "Defense Cuts: Four Navy Programs to Watch Closely," *Forbes*, September 13, 2013, http://www.forbes.com/sites/lorenthompson/2013/09/13/defense-cuts-four-navy-programs-to-watch-closely/.

35. George Nishiyama, "Abe Visit to Controversial Japanese Shrine Draws Rare U.S. Criticism," *Wall Street Journal*, December 26, 2014, http://online.wsj.com/news/articles/SB10001424052702304483804579281103015121712.

36. Michael O'Hanlon, *Healing the Wounded Giant* (Washington, D.C.: Brookings Institution, 2013), 74.

37. Ibid.

38. Ibid., 69.

39. Michèle Flournoy and Janine Davidson, "Obama's New Global Posture," *Foreign Affairs*, July/August 2012, http://www.foreignaffairs.com/articles/137717/michele-flournoy-and-janine-davidson/obamas-new-global-posture.

40. Dan Box, "Collaboration With US Military to Increase," *The Australian*, May 4, 2013, http://www.theaustralian.com.au/national-affairs/collaboration-with-us-military-to-increase/story-fn59niix-1226634960569.

41. Manuel Mogato, "Philippines Offers U.S. Forces Access to Military Bases," Reuters, March 14, 2014, http://www.reuters.com/article/2014/03/14/us-philippines-usa-idUSBREA2D0GE20140314.

42. Dan Box, "Collaboration With US Military to Increase."

43. Michèle Flournoy, "The Smart-Shopping Way to Cut Defense Spending," *Wall Street Journal*, July 7, 2013, http://online.wsj.com/article/SB100014241278873 23419604578575613750348712.html.

44. Hugh White, meeting of the Council on Foreign Relations, October 28, 2013.

45. Matthew Kroenig, "The Case for Overkill," *Foreign Policy*, June 20, 2013, http://www.foreignpolicy.com/articles/2013/06/19/the_case_for_overkill.

46. Matthew Kroenig, "Think Again: American Nuclear Disarmament," *Foreign Policy*, September 4, 2013, http://www.foreignpolicy.com/articles/2013/09/03/think_again_american_nuclear_disarmament

47. Thom Patterson, "Does Cutting U.S. Nukes Really Matter?" CNN, June 19, 2013, http://www.cnn.com/2013/06/19/politics/obama-us-nuclear-strategy.

48. Michael O. Hanlon, "A Moderate Plan for Additional Defense Budget Cuts" (paper, Brookings Institution, February 2013), http://goo.gl/NxjGka.

49. "Russia Builds Missile Defense It Would Deny U.S.," editorial, *Investor's Business Daily*, July 3, 2013, http://news.investors.com/ibd-editorials/070313-662526-russia-builds-armavir-missile-defense-radar.htm.

50. Brendan Bordelon, "Republican Senator Urges East Coast Missile Defense Base," *Daily Caller*, July 24, 2013, http://dailycaller.com/2013/07/24/republican-senator-urges-east-coast-missile-defense-base/.

51. Martin Fackler, "Japanese Minister Proposes More Active Military Presence in Region," *New York Times*, July 26, 2013, http://www.nytimes.com/2013/07/27/world/asia/japanese-minister-proposes-more-active-military-presence-in-region.html.

52. Jennifer Steinhauer and Martin Fackler, "U.S. and Japan Agree to Broaden Military Alliance," *New York Times*, October 3, 2013, http://www.nytimes.com/2013/10/04/world/asia/japan-and-us-agree-to-broaden-military-alliance.html.

53. McCain, "Russians Deserve Better Than Putin."

54. See the reports compiled by LatinAmericanStudies.org, http://www.latinamericanstudies.org/human-rights.htm.

55. Alan Yuhas, "Russian Propaganda Over Crimea and the Ukraine: How Does It Work?" *The Guardian*, March 17, 2014, http://www.theguardian.com/world/2014/mar/17/crimea-crisis-russia-propaganda-media.

56. Chris Buckley, "China Takes Aim at Western Idea," *New York Times*, August 19, 2013, http://www.nytimes.com/2013/08/20/world/asia/chinas-new-leadership-takes-hard-line-in-secret-memo.html.

CONCLUSION

1. Mikheil Saakashvili, "Why the West Must Join the Ukraine Protesters," *Wall Street Journal*, January 28, 2014, http://online.wsj.com/news/articles/SB10001424052702303553204579346560862388416.

2. Teddy, Ng, "Turkey to Buy Chinese Missile Defense System," *South China Morning Post*, September 28, 2013, http://www.scmp.com/news/china/article/1319547/turkey-buy-chinese-missile-defence-system.

3. Saakashvili, "Why the West Must Join the Ukraine Protesters."

WHAT TO DO: RUSSIA

1. Mikheil Saakashvili, "The Tasks Ahead for Ukraine's New President," *Wall Street Journal*, May 28, 2014, http://online.wsj.com/articles/mikheil-saakashvili-the-tasks-ahead-for-ukraines-new-president-1401318064.

2. "Factbox: Western Sanctions Against Russia," Reuters, March 13, 2014, http://www.reuters.com/article/2014/03/13/us-ukraine-crisis-factbox-idUSBREA2C18N20140313.

3. Edward Luttwak, "Weaken Putin With a Russian Brain Drain," *Wall Street Journal*, April 30, 2014, http://online.wsj.com/news/articles/SB10001424052702304518704579523842847892868.

4. Michael E. Brown, "The Alliance Drifted From Its Core Mission—And the World Is Paying the Price," *Foreign Affairs*, May 8, 2014, http://www.foreignaffairs.com/articles/141404/michael-e-brown/natos-biggest-mistake.

WHAT TO DO: CHINA

1. Patrick M. Cronin and Alexander Sullivan, "America and the South China Sea Challenge," *The Diplomat*, May 3, 2013, http://thediplomat.com/2013/05/america-and-the-south-china-sea-challenge/1/.

2. Matthew Pennington, "Obama Drops Asia-Pacific 'Pivot' From U.S. Security Vision," *Japan Times*, May 29, 2014, http://www.japantimes.co.jp/news/2014/05/29/asia-pacific/politics-diplomacy-asia-pacific/obama-drops-asia-pacific-pivot-u-s-security-vision/.

3. Jim Steinberg and Mike O'Hanlon, "Don't Be a Menace to South (China Sea)," *Foreign Policy*, April 21, 2014, http://www.foreignpolicy.com/articles/2014/04/21/obama_china_japan_asia_abe_pivot_rebalance_resolve.

4. "'You'll Be Fired If You Refuse,'"(report, Human Rights Watch, November 4, 2011) http://www.hrw.org/reports/2011/11/04/you-ll-be-fired-if-you-refuse.

5. "Annual Report: China 2103," Amnesty International, May 23, 2013, http://www.amnestyusa.org/our-work/countries/asia-and-the-pacific/china.

6. Howard W. French, "Fast-Growing China Says Little of Child Slavery's Role," *New York Times*, June 21, 2007, http://www.nytimes.com/2007/06/21/world/asia/21china.html.

7. Thomas Lum, "Human Rights in China and U.S. Policy" (report for Congress, Congressional Research Service, July 18, 2011), http://www.fas.org/sgp/crs/row/RL34729.pdf.

8. Michael S. Schmidt and David E. Sanger, "5 in China Army Face U.S. Charges of Cyberattacks," *New York Times*, May 19, 2014, http://www.nytimes.com/2014/05/20/us/us-to-charge-chinese-workers-with-cyberspying.html.

WHAT TO DO: THE NEW AXIS

1. Jonathan Saul and Parisa Hafezi, "Iran, Russia Working to Seal $20 Billion Oil-for-Goods Deal: Sources," Reuters, April 2, 2014, http://www.reuters.com/article/2014/04/02/us-iran-russia-oil-idUSBREA311K520140402.

2. David E. Sanger and William J. Broad, "Iran Is Providing Information on Its Detonators, Atomic Agency Says," *New York Times*, May 23, 2104, http://www.nytimes.com/2014/05/24/world/middleeast/iran-is-providing-information-on-its-detonators-atomic-agency-says.html.

WHAT TO DO: REBUILDING ALLIANCES

1. Matthew Fisher, "NATO Mulls 'More Visible Presence' in Europe," *Leader-Post*, May 20, 2014, http://www.leaderpost.com/news/NATO+mulls+more+visible+presence+Europe/9857024/story.html.

2. Debito Arudou, "Japan Brings Out the Big Guns to Sell Remilitarization in U.S.," *Japan Times*, November 6, 2013, http://www.japantimes.co.jp/community/2013/11/06/issues/japan-brings-out-the-big-guns-to-sell-remilitarization-in-u-s/.

3. Ibid.

4. Dan Lamoth, "More U.S. Missile-Defense Systems in Pacific Possible, Admiral Says," *Washington Post*, May 28, 2014, http://www.washingtonpost.com/world/national-security/more-us-missile-defense-systems-in-pacific-possible-admiral-says/2014/05/28/7f49692c-e66c-11e3-afc6-a1dd9407abcf_story.html.

5. Julian E. Barnes, "Washington Considers Missile-Defense System in South Korea," *Wall Street Journal*, May 27, 2104, http://online.wsj.com/articles/washington-considers-missile-defense-system-in-south-korea-1401233131.

Index